THE
100
BEST
STOCKS
TO BUY IN
2016

THE
100
BEST
STOCKS
TO BUY IN
2016

P ETER S ANDER
AND
S COTT B OBO

A adams media
A VON , M ASSACHUSETTS

Published by
Adams Media, a division of F+W Media, Inc.
57 Littlefield Street, Avon, MA 02322. U.S.A.
www.adamsmedia.com

ISBN 10: 1-4405-8917-8
ISBN 13: 978-1-4405-8917-1
eISBN 10: 1-4405-8918-6
eISBN 13: 978-1-4405-8918-8

Printed in the United States of America.

10   9   8   7   6   5   4   3   2   1

Cover design by Sylvia McArdle.

This book is available at quantity discounts for bulk purchases.
For information, please call 1-800-289-0963.

Contents

Dedication

We continue to dedicate this book to all of you active investors who have the sense of purpose and independence of thought to make your own investing decisions—or at least, to ask the right questions. You continue to be wise enough—and inquisitive enough—to realize that not all the answers can be found in one place—and smart enough to seek the convenience of a good place to start.

Acknowledgments

This year, Peter would like to recognize all of you who have chosen to give us feedback and ask good questions via our "reader response" email address (*ginsander@hotmail.com*). Those comments and questions continue to educate us, too, as well as strengthen our connection with our *100 Best Stocks* community. It feels good—keep it coming. He would like to again recognize his coauthor, research partner, and life friend Scott Bobo, who continually brings his insight and humor to help make complex matters simple, interesting, and fun. And again, he recognizes—and endorses—the good work of Value Line, Inc., and their Investment Survey, which does more than any other known source to turn piles of facts and figures into a simple readable page. Next, no book happens without the added value of exercise to keep a body in shape and a mind clear, and to that end he offers his thanks to his exercise companions. And of course his boys Julian and Jonathan and life partner Marjorie inspire him to do this book year after year.

Scott would like to acknowledge the tireless efforts of his friend and coauthor Peter Sander in setting and keeping a high standard in the research and writing of this series. His diligence is what makes these books and our readers successful. Scott's wife Lorie continues to train Scott in the fine art of dissecting financial statements and has yet to complain about the bread crumbs on the keyboard. Scott's brother and sister, in spite of everything, still pick up the phone when he calls. Finally, Scott would like to acknowledge his mother's fearless spirit as a source of inspiration.

PART I

THE ART AND SCIENCE OF INVESTING IN STOCKS

By Peter Sander

The Art and Science of Investing in Stocks

To our surprise, once again, it didn't happen.

It? What *it?* What didn't happen? In a year when energy prices tanked, ISIS roiled the Mideast, another "Grexit" was threatened, a strong dollar crushed exports, and the San Francisco Giants won the World Series again, just *what* didn't happen?

Actually, there are two *it*'s that didn't happen.

The first *it*: the markets' winning streak didn't end. The stock markets—in the U.S. anyway—forged ahead again, though not so strongly as last year. Those of you who follow the markets or follow our book year after year will know that the markets have finished "up" six straight years. Last year we had once again bet that win streak to end. In fact, all along and through our six-year "history" we've really wanted to test our horses on the sloppy track of a down market.

Didn't happen.

The second *it*: Despite the fact that markets were up, not down, and that we continue to play defensive, which may not prove optimal in an up market—we beat the markets again anyhow. Six straight years, a Sextuple Crown, if you will. We had thought that with the weight we place on U.S. exporters, and industrial and energy-related stocks, we might be doomed to finish out of the money even as the markets won.

That didn't happen, either.

So for another year we'll have to wait and see how well our *100 Best Stocks* lists would run in a down market, because we haven't seen one in the six years since we started putting our horses on the track for the running of that year's 2010 *100 Best Stocks* list.

But most importantly, we still beat the up market. In fact, we scored a 15.0 percent gain versus a 12.7 percent gain in the S&P 500, dividends included; hardly a photo finish, but we'll cash our tickets (a few of them, anyway) and set out to enter the race again for 2016. We'll do our best to put you in the winner's circle again.

* * *

Surely, as the early months of 2015 wore on, we worried about our picks (as we do every year). As mentioned, we've always favored companies that do most of their business overseas. They're a way to play international and especially emerging-market growth while keeping business styles and accounting methods close to home. In fact, international sales generally serve to increase volumes of domestic companies as well; such scale drives down per-unit costs, making these multinational players more profitable.

We like "more profitable." In fact, when you look at the big picture, international growth lies at the heart of how big companies can grow their earnings 10, 12, 15 percent a year against a backdrop of overall economic growth, as measured by GDP, running in the 2–4 percent range. Those of you who have watched the markets for years probably have wondered (or should have wondered, anyway) how stock markets can grow persistently at 8–10 percent for nearly 100 years, while the economy as a whole grows at something not even half of that. Part of it is inflation, but part of it is that major players in the markets find ways to grow their market *share* by buying smaller companies or crowding them out—or by expanding their reach beyond our shores so as to transcend the limits of 2–4 percent U.S. growth. So strong overseas business is not only patriotic in the sense that it brings in valuable income from offshore, helping us fund our insatiable appetites for foreign goods, it also helps stimulate necessary growth in both revenues and profits to help our stocks prosper to the tune of 15 percent (and almost 24 percent last year) as previously described.

The main fly in the ointment comes with the strengthening dollar. When U.S. companies sell in local currency and translate those sales back to U.S. dollars, it can be painful when the value of those local currencies depreciates against those dollars. So we saw the refrain over and over again: "Company X reported a revenue gain of 4 percent, which would have been 8 percent without currency headwinds." Indeed, as the year wore on and we saw such headlines repeated over and over, we began to really wonder if all of our eggs were in the wrong basket and whether we should have picked so many companies with more than 50 percent of sales overseas.

Then there was the energy thing. We had pared our energy holdings over the years as some of the bigger providers had run into growth headwinds, difficulties replacing reserves, and the increased risk of headline disasters like the Deepwater Horizon spill. Despite this trimming, we still had a lot of companies that serviced the energy business directly or indirectly—like Fluor, which builds refineries and other infrastructure; oilfield services giant

Schlumberger; and companies like Praxair that supply specialty materials to the energy industry. Oil prices cratered 50 percent as OPEC and the Saudis in particular essentially tried to put the resurgent U.S. oil business out of business, and we wondered how our *100 Best* list would fare in such an environment—and braced for the worst.

Fortunately, our "excellent" companies trudged through the currency headwinds fairly well for the most part. And the energy thing—well, energy is an *input* cost to a great many of the companies we follow (no surprise!). Too, related collateral damage softened prices in a lot of other commodities as well. Finally, our S&P 500 index benchmark was buffeted by the same headwinds. So, in the end, while some of our energy and commodity-related picks suffered (we'd rather think of it as a buying opportunity), many of our other picks on the *100 Best* list prospered.

The upshot? Markets—both marketplaces and stock markets—can go through twists, turns, ruts, high points, and even backflips from time to time as shifts occur in supply and demand in the different sectors of those markets. But a good list of strong companies with excellent business models, combined with a reasonable diversification (we don't advocate owning all *100 Best Stocks* unless you can afford to; maybe five to ten of our choices will do) should get you through these bumps with flying colors. Owning an excellent business even in a bad environment should pay off in the long term—that is and always will be our thesis and is one of the key pillars of our defensive strategy.

We'll probably stick not only with that thesis but also the sub-theses of picking companies with strong overseas businesses and companies with strong positions in the energy industry.

*   *   *

As we wind down this opening statement we'll share a few other miscellaneous topics on our minds related to this edition and how we connect with you as readers and investors.

First of all, we continue to enjoy your feedback. I (Peter) first offered my e-mail address two years ago (*ginsander@hotmail.com*) as an experiment, and it's worked quite well. We've fielded many well-crafted questions that, frankly, we enjoyed answering. Not only do we appreciate the dialogs, but we learn from them. Keep them coming.

Last year's experiment to work with a slightly tighter production schedule, to feather in more recent news and events into our presentation has worked well. We will continue this schedule and keep things as up to date as possible—but we still know we can't keep up with the Internet. As we've said before, though, the businesses we pick aren't apt to change a whole lot in the six months during which the publisher is assembling, printing, and distributing the book. Our 2015 edition released a bit later than usual as a consequence, but we're trying to keep the original November release schedule.

We continue to be measurement minded. We enjoyed the praise given by "Buffetfan" on Amazon:

> *"Another plus is that they have the courage of their conviction and review the performance of their previous year's stock picks; something not seen too often in other books of this type."*

We agree and appreciate the comment. It's not hard to find investment suggestions, but it's much harder to find advice—or advisors, for that matter—who regularly measure and report their successes and failures. Not only is it good form (especially for us engineer types) to measure the quality of what we're providing, it also helps us understand how well our approach is working. As author Katherine Neville put it in her exquisite novel *The Eight*, "What can be measured can be understood; what can be understood can be altered."

As usual, we continue to produce this book not only to give you our annual selections (fish) but also provide a model for *how* we make our selections (teach you to fish). This Part I narrative has elements of both—and we apologize for parts of it that might seem repetitive, year after year—for those of you faithful enough to buy each year's edition. (For those of you who would like still more insight on how to fish, I'll point you to two of my other works: *The 25 Habits of Highly Successful Investors*, from this publisher, and *All about Low Volatility Investing* from McGraw-Hill.) Anyway, for us, investing is a thought process, which we hope you acquire over time—not just through our investment tenets and philosophies shared in the narrative, but also by watching us *do* it (the *100 Best* list) and ultimately through your own experience.

Speaking of thought process, we noticed ourselves making a couple of quick "acid test" checks when sifting through the universe of thousands of potential companies for the *100 Best* list. We now think that we can recognize a good company—at least one into which to drill down further—by assessing two characteristics.

1. Are dividends meaningful and rising?
2. Is the company buying back shares?

If a company is doing both, it suggests that other business attributes are going well; the company has sufficient capital, management thinks things are improving (else why would they commit capital to dividends and share buybacks?); and finally, it is shareholder oriented. If the company has sufficient capital, things are getting better, and management cares about shareholders, what more do we need to know? (Lots, actually, but it's a good place to get started.) It's like meeting someone new and exciting at a party or online—first impressions are important and things may just click, but you need to find out more.

Finally, some of our best "media" appearances and contacts with the public have come from meeting and presenting the *100 Best Stocks* at investment clubs. We've found investment clubs to be great forums to exchange ideas, insights, and experiences. We also enjoy evaluating investment club portfolios and comparing them to our *100 Best* list. If anyone out there wants to engage us for an investment club meeting, we can work out "consideration" (often just a free lunch; we know you've bought at least one book and we also know we aren't Registered Investment Advisors) and the means, perhaps teleconference or some such. Anyhow, the door is open, contact me (Peter) at the aforementioned e-mail.

As always, enjoy *The 100 Best Stocks to Buy in 2016*; invest long and prosper, and we hope to see you in the winner's circle again.

Beating the Averages—Most of Them, Anyhow

Two years ago, we created a "temporary" analysis and table comparing the performance of the *100 Best Stocks* list against major-sector benchmarks as measured by Lipper, a division of Thomson Reuters and a major supplier of quality financial information and analytics especially for the mutual fund sector. Once again, in 2015, that analysis proved quite interesting—not just because we beat most of the benchmarks once again. While we still call it "Table 0.1" it continues to gain status as a permanent part of our table collection.

In 2013, when we first did the analysis, we came in second, beaten out *only* by the Health/Biotech sector. We were pretty happy with that. Last year, a resurgent European market, a strong tech sector, and surprising strength in the financial sector beat us out; we came in Number Five in a field of 40. Not bad, we gladly accepted that, too. In 2015—drum roll please—nope, we didn't come out Number One this year either, but we moved up a notch to Number Four. As Table 0.1 shows, we lost out only to Health/Biotech (again), Real Estate (but our addition of another REIT helped us, too), and the China Region (which, frankly, surprised us, but we didn't lose out by much). As you can see from the table, our *100 Best* list holds up pretty well against the major market sectors: Therein lies the point.

▼ Table 0.1: Performance Compared to Major Benchmarks

100 BEST STOCKS 2015 COMPARED TO LIPPER MUTUAL FUND INDEX BENCHMARKS

ONE-YEAR PERFORMANCE, APRIL 1, 2014–APRIL 1, 2015

Fund Benchmark	1-year return
Health/Biotech	33.8%
Real Estate	22.2%
China Region	15.8%
100 BEST STOCKS TO BUY 2015	15.0%
Japan Region	14.6%
Science and Technology	13.7%
S&P 500 with Dividends Reinvested	12.7%
General U.S. Treasury	11.1%
Pacific Region	7.1%
Utility	6.8%
Global Large Cap Growth	6.2%
Financial Services	6.1%
Pacific Ex-Japan	6.0%
Global Multicap Growth	5.7%
General U.S. Government	5.1%
Global Multicap Core	4.9%
General Bond	4.7%
Telecommunications	4.5%
Intermediate Municipal Debt	4.2%
Global Large Cap Core	3.6%

Global Large Cap Value	3.1%
Multisector Income	2.4%
Short/Intermediate U.S. Government	1.8%
Global Multicap Value	1.6%
International Large Cap Growth	1.1%
Inflation Protected Bond	1.0%
Short U.S. Government	0.8%
High Yield Bond	0.6%
International Multicap Growth	-0.2%
International Large Cap Core	-0.3%
International Multicap Core	-0.6%
Emerging Markets	-1.6%
International Small/Mid Cap Value	-2.3%
International Small/Mid Cap Growth	-3.1%
International Large Cap Value	-3.3%
International Multicap Value	-3.6%
International Small/Mid Cap Core	-4.1%
European Region	-4.4%
Natural Resources	-18.3%
Latin American	-20.2%
Precious Metals Equity	-23.5%

Source: Lipper/Thomson Reuters, *Barron's Weekly*

A ~~Five~~Six-Year Stretch Run

Last year, we realized that it had been five years since we took over the publication of *The 100 Best Stocks to Buy* series from John Slatter, the previous author. That, and a couple of poignant reader queries, got us to ask ourselves: "So how well did we do?" How well did we achieve the goals of applying solid, value-based, marketplace-based investing techniques and philosophies to picking great companies, the *100 Best* of them for you to invest in? More simply stated, would you have been better off to not buy our book, not take the time to pursue individual stock investing, and throw it over the wall to a low-cost S&P 500 index fund?

We checked this and found the results rather encouraging. If you had invested $1,000 in each stock on each of our lists from 2010 through 2014 ($100,000 total), you would have ended up with $303,461 on your $100,000 investment, compared to $243,899 if you had invested the same $100,000 in an S&P 500 index fund with reinvested dividends. We thought the additional $59,562 in total return was quite worthwhile for having to shell out $16.95 (or less) to buy our book each year.

Like our other "oh-point temporary" table, we got rather fond of the message delivered by this one too, so decided to repeat the performance for the 2015 *100 Best Stocks* list. Now our table covers the six years 2010 through 2015, and as you can see in Table 0.2, we've increased our lead to $74,593 over the plain and simple S&P 500 index over the six years.

▼ **Table 0.2: Performance Compared to Major Benchmarks***

SIX-YEAR PERFORMANCE COMPARISON: *100 BEST STOCKS* VERSUS S&P 500

ANNUAL PERFORMANCE OF EACH *100 BEST* LIST AND COMPOUNDED CUMULATIVE PERFORMANCE

		2010	2011	2012	2013	2014	2015
100 Best Stocks	Gain, percent	**62.5%**	**20.0%**	**5.5%**	**19.2%**	**23.8%**	**15.0%**
	Compounded	62.5%	94.9%	105.6%	145.1%	203.5%	249.0%
	$100,000 invested in 2010	$162,500	$194,919	$205,639	$245,122	$303,461	$348,980
S&P 500	Gain, percent	**44.6%**	**13.1%**	**5.4%**	**15.6%**	**22.4%**	**12.7%**
	Compounded	44.6%	63.5%	72.4%	99.3%	143.9%	174.9%
	$100,000 invested in 2010	$144,600	$163,543	$172,374	$199,264	$243,899	$274,875
Net advantage, $100K invested, *100 Best Stocks*		$17,900	$31,376	$33,265	$45,858	$59,562	$74,106

* For 12-month periods beginning April 1 of previous year, dividends included after 2011

As you can see, over the six years, both lists did quite well, but the *100 Best Stocks* list, when compounded, did 27 percent better through the five-year period. We did not include dividends in our 2010 and 2011 analysis, but especially then, the *100 Best* list pretty much tracked the S&P in terms of return yield, so they don't affect the comparison much. Note also the power of "winning big" in the first year or two of a measurement period. The "beat" was significant in 2010; the *100 Best* performance then never really looked back—a significant illustration of the power of compounding and how much timing can make a difference in long-term portfolio performance.

We'll keep teasing you with the idea that this table is temporary, so you can wonder through the year whether you'll see it again next year. Unless the cost of the paper to print it on skyrockets out of control, it's probably a safe bet. We hope you continue to think our book, for its purchase price, is a safe bet too!

Individual Investor: This Book Is for You

If you bought this book, you're probably an astute and experienced individual investor who invests in individual stocks in individual companies. Are you alone? Heck no. You have more company than ever. In fact, shoved along a bit by the hits most people took in the Great Recession, more and more investors are putting themselves in the driver's seat. Why? It's simple, and easily explained by the old adage: "Nobody cares about your money more than you do."

The trend toward self-directed investing was highlighted in an April 2013 *Wall Street Journal* article entitled "A New Era for Do-It-Yourself Investing." We realize this article might be a bit dated for a 2016 book, but we don't think the figures nor the main message have changed that much.

In the study central to the article, researchers asked mostly middle-tier investors whether they were relying more or relying less on advisors since the 2008–09 financial crisis. Some 50 percent of respondents said "less"; only 21 percent said "more." (The rest said "no change.") They cited a trend toward "investors wanting to be more involved" and toward brokerages offering do-it-yourself services with only occasional help from professional advisors when requested.

Does this mean that everyone is picking their own stocks? No, not necessarily, and not entirely. They may still be using any of among the 14,000 mutual funds or roughly 1,600 exchange-traded fund (ETF) "products" (or hedge funds, if they're wealthy enough) that do the driving for them. But more and more investors are making informed choices themselves; fewer are leaving the choice of those products—or individual stocks, for that matter—to someone else. What's really emerging is more of a hybrid model, where investors are making their own decisions, but sprinkling in some help in the form of professional advice, or professional management given by mutual fund managers, and automatic diversification as given by index funds, ETFs, and other kinds of instruments. These are individually picked investments—with some help along the way.

Where does *The 100 Best Stocks to Buy* fit in? Every edition of *The 100 Best Stocks* is intended as a core tool for the individual investor, especially those investors inclined to buy individual stocks. Most of you probably aren't inclined to buy individual stocks for your entire portfolio—nor should you be unless you have the time and it's your thing to do. However, maybe it makes sense to round out your portfolio with funds and ETFs. Or perhaps it makes sense to round out your ETF and fund portfolio with a few individual stocks of your choosing.

As far as individual stock investing goes, we know that *100 Best Stocks* is hardly the only tool available. Today's explosion of Internet-based investing tools has made this book one of hundreds of choices for acquiring investing information. With the speed of cyberspace, our book will hardly be the most current source. In fact, we know, despite changes we made last year to the publishing schedule, that we're still at least six months out of date. If you check our research, you'll be able to come up with two to three calendar quarters of more current financial information, news releases, and so forth.

So does the delay built into the publishing cycle make our book a poor information source? Not at all. It works because the companies we choose don't change so much and because they avoid the temptation to manage short-term, quarter-to-quarter performance. We chose these companies *because* they have sustainable performance, so who cares if the latest details or news releases are included? In *The 100 Best Stocks to Buy in 2016*, as with all of our previous editions, we focus on the *story*—the story of each company—not just the latest facts and figures.

To that same point, *100 Best Stocks* goes well beyond just being a stock screen or a study of stocks to invest in. Analysis forms the base of *100 Best Stocks*, but it isn't the rigid, strictly numbers-based selection and analysis so often found in published "best stocks" lists. Sure, we look at earnings, cash flow, balance sheet strength, and so forth, but we'll also look far beyond those things. We'll look at the intangible and often subtle factors that make truly great businesses—that is, companies—great. That is, once again, the *story*.

Great companies have good business fundamentals, but what makes them really great is the presence of intangibles and subtleties—the brands, the marketplace successes, the management style, the competitive advantages— that will *keep* them great or make them greater in the future. In our view, *good intangibles today lead to better business fundamentals down the road.*

100 Best Stocks is not a simple numbers-based stock screen like many found on the Internet and elsewhere today. It is a selection and analysis of really good businesses you would want to buy and own, not just for past results, but for future outcomes. Does "future" mean "forever"? No, not any more. While the *100 Best Stocks* list correlates well with the notion of "blue-chip" stocks, the harsh reality is that "blue chip" no longer means "forever."

We feel that the 100 companies listed and analyzed in the pages that follow are the best companies to own for 2016—and generally, beyond. That said, the word "own" has become a more active concept these days. Gone are the days of "own forever," like the halcyon days when Peter's parents, Jerry and Betty Sander, bought their 35 shares of General Motors, lovingly placed the stock certificate in their safe deposit box, and henceforth bought nothing but GM cars. Today, there is no forever; the economy, technology, and consumer tastes change too fast, and the businesses that participate in the economy by necessity change with it. Ownership is a more active concept than it was even 10 or 20 years ago.

So going forward, we offer the *100 Best* companies to own now and for 2016, those that have the best chances of not only surviving but evolving with—or even ahead of—the economy based on their current market position and approach to doing business. We think these are the best companies to (1) stay with or perhaps stay slightly ahead of business change, (2) provide short- and long-term returns in the form of cash and modest appreciation, and (3) do so with a measure of safety or at least reduced volatility so that you can burn your energy doing other things besides staring at stock quotes day and night.

Bottom line: Our intent is simple and straightforward. We provide a list and a set of facts and stories. You take the information as it's presented, do your own assessment, reach your own conclusions, and take your own actions. Anything more, anything less, won't work. You're in charge. And we suspect that you like it that way.

What's New for 2016

For those of you who've stayed with us over the years, this edition will take the same approach as before. For those of you reading for the first time, here are some guidelines and ideas we follow.

First and once again: no changes to the author team of Scott and Peter (we'll introduce ourselves in a minute). Once again, no significant changes to the structure or format of our presentation. Continuing forward is our emphasis on sustainable value, strong market position and other intangibles, and sustainable and growing cash returns to investors, in the form of dividends and share buybacks as well as share appreciation. We continue to take interest in the persistency of dividend increases above and beyond the yield itself, and we continue to stay focused on total shareholder returns. For the most part, we are playing the hand that got us here.

However, although we say every year that our investing style and presentation has remained essentially the same, the style of the best artists, writers, or even software programmers evolves over time. As with any blend of science and art, investing most certainly included, the approach evolves; the style acquires a little of this and a little of that and loses a little of something else as time goes on. Experience matters and is taken into account. Changes in the world investing context and environment factor in. And heck—we're getting older and perhaps a bit wiser. Maybe we see things a little differently than we did six years ago . . . and certainly 35 years ago. All of these factors influence the mix; here are a few directions we've taken recently (or have continued with emphasis) with this edition:

- *Low-volatility bias.* We continue to think it's important to get good returns but also to sleep at night. Steady growth, steady returns, steady dividend increases—that's what we prefer. While we present "beta" as a measure of market correlation, we look deeper into the actual patterns and history of earnings, dividends, cash flow, and yes, share price. If it's a wild ride (or if there are no earnings, cash flows, etc.), we don't get on; we prefer to watch instead. You'll never find the likes of Facebook on our list.

  We know as the markets continue to rise through the years, the chances for corrective "volatility" increase—there isn't a whole lot we can do about that except to stick to our knitting. That said, we've reached outside our normal "core" type of holding just a bit again this year to pick up some lesser-known, smaller-cap, perhaps more volatile names, as some of the mainstream businesses were just a bit too pricey. Mind you, we may have gone outside the traditional blue-chip core, but we continue to not embrace momentum or "story" plays.

- *Still playing defense.* We took a more defensive stance for 2014 and almost wound up with some explainin' to do as the markets forged ahead. We did that again in 2015 and don't think we missed much of what the markets had to offer as a consequence. Our lists continue to be constructed to provide enough growth opportunity to beat the market but also to beat the market in a down market, that is, to be down only 5 percent if the market dropped 10 percent. We continue to take that position. Once again, a number of our *100 Best Stocks* seem fully valued at this juncture. We were nervous about riding them any further. We evaluate all of our picks carefully using our "sell if there's something better to buy" philosophy and try to visualize how they would do "on a sloppy track."

- *Focus on Millennials.* The January 2015 *New York Times* headline summed it up perfectly: "Millennials Set to Outnumber Baby Boomers." There are about 75 million of each, with Millennials counted as being born between 1981 and 1997, and more importantly, with a digital silver spoon in their mouths. Hmmm, we thought. Have we embraced this adequately in our stock picks, given that we like companies with at least steady, and preferably improving, brand strength and loyal customer bases? Millennials are typically typecast as being digitally fluent, preferring unstructured environments, having a taste for customizable products, healthy foods, immediate gratification—all with short attention spans and relatively less loyalty to companies and brands than their non-digital ancestors. We had to ask ourselves, Do they drink Coke? Buy IBM? Eat Big Macs? Wash their clothes with Tide? Go to movie theaters? and a thousand other questions. Are we seeing—or about to see—a major shift in consumer preferences as Millennials gradually take charge of the commercial world? Do our long-standing brands like Coke and Kellogg's Corn Flakes have cachet with these groups like they once did with us older folks? The jury is still out, but we considered every pick (especially consumer brands) in light of its relevance to this group and made a few changes to our list based on this major and gradual demographic and market shift.

- *Another investment product.* In 2014 we tiptoed into the "investment product" space adding a real estate investment trust (REIT) rather unimaginatively called Health Care REIT, Inc. Our goal was to gain the diversification, yield, and defensiveness of a managed portfolio, in this case a portfolio of senior housing and health facilities. Although that investment didn't work out so well for 2014, we doubled down on the approach in 2015 with Public Storage (PSA), another good business built on a foundation of self-storage facilities. Both it and Health Care REIT worked very well in 2015. For 2016, we're adding a new and smaller "mid-cap" REIT—Empire State Realty Trust—that just happens to own the most revered office building in the world: the Empire State Building (how's that for a brand?). Once again, we considered adding other investment products—perhaps an ETF to give us some exposure to the cloud computing and networking space—but didn't do it. Once again we found nothing that really floated our boats (as you'll hear in our later discussion of ETFs, you get the bad stuff with the good, most not focused enough for our purposes). Upshot: We will continue to consider investment products—REITs, other types of investment trusts, funds, ETFs, and others from time to time, but we won't add them unless we (1) understand them, (2) have a specific rationale, and (3) feel that they provide a "*100 Best*" caliber opportunity to deploy your hard-earned cash.

Beyond these ideas, we continued on our value-driven track, looking for the very best businesses to invest in with an emphasis on "sell if there's something better to buy." We didn't respond too much to short-term concerns that affected everyone, like the rising dollar. We thought about bringing some of our "eggs" home and out of foreign baskets to mitigate dollar impacts and reduce foreign event risk somewhat, but figured the dollar thing would stabilize or reverse itself just about the time we made the changes. We consider the headline risk an omnipresent ongoing factor that would nearly equally harm "domestic" investments—we're in a global economy, after all. Finally, while we did take a close look at the energy sector and make a few changes, for the most part we dismissed the recent market disruption as a cycle like many others we put up with in the agricultural and other sectors. In our view, the best businesses will survive, even thrive, in the deepest cycles (as competitors go away, as costs drop, etc.) so we took this view moving forward on energy. More on that in a minute.

About Your Authors

If you're a regular reader of the *100 Best Stocks* series, you've probably seen the following before. It's about us, and not much has changed about us, so feel free to skip this section if it's altogether too familiar—or if it doesn't matter much to begin with.

Peter Sander

Peter is an independent professional researcher, writer, and journalist specializing in personal finance, investing, and location reference, as well as other general business topics. He has written 43 books on these topics, as well as numerous financial columns, and performed independent, privately contracted research and studies. He came from a background in the corporate world, having experienced a 21-year career with a major West Coast technology firm.

He is, most emphatically, an individual investor, and has been since the age of 12 (okay, so Warren Buffett started when he was 11), when his curiosity at the family breakfast table got the better of him. He started reading the stock pages with his parents. He had an opportunity during a "project week" in the seventh grade to read and learn about the stock market. He read Louis Engel's *How to Buy Stocks*, then the preeminent—and one of the only—books about investing available at the time. He picked stocks, and made graphs of their performance by hand with colored pens on graph paper. He put his hard-earned savings into buying five shares of each of three different companies. He watched those stocks like a hawk and salted away the meager dividends to reinvest. He's been investing ever since. (Incidentally, Warren Buffett bought Cities Service preferred shares, Peter bought Burlington Northern preferred shares following much the same principles, and how ironic that Mr. Buffett came to own all of Burlington Northern. Perhaps Peter will come to own a big oil company some day.)

Yes, Peter has an MBA from Indiana University in Bloomington, but it isn't an MBA in finance. He also took the coursework and certification exam to become a Certified Financial Planner (CFP®). By design and choice, he has never held a job in the financial profession. His goal has always been to share his knowledge and experience in an educational way, a way helpful for the individual as an investor and a personal financier to make his or her own decisions.

He has never earned a living giving direct investment advice or managing money for others, nor does he intend to.

A few years ago, it dawned on Peter that he has really made his living finding value, and helping or teaching others to find value. Not just in stocks, but other things in business and in life. What does he mean by value? Simply, the current and potential *worth* of something as compared to its price or cost. As it turns out, he's made a career out of assessing the value of customers (for marketers), places (as places to live), and companies (for investors).

Scott Bobo

Peter and Scott have been friends and colleagues since, roughly, tenth grade (a long time!). Scott has been part of the team for five years now and has been huge not only in identifying the *100 Best Stocks* but also analyzing them and explaining their pros and cons crisply and in plain English so that you can make the best use of the list. Having Scott on the team allows you to get the combined wisdom and observations of two people, not just one, in an arena where one plus one almost always equals something greater than two.

Scott has been an investor since age 14, when he made the switch from analyzing baseball box scores to looking at the numbers and charts in the business section. In his 20-plus years in engineering and technology management, he's learned that a unique product value proposition is important to the success of any company. He has also learned (the hard way) that proper financial fundamentals are critical. From a development manager's perspective, comprehending a new product's risk/reward proposition is one of the keys to a company's success. From an investor's perspective, it's also one of the keys to successful value investing in a dynamic, innovation-driven market.

Scott adds a strong analytical touch. But he is most at home as an applications engineer, explaining how a company's products work and how they apply to a customer's needs. Consequently, and in addition to analytical legwork, Scott really adds an extraordinary and very real-world sense of how a company's products "fit" in the marketplace. Determining whether a company's products are relevant, best-in-class, and have a competitive advantage over others is an oft-overlooked core skill for a value investor. Scott brings this skill to the table in a big way.

How do these diverse experiences of Peter and Scott translate into picking stocks? Just like customers or places to live, we want companies that produce the greatest return, the highest value, *per dollar invested*. And *for the amount of risk taken*. The companies we will identify as among the *100 Best* have, in our assessment, the greatest and most persistent long-term *value*, and if you can buy these companies at a *reasonable price* (a factor that we largely leave out of this analysis because this is a book and prices can change considerably), then these investments deliver the best prospects while keeping the downsides manageable.

Later we'll come back to describe some of the attributes of value that we look for.

A "Low-Volatility" Investing Book

You've heard about—and just read about—the new trend toward low-volatility investing. This term means investing to minimize risk and volatility—to be able to sleep at night and count on your otherwise unpredictable retirement—and achieve decent investing returns all the same. That's the subject of Peter's book *All about Low Volatility Investing* (McGraw-Hill, 2014), and some of the "DNA" from that book has leaked into this one. But that's not what this subsection is about.

What we're getting at here is the low-volatility nature of the sequential editions of this book. We try to keep them useful and relatively simple year after year. The analysis is the same, and for the most part the presentations are the same. Each year we make a few adjustments, pruning away a few stocks and adding a few others. We do that by adhering to our core principles without having any particular number of changes in mind.

When we first took over this series from John Slatter for the 2010 edition, we made 26 changes, not a revolution but perhaps a strong evolution of the philosophy toward core value principles, strong competitive advantages and intangibles, and healthy cash returns. After that first year we went back to more of a fine-tuning mode, changing 14 stocks for the 2011 list, 12 for 2012, and back to 14 for 2013. In 2014 we held the line in a measure of defense and the simple inability to find "better horses," and changed only eight stocks. For 2015 and with the heady gains in the markets (almost 24 percent) we felt that a few more of our horses might be ready to fade and brought in 13 fresh ones for that year's ride.

This year, for the 2016 *100 Best Stocks* list, we replaced ten stocks.

The overall methodology used for analysis and selection of the *100 Best Stocks* remains largely unchanged. We continue to focus on fundamentals that really count, like cash flow, profit margins and balance sheet strength, and those intangibles such as brand, market share, channel and supply-chain excellence, and management quality that really determine success *going forward*. We continue to place more focus on dividends. More and more, especially in today's volatile markets, we feel that investors should get paid something to commit their precious capital to a company; it's a sign of good faith to investors and provides at least some return while waiting for a larger return in the future—or if things go south later on. So once again, 98 of this year's *100 Best* pay at least some dividends. The two "culprits" that don't remain CarMax and Itron. These stocks are included because of other prospects; we can turn our heads the other way on the dividend for a while, but would expect some dividends eventually as the business models mature.

As has become a hallmark feature of our approach, we continue our preference for companies with a track record for regular dividend *increases*. A few years ago we started tracking, for each company, the number of dividend increases or *raises* (yes, you can think of them as comparable to a raise in your own wage or salary) in the past ten years. We are proud to report that of the 98 *100 Best* stocks paying dividends, fully *93* of them *raised* their dividend from 2014 to 2015. Of the 93, *46* of them have raised their dividends in each of the past ten years, and 21 more have raised them each of the past eight or nine years (most of these took a year or two off during the Great Recession), adding up to 67—or two-thirds—of our stocks able and willing to give you annual raises. Pretty good stuff, in our view.

As in all editions, we review the performance of our 2015 picks in some detail, and continue with our "stars" lists identifying the best stocks in six different categories:

1. Yield Stars (stocks with solid dividend yields—Table 6)
2. Dividend Aggressors (companies with strong and persistent records and policies toward dividend *growth*—Table 6.1)
3. Safety Stars (solid performers in any market—Table 7)
4. Growth Stars (companies positioned for above-average growth—Table 8)
5. Prosperity Stars (formerly Recovery Stars—companies poised to do particularly well in a strong economy—Table 9)
6. Moat Stars (companies with significant sustainable competitive advantage—Table 10)

So, if you're an investor partial to any of these factors, such as safety, these lists are for you.

2014–2015: A Little Slower This Year—But the Beat *Still* Goes On

Now comes the part of this narrative where we diagnose what went on in the year gone by and attempt to turn that into a prognosis for the coming year. Always a challenge.

It was a year of change and transition, but one thing that didn't change was the persistent march forward of the stock markets—the U.S. markets, anyway. The benchmark S&P 500 index advanced 10.5 percent not including dividends during our measurement year April 1, 2014, to April 1, 2015—far short of the 22.4 percent rise in 2014 but impressive just the same. For the year, we noted six factors that drove the markets:

- *Continuing accommodative Fed policy.* The Fed ended its "QE3" Quantitative Easing program, whereby it injects money into the U.S. economy by buying bonds, in October 2014. Early on that was expected to create a fair amount of market angst as it would temper increases in the money supply and bring on a rise in interest rates. The markets sold off anticipating this, but nothing really changed when the QE "punch bowl" was removed—probably because everyone knew it was coming and it had already been priced into the markets. There may be more "angst" to come when the Fed decides to raise interest rates more directly, which could come as soon as late 2015. The markets, particularly some of our dividend-paying stocks, which essentially compete with bond yields, have sold off again somewhat in anticipation. As 2016 unfolds the real questions will be how much interest rates are raised, how fast, and whether the markets have again priced it in. Fedwatchers: stay tuned.

- *Recovery in Europe.* We were pretty jazzed about Europe through the first part of 2014. The more precarious parts of the European region—aside from the Ukraine—had stopped giving us nerve-wracking headlines for the moment. We expected Europe to become a positive factor in world demand for things such as cars, machinery, consumer staples, and other products—a mild tailwind instead of a headwind. But alas, those headlines started to creep in again, especially for Greece, and weakening of the euro versus the dollar once again dampened European customer demand for U.S. goods. Europe went from being a positive to being a negative for most of our U.S.-based exporters doing business there.

- *Strength in U.S. manufacturing.* Although it is slowing some, we still see a steady, if not ground-shaking, reshoring of manufacturing to American soil. Companies finally got the memo that it isn't just about labor costs—long, inflexible supply chains and the inability to control quality negate the savings, sometimes in a big way. Chinese labor costs are going up, and improved availability and declining costs of U.S. energy resources, especially natural gas, are helping even more. True, some supply chains, especially for electronics products, simply aren't deep enough to support U.S. manufacturing. Still, some 13.5 percent of U.S. manufacturers, according to a poll done by the MIT Forum for Supply Chain Innovation, planned to move some manufacturing back to the U.S. in 2015 compared to 21 percent previously. So while the strength of the trend moderated, it was still present for the year. Many of our companies, like W.W. Grainger and Illinois Tool Works, benefit from reshoring.

- *Persistence of share buybacks.* Companies have accumulated huge hoards of cash, as they have learned how to manage expenses and leverage their infrastructure to produce more for less. Although a big chunk of that cash is parked overseas for tax reasons, companies continue to actively buy back shares, producing rather silent but persistent returns to existing shareholders. S&P's Howard Silverblatt estimates that S&P 500 companies bought back an estimated $553 billion in 2014, ahead from $475 billion in 2012 and only lagging the $589 billion repurchased in 2007. More than half the companies on our *100 Best Stocks* list could be classified as "buyback aggressors," retiring 10–20 percent and as much as 50 percent of outstanding float since 2004. This, of course, serves to increase returns, both to the shareholders who sell and to those who remain to enjoy a higher rate of return on the remaining shares. We did see a moderation of that trend as the year went on, as some of our more financially sensitive companies (like our REITs), anticipating higher interest rates, chose to "deleverage" their balance sheets by paying off debt instead. We also saw share buybacks pull back in the energy industry because of new uncertainties, and—possibly due to high share prices—a few of our companies reduced buybacks in favor of cash dividends paid outright to shareholders.

- *Energy price collapse.* The U.S. oil price benchmark peaked in June 2014 at just over $107 per barrel, but increased supply (mostly from the U.S.) and flat demand began to eat away at this price. Then in November OPEC, led by Saudi Arabia, announced their plans to essentially "flood" the markets with cheap oil, mostly (in our view, not their stated intention) to drive more expensive domestic "fracking" operations to the sidelines to preserve their market share. This aggravated the oversupply of oil and threw a lot of domestic drilling activities into question. Oil producers and field service companies, large and small, took a hit in revenues and to their bottom lines as production volumes declined. This "cycle" (and that's what we believe it to be; lower prices will spur demand and restrain production, bringing prices to a higher equilibrium eventually) hurt the stocks of oil producers and all who service them, and we have several companies in this industry on our list. We feel we had picked "best in breed" choices originally, and such choices, like Chevron and Schlumberger, took a small hit but appear to be adjusting to the change appropriately. Still, the cycle isn't over, and there could be some collateral damage to other sectors and the economy at large if big and small oil stop investing in their projects long term.

- *Moderating commodity prices.* We tend to like companies that add value to raw commodities, turning them into high-quality finished products for the global marketplace. As such, our *100 Best* list tends to be sensitive to commodity prices, although we have a few key plays in companies that provide such commodities, like Mosaic, Schnitzer Steel, and our energy picks. Commodity prices had already been soft earlier in the year due in part to the slowdown in China; the downturn accelerated when the oil price started tanking in mid-2014, especially in mined commodities like iron ore and copper. While our thesis continues that lower commodity input costs will help a majority of our businesses (save for the likes of Mosaic and Schnitzer), the benefits lag the event, as many finished products producers "hedge"—that is, lock in input prices through futures contracts—this time causing them to pay more for certain inputs than they would by buying on the "spot" market. So we didn't see that much benefit for 2014 but expect more benefit to hit bottom lines in 2015 and beyond.

- *Weaker growth in China.* A combination of domestic policy, saturation in big cities (just how many more high rises can you fit into a small space?), and what we think is a global drop in the demand for manufactured "stuff"—physical goods—furthered the softness in China's economic growth rate, down to 7.4 percent in real GDP terms from 7.7 percent in 2013 and the 9–10 percent range a few years ago. This may not seem like much, but just the loss of 0.3 percent meant roughly $50 billion or so less in new demand than if the growth rate had remained constant. This moderation played a part in soft energy and commodity demand worldwide, and in agricultural and certain other U.S. exports, which hurt some parts of the stock market (and our *100 Best* list) to a degree.

Report Card: Recapping Our 2015 Picks

As mentioned at the outset, we were more than pleased (somewhat surprised, really) at the 12.7 percent gain, including dividends, enjoyed by the S&P 500. As we had gone into the year, as usual, with a slightly more defensive position, and as we tend toward more dividend-paying stocks (our yield was 2.3 percent versus 2.1 percent for the S&P), we were afraid, once again, that we might miss the boat just a little and underperform the S&P.

That didn't happen. We were up 15.0 percent including dividends.

At this juncture, we'll do a short refresher on how we evaluate our gains. There are many ways to evaluate the performance of a group of stocks over time. Some are simplistic, such as simply averaging the percent gain in each share price. But such a method may not weight a portfolio very realistically, for it assumes you buy the same number of shares of W.W. Grainger at $250 as you would Daktronics at $12. We continue to feel it's better to take the approach of an investor with $100,000 to invest—who invested $1,000 in each of the *100 Best Stocks* across the board, regardless of share price. Sure, you end up with some weird quantities of shares in your portfolio, but the portfolio, and thus the performance metrics, isn't weighted in favor of more expensive stocks.

The Bottom Line

If you had invested $100,000 in our *100 Best Stocks 2015* list on April 1, 2014—$1,000 in each of the 100 stocks—you would have ended up with $112,703 on April 1, 2015, not including dividends paid during that period. That's a 12.7 percent gain. Including dividends of some $2,305, you would have ended up with $115,008. The S&P, as measured by the buyable SPDR S&P 500 ETF Trust, was ahead just 12.5 percent, including dividends ($112,491) during that period—a clear victory for us requiring no binoculars or photo finish to determine.

Winners and Losers

At this point, we'll give a short overview of what really worked and what didn't within the *100 Best Stocks 2015* list. First, the winners:

▼ Table 1: Performance Analysis: 100 Best Stocks 2015

TOP WINNERS, 1-YEAR GAIN/LOSS, APRIL 1, 2014–APRIL 1, 2015; * = NEW FOR 2015

		Price 4/1/2014	Price 4/1/2015	% change	Dollar gain per $1,000 invested
Allergan	AGN	$123.74	$240.00	94.0%	$939.55
Southwest Airlines	LUV	$23.61	$44.30	87.6%	$876.32
Kroger	KR	$43.62	$76.66	75.7%	$757.45
Apple	AAPL	$76.25	$124.43	63.2%	$631.87
ResMed (*)	RMD	$44.69	$71.78	60.6%	$606.18
Fair Isaac	FICO	$55.32	$88.72	60.4%	$603.76
Sigma Aldrich	SIAL	$93.38	$138.25	48.1%	$480.51
CarMax	KMX	$46.80	$69.01	47.5%	$474.57
UnitedHealth Group	UNH	$81.84	$118.29	44.5%	$445.38
Ross Stores	ROST	$72.90	$105.30	44.4%	$444.44
CVS Health	CVS	$74.86	$103.21	37.9%	$378.71
Nike	NKE	$73.86	$100.33	35.8%	$358.38
Costco Wholesale	COST	$111.68	$151.50	35.7%	$356.55
Target Corporation	TGT	$60.57	$82.07	35.5%	$354.96
Whirlpool	WHR	$149.46	$202.06	35.2%	$351.93

Aetna	AET	$74.97	$99.15	32.3%	$322.53
Quest Diagnostics	DGX	$57.92	$76.35	31.8%	$318.20
Health Care REIT	HCN	$59.60	$77.36	29.8%	$297.99
Time Warner	TWX	$65.33	$84.44	29.3%	$292.51
Wal-Mart	WMT	$42.07	$54.23	28.9%	$289.04

This year, our "winning percentage" of 79 winners out of 100 picks was off a bit from our record high of 89 last year. That's probably not too surprising given the overall year's performance was somewhat below that of the 2014 year.

Our biggest winners are, of course, the two takeovers (we had been averaging one takeover a year; this year we had both Allergan and Sigma-Aldrich "taken out" by bigger fish), but more presciently, a lot of our top winners recovered from previous doldrums or periods of flat performance. Market pros call it a "hockey stick" pattern when a stock flatlines for a period while performance improves, then the share price finally springs to life. Such a "hockey stick" pattern could describe Southwest (continuing from last year), Kroger, Fair Isaac, CarMax, Costco, and Quest Diagnostics among many on our *100 Best* list. This is not uncommon; it can take a while for solid performance to set in and for professional money managers to discover these improved "corners" of the market. We also had a couple of notable turnarounds—Apple (it was our worst pick for 2014, believe it or not) and Target, which emerged from its late-2013 credit card hack with flying colors. On this "winners' circle" list we see few patterns of businesses or business types, but we do see some particular strength in retail. We were disappointed that only one of our new picks (ResMed) made the Top Winners list (especially since we had five new picks on our Top *Losers* list!).

Now, for the losers:

▼ **Table 2: Performance Analysis: 100 Best Stocks 2015**

TOP LOSERS, 1-YEAR GAIN/LOSS, APRIL 1, 2014–APRIL 1, 2015; * = NEW FOR 2015

		Price 4/1/2014	Price 4/1/2015	% change	Dollar gain/loss per $1,000 invested
Deere	DE	$90.80	$87.69	-3.4%	$(34.25)
Grainger, W.W.	GWW	$252.66	$235.81	-6.7%	$(66.69)
AT&T	T	$35.07	$32.65	-6.9%	$(69.00)
Storage Technology	STX	$56.16	$52.03	-7.4%	$(73.54)
Mosaic	MOS	$50.00	$46.06	-7.9%	$(78.80)
Praxair	PX	$131.82	$120.74	-8.4%	$(84.05)
Devon Energy (*)	DVN	$66.93	$60.31	-9.9%	$(98.91)
ConocoPhillips	COP	$70.35	$62.26	-11.5%	$(115.00)
Chevron	CVX	$118.91	$104.98	-11.7%	$(117.15)
Schlumberger	SLB	$97.96	$83.44	-14.8%	$(148.22)
IBM	IBM	$192.49	$160.50	-16.6%	$(166.19)
Valmont Industries	VMI	$148.84	$122.88	-17.4%	$(174.42)
Ralph Lauren (*)	RL	$160.93	$131.50	-18.3%	$(182.87)
Philips N.V. (*)	PHG	$35.16	$28.34	-19.4%	$(193.97)
Eastman Chemical	EMN	$86.21	$69.26	-19.7%	$(196.61)
Total S.A.	TOT	$65.60	$50.01	-23.8%	$(237.65)
Daktronics (*)	DAKT	$14.39	$10.81	-24.9%	$(248.78)
FMC Corporation	FMC	$76.56	$57.25	-25.2%	$(252.22)
Fluor	FLR	$77.73	$57.16	-26.5%	$(264.63)
Schnitzer Steel (*)	SCHN	$28.85	$15.86	-45.0%	$(450.26)

Our Top Losers list was dinged by five of our 13 companies new to the 2014 list (okay, we're *long-term* investors!). But the pattern of loss was pretty easy to see in companies affected by the energy market disruption (Fluor, Chevron, ConocoPhillips, Devon Energy, Total S.A., Schlumberger, Praxair), and related disruption in other commodities (Schnitzer, Eastman, Mosaic, FMC). Others were hurt more by the reversal in Europe (Philips N.V., Total S.A. again, and Ralph Lauren) and the weak dollar in general. We'll discuss our adjustments for 2016 shortly. We did prune a few but not too many issues from this "losers" list, expecting factors that put them there to reverse eventually (by 2016, we hope!)

Value—Now More Than Ever

Those of you who take in our book every year have seen this before, but we remain steadfast in the principles of value investing.

For intelligent investors, chasing the latest fad doesn't work; buying something and locking it away forever doesn't work anymore, either. Investors must make intelligent choices based on true value and follow those choices through time and change. It all points to taking a value-oriented approach to investing and to staying modestly active with your investments.

The next obvious task is to define what we mean by a "value" approach. Essentially, it is to think of buying shares in a company as buying the company itself; it is about putting yourself in an entrepreneurial frame of mind, not just an investment frame of mind. Would you want to own that business? Why or why not?

Fundamentally, whether or not you want to own the business depends on two factors: first, the returns you expect to receive on your investment in the near- and long-term future, and second, the risk you'll take in generating those returns. Fortunately, the third factor the prospective entrepreneur must consider—"Do I have the time for this?"—is less of an issue for the investor.

You are looking for tangible value—tangible worth—for your precious, scarce, and hard-earned investment capital. That return can come in the form of immediate cash returns (dividends), longer-term cash returns (dividends and especially growing dividends), or as growth in the value of assets longer term. If you realize your return in the form of owning a share of a larger company eventually, that's still a legitimate return. Cash flow received later in the form of a higher share price or a takeover is still cash return; it is just less certain because of the forces of change that may take place in the interim. It is also theoretically worth less because of the nature of discounting—a dollar received tomorrow is worth more than a dollar received 20 years in the future.

The point: Many investment experts distinguish between "value" and "growth" investing; in fact, mutual funds are often classified as being one or the other. We dismiss this separation; growth can be an essential component of a firm's value. That growth can come either in the form of asset values or cash returns—i.e., growing dividends.

Value also implies safety. The safety comes in three forms. First is the fundamental quality and soundness of the firm's financial fundamentals—that is, income, cash flow, and the balance sheet. Value companies have plenty of reserves, a large enough *margin of safety*, to weather downturns and unforeseen events in the marketplace. Second, they have strong enough intangibles (brands, market position, supply-chain strength, etc.) to *maintain* their position in that marketplace and generate future returns. When we say this year, as we did last year, that our list should fare better in a *down* market than the S&P 500 as a whole, it's these safety factors, and particularly the intangibles, that support our premise.

Third, if you're really practicing value-investing principles, you buy these companies at reduced prices, when the markets are down, when the company is out of favor. You're looking for situations where the price is less than what you perceive to be the value, although calculating the value that precisely is elusive. When you "buy cheap" you provide another margin of safety; that margin makes it less likely that the stock will drop further. It gives you room for error if you turn out to be wrong about a choice. Again, it's much like buying a business of your own—you want to pay as little as possible in case things don't turn out as you'd expect. In today's markets, admittedly it's hard to buy cheap, but many of the ten new adds for 2016, for the moment at least, appear to have value relative to the market and the other choices we could have made, although are hardly in bargain territory. Sell when there's something better to buy.

Stay Active

What do we mean by "stay active?" Staying active means that you should remain abreast of your investment and, like any business you own, keep an eye on its performance. Periodically review it as you would your own finances to see if it is making money and generally doing what you think it should be doing. You should keep an eye on company-related news, financials, earnings reports, and so forth—it's all part of being an individual investor and owner of companies.

Beyond that, time permitting, you should listen in on investor conference calls (usually at earnings announcements) to see what management has to say about the business. In addition, you should watch your business in the marketplace. See how many people are going to your local Starbucks and whether they are enjoying the experience, and look for other signs of excellence. We're not talking about constantly monitoring the stock price. Instead, we're suggesting an oversight of the business as though it were one you happen to own that, while professionally managed, requires an occasional glance to make sure everything is still acting according to your best interests. We also recommend a periodic review—at least annually—of whether your investments are still your best investments. Evaluate each investment against its alternatives. If you still perceive it to be the best value out there, keep it. If not, consider a swap for something new. Sell if there's something better to buy.

The 100 Best Stocks for 2016: A Few Comments

We're still betting on a gradual and relatively steady recovery as we head into 2016. Tailwinds include continued accommodative monetary policy even with the gradual rise in interest rates (we're betting on the Fed to keep this gradual, visible, and moderate), cheaper energy (which acts like a tax cut for the greater economy, though causing pain in the oil patch and related industries), and an expanding reality and mentality that U.S.-based manufacturing can and does work. The strong dollar, which has been a headwind, is also hurting the balance of trade, as exports are more expensive to their buyers and imports are less expensive to U.S. citizens. This is offset somewhat by cheaper oil, and we also think it will restrain the Fed, as higher interest rates strengthen the dollar. For that reason, we are cautious about the trade balance and how it will affect our businesses, but we realize that the trade balance is a source of stability and instability at the same time.

It's a presidential election year, and that usually means good things, although with today's Washington gridlock it's more of a wait-and-see. Although we'd like to see this happen faster, we still see a continued semi-subconscious adjustment away from low value–add industries toward a back-to-basics, make-things-that-people-need mentality; with capital allocated to things like research labs and factories, not housing and real estate.

Still of continuing concern is the rapid and still-uncontrolled rise in health-care costs. Recent data showed that almost half the jobs created since the trough of the Great Recession are in health care–related fields. Health-care businesses should prosper, but health care also acts like a tax for the rest of us—unless we start exporting health care in a meaningful way (many of the companies we choose in the sector do export health care in the form of pharmaceutical products or health-care technologies). The Affordable Care Act made some important structural changes and expanded the reach of covered health care, but basically kicked the can down the road so far as health-care costs are concerned. We think this could start to be a real drag on the economy in 2016 and especially beyond.

While lower energy prices have kept inflation in check (which should also attenuate interest rate hikes), we still see more inflation at a personal level than we'd like, and wonder sometimes just what numbers the Fed and

Bureau of Labor Statistics are really looking at. Anyone who has bought meat, airline tickets, hotel accommodations—not to mention health insurance—knows what I'm talking about. We wonder where we would be without cheap energy, and as suggested earlier, we do think energy prices will gradually rise to something close to their previous equilibrium, as supply adjusts and demand continues its steady, if moderate, rise.

America is the great nation of consumers; with some 69 percent of economic activity arising from consumption, this country is far and away the leader in that department. Although the gap closed a bit in 2015, we continue to wonder if that is sustainable. (China is 35 percent, Japan is 61 percent, Germany is 58 percent—you get the idea.) We also fret about the growing income gap (clearly the rich are getting richer at the expense of everyone else); that the second-largest category of job increases was in food service, retail, and hospitality suggests that the benefits of economic recovery aren't as helpful to some as others; and that good-paying jobs still exit our shores. We were particularly pained by a recent news story about Disney replacing 250 good-paying IT jobs with insourced overseas workers brought from India to work in U.S. locations at a 25 to 49 percent in wage savings. Disney also forced the displaced workers to train their replacements! We don't think such behavior aligns with the intended use of H-1B visa rules, which are intended to allow hiring for jobs where no adequate U.S. resources are available. (Some of you have asked over the years why we don't include Disney on our *100 Best* lists—actions like this would be part of the answer.)

All of this takes us to the usual place: We stick to companies with great business models, that have brand, marketplace, and financial strength sufficient to master the crosscurrents of change and the emergence of megatrends. We do factor such megatrends as the cloud, the demise of paper in the workplace, the "always-on" nature of personal connectivity (and the prospect of marketers taking advantage of it), the availability of health care for everyone—and now the emergence of the Millennial generation. We've wanted to see a megatrend toward more energy wisdom; that one's been put on hold by cheap energy and new domestic energy supplies, although we're still betting on it for the longer term. We continue to see a "national" economy, where large national brands gradually usurp local favorites, providing extra lift for big brands and big names like Coke and Smucker's and Tiffany. (We do, however, especially with Millennials in mind, watch for localization trends in key industries like food processing; the beer industry, where local microbrews have gained significant share, provides an example.) For 2016, as always, we look for companies with good business models, which produce high value–add things that people (or companies) need, do it efficiently, and generate a lot of cash. Good businesses.

Not just companies that make a lot of money, but good businesses with a sustainable future. We think our "core" list is still pretty good regardless of what the market does; this year we've made ten changes taking in some of the themes we've mentioned previously, or simply switching horses where we felt it made sense. Sell when there's something better to buy. As is our custom, we'll start with the companies removed from the 2015 list:

▼ **Table 3: Companies Removed from 2015 List**

Company	Symbol	Category	Sector
Allergan	AGN	Aggressive Growth	Health Care
Devon Energy	DVN	Aggressive Growth	Energy
Fluor Corporation	FLR	Aggressive Growth	Heavy Construction
FMC Corporation	FMC	Aggressive Growth	Materials
Kellogg	K	Growth and Income	Consumer Staples
McDonald's	MCD	Aggressive Growth	Restaurants
PepsiCo	PEP	Conservative Growth	Consumer Staples
Philips N.V.	PHG	Growth and Income	Industrials
Sigma-Aldrich	SIAL	Aggressive Growth	Industrials
Southern Co.	SO	Growth and Income	Utilities

This year, our "takedowns" follow a few themes already presented. First, and most obvious, we lost Allergan and Sigma-Aldrich to acquisitions. Then, we made a few adjustments based on recent happenings in the energy and commodity patch. Devon Energy, a domestic and fracking play we added just last year, had to be reluctantly removed after only one year on the list; this is one of those cases where we like the core business, but the marketplace and business model shifted in a big enough way to give us cold feet—it wouldn't surprise us if Devon finds its way onto our list again down the road. FMC (minerals) and Fluor (a big stake in energy and refining infrastructure—too many players in this business) also took leave of our list.

But our fine-tooth comb was really directed at companies that would feel increased pain in an atmosphere where Millennials have become demographically dominant. The research is abundant; summing it up, among other things Millennials like customization and personalization, are health conscious, change preferences rapidly (brought on in part by rapid-fire social media; less loyal is another way to put it), like edgy new things, embrace and use information technology for everything, and tend *not* to do things the way Mom and Dad always did them. We looked through our list at companies that would have trouble dealing with this shift. Would Millennials buy IBM and embrace its heritage and brand? Would Millennials consume traditional breakfast cereal? Soft drinks? Mass-produced food and drinks? Packaged foods? Small mass-produced hamburgers in a plastic-y environment with a PlayPlace behind them? We weren't so sure and did comb out a few companies after looking through this lens, some of which might have given us too much duplication anyway. For 2016, Kellogg, McDonald's, and PepsiCo came off the list because we see them as less than ideally positioned with Millennials. In the case of McDonald's, we think it is actually starting to hurt sales. We're likely not done making changes to the *100 Best* list to embrace this demographic shift; stay tuned next year.

Two more companies left our list—Philips N.V. and Southern Company—and both deserve explanation both for the action and as a model of how we think. Philips N.V. was added to the list last year as we sought a little more presence in foreign-based companies, though we were somewhat fearful still because foreign companies are big, complex, and hard to understand, particularly financially. Philips languished through the year and entered a big restructuring phase that appears poised to cut out its most interesting product line: LED lighting. When we looked at the company this year we did not understand the restructuring, and our attempts to decipher the business with all of its currency translations and effects, English translations, and broad but not very insightful "strategic direction" statements . . . Well, we decided we didn't understand this company after all. When we don't understand a company, it doesn't get a place on our *100 Best* list, and we've stepped back on including foreign companies as a strategy on this list (although we did add another one for 2016; stay tuned).

Finally, Southern Company just didn't seem to be where the puck was going in the utility space, with its reliance on coal and nuclear power. The industry is shifting to natural gas and more toward solar and wind as alternative power sources; Southern not only was invested in the "old" technology but has had some major failures in getting a new nuclear plant online and in rolling out a new coal gasification plant. Sell when there's something better to buy—and we switched horses to CenterPoint Energy, another geographically Southern utility with a more progressive business model. We tend to favor business models that keep up with the times. Incidentally, we kept our NextEra and Otter Tail Corporation picks, as we see these utilities as well positioned in the current and future environment.

Sell when there's something better to buy. So we did that in ten cases, and here they are:

▼ Table 4: New Companies for 2016

CenterPoint Energy	CNP	Growth and Income	Utilities
Cincinnati Financial	CINF	Growth and Income	Financials
Empire State Realty Trust	ESRT	Growth and Income	Real Estate
Fresh Del Monte	FPD	Conservative Growth	Consumer Staples
Hillenbrand Inc.	HI	Aggressive Growth	Industrials
International Flavors & Fragrances	IFF	Aggressive Growth	Consumer Staples
Novo Nordisk	NVO	Aggressive Growth	Health Care
RPM International	RPM	Aggressive Growth	Basic Materials
Timken Company	TKR	Aggressive Growth	Industrials
WD-40 Company	WDFC	Aggressive Growth	Industrials

Now the real fun begins—typically introducing our new picks is one of the more enjoyable and rewarding parts of creating this narrative.

First, we'll admit right off the bat . . . this was hard to do this year! "Sell when there's something better to buy" continues to rule the day, but the second part of that equation, finding companies better to buy, was a challenge this year. When we made the selections, stocks were at an all-time high, and the challenge, once again—greater than usual—was to find corners of the market that seemed to have potential nevertheless. We went through a great many choices to come up with this year's list, and Table 4 shows the result.

Easy to explain is CenterPoint Energy: It's a quid pro quo replacement for Southern Company as just described. We decided to re-up Cincinnati Financial, in the property/casualty insurance business, for another tour of duty; we had just scratched it last year for valuation reasons and replaced it with Allstate, but now we've decided we like this P/C model and the Berkshire Hathaway approach of profiting off the "float" sufficiently well that we could and should have two such companies on the list.

Empire State Realty Trust is a small (really, mid-cap) REIT designed to extend our REIT portfolio with prime New York–area properties and a strong potential growth component as the company finishes major retrofit and "green" enhancement projects. Fresh Del Monte is a play on healthy Millennial tastes and a state-of-the-art logistics system. Hillenbrand, RPM

International, and Timken are from those mid-cap corners of the market, small to medium-sized established businesses with strong niches, brands, and financials thus derived. International Flavors & Fragrances is an excellent niche play we wish we had decided on sooner, but it exhibits the strengths we like even though others have found it. Novo Nordisk at once replaces Allergan in the Health Care sector and gives us that overseas company we lost by cutting Philips N.V. (neither reason per se is why we picked it), and has a strong growth story in the unfortunately robust diabetes treatment market. Finally, WD-40 is a heralded brand that seems ripe for expansion by this particularly well-managed company.

As you can see from Table 5, our sector weighting didn't really change that much: one fewer in the Energy and Heavy Construction sectors for reasons already clear, another toe in the Financials water with Cincinnati Financial, not too risky as it's a known quantity headquartered far from the wolves of Wall Street, and another lot next door bought in the Real Estate sector. Our other moves were largely replacements.

▼ **Table 5: Sector Analysis and 2015 Change by Sector**

Sector	On 2015 list	Added for 2016	Cut from 2015	On 2016 list
Business Services	2			2
Consumer Discretionary	5			5
Consumer Staples	13	2	-2	13
Consumer Durables	1			1
Energy	7		-1	6
Entertainment	1			1
Financials	4	1		5
Health Care	14	1	-1	14
Heavy Construction	1		-1	0
Industrials	15	3	-2	16
Information Technology	8			8
Materials	6	1	-1	6
Real Estate	1	1		2

Restaurants	2		-1	1
Retail	9			9
Telecommunications Services	3			3
Transportation	5			5
Utilities	3	1	-1	3

Yield Signs

We continue to like dividend-paying stocks. We like stocks that pay meaningful dividends, and especially stocks that have a tendency to raise their dividends over time.

With dividend-paying stocks, especially those inclined to raise their dividends, you get an attractive yield from the day you buy the stock, but you'll also get handsome raises over time. As we reported earlier, 93 of the 98 dividend-paying stocks on the 2015 *100 Best* list raised their dividends in 2014, and 46 of those have raised their dividends in each of the past ten years. We like this. We like it a lot. A company that raises its dividend 10 percent will roughly double the payout in just seven years. (Calculation? Rule of 72—divide the percent increase into 72 and you'll get the number of years it takes to double: 72/10 equals 7.2 years.) You could end up with twice the income in addition to any gains or growth in the price of the stock.

DIVIDEND-PAYING, DIVIDEND-RAISING STOCKS—NOW AND FOREVER

The Rule of 72 and dividend-paying stocks lessons should be taken to heart by prudent investors, particularly those who fret about the effects of rising interest rates on their income-oriented investments (and who follow such fret in the financial media). When interest rates rise, bond prices fall, as the implied yield must adjust somehow; that is, a bond that generates a fixed-income stream is worth relatively less in a higher interest–rate environment. Often, as we've seen, dividend-paying stocks take a tumble along with their bond brethren anytime even the rumor of rising interest rates is unsheathed. But the rising dividend provides the difference, and we feel that most of the investing world, particularly those attempting to build a comfortable retirement stream, should take note.

If you invest in a bond over a ten-year period, that bond will pay back its original principal at the end of the ten years, plus the interest as prescribed initially when the bond is sold. Nothing more, nothing less—so long as you wait ten years assuming no default—and you might not get your original principal if you decide to sell the bond sooner in a rising interest-rate environment (note that the interest payments don't go up; only that the bond value goes down).

If you invest in a dividend-paying stock with a persistent dividend raise policy and track record, as some two-thirds of the *100 Best* list represents, you enjoy the benefits of—and the protection of—the rising dividend. If your company raises its dividend 10 percent each year, the dividend will double in 7.2 years, and if it's paying 3 percent today, that implies 6 percent in 7.2 years—or a doubling in the stock price if the same yield is maintained (which is affected by a lot of factors besides the yield). If your company raises its dividend only 5 percent each year, it doubles in 14.4 years but is still up roughly 70 percent in the ten-year period just described. That's still a handsome gain in payout as well as giving solid potential for stock appreciation.

This favorable scenario simply does not exist for bonds. Bonds may be a bit more safe, as the interest payments are less likely to be cut (a cut is a default) and will be paid before dividends. But when we put a stock on the *100 Best* list, we feel that not only is the dividend itself fairly secure, but so is the potential for increase. We should also add that dividends receive favorable tax treatment for those of you holding investments outside of retirement accounts.

We continue to feel that investing in dividend-paying, dividend-growing stocks is the best way to save for a financially secure future.

In the beginning of this narrative, we mentioned the two key indicators that suggest a good stock for further analysis: strong and growing yield, and persistence of share buybacks. Like that pretty face at a party, those two features suggest that we should learn the rest of the story. We continue to focus on those healthy companies willing to not only share a portion of their profits but also to give you, the investor, a periodic raise to recognize the value of your commitment of precious investment capital. In that spirit, in our presentation format we show the number of dividend increases in the past ten years in the header right after Current Yield. We know of no other financial publication that does this.

We also present the Dividend Aggressors list in our Stars lists, which you'll see shortly. Dividend Aggressors are companies with substantial payouts that are also growing those payouts at a persistent and substantial rate. They have indicated through both words and performance that they continue to do so and have the resources to do it. So it isn't enough to raise the dividend each year by just a penny; it must be substantial. It also isn't enough to raise the dividend each year but still only be yielding 0.5 percent. There are lists of "dividend achievers" floating around on the Internet, and there are even a few funds constructed around a dividend achievers index. Our Aggressors are—well—a bit more aggressive.

The climate for dividend growth continues to be favorable. Standard & Poor's estimates that dividends for its 500 will rise some 9.0 percent in 2015, which has dropped a bit since 2014's 9.9 percent. Part of the reason is the addition of a few new non-payer stocks to the S&P 500 index such as Facebook and Michael Kors, but part may be that growth has simply hit a ceiling—but a 9 percent ceiling isn't too bad as the previous sidebar suggests. We see no "fade" in this figure going forward, as companies are swimming in cash ($1.4 trillion for the 500 in early 2015). Rather than commit to expensive wages or business investments that might not pan out, they are simply returning cash to previously starved shareholders. This may be further helped along by lower energy and commodity input prices as they become baked into company performance.

Dancing with the Stars

We continue developing and sharing our "star" categories—groups of stocks, essentially the "best of the best" in categories we chose to highlight—yield stars, dividend aggressors, safety and stability stars, growth stars, prosperity stars, and moat stars. We provide these stars lists because we know that every investor has his or her own preferences, and thus there are no "best" stocks within our "best" list; that is, there is no number one, two, and so on within the list.

Table 6 shows the top 20 stocks on our *100 Best* list by percentage yield as of mid-2015:

▼ **Table 6: Top 20 Dividend-Paying Stocks**

Company	Symbol	Projected 2015 dividend	Yield %	Dividend raises, past 10 years
AT&T	T	$1.88	5.3%	10
Health Care REIT	HCN	$3.30	5.3%	10
Total S.A.	TOT	$2.80	4.4%	8
Verizon	VZ	$2.24	4.3%	9
Otter Tail Corporation	OTTR	$1.23	4.1%	5
ConocoPhillips	COP	$2.92	4.0%	9
Seagate Technology	STX	$2.16	4.0%	9
CenterPoint Energy (*)	CNP	$0.99	3.9%	10
Chevron	CVX	$4.40	3.9%	10
Kimberly-Clark	KMB	$3.52	3.5%	10
Cincinnati Financial (*)	CINF	$1.82	3.4%	10
Clorox Company	CLX	$3.00	3.4%	10
General Electric	GE	$0.92	3.4%	8
Paychex	PAYX	$1.52	3.4%	8
General Mills	GIS	$1.67	3.3%	10
Sysco	SYY	$1.20	3.3%	10
Public Storage	PSA	$5.92	3.3%	9
Coca-Cola	KO	$1.32	3.2%	10
Procter & Gamble	PG	$2.60	3.2%	10
Daktronics	DAKT	$0.50	3.1%	7

Table 6.1 shows our list of Dividend Aggressors for 2016:

▼ **Table 6.1: Dividend Aggressors: Companies with Strong Dividend Track Records**

Company	Symbol	Estimated 2015 dividend	Yield %	Dividend raises, past 10 years
3M Company	MMM	$4.10	2.6%	10
AT&T	T	$1.88	5.3%	10
Chevron	CVX	$4.40	3.9%	10
Clorox Company	CLX	$3.00	3.4%	10
Coca-Cola	KO	$1.32	3.2%	10
General Mills	GIS	$1.67	3.3%	10
Health Care REIT	HCN	$3.30	5.3%	10
Johnson & Johnson	JNJ	$2.92	3.0%	10
Kimberly-Clark	KMB	$3.52	3.5%	10
NextEra Energy	NEE	$3.08	2.9%	10
Norfolk Southern	NSC	$2.36	2.4%	10
Procter & Gamble	PG	$2.60	3.2%	10
Public Storage	PSA	$5.92	3.3%	9
Scotts Miracle-Gro	SMG	$1.85	3.1%	6
Seagate Technology	STX	$2.16	4.0%	9
Target Corporation	TGT	$2.15	2.8%	10
United Parcel Service	UPS	$2.92	2.9%	10
Valero	VLO	$1.60	2.9%	9
Verizon	VZ	$2.24	4.3%	9
Wells Fargo	WFC	$1.48	2.8%	8

REMEMBER, THERE ARE NO GUARANTEES

While dividends and especially high yields are attractive, investors must remember that corporations are under no contractual or legal obligation to pay them! Interest payments on time deposits and bonds are much more clearly defined, and failure to pay can represent default. With dividends, there is no such safety net. Companies can—and do—reduce or eliminate dividends in bad times, as most strikingly observed with BP in the wake of the Deepwater Horizon Gulf spill disaster in 2010 and most bank stocks after the 2008 dive. More recently, energy price declines have hurt many U.S. oil producers, particularly more indebted ones engaged in the more expensive "fracking" process—and many of these players have cut or omitted dividends mostly in early 2015. Dividend investors should therefore keep an eye out for changes in a company's business prospects and shouldn't put too many eggs in a single high-yielding basket. On the flip side, as investors become more conscious of returns, and as corporate management teams become more aware of such investor consciousness, we've seen a lot of companies loudly trumpet their recent dividend increases to their investors and the investing public. It's a nice sound that we hope to continue to hear.

Safety Stars

Safety stars are companies we think will hold up well in volatile and negative stock markets as well as recessionary economies. They have stable products and customer bases, and long traditions of being able to manage well in downturns. We made one small change, subbing in Bemis for the relatively higher-flying J.M. Smucker. Several others, including the likes of Colgate-Palmolive, Coca-Cola, and Procter & Gamble from the remainder of the *100 Best* list would probably qualify.

▼ Table 7: Top 10 Stocks for Safety and Stability

Company	Symbol
Aqua America	WTR
Becton, Dickinson	BDX
Bemis	BMS
Campbell Soup	CPB
Clorox Company	CLX
General Mills	GIS
Johnson & Johnson	JNJ

Kimberly-Clark	KMB
McCormick & Co.	MKC
Sysco	SYY

Growth Stars

Looking at the other side of the coin, we picked ten stocks we feel are especially well positioned to grow, even in a negative economy and especially in a positive one. We made one change, bringing in the growth engine Novo Nordisk in place of Daktronics, whose growth prospects are there but appear more muted at present.

▼ Table 8: Growth Stars: Top 10 Stocks for Growth

Company	Symbol
Apple	AAPL
CarMax	KMX
Corning	GLW
Harman International	HAR
Nike	NKE
Novo Nordisk	NVO
ResMed	RMD
Seagate Technology	STX
Starbucks	SBUX
Visa	V

Prosperity Stars

Two years ago we shifted into post–Great Recession gear, replacing our "recovery stars" list with a "prosperity stars" selection. For this year we removed Allergan (due to acquisition) and Fluor, due to weak performance and ties to the energy industry; we added GE and recent pick and dark horse Schnitzer Steel, which stands to benefit from any gain in the metals markets as, being in the recycling business, we think it will run ahead of miners in a recovery.

▼ **Table 9: Prosperity Stars: Top 10 Stocks for a Growing Economy**

Company	Symbol
CarMax	KMX
DuPont	DD
General Electric	GE
Grainger, W.W.	GWW
Illinois Tool Works	ITW
Schnitzer Steel	SCHN
Southwest Airlines	LUV
Steelcase	SCS
Tiffany	TIF
Whirlpool	WHR

Moat Stars

Finally, we get back to one of the core tenets of value investing—the ability of a company to build a sustainable and unassailable competitive advantage. Value investing aficionados call such an advantage a "moat," for it represents a barrier to entry for competitors that will likely preserve that advantage for some time. The moat can come in the form of technology, the use of technology, a brand, enduring customer relationships, channel relationships, size or scale, or simply a really big head start into a business that makes it hard or even impossible for competitors to catch up. The appraisal of a moat is hardly an exact science; here we give our top ten picks based on the size and strength (width?) of the moat. For this year we removed Sysco and W.W. Grainger, as, while they're market-share leaders in their businesses, they still have relatively small market shares (as came to light in the Sysco/U.S. Foods presentation to the FTC on their proposed merger). We added WD-40, and McCormick, which both clearly dominate their niche and have a huge lead on any potential competition.

▼ Table 10: Moat Stars: Top 10 Stocks for Sustainable Competitive Advantage

Company	Symbol
Apple	AAPL
Coca-Cola	KO
McCormick & Co.	MKC
Monsanto	MON
Pall Corporation	PLL
Ralph Lauren	RL
Starbucks	SBUX
Tiffany	TIF
Visa	V
WD-40 Company	WDFC

What Makes a Best Stock Best?

In this year's opener, we proclaimed that we could identify a good *100 Best* candidate on two simple features: increasing dividend and declining share counts. But these, of course, aren't the whole story: Where do we go from there? What comes next? What is it that defines excellence—sustainable excellence—among companies? That's been a topic of considerable debate for years, and with all the study that's gone into it, nobody has hit upon a single formula for deciphering undeniable excellence in a company. That may seem amazing at first, but when you think about it, it isn't.

"Excellence" isn't as scientific as most of us would like or expect it to be. Much like finding your "match" and life partner, it defies data and mathematical formulation. Take the square of net profits, multiply by the cosine of the debt-to-equity ratio, add the square root of the revenue-per-employee count, and what do you get? Some nice numbers, but not a clear picture of how the company works or how a company will sell its products to customers and prosper going forward. And you certainly wouldn't want to select your ideal "match" this way.

Fundamentals such as profitability, productivity, and asset efficiency tell us how well a company has done in the marketplace and, by proxy, how well it is managed. Fundamentals are about what the company has already achieved and where it stands right now, and if a company's current fundamentals are a mess (or your potential partner is in bankruptcy court)—

stop right now; there isn't much point in going any further.

In most cases, what really separates the great from the good are the intangibles, the "soft" factors of market position, market acceptance, customer "love" of a company's products, its management, its aura. These features create competitive advantage, or "distinctive competence," as an economist would put it, that cannot be valued. Furthermore, and most importantly, they are more about what a company is set up to achieve in the future. When you think about it, it's the intangibles that provide the spark for most of our personal matches, too.

To paraphrase Buffett at his best: Give me $100 billion, and I could start a company; but I could never create another Coca-Cola.

What does that mean? It means that Coca-Cola has already established a worldwide brand cachet; the distribution channels, customer knowledge, and product development expertise cannot be duplicated at any cost. When companies have competitive advantages that cannot be duplicated at any cost, they have an enduring grip on their markets. They can charge more for their products. They have a moat that insulates them from competition or makes it much more expensive for competitors to participate. They're perceived by loyal customers as having top-line products worth paying more for.

A company with exceptional intangibles can control price and, in many cases, can control its costs.

Strategic Fundamentals

Let's examine a list of strategic fundamentals that define, or keep score of, a company's success. This list can be used as a checklist, although it's hard to find a company that shows excellence in all of these areas.

Are Gross and Operating Profit Margins Growing?

We like profitable companies; who doesn't? But what really counts is the size of the margin and especially the growth. If a company has a gross margin (sales minus costs of goods sold) exceeding that of its competitors, that shows that it's doing something right, probably with its customers and/or with its costs. But competitive analysis is elusive; there is no dependable source of "industry" gross margins, and comparing competitors can be difficult because no two companies are exactly alike; it's easy to mix apples and oranges.

We like to see what direction gross margin is moving in—up or down. A growing gross margin also signals that the company is doing something right and is gaining strength in its markets and/or its supply chain. That isn't perfect, either; as the economy moved from boom to bust, many excellent companies reported declines in gross and especially operating margins (sales minus cost of goods sold minus operating expenses) as they laid off workers and used less capacity. Still, in a steady-state environment, it makes sense to favor companies with growing margins. In a declining market, companies that can *protect* their margins will come out ahead.

DOES A COMPANY PRODUCE MORE CAPITAL THAN IT CONSUMES?

Make no mistake about it—we like cash. Pure and simple, we also like it when a company produces more cash than it consumes.

At the end of the day, cash generation is the simplest measure of whether a company is being successful, especially over the long term. Sure, if a company buys an airplane or opens a factory or a bunch of stores in a given quarter, it will be cash-flow negative. But that should be a temporary thing; over the long haul, it should produce, not consume, cash. Companies that continually have to borrow or sell shares to raise enough cash to stay in business are on the wrong track.

So how do you determine this? You'll have to become familiar with the Statement of Cash Flows or equivalent in a company's financial reports. "Cash flow from operations" is usually positive and represents cash booked from sales less cost of goods sold, with adjustments for noncash items like depreciation and for increases or decreases in working capital. In simple terms, is the cash going into the cash register from the daily operations of the business?

"Cash used for investing purposes" or similar is a bit of a misnomer and represents net cash used to "invest" in the business—usually for capital expenditures, but also for short-term noncash investments like securities and a few other smaller items usually beyond scope. This figure is typically negative unless the company sells some part of its infrastructure. Over the long haul, cash generated from operations should well exceed cash used to invest in the business.

Companies in expansion mode may not show this surplus, and that's where "cash from financing activities" comes in. That's the cash generated from issuing debt or selling securities—or paying off debt or repurchasing shares, if things are going well—and dividends are included here as well. Again, a successful company will produce more cash—capital—from the business than it consumes, just as a successful household does the same, or else it goes into debt. Smart investors track this surplus over time.

ARE EXPENSES UNDER CONTROL?

Just like your household, company expenses should be under control, and anything else, especially without explanation, is a yellow flag.

The best way to test this is to check whether the "Selling, General, and Administrative" expenses (SG&A) are rising, and more to the point, rising faster than sales. If so, that's a yellow, not necessarily a red, flag, but if it continues, it suggests that something is out of control, and it will catch up with the company sooner or later. In a downturn, companies that are able to reduce their expenses to match revenue declines scored more points, too.

IS WORKING CAPITAL UNDER CONTROL?

Working capital is a hard concept to grasp—even for small entrepreneurs who live with its ups and downs on a daily basis. Insufficient working capital is one of the biggest causes of death for small businesses, and working capital and especially changes in working capital can signal success or trouble.

Using a simple analogy, working capital is the circulatory lifeblood of the business. Money comes in and money goes out, and working capital is what circulates in the veins in between. In its purest sense, it is cash, receivables, and inventory, less short-term debts. It's what you own less what you owe aside from fixed assets like plant and equipment.

If receivables are increasing, that sounds like a good thing—more people owe you more money. But if receivables are rising and sales aren't, that suggests that people aren't paying their bills, or worse, the business has to finance more to achieve the same level of sales. Similarly, a rise in inventory without a rise in sales means that it costs the business more money—more working capital—to do the same amount of business. That costs twice, because unless the firm is lucky, more inventory means more obsolescence and potentially more deep-discount sales or more writeoffs down the road.

So a sharp investor will check to see that major working capital items—receivables and inventory—aren't growing faster than sales; indeed, a company that generates more sales with a decrease in working capital is becoming more productive.

IS DEBT IN LINE WITH BUSINESS GROWTH?

Like many other "fundamentals" items, you can tear your hair out looking at debt figures and trying to decide whether they're in line with asset levels, equity levels, and industry norms. A simpler test is to check and see whether long-term debt is increasing or decreasing, and in particular, whether it is increasing faster than business growth. Gold stars go to companies with little to no debt, and to companies able to grow without issuing mountains of long-term debt. It's also worth checking to make sure the company isn't simply issuing debt to buy back shares—a little of this is okay, but some companies take on expensive debt just to increase per-share earnings (and management bonuses). This isn't a good strategy; in fact, it isn't a strategy at all.

Is Return on Equity Steady or Growing?

Return on equity (ROE) is another of those hard-to-grasp concepts, and another subjective measure when valuing assets and earnings. But at the end of the day, it's what all investors really seek: a return on their capital investments.

Like many other figures pulled from income statements and balance sheets, an ROE number, without any context, is hard to interpret. Does a 26.7 percent ROE mean, in itself, that a company is excellent? The figure sounds healthy, to be sure—it's a heck of a lot better than investing your money in a CD or T-bill. But because earnings and asset values are subjective, it may not represent true success. In fact, a company can increase ROE simply by borrowing money (yes!) and investing it into the business, even if it isn't invested as productively as other previous funds were invested. The math is complicated; we won't go into it here.

So the true test of ROE success is to check whether it is steady or increasing. Increasing—that makes sense. Why *steady*? Because if a company makes profits in a previous period and reinvests them in the business, that amount of money becomes part of equity (retained earnings). If the company reinvests productively, it will produce more returns, and ROE will at least keep up. If the company can't reinvest those earnings productively, ROE will drop—and perhaps it should be paying the earnings to you as dividends instead of investing them unproductively in the business. So if ROE is steady, the company still has good investments to make, and management is probably doing the right thing.

We should note that many investment analysts today prefer "Return on Invested Capital" (ROIC) as a metric over ROE. ROIC is return, or profit, divided by total equity *plus* debt. This gets you past the distortions that adding debt to the balance sheet might cause. Since the traditional balance sheet equation holds that "Assets = Liabilities + Capital," you can simply use total assets as the denominator—essentially the measure is "return on assets." Some analysts prefer to go farther by removing the cash balance from the asset denominator, to reflect the assets deployed and in use to generate returns and to get around the distortions of large reserve capital infusions often found at startup companies.

Does the Company Pay a Dividend?

Different people feel differently about dividends, and as previously described, we place great emphasis on dividend-paying stocks and especially those that *grow* their dividends. After all, save for the eventual sale of the company to someone else, a dividend is the only true cash that an investor will realize from buying a stock in a corporation, other than by selling the stock. At least in theory, investors should receive some compensation for their investments once in a while.

Yet, many companies don't pay dividends or don't pay dividends that compete very effectively with fixed-income yields. Why do investors put up with this? Because, in theory anyway, a company in a good business should be able to reinvest profits more effectively than the investor can (or else why would the investor have bought the company in the first place?). Investors trust that reinvested profits will eventually bring the growth in company value that will be reflected in the share price, or eventual takeover, or an eventual payment of a dividend or, better yet, growth in that dividend.

That's the theory, anyway, but there are still lots of companies that get away with paying no dividend at all. Can we tolerate this? Yes, if a company is really doing a great job with their retained profits, like Apple before they started paying dividends three years ago, or CarMax. But we favor companies that offer at least something to their investors in the short term, some return on their hard-earned and faithfully committed capital. If nothing else, it keeps management teams honest and shows that management understands that shareholder interests are up there somewhere on the list of priorities. And getting an ever-*increasing* dividend—and owning a stock that has most likely appreciated because the dividend has increased—is like having your cake and eating it, too: a true favorite among investors, as noted in our previous sidebar (Dividend-Paying, Dividend-Raising Stocks—Now and Forever).

Strategic Intangibles

When you look at any company, perhaps the bottom-line question follows the Buffett wisdom: If you had $100 billion in cool cash to spend (and we'll assume the genius intellect to spend it *well*), could you re-create that company?

If the answer is yes, it may still be a great company, but it may not be great enough to fend off competition and keep its customers forever. If the answer is no, the company truly has something unique to offer in the marketplace, difficult to duplicate at any cost. That distinctive competence, that sustainable competitive edge—whatever it is, a brand, a trade secret, a lock on distribution or supply channels—may be worth more than all the factories and high-rise office buildings and cash in the bank a company could ever have.

What we're talking about are the intangibles, the "soft" factors that make companies unique and that add up to more than the sum of their parts, the factors that ultimately drive future revenues. Intangibles not only define excellence, they define the future, while fundamentals mainly define the past. Seven key intangibles follow, although you'll think of more, and some industries may have some unique ones of their own, like intellectual property in the technology sector.

Does the Company Have a Moat?

A business moat performs much the same role as its medieval castle equivalent—it protects the business from competition. Whatever factors create the moat, ultimately those are the factors that prevent you, with your $100 billion, from taking their business. Moats are usually a combination of brand, product technology, design, marketing and distribution channels, and customer loyalty all working together to protect a company. A moat doesn't just protect the existence of a company, it helps it command higher prices and earn higher profits.

Whether a company has a narrow moat, a wide moat, or none at all is a subjective assessment for you to make. However, you can get some help at Morningstar (*www.morningstar.com*), whose stock ratings include an assessment of the moat.

Coca-Cola has a moat because of the sheer impossibility of surpassing its brand and brand recognition worldwide. CarMax has a moat because it is further along in putting retail-style dealerships on the ground and applying management information technologies to its business than anyone else; it would take years for a competitor to catch up. Tiffany has a moat because of its immediately recognized brand and elegantly simple, stylish brand image and the enduring and timeless panache around that. WD-40 has a moat because it's virtually the only game in town and the only recognized brand for its relatively simple product. The Moat Stars list presented earlier identifies the top ten stocks with a solid and sustainable competitive advantage.

Does the Company Have an Excellent Brand?

It's hard to say enough about brand, especially in today's fast-moving, highly packaged, highly national and international marketplace. A strong brand means consistency and a promise to consumers, and consumers sold on a brand will prefer it over any other, almost regardless of price. People still buy Tide; Starbucks is still synonymous with high quality and ambience. Good brands command higher prices and foster loyalty, identity, and even customer "love."

Ask yourself if a company has a sought-after brand, a brand customers would pay extra to buy or align with, a brand that would be difficult to duplicate at any cost. Would customers rather fight than switch? Think about Starbucks, Coca-Cola, Allstate, Tiffany, Smucker's, Ralph Lauren, Scotts, or Nike, or the brands within a house, like Minute Maid (Coke), Tide (P&G), Mark Levinson (Harman International), KitchenAid (Whirlpool), or Teflon (DuPont).

Is the Company a Market Leader?

Market leadership usually—but not always—goes hand in hand with brand. The trick is to decide whether a company really leads in its industry. Often—but not always—that's a factor of size. The market leader usually has the highest market share, and the important point is that it calls the shots with regard to price, technology, marketing message, and so forth—other companies must play catch-up and often discount their prices to keep up. Apple is a market leader in digital music, Monsanto in systematized agriculture, Nike in sports apparel, and Starbucks in beverages—and so forth.

Excellent companies tend to be market leaders, and market leaders tend to be excellent companies. However, this relationship doesn't always hold true—sometimes the nimble but smaller competitor is the excellent company and *headed for* market leadership. Examples like CarMax, Perrigo, Valero, and Southwest Airlines can be found on our list.

Does the Company Have Channel Excellence?

"Channels" in business parlance means a chain of players to sell and distribute a company's products. It might be stores, it might be other industrial companies, it might be direct to the consumer. If a company is considered a top supplier in a particular channel, or a company has especially good relations with its channel, that's a plus.

Excellent companies develop solid channel relationships and become the preferred supplier in those channels. Companies such as Patterson, Deere, Fair Isaac, McCormick, Nike, Novo Nordisk, Procter & Gamble, Scotts Miracle-Gro, Sysco, WD-40, and Whirlpool all have excellent relationships with the channels through which they sell their product.

DOES THE COMPANY HAVE SUPPLY-CHAIN EXCELLENCE?

Like distribution channels, excellent companies develop excellent and low-cost supply channels. They are seldom caught off-guard by supply shortages and tend to get favorable and stable prices for whatever they buy. This is often not an easy assessment unless you know something about a particular industry. Fresh Del Monte, Nike, Target, and Procter & Gamble again, are examples of companies that have done a good job managing their supply chains.

DOES THE COMPANY HAVE EXCELLENT MANAGEMENT?

It's not hard to grasp what happens if a company *doesn't* have good management: Performance fails, and few inside or outside the company respect the company. It's not easy for an investor to determine if a management team does a good job or acts in shareholder interests. Clues can include candor and honesty and the ability of company management to speak in accessible, easily understood terms about the company and company performance (it's worth listening to conference calls as a resource). A management team that admits errors and eschews other forms of arrogance and entitlement (i.e., luxury perks, office suites, aircraft) is probably tilting its interests toward shareholders, as is the management team that can cough up some return to shareholders once in a while in the form of a dividend.

This may be the most subjective and elusive assessment of all, as few investors work with these folks on a daily basis. Still, over time, you can garner a strong hunch about whether a management team is effective and on your side. We're reluctant to keep mentioning WD-40 in this section, but a trip through their website and especially their "values" page (*www .wd40company.com/about/values/*) will give you (as it gave us) comfort with their management style. Of course, be careful: It can be difficult to separate the "business B.S." from the true indicators of excellence; it becomes largely a matter of gut feel and personal assessment of what they say—again, we're back to what it takes to make that relationship "match."

Are There Signs of Innovation Excellence?

This question seems pretty obvious, but it's not just about the products that a company sells. True, if the company is leading the industry in innovation, that's usually a good thing, for "first to market" definitely offers business advantages.

The less obvious part of this question is whether the company makes the best *use* of technology to make operations and customer interfaces as efficient and effective as possible. Southwest Airlines may have missed our list in the past because of the difficulty of achieving excellence in an industry where players can't control prices or costs. While airlines have enjoyed better times, we still don't like them in general—but Southwest continues to make our list today, not only because of brand and management excellence, but also innovation excellence. Why? Simply because, after all of these years, amazingly, it still has the best, simplest, easiest-to-use flight booking and check-in in the industry. Sometimes such innovations mean a lot more than bringing new, fancy products and bells and whistles to the market. You can also look to Apple, CarMax, CenterPoint Energy, Daktronics, FedEx, Itron, Novo Nordisk, ResMed, Steelcase, UPS, and Visa on our list for more obvious examples of companies that have deployed technology and innovative customer interfaces to achieve sustainable competitive advantage.

Choosing the *100 Best*

With all of this in mind, just how was this year's *100 Best Stocks* list actually chosen?

The answer is more subtle than you might think. If we could give you a precise formula, you wouldn't need this book. You'd be able to do it yourself. In fact, every investor would be able to do it on his or her own. Our book would simply be the result of yet another stock screener, and every investor would invest in the same stocks. Is that a feasible or practical solution? Hardly. Everyone would scramble to buy the same 100 best stocks. The prices would be sky high, and the price of other stocks would melt to nothing.

SIGNS OF VALUE

Following are a few signs of value to look for in any company. This is not an exhaustive list by any means, but it's a good place to start:

- » Rising dividends
- » Declining share count
- » Gaining market share
- » Can control price
- » Loyal customers
- » Growing margins
- » Producing, not consuming, capital (free cash flow)
- » Steady or increasing ROE
- » Management forthcoming, honest, understandable

SIGNS OF UNVALUE

. . . and signs of trouble, or "unvalue":

- » Declining margins
- » No brand or who-cares brand
- » Commodity producer, must compete on price
- » Losing market dominance or market share
- » Can't control costs
- » Must acquire other companies to grow
- » Management in hiding, off message, making excuses, difficult to understand, or in the news for all the wrong reasons

Fortunately or unfortunately, however you want to look at it, creating a comprehensive investing "formula" or screener just can't be done. There are so many fundamentals, so many intangibles, and so many unknown and unknowable weighting factors to combine the fundamentals and intangibles that—well—it just wouldn't work. No screener could re-create the subtle judgment that gets applied to the cold, hard facts. It's that judgment, the interpretation of the facts and intangibles, that makes it worth spending money on a book like ours.

While we didn't apply a specific formula or screener to the universe of stocks, we did take a few measurable factors into account to narrow the list from thousands to a few hundred issues. Those factors came from several sources, but at this point we must tip our cap to Value Line and the research and database work they do as part of The Value Line Investment Survey. If you aren't familiar with Value Line, it's worth a look for any savvy individual investor, either online at **www.valueline.com** or, in many cases, at your local library. It is an excellent resource.

When to Buy? Consider When to Sell

We've said it over and over: Sell when there's something better to buy.

Selling is hard. So is removing something from our *100 Best* list (unless it became part of a takeover transaction). If it's hard to figure out when to buy a stock, it's even harder to figure out when to sell. People tend to get married to their investment decisions, feeling somehow that if it isn't right, maybe time will help and things will get better. It's human nature.

Or they're just too arrogant to admit that they made a mistake. That's also human nature.

There are lots of reasons why people hold on to investments for too long a time.

Here's the fundamental truth: Buying and selling should be much the same process. Let's look at it from the point of view of selling. When should you sell? Simply, as we've said repeatedly, when there's *something else better to buy*. Something else better for future returns, something else better for safety, something else better for timeliness or fit with today's go-forward worldview; a *megatrend* as we've referred to it. That something else can be another stock, an index fund, or a house, or any kind of investment. It can also be cash—sell that stock when . . . when what? When cash is a better investment. Or when you need the money, which is another way of saying that cash is a better investment—at least it's safer for the time being.

Similarly, if you think of a buy decision as a best possible deployment of capital because there's no better way to invest your money, you'll also come out ahead. It really isn't that hard, especially if you've done your homework. And it's also made easier if you avoid rash overcommitments; that is, you avoid buying all at once in case you've made a mistake or in case better prices come later down the road.

ETFs: Different Route, Same Destination (Almost)

The 100 Best Stocks to Buy series continues to be about—well—the 100 best individual companies in which you can buy shares to build into your investment portfolio. The objective is to use these selections as a starting point to build a customized portfolio of your very own, a portfolio that earns decent, better-than-market, long-term returns from excellent companies while—because they're excellent companies—taking less risk than you would with most investments. Because you're doing it yourself, you save money on fees and expenses and come away with the pride of ownership of doing it yourself.

That said, not everyone has the time or inclination to do this this. Not everyone wants to sail through the treacherous channels of company financial information and the foggy mysteries of intangibles and marketplace performance to figure out which companies are really best to own and to keep a finger on the pulse to make sure they stay that way. You may want to own individual stocks. But just as buying a kit makes many aspects of building a new outdoor deck easier, so does buying a stock "kit": a product or package of stocks to do what you might otherwise have to struggle through on your own. If you could get such a kit product cheap enough and aligned to your needs, then why wouldn't you? It will save time, and you'll be firing up the barbecue and enjoying those outdoor parties with your friends a lot sooner. Or, perhaps at the risk of more tiring analogies, buying individual stocks is like ordering à la carte from a menu. You're not sure if what you're getting works together, so why not do a *prix fixe* to let the chef do some of the driving? Okay, enough . . .

Such is the impulse to find investment products—packages, *prix fixe* menus—that mimic the performance of the *100 Best* stocks. Honestly, we would love it if some fund company would come to us and "buy" our index to build a fund you could buy, but that hasn't happened yet. However, in that spirit—and because we've written a lot about the merits of individual stock versus fund investing before—we'd like to offer this special section about using exchange-traded funds (ETFs) as a path to own portfolios crafted with many of the *100 Best Stocks* principles in mind.

The ETF Universe

We're talking about ETFs here, not traditional mutual funds. Although total traditional mutual fund assets still outweigh ETF-held assets by a factor of eight to one, traditional mutual funds are more expensive and haven't performed as well as ETFs—or the market benchmarks—over time. So we

will limit this discussion to ETFs, but if you're ▸
advisor or are limited to traditional funds thr
other investment platform, the discussion car
too.

ETFs are packaged single securities tradi
than directly through a mutual fund comp
securities that track the composition of specia.,
most ETFs (excluding "actively managed" ETFs) there are no ru...
making individual stock purchase or sale decisions. The fund follows the
index.

These indexes started out as broad, bland, and obvious—the first ETF,
the SPDR S&P 500 ETF Trust, has tracked the S&P 500 index since 1993.
Since that inception, hundreds of new indexes have been created to track
everything from broad baskets of stocks to the price of certain commodities
in Australian dollars. Two years ago we made an attempt to identify the
indexes—and the funds built around them—that mimic *100 Best Stocks*
principles.

As of early 2015, there are about 1,600 exchange-traded products, of
which about 1,400 are ETFs and 200 are so-called "exchange-traded notes,"
or ETNs, which are actually fixed-income securities adjusted in value to
track an index without actually owning the components of the index.
Growth in the ETF space has slowed as recently some funds have closed due
to the lack of interest; the total number has stayed relatively constant over
the past two years. Total assets were about $2 trillion, or 13 percent of the
total "fund" market at the end of 2014. There are generalized and specialized
ETFs covering stocks, bonds, fixed-income investments, commodities, real
estate, currencies, and the so-called "leveraged and inverse" funds designed
to achieve specialized investing objectives. Within each of those groups, the
segments available could fill a chapter in and of themselves with divisions by
market cap, style (growth versus value), industry, sector, strategy, country,
and region—just to name a few.

ETF Advantages

There are numerous advantages of ETFs over traditional funds—reasons
why they are "where the puck is going" in packaged investments:

search. ETFs are relatively easy to understand and easy to screen commonly found screening tools at online brokers.

nsparency. It's easy to learn what individual stocks an ETF owns and what comprises the underlying index, both through the online portals and through the index providers' websites. (Want to know what's in the Focus Morningstar Health Care Index? Just put the index name into a search engine, and you'll find out.)

- *Low fees, low cost.* Fees typically range from 0.1 percent for the most generic index funds to 0.2–0.8 percent for more specialized funds— about half of the typical figures found in traditional mutual funds. One fund provider—Vanguard—has traditionally been the lowest cost provider in this regard.
- *Easy to buy and sell.* It's like buying and selling an ordinary stock.
- *Easy to match your objectives and style.* New funds are showing up every day, and many match a quality, low-volatility, value-oriented style we're aligned with.

Dining with the 100 Best: A Special ETF Menu

Our *100 Best Stocks* list doesn't really follow any investment style. It isn't just growth or value. It isn't just large cap, it isn't just high yield, nor is it just tied to certain industries or sectors of the economy. It is a blend of excellent companies in the right businesses, doing well in those businesses, with a potential for strong, steady, and growing investor returns. There is no index or any other screenable classification to select those companies. If there were, there'd be little reason to publish this book.

So as we search for ETFs that run with the same tailwinds as our *100 Best* list, we start with the name of the fund and the index that the fund follows. "Dividend Achievers" or "Buyback Achievers" tells us we're looking on the right part of the menu. Then we dig in and look at the actual portfolio composition (again, most investing portals and brokerage sites let you do this—we use Fidelity (*www.fidelity.com*). If we see lots of *100 Best* stocks on the list, it confirms that we're on the right track.

Two years ago we selected eight ETFs that we thought most closely followed our *100 Best* style and principles, and could be used to build or supplement parts of your portfolio. For the second year in a row, we reviewed the list of available funds and found no others that fit better than what we had. We share the list in the following table, and in the typical spirit of our presentations, we show the performance of these eight funds during our measurement period.

This year, we were somewhat surprised that three of our eight funds actually *beat* the 15.0 percent total return performance enjoyed by the 2015 *100 Best Stocks* list, although as you can see from the table the margin of victory for the second two was slight. It's possible that these funds were a bit more weighted in the successful Health Care and Financials sectors, with less weighting in Industrials and Consumer Staples than on our list. This performance gave us optimism that you can track *100 Best* performance in a fund at least to an extent; we might suggest at least the top funds as candidates to round out or build a portfolio for investors reluctant to invest in individual stocks.

Selecting ETFs is an art in itself and was covered in a now dated but still relevant earlier book we did in this series called *The 100 Best ETFs You Can Buy 2012*. Unfortunately, that book didn't find a large enough market to be updated each year, but it is still useful in its original form and is still available. There are many other ETF resources, again at your online broker or through a specialized ETF portal called ETFdb (*www.etfdb.com*). This portal and its classification page (*www.etfdb.com/type*) can be helpful in finding individual ETFs that suit your taste.

We'll leave the ETF discussion here for this year; the good news (which appears to have gotten better) is that you can invest in ETFs and still follow the *100 Best* style. Now we invite you to accompany us in the unveiling of *The 100 Best Stocks to Buy in 2016*. Drum roll, please.

ETF	Symbol	Sponsor	Total assets	Expense ratio (%)	Price 4.1.2014	Price 4.1.2015	% gain Share value	2014–5 dividend	Yield %	Total return	What attracted us:
iShares MSCI USA Minimum Volatility Index Fund	USMV	Blackrock	$2.5B	0.15%	$35.83	$41.16	14.9%	$0.76	2.1%	17.0%	Low-volatility focus, lots of 100 Best Stocks, low cost
PowerShares S&P 500 High Quality Portfolio	SPHQ	Invesco	$533.54M	0.29%	$20.54	$23.36	13.7%	$0.39	1.9%	15.6%	Growth and stability of dividends, lots of 100 Best
PowerShares BuyBack Achievers Portfolio	PKW	Invesco	$3.0B	0.68%	$42.98	$49.16	14.4%	$0.53	1.2%	15.6%	Compelling strategy, strong long-term results
100 Best Stocks 2015 Portfolio										15.00%	
PowerShares S&P 500 Low Volatility Portfolio	SPLV	Invesco	$4.9B	0.16%	$33.70	$37.77	12.1%	$0.85	2.5%	14.6%	Low-volatility focus, lots of 100 Best Stocks, low cost
SPDR S&P Dividend ETF	SDY	State Street	$13.6B	0.35%	$71.23	$77.87	9.3%	$3.75	5.3%	14.6%	Diverse portfolio, "Dividend Aristocrats" Index
iShares Dow Jones Select Dividend Index Fund	DVY	Blackrock	$14.9B	0.39%	$72.56	$77.91	7.4%	$2.50	3.4%	10.8%	Growth plus income, lots of 100 Best Stocks
First Trust Morningstar Dividend Leaders Index Fund	FDL	First Trust	$926.7M	0.45%	$22.38	$23.25	3.9%	$0.82	3.7%	7.6%	Lots of 100 Best Stocks
Market Vectors Wide Moat ETF	MOAT	Van Eck Global	$929M	0.49%	$29.24	$30.16	3.1%	$0.42	1.4%	4.6%	Compelling strategy, new fund, low cost

Part II

THE 100 BEST STOCKS TO BUY

The 100 Best Stocks to Buy

Index of Stocks by Company Name (*New for 2016)

Company	Symbol	Category	Sector
3M Company	MMM	Conservative Growth	Industrials
—A—			
Aetna	AET	Conservative Growth	Health Care
Allstate	ALL	Conservative Growth	Financials
Apple	AAPL	Aggressive Growth	Consumer Discretionary
Aqua America	WTR	Growth and Income	Utilities
Archer Daniels Midland	ADM	Conservative Growth	Consumer Staples
AT&T	T	Growth and Income	Telecommunications Services
—B—			
Becton, Dickinson	BDX	Conservative Growth	Health Care
Bemis	BMS	Conservative Growth	Consumer Staples
—C—			
Campbell Soup	CPB	Conservative Growth	Consumer Staples
CarMax	KMX	Aggressive Growth	Retail
CenterPoint Energy*	CNP	Growth and Income	Utilities
Chevron	CVX	Growth and Income	Energy
Cincinnati Financial*	CINF	Growth and Income	Financials
Clorox Company	CLX	Conservative Growth	Consumer Staples
Coca-Cola	KO	Conservative Growth	Consumer Staples
Colgate-Palmolive	CL	Conservative Growth	Consumer Staples
Comcast	CMCSA	Aggressive Growth	Telecommunications Services
ConocoPhillips	COP	Growth and Income	Energy
Corning	GLW	Aggressive Growth	Information Technology
Costco Wholesale	COST	Aggressive Growth	Retail
CVS Health	CVS	Conservative Growth	Retail
—D—			
Daktronics	DAKT	Aggressive Growth	Technology
Deere	DE	Aggressive Growth	Industrials
DuPont	DD	Growth and Income	Materials
—E—			
Eastman Chemical	EMN	Conservative Growth	Materials
Empire State Realty Trust*	ESRT	Growth and Income	Real Estate

Index of Stocks by Company Name (continued)

Company	Symbol	Industry	Sector
—F—			
Fair Isaac	FICO	Aggressive Growth	Business Services
FedEx	FDX	Aggressive Growth	Transportation
Fresh Del Monte*	FPD	Conservative Growth	Consumer Staples
—G—			
General Electric	GE	Growth and Income	Industrials
General Mills	GIS	Growth and Income	Consumer Staples
Grainger, W.W.	GWW	Conservative Growth	Industrials
—H—			
Harman International	HAR	Aggressive Growth	Consumer Discretionary
Health Care REIT	HCN	Growth and Income	Health Care
Hillenbrand, Inc.*	HI	Aggressive Growth	Industrials
Honeywell	HON	Aggressive Growth	Industrials
—I—			
IBM	IBM	Conservative Growth	Information Technology
Illinois Tool Works	ITW	Conservative Growth	Industrials
International Flavors & Fragrances*	IFF	Aggressive Growth	Consumer Staples
Itron	ITRI	Aggressive Growth	Information Technology
—J—			
J.M. Smucker	SJM	Growth and Income	Consumer Staples
Johnson & Johnson	JNJ	Growth and Income	Health Care
Johnson Controls	JCI	Conservative Growth	Industrials
—K—			
Kimberly-Clark	KMB	Growth and Income	Consumer Staples
Kroger	KR	Conservative Growth	Retail
—M—			
Macy's	M	Aggressive Growth	Retail
McCormick & Co.	MKC	Conservative Growth	Consumer Staples
McKesson	MCK	Conservative Growth	Health Care
Medtronic	MDT	Aggressive Growth	Health Care
Microchip Technology	MCHP	Aggressive Growth	Technology
Monsanto	MON	Aggressive Growth	Industrials
Mosaic	MOS	Aggressive Growth	Materials

Index of Stocks by Company Name (continued)

Index of Stocks by Company Name (continued)

CONSERVATIVE GROWTH

3M Company

Ticker symbol: MMM (NYSE) □ S&P rating: A- □ Value Line financial strength rating: A++ □ Current yield: 2.5% □ Dividend raises, last 10 years: 10

Company Profile

The 3M Company, originally known as the Minnesota Mining and Manufacturing Co., is now a $32 billion diversified manufacturing technology company with leading positions in industrial, consumer and office, health care, safety, electronics, telecommunications, and other markets. The company has operations in 30 U.S. states and in more than 70 countries and serves customers in nearly 200 countries; 63 percent of the company's sales are international. 3M also operates 36 laboratories worldwide and spends about 5.6 percent of revenues on R&D. Due to the breadth of their product line and the global reach of their distribution, the company has long been viewed as a bellwether for the overall health of the world economy.

3M's operations are divided into five business segments (approximate revenue percentages in parentheses):

- The Industrial business (34 percent) serves a variety of vertical markets, including automotive, automotive aftermarket, electronics, paper and packaging, appliance, food and beverage, and construction. Products include industrial tapes, a wide variety of abrasives, adhesives, specialty materials, filtration products, closures, advanced ceramics, automotive insulation, filler and paint system components, and products for the separation of fluids and gases.

- The Safety and Graphics business (18 percent) serves a broad range of markets that increase the safety, security, and productivity of workers, facilities, and systems. Major product offerings include personal protection, like respirators and filtering systems, safety and security products such as reflectorized fabrics and tapes, energy control products, traffic control products including sheeting for highway signs, building cleaning and protection products, track and trace solutions, and roofing granules for asphalt shingles.

- The Health Care business (17 percent) serves markets that include medical clinics and hospitals, pharmaceuticals, dental and orthodontic practitioners, and health information systems. Products and services include medical and surgical supplies, skin health and infection prevention products, drug delivery systems, dental and orthodontic products, health information systems, and antimicrobial solutions.

■ The Electronics and Energy segment (17 percent) serves the electrical, electronics, communications, and renewable energy industries, including electric utilities. Products include electronic and interconnect solutions, microinterconnect systems, high-performance fluids and abrasives for semiconductor and disk drive manufacture, high-temperature and display tapes, telecommunications products, electrical products, and optical film materials that support LCD displays and touch screens for monitors, tablets, mobile phones, and other products.

■ The Consumer segment (14 percent) serves markets that include retail, home improvement, building maintenance, office, and other markets. Products in this segment include office supply products such as the familiar Scotch tapes, Post-it notes, Scotch-Brite cleaning abrasives, stationery products, construction and home improvement products, home-care products, protective material products, and consumer health-care products. This segment grew considerably with the 2012 acquisition of the Avery Dennison office products line.

Financial Highlights, Fiscal Year 2014

A crosscurrent of innovations, small acquisitions, focus on emerging markets and higher-margined businesses, and currency headwinds delivered a solid "golf clap" performance in FY2014. Revenues rose a moderate 3.1 percent, while net earnings rose a more robust 7 percent and per-share earnings, helped along by a healthy 4 percent share buyback, rose a bit more than 11 percent. The outlook for FY2015 and beyond is much the same: moderate revenue growth in the 1–4 percent range depending on currency effects, with earnings growth in the 4–8 percent range and per-share net growth in the 9–11 percent range. The dividend was raised 34 percent in FY2014; we expect a continuation of healthy dividend raises and share buybacks over the near term.

Reasons to Buy

3M is a classic, maybe slightly better-than-classic "golf clap" stock. Steady performance, steady gains every year, few threats, and little change to worry about. The company makes many steady-selling products essential to manufacturing and day-to-day operations of other companies and organizations and seemingly essential to most of us, e.g., Post-it notes and Scotch tape. The company appears to do better than the markets during strong periods and also holds value better than most during downturns. There is a persistent focus on innovation here, both in its products and in its internal operations and marketing—and it's more the slow, steady than a flash-in-the-pan variety. Cash flows are strong and growing, and are shared liberally with shareholders.

Reasons for Caution

3M is, and always will be, vulnerable to economic cycles, although as we pointed out, the business holds up pretty well in down cycles. We also worry that 3M could go on an acquisition rampage to boost growth, but so far have been comfortable with the types of acquisitions the company has made. The markets have recently seen more in the company's success, which has driven the share price up to new highs We still think there's value here—we suggest placing a Post-it on this page to pick up a few shares when the price is right.

SECTOR: **Industrials** ❑ BETA COEFFICIENT: **1.10** ❑ 10-YEAR COMPOUND EARNINGS PER-SHARE
GROWTH: **10.0%** ❑ 10-YEAR COMPOUND DIVIDENDS PER-SHARE GROWTH: **6.5%**

		2007	2008	2009	2010	2011	2012	2013	2014
Revenues (mil)		24,462	25,269	23,123	26,662	29,611	29,904	30,871	31,821
Net income (mil)		4,096	3,460	3,193	4,169	4,283	4,445	4,659	4,956
Earnings per share		5.60	4.89	4.52	5.75	5.96	6.32	6.72	7.49
Dividends per share		1.92	2.00	2.04	2.10	2.20	2.36	2.54	3.42
Cash flow per share		7.29	6.65	6.15	7.43	7.85	8.35	9.09	10.02
Price:	high	97.0	84.8	84.3	91.5	98.2	95.5	140.4	168.2
	low	72.9	50.0	40.9	68.0	68.6	82.0	94.0	123.6

Website: *www.3m.com*

Aetna Inc.

Ticker symbol: AET (NYSE) ❑ S&P rating: A ❑ Value Line financial strength rating: A ❑ Current yield: 0.9% ❑ Dividend raises, past 10 years: 4

Company Profile

Founded in 1853, Aetna is one of the nation's longest-lived insurers and a leading provider of health insurance benefits. The company's three distinct businesses are operated in three divisions. Health Care provides a full assortment of health benefit plans for corporate, small business, and individual customers, including PPO, HMO, point-of-service, vision care, dental, behavioral health, Medicare/Medicaid, and pharmacy benefits plans. The Group Insurance business provides group term life, disability, and accidental death and dismemberment insurance products primarily to the same sort of businesses that might sign up for its health plans. The Large Case Pensions business administers pension plans for certain existing customers.

The health-care business is by far the largest segment and the focal point of our selection of this company. The business touches some 46 million individuals; of $58 billion in 2014 revenues, about 38 percent is Government including Medicare Advantage and Medicaid; 32 percent is Large Group Insured and 18 percent is Small Group and Individuals. Driven in part by the Affordable Care Act, the Government segment has risen rapidly from 22 percent since 2010.

Obviously, the company is a big player in the Affordable Care Act and its related reforms. While future outcomes are uncertain, much of its majority base in providing employer coverage is left relatively intact. Prior to the ACA as now, Aetna has proven itself to be a pacesetter among insurance providers, mainly through its support and innovations in the area of consumer-directed health care.

For example, with Aetna's consumer-directed HealthFund plans, subscribers become responsible for a portion of their own health-care costs and are given the tools to shop for health-care alternatives and maximize preventive care. Aetna originally led the way with some of the first health savings account–compatible products in 2001. Since then the company has led the industry in developing tools, such as the Aetna Navigator price transparency tool designed to help patients evaluate the cost and outcomes of procedures in different geographies. The company also has championed patient- and doctor-accessible medical records and other techniques for making health-care delivery more efficient— as they put it, "Industry-leading use of patient data and new connections [to help] you play a greater, more informed role in your own health." The company estimates that now 60 percent of patients want to "take charge" of their care, and 80 percent believe that "consumerism in health care is good for Americans."

Aetna is a big believer in the use of analytics—using a "big data" approach to predict the types of medical conditions their covered clients are likely to encounter in the coming years based on correlations among contributing factors in their large data pool. More generally, the company follows an industry trend to focus less on "episodic" care at a medical facility toward more long-term wellness—a "health plus health care" model. Obviously, being able to tell a particular patient how to avoid a predicted condition is a big win for both parties. Predictability permits the company to assemble coverages appropriate to the patient's needs, saving money for both the company and the client.

Over the years, the company has made several, mostly small acquisitions on the international front and in health administration, and plans to grow internationally as well as with new health concepts such as population health.

Financial Highlights, Fiscal Year 2014

Despite ongoing uncertainties with the Affordable Care Act, and helped along by the acquisition of insurance provider and service provider Coventry, revenues grew some 21 percent in FY2014. Earnings were attenuated somewhat by a higher tax rate (7 percent higher) and the combined effects of more Affordable Care Act patients and post-recession "deferred maintenance" that drove care volumes (thus, costs) higher—net income only advanced 11 percent for the year. Revenue expansion through FY2016 is projected in the 7–8 percent range; net income is projected ahead about 5 percent for FY2015 rising to about 9 percent in FY2016, so somewhere near $8.00 per share. The company has actively raised its dividend and has steadily retired shares—about 35 percent of them in ten years—and should continue along this path. There are many shifting currents for the long term. Mergers and acquisitions are reducing the number of players in this space. The company projects a modest decline in large and "gold-plated" employer-sponsored health plans. The "Cadillac tax" on such plans will take effect in 2018, and there are possible changes in the deductibility of such plans; the company is responding by taking a leadership role in government plans, insurance exchanges, and in moving more employers to insurance exchanges (resembling a school voucher plan). To that mix, add the fact that the population continues to age and expand Medicare rolls, fixed-payment Accountable Care Organizations, and numerous changes to the cost side, and you have a dynamic mix that bears watching over time.

Reasons to Buy

We feel that Aetna continues to pace the pack in terms of both business and technology innovation, and as such will not only adapt faster to the new ACA environment but will also lead the way more generally in information-driven health care and health-care utilization. The company has its strategies right, is positioned to lead the way, and has declared its intentions to evolve from an "insurance" company to a "health-care" company providing more integrated, efficient, cost-effective solutions as we move through the decade.

The company's financials remain solid, with strong earnings and cash-flow levels and trends and significant cash reserves. The recent focus on dividend increases (obvious from the following chart) and continued aggressive share buybacks also bode well. In all, Aetna is probably one of the safer bets on our *100 Best* list.

Reasons for Caution

The complete effects of health-care reform have yet to become fully visible, and it could turn out that the ACA and other initiatives leave the company with a more expensive base of insured—with a lag in ability to recover that cost. That said, the company is well positioned to draw on its analytics to make relatively quick adjustments. Public and governmental scrutiny of health insurers has never been higher, and burgeoning health-care costs can be difficult for even a company of Aetna's capability and influence to manage. That said, new utilization management initiatives like Medicare's efforts to reduce unnecessary admissions and procedures will have collateral benefits for private insurers as well. The stock price has risen aggressively since mid-2012, making it important to seek good entry points.

SECTOR: **Health Care** ❑ BETA COEFFICIENT: **0.96** ❑ 10-YEAR COMPOUND EARNINGS PER-SHARE GROWTH: **27.5%** ❑ 10-YEAR COMPOUND DIVIDENDS PER-SHARE GROWTH: **37.0%**

	2007	2008	2009	2010	2011	2012	2013	2014
Revenues (mil)	27,600	30,951	34,765	34,246	33,700	36,596	47,295	58,003
Net income (mil)	1,842	1,922	1,236	1,555.5	1,850	1,658	2,058	2,330
Earnings per share	3.49	3.93	2.75	3.68	5.15	5.14	5.86	6.68
Dividends per share	0.04	0.04	0.04	0.04	0.45	0.73	0.80	0.90
Cash flow per share	4.36	5.07	3.83	5.20	6.25	6.43	7.24	8.49
Price: high	60.0	59.8	34.9	36.0	46.0	51.1	69.5	91.9
low	40.3	14.2	16.7	25.0	30.6	34.6	44.4	64.7

Website: *www.aetna.com*

CONSERVATIVE GROWTH

Allstate Corporation

Ticker symbol: ALL (NASDAQ) □ S&P rating: A- □ Value Line financial strength rating: A+ □ Current yield: 1.7% □ Dividend increases, past 10 years: 6

Company Profile

We initially decided we'd be in good hands with Allstate with the 2015 *100 Best Stocks* list, and we were right. The large insurer rewarded us with a 28 percent gain for the measurement year.

Admittedly, although we're not too hot on financial stocks in general, we've come to like the property-casualty insurance business. Collect the premiums, invest the "float" (money held in advance of casualty loss payouts, with some for profits) in the financial markets for *more* profit, and walk away doubly happy. A certain investing icon from Omaha, Nebraska, who goes by the initials W.B. has been doing this successfully for years. So why shouldn't we?

For years we had a smaller but solid niche player, Cincinnati Financial, on our *100 Best* list. After a long and successful stretch run, we decided to switch horses to Allstate. Why? Allstate is much larger and more recognized as a brand and broadens the offering considerably into the branded consumer and retail insurance space. The primary business is property/casualty (auto and home, mainly) and some commercial lines, but the company also sells life insurance, annuities, and accident and health insurance. But guess what—we plan to ride the Cincinnati Financial horse once again—we've decided that indeed there's room for two horses in this race.

Allstate is the nation's largest publicly held, full-line "P/C" provider, offering the gamut of auto, home, renters, and business insurance, with an entry into the life insurance, retirement, and annuity market as well. The company serves 16 million households through a network of 35,000 Allstate-exclusive agents with almost a billion and a half policies in force, and prides itself on its four-tiered brand and channel strategy for delivering choice and advice to customers where, when, and how they want it.

The company sells its own Allstate product through 9,300 exclusive agencies and its "Encompass" sub-brand through independent agencies and estimates that the Allstate brand alone owns 19 percent of the traditional P/C market. The company owns and operates the e-commerce insurance portal Esurance and also sells its product direct, along with other insurance brands, through its "Answer Financial" phone portal for self-directed consumers looking for choices. That said, the lion's share of premiums ($25.7 billion, or 92 percent of policies in force) is earned through the Allstate brand, while Encompass and Esurance contribute about $1.2 billion, or 4 percent each. By product line, auto leads the way with about two-thirds of premium dollars, homeowners with 24 percent, with the rest coming from life, commercial, and other business lines. Increasingly, the company is using analytics to "microsegment" and tune the premium/cost mix.

Financial Highlights, Fiscal Year 2014

Allstate continued to ride expanding market share, strong pricing, and a favorable loss environment to a 4.7 percent gain in premiums earned after a 4.2 percent gain in the prior year. The loss ratio (losses to premiums earned) notched back up to a more normal 68 percent, but this is still much lower than the low-to-mid 70s readings earlier in the decade. Investment income continued strong. But a much higher effective tax rate reduced net income by 18 percent from 2013 and per-share earnings dropped from $5.70 to $5.42. The company expects stronger revenue gains in the 5–7 percent range through FY2016. This increase in revenues, a reduction in operating expenses, and continued share count reductions are expected to drive per-share earnings ahead as much as 8 percent in FY2016. All of this, of course, assumes steady-state casualty losses and investment income. Cash payouts to shareholders look to stabilize and increase steadily, and the company has been aggressive in reducing share counts—about 2 percent retired per year now, after several years in the 6 percent range; the company has retired 40 percent of its shares since 2004.

Reasons to Buy

We like the market position, brand strength, channel strategy, increased stability, and upside potential both in underwriting and in investment performance. The company has sold some underperforming operations (including Lincoln Benefit Life) and has gained a solid strategic foothold on its reputation, brand, and channel strategy. Esurance and other "direct" models are gaining traction, while the company is also offering a better product mix and better cross-selling opportunities through its traditional agencies.

The Allstate brand is ever stronger, turning from a slight negative years ago to a solid positive through stronger advertising, product offering, and general branding initiatives. The company now proudly places its name on "adjacent" businesses such as Allstate Roadside Services; another branding example is found in the new "Package" policy, combining auto and homeowners into a single policy sold under the Encompass brand. While improving the top line through such initiatives, there is also clearer focus on expenses, the bottom line, stability, and overall shareholder returns going forward; in our view Allstate has become a solid blue-chip performer in a difficult industry with a pretty decent upside going forward.

Reasons for Caution

Competition is stiff and another hurricane-infested year like 2005 could also hurt, although Allstate is more geographically diverse than some of its competitors. Interest rates on the industry's traditional investment instruments may continue to be weak for some time, and a major stock or bond market correction could hurt too. For years, the brand suffered from a reputation for poor claims performance and a sales-y approach. Although the company is more aware of its relatively erratic past and seems to be doing something about it, the prior volatility of its results in revenues, earnings, and especially dividends paid is hard to ignore. Too, the stock price may have expanded faster than its prospects; entry points should be chosen carefully.

SECTOR: **Financials** ❑ BETA COEFFICIENT: **0.98** ❑ 10-YEAR COMPOUND EARNINGS PER-SHARE GROWTH: **3.0%** ❑ 10-YEAR COMPOUND DIVIDENDS PER-SHARE GROWTH: **1.0%**

		2007	2008	2009	2010	2011	2012	2013	2014
Property/Casualty premiums (mil)		27,233	26,967	26,194	25,957	25,942	26,737	27,618	28,929
Net income (mil)		4,993	1,445	1,976	1,535	699	2,143	2,559	2,265
Earnings per share		6.47	3.22	3.47	2.83	1.34	4.34	5.70	5.42
Dividends per share		1.49	1.64	1.01	0.80	0.83	1.09	0.75	1.12
Underwriting inc. per share		3.12	(1.96)	(0.58)	(0.58)	(4.19)	2.49	4.95	4.22
Price:	high	65.9	52.9	33.5	35.5	34.4	42.8	54.8	71.5
	low	48.9	17.7	13.8	26.9	22.3	27.0	40.7	49.2

Website: *www.allstate.com*

Apple Inc.

Ticker symbol: AAPL (NASDAQ) ◻ S&P rating: AA+ ◻ Value Line financial strength rating: A++ ◻ Current yield: 1.5% ◻ Dividend raises, past 10 years: 3

Company Profile

Apple has traditionally been one of the more fascinating analyses we do each year, and this year is no exception. Commentary from investors large and small and supporters and pundits deep and wide continues almost unabated on whether the company is still a superhero among modern enterprises or has lost its edge and is headed to the boring ranks of other graying technology firms. At the end of the day, the decision is whether the rapid transformation of this company into a cash-bearing value stock makes up for a slowdown in innovation and its previous power to not only lead but define markets. If you take the view that cash is king, this company has a lot to offer either way—as much if not more now than ever.

Apple has gone from being a niche supplier of high-end gadgets to a familiar bellwether of consumer technology and industrial design (recently added to the Dow Jones Industrial Average, by the way). Their products have become and continue to be bellwethers in all major consumer segments from preteen to seniors. The company designs, manufactures, and markets personal computers, tablet computers, portable music players, cell phones, and related software, peripherals, downloadable content, and services. The company added the digital watch to its portfolio in mid-2015. It sells these products through its own retail stores, online stores, and third-party and value-added resellers. The company also sells digital content through its iTunes store. The company has become a big player in the "digital wallet" mobile payment space, with its Apple Pay apps and network. And finally, and perhaps most remarkably of all, the company is rumored to be considering a move into the automobile business.

The company's products have become household names: The iPhone, iPod, iPad, and MacBook are just some of the company's hardware products. While the software may be less well-known, iTunes, QuickTime, OSX, and the emerging iCloud are important segments of the business, each with its own revenue stream. And who knows—is there an iCar just around the corner?

It's hard to imagine the current consumer tech landscape without Apple's presence at the top of the heap. Its product line, while comparatively narrow, is focused on areas where the user interface is highly valued. Apple has leveraged this focus on the user experience into a business that is far and away the most profitable in the industry.

Apple has become a case study in creating extraordinary value through innovation, innovative leadership, and marketing excellence. But while wildly successful, the company came upon a test anticipated for some time: the passing of Steve Jobs in October 2011. Steve was clearly the driving and leading force in Apple's innovation, style, and success (for more on this leadership style, we refer you to coauthor Peter Sander's recent book *What Would Steve Jobs Do?*). There had been some doubts that the momentum could be maintained in the absence of this unique guiding light and under the current CEO Tim Cook—the concern being whether his quiet, operationally focused style could bring the same leadership, innovation, and excitement into the marketplace as Mr. Jobs. Innovations since then haven't had the same scale—the latest iPhones are bigger more than better, and we think the watch is a novelty. But with Apple Pay, the iCloud, the automobile, and who knows what else waiting in the wings, and with the financial and operational results recently delivered, we no longer worry so much about slippage into techno-mediocrity under Mr. Cook.

Among other developments, the company recently split its shares a massive seven for one, and has, in part due to shareholder activist pressures, stepped up its cash returns to shareholders, now rumored to be planning up to a cumulative $200 billion to be delivered in the form of dividends and share buybacks by the end of 2018. This is more than the value of all but a few of the largest corporations on earth.

Financial Highlights, Fiscal Year 2014

The numbers remain the envy of the corporate world. On a huge $170 billion revenue base, the company managed to turn in a 7 percent growth in FY2014 revenues. Profits hit $39 billion for the year, also up just under 7 percent. We don't usually say much about quarterly profits, but Apple turned in a record $18 billion in profits for the FY2015 first quarter, and is off to the races for a 32 percent gain in net profits for FY2015 on sales ahead some 29 percent for the year. After this phenomenal year, FY2016 looks to come in incrementally ahead—something in the 5 percent range for both revenues and profits—normally not too exciting but pretty significant considering the size and enormous FY2015 leap forward (yes, China is a big factor in this). We expect dividend increases and especially share buybacks to continue large, with about 100 million shares retired each year on a 5.8 billion share base. The company has already retired about 13 percent of its shares since FY2012.

Reasons to Buy

Two hundred billion returned to shareholders over a four-year period? That's incredible. How could Apple not be a *100 Best* stock? We certainly like the result, but mostly we continue to admire (and believe in) the business and innovation excellence that got Apple there.

Apple's most well-known product, the iPhone, seems ubiquitous. You probably have one. Everyone you know has one. They're everywhere, and you can be forgiven for thinking that the market for this product is saturated. Everyone thought it was getting too expensive as lower-priced Android products started to flood the market. And everyone wondered what would happen in China. But the truth is, by lowering prices, improving quality, and gradually improving feature sets, the iPhone is once again dominating the smartphone market, and better yet, it's doing very well in China—can you believe that China iPhone shipments may soon exceed those in the U.S.? And as we know, the company's iPhone and tablet leadership brings along sales in other product categories and connects well with new app-based services like Apple Pay as well as the now industry standard iTunes.

And that's just shipment volumes—the profitability and cash-flow story is even better. Yes, net profit margins fell a bit when the company introduced the iPhone 5 and 5s a few years ago; that was a deliberate attempt to compete with the new products and maintain the installed base for future upgrades. Net profit margins of over 22 percent for a company of this size alone are remarkable, and suggest that the company's products are far from becoming commoditized. And margins are expected to grow slightly through the end of the decade. On the shareholder return front, thanks to Carl Icahn and others, Apple has taken steps to address the vocal critics of their massive cash hoard. Shareholders have already benefitted as described and will continue to do so as the company places new emphasis on returning cash.

While many are concerned about Apple's ability to innovate, and while there has been somewhat of a slowdown in the creation of whole new businesses, like iPods and tablets and a complete restructuring of the smartphone business, we haven't given up on such innovations. We feel that Apple still has room to create some blockbusters in the "wearable" technology space—smartphone technology integrated into clothing, for example, and in flexible display technologies (see Corning, another *100 Best* pick). Apple Pay, its venture into the financial transaction space, could also be huge, and a big driver for sales of compatible hardware as well. We foresee other major "vertical" applications of iPhone form and technology in cars (check out "CarPlay") and in the health-care space for remote patient monitoring and such. And cars themselves too, if you look further down the curve. Breakthrough technologies in the TV space have been talked about for some time; while not gaining much traction to date, we could still tune in to some upside in that lucrative space.

The seven-for-one split in mid-2014 created no change in real share value, but the shares appear more affordable and a better fit for smaller investor accounts.

Reasons for Caution

Phones, in our view, will never be as profitable on a per-unit basis for Apple as they were through 2012, but they still deliver plenty of profit on a unit basis. Apple delivered a user experience that no one else could touch initially, but the Android platform, led by Samsung hardware offerings, has caught up in many major markets. Revolutionary year-to-year advances—at least in the traditional handheld part of the category—seem unlikely. In other categories, there is some concern about competition and price erosion in the tablet space, but production efficiencies and scale should help offset at least some of this.

In the main, we continue to admire Apple's ability to generate income, and now, to distribute it to shareholders. The franchise is the world's most valuable in market capitalization—and deservedly so. But nobody can sit on their laurels, especially when their laurels are this high off the ground and in plain sight of every competitor. Apple will need to continue to feed the innovation machine. And, not surprisingly, the stock price has reflected most of this success and future opportunity—but fairly in our opinion. Choose entry points carefully.

SECTOR: **Consumer Discretionary** ❑ BETA COEFFICIENT: **0.84** ❑ 10-YEAR COMPOUND EARNINGS PER-SHARE GROWTH: **70.5%** ❑ 10-YEAR COMPOUND DIVIDENDS PER-SHARE GROWTH: **NM**

	2007	2008	2009	2010	2011	2012	2013	2014
Revenues (bil)	24.0	32.5	36.5	65.2	108.2	156.5	170.9	182.8
Net income (bil)	3.5	4.8	5.7	14.0	25.9	41.7	37.0	39.5
Earnings per share	0.56	0.77	0.90	2.16	3.95	6.31	5.66	6.45
Dividends per share	—	—	—	—	—	0.38	1.63	1.82
Cash flow per share	0.62	0.85	1.02	2.35	4.26	6.85	6.96	8.09
Price: high	29.0	28.6	30.6	46.7	61.0	100.7	82.2	119.8
low	11.7	11.3	11.2	27.2	44.4	58.4	55.0	70.5

Website: *www.apple.com*

Aqua America, Inc.

Ticker symbol: WTR (NYSE) ❑ S&P rating: A+ ❑ Value Line financial strength rating: A ❑ Current yield: 2.5% ❑ Dividend raises, past 10 years: 10

Company Profile

If you're like most people, by the time you landed on Water Works as you circled the Monopoly board, you had already deployed your investment capital elsewhere and weren't so excited about its modest growth and yield prospects. You can't build houses or hotels on Water Works, and the monopoly power for owning it in tandem with the Electric Company doesn't seem as powerful as other investments on the board. So you may have passed it up.

Well, times have changed since Monopoly was created. The strategic importance of water, the efficiencies of operating water utilities across a wide geography, and their stability as investments (we didn't care so much about that in Monopoly), have made water utilities a more desirable investment, one for which you might just have plunked down $150 as you circled the board.

"Water Works," in this case, is Aqua America, Inc., a U.S.-based publicly traded water and wastewater utility, serving approximately 3 million customers in eight states: Pennsylvania, Ohio, North Carolina, Illinois, Texas, New Jersey, Indiana, and Virginia, operating 1,447 public water and 187 wastewater treatment systems. Like many modern utilities, the company also owns a nonregulated subsidiary supplying industrial water and services with a new and special emphasis on the Pennsylvania, Texas, and Ohio shale industries. As an example, in mid-2012, the company and a partner deployed a new water pipeline specifically to serve Marcellus shale operators, eliminating some 4,000 water truck trips every two months.

The company has pursued growth aggressively through acquisitions, bringing in nearly 200 acquisitions and growth ventures in the past ten years. Another 16 small water utilities were added in 2014, and the company purchased two small utility services businesses as well, one a consulting company and one that inspects, cleans, aligns, and televises sewer and storm drain systems. Normally we're not too thrilled with growth-by-acquisition strategies, but in this case it makes sense because a lot of local public jurisdictions and private operators see the logic in turning smaller plants over to a larger company, where economies of scale and management can take effect. That, in essence, is Aqua America's strategy, and we like it.

Financial Highlights, Fiscal Year 2014

Acquisitions and a few divestitures make true revenue and earnings trends hard to capture, but overall the company grew revenues 1.5 percent on a 1.3 percent growth in the customer base. Earnings, which had jumped substantially in FY2013 mostly due to new unregulated sales to the shale energy industry, rose about 4.3 percent. Although unusually cold weather in both 2013 and 2014 hurt a bit, and with some contraction in the shale supply business, favorable pricing and continued economies of scale work the other way; revenues are projected ahead in the 2.3 percent range in both FY2015 and FY2016 and net earnings should grow a bit faster. The company has raised its dividend for 23 straight years, and may accelerate those dividend increases in the short term based on its strong cash flows.

Reasons to Buy

In the midst of a raging bull market, we continue to keep Aqua on our *100 Best* list in defense against the next pullback—we'd like to have a few choices that will likely be relatively immune from such an event. That, plus an interest in steadily growing cash returns, fuels our interest in Aqua America. The company is a relatively small and simple business compared to a lot we look at. It occupies a strategic position in a key utility area, especially as more water works become available as public sector operations are trimmed. The company is earning the maximum return on equity allowed by regulators, suggesting a "best in class" operating effectiveness; it is also beginning to expand the use and strength of its brand. The stock has a low beta of 0.42, indicating stability and persistently growing earnings and dividends. The payout percentage—dividends as a percent of net profits—has trended downward, and that, along with strong cash flow, suggests a pickup in the size of dividend increases into the 8–10 percent range annually.

Reasons for Caution

Water distribution requires a lot of expensive infrastructure, and a lot of the current infrastructure is old; in fact, the need to replace infrastructure is one reason some smaller utilities are selling out to Aqua America. Such replacement costs, particularly with the severe winters we've been having, could be high and a drag on earnings in the short term, but the company has managed them well as evidenced by a decline in long-term debt as a portion of total capitalization despite these capital expenditures. Big plans made to deliver water to shale operators may be attenuated by recent energy price declines as well.

Overall, we chose this investment in part due to its relatively inelastic demand and steady earnings and cash flow into the future even in bad economic times; however, Aqua may participate less in economic growth and rising equity markets than other stocks we choose. This isn't necessarily a negative; it's just good to know the temperature of the water you're getting into.

SECTOR: **Utilities** ▫ BETA COEFFICIENT: **0.42** ▫ 10-YEAR COMPOUND EARNINGS PER-SHARE GROWTH: **8.5%** ▫ 10-YEAR COMPOUND DIVIDENDS PER-SHARE GROWTH: **7.5%**

	2007	2008	2009	2010	2011	2012	2013	2014
Revenues (mil)	602.5	627.0	670.5	728.1	712.0	757.8	768.6	780
Net income (mil)	95.0	97.9	104.4	124.0	144.8	153.1	205.1	213.9
Earnings per share	0.57	0.58	0.62	0.72	0.83	0.87	1.15	1.20
Dividends per share	0.38	0.41	0.44	0.47	0.50	0.54	0.58	0.63
Cash flow per share	1.10	1.14	1.29	1.42	1.45	1.51	1.82	1.90
Price: high	21.3	17.6	17.2	18.4	19.0	21.5	28.1	28.2
low	15.1	9.8	12.3	13.2	15.4	16.8	20.6	22.4

Website: *www.aquaamerica.com*

CONSERVATIVE GROWTH

Archer Daniels Midland Company

Ticker symbol: ADM (NYSE) ▫ S&P rating: A ▫ Value Line financial strength rating: A+ ▫ Current yield: 2. 3% ▫ Dividend raises, past 10 years: 10

Company Profile

ADM is one of the largest food processors in the world. It buys corn, wheat, cocoa, oilseeds, and other agricultural products and processes them into food, food ingredients, animal feed and ingredients, and biofuels. It also resells grains on the open market. Rather than the finished consumer products most food processors are known for, ADM produces and distributes intermediate components for food product manufacture and is by far the largest publicly traded company in this business. Among the more important products are vegetable oils, protein meal and components, corn sweeteners, flour, biodiesel, ethanol, and other food and animal feed ingredients. For-eign sales make up about 51 percent of total revenue.

The company is highly vertically integrated and owns and maintains facilities used throughout the production process. It sources, transports, stores, and processes agricultural materials in more than 79 countries on six continents, with 270 processing plants and its own extensive sea/rail/road network. The company owns 26,400 rail cars, 1,700 barges, 8 ocean vessels, and a fleet of trucks.

The company operates in four business segments: Oilseeds Processing (39 percent of FY2014 sales), Corn Processing (14 percent), Agricultural Services (46 percent), and Other (less than 1 percent). The Oilseeds Processing unit processes soybeans, cottonseed, sunflower, canola, peanuts, and flaxseed into vegetable oils and protein meals for the food and feed industries. Crude vegetable oils are sold as is or are further refined into consumer products, while partially refined oils are sold for use in paints, chemicals, and other industrial products. The solids remaining from this processing are sold for a number of applications, including edible soy protein, animal feed, pharmaceuticals, chemicals, and paper.

The Corn Processing segment milling operations (primarily in the United States) produce food products too numerous to list but include syrup, starch, glucose, dextrose, and other sweeteners. Markets served include animal feeds and the vegetable oil market. Fermentation of the dextrose yields ethanol, amino acids, and other specialty food and feed products. The ethanol is processed for beverage stock or industrial use as the base for ethanol-blended gasoline and other fuels.

The Agricultural Services segment is the company's storage and transportation network. This business is primarily engaged in buying, storing, cleaning, and transporting grains to/from ADM facilities and for export. It also resells raw materials into the animal feed and agricultural processing industries.

The Other segment engages primarily in financing and financial activities, including commodity futures and merchant activities.

In early 2015, ADM completed the acquisition of German natural flavorings and specialty ingredients producer WILD Flavors GmbH. This unit, which will be reported as a separate segment starting in 2015, supplies fruit-containing flavor systems for energy and sport drinks, teas, and other foods and beverages, as well as flavorings for other consumer products like oral care products. This new unit will also include ADM's existing nutrients product lines, including specialty proteins and natural health and nutrition products like natural-source Vitamin E and Omega-3 DHA, and signals a foray into more specialized "value-add" businesses than ADM's traditional core. Bad news for you chocaholics—the company also sold its chocolate-and cocoa-processing business during the year. It also sold its South American fertilizer business to Mosaic, also a *100 Best* stock, in an effort to focus on core and high value–add businesses.

Financial Highlights, Fiscal Year 2014

Acquisitions, spinoffs, currency effects, fluctuating prices, and fluctuating costs of agricultural commodity inputs make any yearly comparison of ADM results challenging, but the FY2014 is more difficult than most. Lower average sales prices and the disposal of the cocoa business sprung an almost 10 percent drop in revenues—the company attributes almost all of that to lower average sales prices driven by market conditions and currency effects. Normally we'd brace ourselves for a horrible profit performance, but that was not the case. Agricultural commodity prices dropped during the year; in fact, cost of goods sold decreased 11 percent in the same period. That, and operational cost improvements and lower energy prices, led to a record net profit of over $2.2 billion, some 67 percent ahead of FY2013. In this business, it's not so much the sales as value add and profits that count. The net profit margin, while tiny, skyrocketed from 1.5 percent to 2.8 percent. Acquisitions and moderate price strengthening should produce revenue gains in the 2–3 percent range through FY2016, while net profit margins are expected to hold fast, with earnings gains in the 1–3 percent range for the next couple of years. That may not sound like much, but holding FY2014's large gain intact is a good thing. Cash flows and the balance sheet are strong, reflecting that the company raised its dividend 28 percent in 2014 and appears poised for decent increases in the near term.

Reasons to Buy

Agriculture is still a key strategic business on a global basis, and increased demand for food and especially middle-class Western diets from emerging-market customers bodes well. The company is and has been a strong player in the biofuels industry. While uncertainties continue in the ethanol and biofuels segment, the company's experience and scale in ethanol and biodiesel are strong positives, and the company should win as other smaller players exit the market.

There are four major suppliers that dominate the world market for commodity foodstuffs: Archer, Bunge, Cargill, and Dreyfus—the "ABCD" of world foods. Growth through selective acquisitions is an important factor to success in this business—if you miss an attractive opportunity, you can be reasonably certain one of your competitors will not. ADM continues to grow its presence in the emerging markets of Asia, South America, and Eastern Europe. Sales growth outside the United States has far outpaced domestic growth, and ADM's presence and extensive transportation capability give it a decided advantage over its smaller competitors, many of which are focused only in certain markets or certain industries. The company is fine-tuning its business mix, disposing of smaller low-margin product lines in favor of a higher value add in the food chain with the addition of WILD. We like the solid track record for growth in dividends and overall shareholder value.

Reasons for Caution

We've seen how agricultural cycles and production can negatively impact this company, but we expect that the worst is over. Still, there's a cyclical—even a volatile—component that's hard to ignore (that said, the beta of 0.88 suggests some safety, even though that changed from 0.70 last year and 0.47 two years ago). The WILD acquisition may signal a move to the "wild" side in more specialized, less commoditized business, which seems like a good strategy but does add some risk. The stock price has woken up from its doldrums, a sign that the markets have recognized its steady progress and niche strength, but that makes new investments more vulnerable to poor conditions like those seen in 2012 and 2013. Entry points should be picked carefully.

ADM is heavily invested in the corn-ethanol-fuel processing chain. Ethanol has always existed at the very margins of the transportation fuels market, and continued softness in demand and lower prices for gasoline could have a disproportionate effect on the profitability of ethanol, although the price/cost balance remains intact so far. Federal government policy toward ethanol subsidies and ethanol imports (primarily sugar-based ethanol from Brazil) both bear watching. Finally, the company does produce that nasty-sounding but in fact relatively benign high fructose corn syrup; a pickup in nutritional health sentiment in the food and especially the beverage industry won't help.

SECTOR: **Consumer Staples** ❑ BETA COEFFICIENT: **0.88** ❑ 10-YEAR COMPOUND EARNINGS PER-SHARE GROWTH: **11.5%** ❑ 10-YEAR COMPOUND DIVIDENDS PER-SHARE GROWTH: **14.0%**

		2007	2008	2009	2010	2011	2012	2013	2014
Revenues (mil)		44,018	69,816	69,207	61,692	80,676	89,038	89,804	81,201
Net income (mil)		1,561	1,834	1,970	1,959	2,036	1,496	1,342	2,248
Earnings per share		2.38	2.84	3.06	3.06	3.13	2.26	2.02	3.43
Dividends per share		0.43	0.49	0.54	0.58	0.62	0.69	0.76	0.96
Cash flow per share		3.51	3.97	4.21	4.49	4.54	3.56	3.42	4.80
Price:	high	47.3	48.9	33.0	34.0	38.0	33.5	44.0	53.9
	low	30.2	13.5	23.1	24.2	23.7	24.5	27.8	37.9

Website: *www.adm.com*

GROWTH AND INCOME

AT&T Inc.

Ticker symbol: T (NYSE) ❑ S&P rating: BBB+ ❑ Value Line financial strength rating: A++ ❑ Current yield: 5.7% ❑ Dividend raises, past 10 years: 10

Company Profile

Measured by revenue, AT&T continues to be the largest telecommunications holding company in the U.S. Although known for years as the center of the wireline local and long-distance telecom service, it has evolved to be the largest provider of wireless, commercial broadband, and Wi-Fi services in the United States and has become a large player in consumer broadband services with its ISP service and U-verse bundle product.

At 56 percent of total revenues, the AT&T Wireless subsidiary has emerged as the largest segment, providing voice, data, and text through its familiar wireless service. Wireless *data* continues to be the biggest growth driver—and why not—as more and more of us, especially under the age of 40, consume ever larger chunks of data on our smartphones and as people of all groups sign up for data-everywhere plans for their tablets. Some 85 percent of postpaid smartphone subscribers have a data plan, up from 67 percent two years ago, and 50 percent have opted for plans with 10gb or more per month of data.

Wireline, in total, and including new and "classic" forms of wireline, accounts for 44 percent of the business. Included is the strategically important Wireline Data/Managed IT Services—whose servers and trunk lines account for a major part of the global Internet—which now account for 28 percent of the sales mix. The traditional wireline voice subsidiaries—the part that descended from the old "Ma Bell" of decades ago, now account for only 16 percent of revenues and offer services in 13 states, and the wireless business provides voice coverage primarily for traveling U.S. customers and U.S. businesses in 220 countries.

Business customers account for more than 54 percent of total revenues; AT&T is a leader in this traditionally more loyal segment. Recent growth in the business base of 4.1 percent in FY2014 outpaces the 2.9 percent growth rate overall, suggesting that this base is financially more robust than the more price-competitive consumer segment these days. With the acquisition of DirecTV, the company is shifting its reporting segments to have four, defined more by market than product: Business (wireline/wireless), Consumer Mobility, U.S. Video & Broadband, and International Voice & Mobility. No specific figures have been offered for these segments thus far.

The company has long been focused on offering one-stop-shopping services—wireline, data, wireless, and other services with one price on one bill—a "premier network experience" in the company's own words. These efforts have had varying success, but the U-verse product, an IP-based bundling of TV, data, and voice services turning the TV, the PC, and the cell phone into integrated display and transaction devices, is a particularly important development.

In mid-2014 the company made an unsolicited $48.5 billion offer ($67.1 billion including assumed debt) for satellite TV provider DirecTV in a play to expand TV, content, and bundled offerings. The deal closed in July 2015, making AT&T not just the world's largest TV provider but also adding satellite as a major delivery path to add to wired and wireless networks. DirecTV adds video content to deliver on its other lucrative platforms: wireless data and U-verse. The company estimates that over 50 percent of its network traffic *today* is video, and you can see where this puck is going with the DirecTV acquisition. The company has also acquired Nextel Mexico; with DirecTV and other acquisitions, the company will become a major player in the Latin America market.

Financial Highlights, Fiscal Year 2014

Although the wireless data subsegment is promising, overall this type of company will never experience double-digit growth. But even slow, steady, single-digit growth makes for good business when you're this big and you generate this much cash—some $31 billion in the most recent year alone.

The wireless business did fairly well in FY2014. During the year, AT&T delivered the company's best-ever full-year postpaid churn at only 1.04 percent, demonstrating customer loyalty especially in its solid business-account base, and added nearly twice as many postpaid subscribers—about 3.3 million—as it did in 2013. Also, mobile pricing trends, after price cuts during 2014, began to improve as the company initiated its "Next" platform, allowing customers to upgrade more often for a small fee. U-verse high-speed Internet connections were ahead almost 18 percent and video connections were up almost 9 percent. Business solutions revenues advanced 11 percent, while traditional wireline connections dropped about 14 percent.

In total, FY2014 revenues ticked up almost 3 percent, better than the previous year's 1 percent increase. Earnings, tempered by more competitive pricing particularly on the company's family-oriented "share" plans, slumped about 3 percent, although buybacks kept per-share earnings constant. FY2015 and FY2016 revenues, not including the DirecTV acquisition, look poised to advance about 2 percent annually, with earnings and per-share earnings advancing a similar amount. Share buybacks should continue but at a more moderate pace as DirecTV is absorbed; the dividend should increase at its very predictable 4 cents per share per year pace. We hope for good customer and cost synergies with DirecTV, but don't have those numbers plugged in yet.

The company continues to invest heavily in spectrum, acquiring $18 billion worth in a recent government auction on top of its acquisition of Leap Wireless.

Reasons to Buy

We think all core businesses are healthy, and DirecTV, as mentioned, will add some customer and operating leverage. Beyond that, we think wireless data consumption is on an unstoppable rise—almost as addictive as caffeine is to our Starbucks customer base (another *100 Best* stock) and destined to grow as text evolves to Instagram picture transmissions among teenagers, as people watch more movies on their phones (admittedly, we still don't get this trend), and so forth. This part of the business is growing 16–20 percent per year, and aside from capital investments, many of which have been already made, much of this drops to the bottom line. The company continues to grow (and aggressively market) the U-verse product bundle and has overcome some technology barriers giving it more reach, and increasing volumes offer operating leverage over the longer run. More conceptually, we are evolving to a 24/7 connected, always-on world where, for instance, real-time health monitoring can be done from everywhere, and AT&T will play a big part of that.

Likewise, shareholder cash returns will continue to be above average, with a strong dividend payout, regular increases, and steady share buybacks all funded by strong cash flows. While DirecTV does add some acquisition risk and competition is intense, the company is generally a safe play with a beta of only 0.42.

Reasons for Caution

Aside from the DirecTV acquisition and its related risks and dilution of management bandwidth, competition is the main worry. Markets, market analysts, and company analysts continue to fret about subscriber growth, but as suggested earlier, the company now views "better" as better than "more," and is focused on its business customers too—we like that approach. Still, competition also can hurt revenues and profits from existing customers, and we've seen some mild signs of increased price competition, especially from minority players T-Mobile and Sprint, that bear watching. While the company has successfully built out a quality set of networks, capital expenditures in this sort of business continue to be a factor and could stress cash-flow growth, especially with the pending acquisitions.

We'll also add one more downside attribute we don't bring up often: In researching this company, we feel the investor materials are unnecessarily complicated—either the company is too complex to consider as an investment, or the materials aren't presented as well as they could be. We're opting for the latter at this moment but if the revised market segment reporting and a few other clarifications don't happen, AT&T could be dropped from next year's list. We hate to drop a good company because of a bad presentation, but we also choose to invest in what we understand. We serve this up not only as a criticism of AT&T but as a lesson to all investors.

SECTOR: **Telecommunications Services** ❑ BETA COEFFICIENT: **0.42** ❑ 10-YEAR COMPOUND
EARNINGS PER-SHARE GROWTH: **3.5%** ❑ 10-YEAR COMPOUND
DIVIDENDS PER-SHARE GROWTH: **4.0%**

	2007	2008	2009	2010	2011	2012	2013	2014
Revenues (bil)	119.0	124.0	123.0	124.4	126.7	127.4	158.8	132.4
Net income (mil)	16,950	12,867	12,535	13,612	13,103	13,698	13,463	13,056
Earnings per share	2.76	2.16	2.12	2.29	2.20	2.33	2.50	2.50
Dividends per share	1.42	1.60	1.64	1.68	1.72	1.76	1.80	1.84
Cash flow per share	5.36	5.56	5.46	5.60	5.31	5.70	6.10	6.04
Price: high	43.0	41.9	29.5	29.6	31.9	38.6	39.0	37.5
low	32.7	20.9	21.4	23.8	27.2	29.0	32.8	31.7

Website: *www.att.com*

CONSERVATIVE GROWTH

Becton, Dickinson and Company

Ticker symbol: **BDX (NYSE)** ❑ S&P rating: **BBB+** ❑ Value Line financial strength rating: **A++** ❑ Current yield: **1.7%** ❑ Dividend raises, last 10 years: **10**

Company Profile

Gotten a flu shot or any other "delivery" of medicine lately? Chances are the "device" used to make the delivery had a prominent "B-D" logo on the package. That doesn't stand for "Bad–Day"—but rather "Becton, Dickinson," one of the premier medical supply and technology companies on the planet.

Becton, Dickinson is a global health-care technology player focused on improving drug delivery, enhancing the diagnosis of infectious diseases and cancers, and advancing medical lab work and drug discovery. The company develops, manufactures, and sells medical supplies, devices, laboratory instruments, antibodies, reagents, and diagnostic products through its three segments: BD Medical, BD Diagnostics, and BD Biosciences. These products are sold to health-care institutions, life science researchers, clinical laboratories, the pharmaceutical industry, and the general public. International sales account for about 59 percent of the total. The B-D brand is found throughout the range of clinics, medical offices, and hospitals and is well recognized in the medical community.

The company operates in three worldwide business segments: Medical (54 percent of FY2014 sales), Biosciences (14 percent), and Diagnostics (32 percent).

The BD Medical segment produces a variety of drug-delivery devices and supplies, including "sharps" (hypodermic needles and syringes) and related disposal products, infusion therapy devices, intravenous catheters, insulin injection systems, regional anesthesia needles, diabetes care systems, and prefillable drug-delivery systems for pharmaceutical companies.

BD Diagnostics offers system solutions for collecting, identifying, and transporting blood and other specimens, as well as instrumentation for analyzing these specimens. Testing systems include those for sexually transmitted diseases, microorganism identification and drug susceptibility, and certain types of cancer screening. The business also provides customer training and business management services.

BD Biosciences provides research tools and reagents to accelerate the pace of biomedical discovery. Clinicians and researchers use BD Biosciences' tools to study genes, proteins, and cells to understand disease, improve technologies for diagnosis and disease management, and facilitate the discovery and development of new therapeutics. Products include reagents, fluoroscience cell-activated sorters and analyzers, monoclonal antibodies and kits, and cell imaging and reagent solutions, among others.

In mid-2014, the company took a bold step into the health-care delivery and quality market through the announced acquisition of CareFusion, a global provider of automated tools and systems designed to reduce patient medication errors and to prevent care-associated infections. These areas have become increasingly important as patient volumes increase and as Medicare and other payers scrutinize and cut back on payments for readmissions and other follow-on care that could have been avoided. The acquisition is sizeable, adding some 45 percent to the revenue and capitalization base and about 33 percent to total net income, before acquisition synergies. As of mid-2015 the merger was yet to close but is believed to be a solid step forward for the company into an increasingly important area of health-care delivery.

Financial Highlights, Fiscal Year 2014

Aside from the CareFusion acquisition, FY2014 was another solid year for B-D, even with the negative impact of the rise in the U.S. dollar. Revenues advanced about 5 percent, while net earnings continued a long-term trend of outpacing sales growth with a 7 percent rise. Both figures would have been better with a constant exchange rate. With currency effects and the unknowns (and size) of the acquisition, next year's figures are hard to predict. While accretive, CareFusion may appear to dilute B-D's strong profit margins (net profit margin for B-D is about 15 percent while CareFusion is about 11 percent), but we anticipate synergies and growth to be a net positive. We should also note that dividend increases are not only steady but large, typically 10 percent per year, and the company plans to continue that pattern, a strong internal signal for anticipated solid and steady financial growth in the future.

Reasons to Buy

With or without CareFusion, Becton, Dickinson continues to be a classic "blue-chip" company, as recession-proof as any stock on our list. Prior to the acquisition, the company offered steady and substantial growth potential, especially in earnings, cash flow, and dividends. Double-digit operating and net profit margins exceed industry benchmarks. While it adds some risk and possible income dilution, we see the CareFusion acquisition as a "where the puck is going" play, and once digested, it should be a positive, especially given management's solid track record.

Reasons for Caution

CareFusion is a big bet and one that lies a bit outside of the core supplies and diagnostics business, hence there's some additional risk here. As a consequence, considering the risk and a tripling of long-term debt to finance the acquisition, Standard & Poor's downgraded BDX's long-term debt rating from "A+" to "BBB+" in late 2014. While we do embrace the technology advance and the deeper venture into the "quality of care" arena, we share the view that risk has increased somewhat along with opportunity.

Too, one must continue to be wary of the possible distortions in demand, supply, pricing, and quantity of health care consumed, given the Affordable Care Act and the adaptation of the health-care community to that and subsequent legislation. The trend toward greater cost management among care providers gives another possible "nega-trend" in its core business to consider. All said, Becton continues to be one of the best, safest, steadiest, and most well-managed players in the segment.

SECTOR: **Health Care** ❑ BETA COEFFICIENT: **0.87** ❑ 10-YEAR COMPOUND EARNINGS PER-SHARE GROWTH: **11.5%** ❑ 10-YEAR COMPOUND DIVIDENDS PER-SHARE GROWTH: **16.5%**

		2007	2008	2009	2010	2011	2012	2013	2014
Revenues (mil)		6,560	7,156	7,160	7,372	7,828	7,708	8,054	8,446
Net income (mil)		978	1,128	1,220	1,185	1,272	1,123	1,159	1,236
Earnings per share		3.84	4.46	4.95	4.94	5.61	5.36	5.81	6.25
Dividends per share		0.98	1.14	1.32	1.48	1.64	1.80	1.98	2.18
Cash flow per share		5.82	6.60	7.13	7.25	8.27	8.30	8.79	9.37
Price:	high	85.9	93.2	80.0	80.6	89.4	80.6	110.9	142.6
	low	69.3	58.1	60.4	66.5	72.5	71.6	78.7	105.2

Website: *www.bd.com*

CONSERVATIVE GROWTH

Bemis Company, Inc.

Ticker symbol: BMS (NYSE) ❑ S&P rating: A ❑ Value Line financial strength rating: A ❑ Current yield: 2.4% ❑ Dividend raises, past 10 years: 10

Company Profile

You open a stick of string cheese. You pull the little tab at the end and out pops the stick of cheese, which had been happily stored in its little plastic sack through thousands of miles of trucks, warehouses, more trucks, a stockroom or two, the store, your refrigerator, and now maybe your lunch bucket or bag. You enjoy the string cheese with a sandwich made from lunchmeat packaged in a little zippered plastic bag. Afterward, you take your regular dose of allergy medication, packed up in one of those 12-tablet plastic trays with a metal foil backing to tear through.

Who makes this stuff? Did you ever stop to think about it? How it makes our lives easier, as well as those of manufacturers and distributors of these products? Neither had we, until our search for strategic and vital niche holders led us to one of the other companies in Kimberly-Clark's quiet and productive original hometown of Neenah, WI.

"Freshness," "Convenience," and "Performance" are the three buzzwords that adorn the company's homepage, and they go a long way to explain their value add in the food chain. Bemis makes all kinds of "inspired packaging solutions," mainly for the food, beverage, health and hygiene, building materials, and chemicals markets. Flexible packaging products include bags, wraps, and containers, many with a pressure-sensitive or zipper closure, all set up to be filled with standard packaging line equipment and all labeled for the client's products. "Raw" packaging materials roll out of 60 facilities to the end of packing lines in 11 countries. About 34 percent of sales are international; most of that is in Latin America, China, and Australia.

In 2014 Bemis sold its line of pressure-sensitive materials used in its own packaging but also sold into the printing, graphic design, and technology markets. The company had previously sold four paper-packaging plants to Hood Packaging Co.—plants that make items like paper bags for pet foods. Both sales represent a sustained effort to adjust the business mix toward higher-margin businesses.

The company believes that its leadership position "rests on its strong technical foundation in polymer chemistry, film extrusion, coating and laminating, printing and converting" and that "material science continues to be the primary instrument for creating sustainable competitive advantage."

Financial Highlights, Fiscal Year 2014

As numbers go, FY2014 comparisons aren't so meaningful due to the divestiture of the Pressure Sensitive materials business. Reported revenues dropped 14 percent, but "organic" growth, taking out currency effects and divestitures, was estimated just north of 4 percent, a decent growth rate for this type of business. The real uptick was in gross and net profit margins; net profit margins advanced from the mid-4 percent to the mid-5 percent range, again quite healthy for this sort of business and reflecting the results of the divestiture margin enhancement strategy. Lower materials input costs helped as well. The fact that net earnings stayed roughly flat despite the revenue drop again attests to the strategy.

Going forward, the company expects sales, again digesting divestitures and currency effects, to remain roughly flat in FY2015 with another 4 percent upturn driven largely by international growth, in FY2016. With moderate buybacks and continued margin improvements, per-share earnings should advance 8–13 percent each year. Dividends will rise and share counts should fall slowly and steadily.

Reasons to Buy

This is not an exciting company, but it is a strong niche player providing critical packaging technologies to the industries it serves. New and innovative food-packaging designs are becoming more desired as convenience and quality outweigh cost as a priority in most consumer markets these days. The new packaged salads are a good example of packaging for a product not packaged before; new ziplock containers for lunchmeats, cheeses, etc., show how the package is moving up the value-add scale. The company has a significant beachhead in growing Latin American markets, China, and Australia and is investing in new technologies and applications such as package design enhancements for microwaving, easy-open packages for elderly customers (we continue to applaud this one!), and new technologies and delivery systems for the health-care and pharmaceutical industries. We like the strategy of fine-tuning the business mix toward more profitable, higher value–add packages, and the company seems to be executing it well and getting the desired results from it. Cash flow and cash returns to shareholders are steady and increasing; the issue continues to have appealingly low volatility and is generally a good defensive play.

Reasons for Caution

To a degree, Bemis is exposed to price volatility in both food and energy and to the economy in general. When food prices rise, consumers get more sensitive to price and may hesitate to pay for convenience packaging—I'll choose and boil my own Brussels sprouts, thank you; no boiling bags for me. When energy prices go up, that does bad things to plastic resin prices, and this company makes almost everything it sells out of plastic. Aside from those two downsides, which are partially offset by niche strength (price wars in their product space aren't much of a concern), Bemis is a safe, steady, and well-managed—if not exciting—business.

Last year we predicted that the "stock price would wake up to the contents of this package"—and indeed it has, with a nice 18 percent gain for the year, not including the dividend. Such gains make it more important to find good entry points.

SECTOR: **Consumer Staples** ❑ BETA COEFFICIENT: **0.62** ❑ 10-YEAR COMPOUND EARNINGS PER-SHARE GROWTH: **3.5%** ❑ 10-YEAR COMPOUND DIVIDENDS PER-SHARE GROWTH: **6.0%**

		2007	2008	2009	2010	2011	2012	2013	2014
Revenues (mil)		3,649	3,779	3,515	4,835	5,323	5,139	5,030	4,344
Net income (mil)		181.6	166.2	147.2	203.3	212.4	225.3	237.0	233.1
Earnings per share		1.74	1.65	1.38	1.83	1.99	2.15	2.28	2.30
Dividends per share		0.84	0.88	0.90	0.92	0.96	1.00	1.04	1.08
Cash flow per share		3.38	3.29	2.81	3.84	3.87	3.66	4.19	4.21
Price:	high	36.5	29.7	31.4	34.3	34.4	33.9	42.3	47.2
	low	25.5	20.8	16.8	25.5	2.2	29.5	33.7	34.3

Website: *www.bemis.com*

CONSERVATIVE GROWTH

Campbell Soup Company

Ticker symbol: CPB (NYSE) □ S&P rating: BBB+ □ Value Line financial strength rating: B++ □ Current yield: 2.7% □ Dividend raises, past 10 years: 9

Company Profile

Campbell Soup Company is the world's largest, as they like to say, maker of "real food that matters for life's moments." To most of the free world, that still translates to soup and the ubiquitous pop-culture-iconic Campbell's Soup can. But there is a lot more to this story.

While there are 17 such brands under the Campbell's North American roof, the original Campbell's Soup is still far and away the most important. The company owns 60 percent of the prepared-soup market. Their three top soups are three of the top ten grocery products sold in the United States every week. Approximately 80 percent of U.S. households purchase the soup, and the average inventory on hand is six cans. Few brands have enjoyed such penetration and loyalty.

The company has five reporting segments. To highlight the company's own vision of breadth beyond soup, the former U.S. Soup division (including U.S. Sauces) is now referred to as the Simple Meals division and accounts for 35 percent of sales with a stronger targeting and message around the concept of convenience. Other divisions include U.S. Beverages (9 percent), Global Baking and Snacking (30 percent), International Simple Meals and Beverages (11 percent), and Bolthouse and North America Foodservice (17 percent). Within each segment reside the many familiar brands that constitute the business: Swanson, Prego, Goldfish, SpaghettiOs, Pace, V8, Pepperidge Farm, Bolthouse Farms, Arnott's, Wolfgang Puck, and of course, Campbell's, which still accounts for 26 percent of total company sales.

One might observe that their business structure is aligned to geography as much as to product family. Following a more general U.S. business trend to "get the geography out" of the org chart and focus exclusively on product families instead, Campbell announced a restructuring in early 2015 into three business units (with estimated portions of revenues and profits in parentheses): Simple Meals and Beverages (55 percent of sales, 70 percent of earnings), Global Biscuits and Snacks (33 percent, 25 percent), and Packaged Fresh (which includes Bolthouse Farms, and its newest and fastest-growing segment—currently 11 percent of sales and 5 percent of operating earnings). The restructuring also comes with $200 million in overhead cost reductions.

Campbell's products are distributed to 120 countries worldwide and are sold through its own sales force and through distributors. U.S.-based operations accounted for 78 percent of revenue in FY2014. Products are manufactured in 18 principal facilities within the United States and in 13 facilities outside the country. The company's growth strategy has evolved toward greater innovation in product marketing and brand recognition and new packaging designed to broaden use in today's fast-paced economy, as well as a healthy dose of internationalization. Campbell's $1.55 billion cash purchase of Bolthouse Farms in 2012 gave the company a strong presence in the important and growing "super premium" healthy beverage and dressings segment. Bolthouse, based in Bakersfield, CA, is best known for its line of natural carrot snacks and vegetable and fruit juice matching offerings by Odwalla and others—and often beating them on price. Bolthouse gives the company better exposure to Millennials, a market not well addressed by Campbell's traditional brands. In 2013, the company also acquired Plum Organics, a maker of organic foods for infants and young children, and the Kelsen Group, an international producer of gourmet cookies, including those tins of Danish butter cookies, one of our favorites—which, incidentally, also gives the company an expanded sales channel for its Pepperidge Farm and Arnott's brands.

The company recognizes "seismic shifts" in its markets—not just economic shifts but big changes in consumer needs and preferences. Consumers want greater nutrition and transparency with respect to ingredients and food origins. They want to know the impact on diet and health. They want greater convenience without sacrificing diet and health. And the demographics have shifted—there are 80 million so-called Millennials and 60 million Latinos in the U.S. market—all of whom amplify these trends.

Generally the company is recognizing the need for marketable innovations and is answering that challenge with these noted acquisitions and other new products such as Campbell's Skillet Sauces, Slow Cooker and Oven Sauces, V-8 Protein Bars, and the like. Their market research suggests the well-known desire for better nutrition and more "natural" ingredients, but also captures that in-home dinner meals are back on track, growing 8.3 percent annually—but only 33 percent are made from scratch and 68 percent are planned within one hour of eating (sound familiar?).

Financial Highlights, Fiscal Year 2014

FY2014 cooked up an "okay" performance for Campbell. Revenues, helped along a bit by acquisitions, rose 2.7 percent, while higher input costs and supply-chain costs dinged net earnings, which rose about 1.8 percent, even with lower advertising and marketing costs. Too, both figures would have been healthier without currency effects. Restructuring and continued input cost pressure will attenuate revenues and earnings for the next two years; most forecasts put both on a fairly flat to slightly downhill run. As we'll describe next, our "good tastes" for Campbell come chiefly for what happens after that. In the meantime, modest dividend increases and share repurchases should juice investor returns just a bit.

Reasons to Buy

We continually swim against the investment current with our Campbell pick, and in this year when we've abandoned two other key food and beverage players, Kellogg and PepsiCo, we're still hanging on to Campbell. Why? Mainly because their approach to innovation resonates with us—as it has for others since the company has been named to the Forbes 100 Most Innovative Companies list. We think innovation is the key to survival particularly as markets evolve to the tastes of the new Millennial generation.

Then there's the usual: core brand and brand strength. Campbell owns the number one or number two position in each of the product categories in which it participates. It dominates the $4 billion U.S. soup market and is making headway in key foreign markets too. Cash cows are always a good thing to have as you step forward into the marketing "beyond."

Campbell isn't trying to capture the remaining 40 percent of the soup market that it doesn't own; it's trying to grow the overall size of the market and letting its 60 percent share do the talking. The strategy, well known in the food industry, is to maintain and slowly grow its core brands while generating new growth, leveraging distribution and sales channels, and increasing brand presence through new products often not directly associated with the Campbell brand. The strategy sounds pretty tasty to us.

Reasons for Caution

Even with the recent emphasis on innovation, the company's brands and core customer base are aging, and adoption of new products may continue to prove slow, especially among the younger set. As others, like Coca-Cola, have found out over the years, there are risks inherent with tinkering with a long-established brand such as Campbell's. We would hope that Campbell succeeds with its new ventures without pulling the rug out from under the old ones. We still like Cream of Mushroom on a rainy day, even if we have no idea what it's made of.

SECTOR: **Consumer Staples** ❑ BETA COEFFICIENT: **0.34** ❑ 10-YEAR COMPOUND EARNINGS PER-SHARE GROWTH: **5.5%** ❑ 10-YEAR COMPOUND DIVIDENDS PER-SHARE GROWTH: **6.5%**

		2007	2008	2009	2010	2011	2012	2013	2014
Revenues (mil)		7,867	7,998	7,586	7,676	7,715	7,707	8,052	8,268
Net income (mil)		771	798	771	842	846	783	786	800
Earnings per share		1.95	2.09	2.15	2.45	2.54	2.44	2.48	2.53
Dividends per share		0.82	0.88	1.00	1.05	1.15	1.16	1.16	1.25
Cash flow per share		2.78	3.07	2.87	3.25	3.48	3.35	3.82	3.53
Price:	high	42.7	40.8	35.8	37.6	35.7	37.2	45.8	46.7
	low	34.2	27.3	24.8	24.6	29.7	31.2	34.8	39.6

Website: *www.campbellsoup.com*

AGGRESSIVE GROWTH

CarMax, Inc.

Ticker symbol: KMX (NYSE) ❑ S&P rating: NR ❑ Value Line financial strength rating: B+ ❑ Current yield: Nil ❑ Dividend raises, past 10 years: NA

Company Profile

"The Way Car Buying Should Be." That's the slogan used by this clean-cut chain of used vehicle stores and superstores and its new big-box, retail-like model for selling cars. CarMax buys, reconditions, and sells cars and light trucks at 144 retail centers in 73 metropolitan markets, mainly in the Southeast, Midwest, and California, but is gradually moving to a more nationwide footprint. The company specializes in selling cars that are under six years old with less than 60,000 miles in excellent condition; the cars are sold at a competitive price, typically in the $10,000 to $34,000 price range, for their condition in a no-haggle environment. The price is the price; the emphasis is on the condition of the vehicles and on a helpful and friendly sales and transaction process. Sales representatives are compensated for cars they sell, but not in such a way that drives them to push the wrong car on a customer. The company sold some 582,282 used vehicles in FY2014, up 11 percent from FY2013 and up 42 percent from the 408,080 sold in FY2011. The average selling price for 2014 was $19,897, up 2.5 percent from the previous year, and the average gross margin was $2,179 per vehicle.

CarMax is gaining footholds in new markets such as Philadelphia, Denver, and the D.C. area, and most reports suggest they are gaining market share in the markets they serve with a high degree of customer satisfaction. CarMax opened 13 new superstores in each year 2014 and 2015; in 2016 they plan to open 14 new stores, five of which will touch new markets in Minneapolis-St. Paul, Boston, Tallahassee and Gainesville, Florida, and Peoria, Illinois, as well as strengthening other market centers in Denver, the D.C. area, and Houston. The company is also testing small-format stores in markets like Harrisonburg, VA, and Jackson, TN.

The health of the economy and consumer spending have swung car buying into a higher gear, but with newfound consumer prudence. Many of these purchases are heading to the one- to six-year-old used car sector of the business, where prices are 40–60 percent lower than comparable new cars. In addition to "retail" used car sales, CarMax is a big player in auto wholesaling, having moved about 376,000 units mostly taken in trade; the company is the world's largest used car buyer. The company also earns income through its financing unit, known as CarMax Auto Finance, or CAF.

CarMax also has service operations and sells extended warranties and other products related to car ownership. The company has state-of-the-art web-based and mobile tools as well as other aids designed to make the car selection, buying, and ownership experience easier. As CarMax puts it, customers request four things when they buy a car:

1. Don't play games
2. Don't waste my time
3. Provide security
4. Make car buying fun

The company's offering is aimed at reducing these concerns and providing the right experience. The offering continues to be unique in the industry, and competitors would have a long way to go to catch up.

Financial Highlights, Fiscal Year 2014

It was a good market overall for selling cars, with new car sales running at a 17 million annual rate—at the high end of the cyclical range. For the year ending February 28, 2015, which the company calls FY2015 but we will refer to as "2014" because most activity occurred in that year, same-store used vehicle sales were up 7 percent, total unit volume was 10.5 percent higher, and used vehicle revenue was 13.3 percent higher—driving total revenues, which include auction and financing revenues, 13.5 percent higher for the year. Success factors included favorable financing, a significant growth in online and mobile vehicle shopping activity, and higher conversion rates in the store with an assortment of physical and process tweaks.

The gross margin per used vehicle stayed relatively flat at $2,179 versus $2,171 in 2013, but favorable business trends in the auction market and financing drove overall operating margins up from 4.7 percent to 5.1 percent and net earnings up 18 percent. An aggressive buyback program retired some 5.6 percent of the float and drove per-share earnings about 30 percent higher. For 2015, the company projections call for a 15–16 percent increase in per-share net on a 10–11 percent revenue increase; the earnings growth rate attenuates somewhat to 10–12 percent in 2016 on a 10 percent revenue increase.

The company announced its first share buyback program in 2012 and has expanded it every year since then, clearly set up as a shareholder return vehicle in lieu of dividends; CarMax is one of only two companies on our *100 Best* list that doesn't pay a dividend. Since then they have retired 11 percent of the float; a current $2.4 billion authorization may get them as far as retiring 20–22 percent of their float in the next few years depending on share prices.

Reasons to Buy

Quite simply, CarMax continues to be a buy if you believe the traditional dealer model is broken and if you believe people will continue to see value in late-model used vehicles.

Additionally, CarMax brings the latest in business intelligence and analytic models to the car-marketing process, in procurement, merchandising, pricing, and selling the vehicles. Do green Jeep Cherokees sell well in Southern California? Then let's find some, put them on the lot there, and set a market-based price. KMX is well ahead of the industry in making analysis-based supply and selling decisions and has quite successfully deployed analytic tools to adjust prices and inventories quickly to market conditions, a competency that bodes well for the future.

While the auto industry has recovered to the 17 million new car rate this year, the used car business is also strong—and much larger—at 39 million used cars sold annually. CarMax is increasingly a big player, taking market share from traditional used car dealers, but there's fertile ground to capture more. The company estimates that it has only 5 percent of the current market for zero-to-ten-year-old used vehicles in markets in which it operates, and only 3 percent of the total nationwide—all while being the largest player and twice the size of the nearest competitor.

The company is positioned well both for organic growth through market share and for geographic growth; there is still plenty of fertile ground for new growth, especially in the Northeast and Northwest and smaller metro areas. The footprint is slowly but surely becoming a nationwide one, which will not only help volumes but also brand recognition, pricing power, buying power, and cost absorption. The small-format store test, if successful, could add to this.

Finally, we like the aggressive and consistently executed share repurchase program.

Reasons for Caution

CarMax will always be somewhat vulnerable to economic cycles, the availability of credit, and the availability of quality used vehicles to resell. We should note that vehicle availability is less of a concern for the moment, as the Great Recession recedes into the past and vehicle leasing has come on strong again—a great source of late-model used cars. A new trend toward longer six- and seven-year new car financing periods may keep people in their cars longer, but it may also incentivize people to buy used to avoid the long financing period in the first place. As this company is still in the growth phase, and new dealerships involve putting lots of new cars on the ground, working capital needs are extensive, long-term debt has risen, and cash returns to shareholders have not met our norms; however, the new share repurchase program takes a big step toward fixing that. Finally, investors have finally seen the headlights on this top-notch retail model, and have bid the share price up accordingly—shop carefully.

SECTOR: **Retail** ❑ BETA COEFFICIENT: **1.65** ❑ 10-YEAR COMPOUND EARNINGS PER-SHARE
GROWTH: **15.0%** ❑ 10-YEAR COMPOUND DIVIDENDS PER-SHARE GROWTH: **NA**

	2007	2008	2009	2010	2011	2012	2013	2014
Revenues (mil)	8,200	6,974	7,400	8,975	10,004	10,963	12,574	14,269
Net income (mil)	182.0	59.2	281.7	380.9	413.8	425.0	492.6	583.9
Earnings per share	0.83	0.27	1.26	1.67	1.79	1.87	2.16	2.68
Dividends per share	—	—	—	—	—	—	—	—
Cash flow per share	1.05	0.52	1.52	1.95	2.19	2.0	2.70	3.35
Price: high	29.4	23.0	24.8	30.0	37.0	38.2	53.1	68.7
low	18.6	5.8	6.9	18.6	22.8	24.8	38.0	42.5

Website: *www.carmax.com*

GROWTH AND INCOME

NEW FOR 2016

CenterPoint Energy, Inc.

Ticker symbol: CNP (NYSE) ❑ S&P rating: A- ❑ Value Line financial strength rating: B++ ❑ Current yield: 4.9% ❑ Dividend raises, past 10 years: 10

Company Profile

"Sell when there's something better to buy" is our guiding philosophy and mantra for removing and replacing companies on our *100 Best* list each year. Sometimes we cut a company from our list with a specific replacement from the same industry in mind; other times we make a cut and find something better to fill the spot from a wide assortment of other choices.

CenterPoint Energy is a case of the former; we were looking for something to replace Southern Company, an old favorite that seemed mired in the muck trying to get its new nuclear units and a new coal gasification unit online. Moreover, it just seemed to be yesterday's coal-burning, nuclear-ambitious utility in a world that has moved forward into new energy sources, smart grid technologies, conservation, and new business models. It wasn't easy to replace SO's steady performance and 4.5 percent yield—but with CenterPoint, we think we've modernized and improved our hand, and have a better current yield to boot.

CenterPoint Energy is in the electricity delivery (not production, but delivery) business, serving over 2.2 million customers in a 5,000-square-mile service territory in the greater Houston area, and is in the retail gas delivery business, serving more than 3.3 million metered customers in Louisiana, Arkansas, Minnesota, Mississippi, Oklahoma, and Texas (including Houston); it is the fifth-largest gas distribution company in the U.S. by customer base. It is also in the gas *production* business, with a 55 percent interest in a master limited partnership called Enable Midstream Partners, which produces and distributes wholesale gas and some oil mainly from Texas and Oklahoma. Finally, the company operates an unregulated CenterPoint Energy Services arm, which sells gas to commercial, industrial, and wholesale customers throughout most of the eastern half of the U.S. and provides an assortment of consulting services for other utilities.

CenterPoint intrigues us because, first, it does not own generating assets but instead distributes electricity to its customers produced by some 18 providers, some green. It owns the wires, the meters, and the customer contact, while such messy problems as fuel costs and environmental risks are left to someone else. Second, in its distribution business, the company has learned to use technology to drive efficiency and improve the customer experience, with advanced implementations of smart grids, smart metering, and other technologies from companies like Itron, Inc. (another *100 Best* pick). The company has installed smart meters for almost all its customer base, automating meter reading and frequent readouts on electricity use. Customers are never left in the dark for long—these technologies manage the grid to reduce consumption, access the least expensive source, and keep the lights on more reliably—and when that fails, the company has also learned how to hook up with customer smartphones and media to quickly advise of service interruptions or other important announcements.

Finally, we liked the idea of a gas distributor acquiring some upstream assets to control costs and assure supplies—only it backfired as energy prices cratered in late 2014. While in the short term this represents bad news, we feel that it also creates a buying opportunity for this company at an attractive yield and price.

Electricity transmission and distribution accounts for 26 percent of FY2014 revenue; gas distribution accounts for 38 percent, and the unregulated gas sales and services unit accounts for 36 percent.

Financial Highlights, Fiscal Year 2014

With the limited partnership interest and the large unregulated sales unit, revenues and earnings can vary more widely than with most large utilities. Revenues for FY2014 rose almost 14 percent over FY2013, but lower energy prices will keep revenues roughly flat in FY2015. Earnings rose about 13 percent, mostly in line with revenues, but are projected to fall substantially, about 25 percent, to $455 million or about $1.00–$1.10 per share, for FY2015, mostly due to Enable. The dividend, which by policy was to be grown in the 8–10 percent range, is still well covered for FY2015, although the company will scale back increases to a more moderate 4–5 percent for the time being. Revenues appear to be poised to grow in the 4–5 percent range for FY2016; earnings are projected about 10 percent higher but still below FY2013 levels. Again, it makes sense to watch cash flows carefully when judging dividend payment capacity, and cash flows are just fine. Depletion and depreciation allowances typically create a big gap between cash flow and earnings for this type of company. That said, returns from the Enable partnership bear watching.

Reasons to Buy

CenterPoint is a progressive-minded utility located in a high-growth market that simply cannot do without large amounts of electricity. We look at the electricity business as a key business anchor with decent growth prospects; in addition, the gas business should do very well once natural gas prices recover. We like their positioning as a low-cost producer and wholesaler in the gas business with a built-in outlet in the regulated business for their product. We expect that management will eventually return to its 8–10 percent dividend growth philosophy and think CenterPoint combines the safety and yield of a quality utility with a bit of appreciation potential in the energy production and nonregulated distribution business.

Reasons for Caution

If natural gas prices don't recover, that could spell trouble for the Enable arm . . . although lower input costs would help the distribution arms somewhat. Too, a protracted slowdown in the energy economy could temper Houston's growth, creating a soft patch in its own right. To an extent, CenterPoint is a bet on a recovering energy industry, albeit with a strong base in its distribution businesses to balance the risk.

SECTOR: **Utilities** ❑ BETA COEFFICIENT: **0.35** ❑ 10-YEAR COMPOUND EARNINGS PER-SHARE GROWTH: **8.0%** ❑ 10-YEAR COMPOUND DIVIDENDS PER-SHARE GROWTH: **9.0%**

	2007	2008	2009	2010	2011	2012	2013	2014
Revenues (mil)	9,623	11,322	8,281	8,765	8,459	7,452	8,106	9,226
Net income (mil)	399	447	372	442	546	581	536	611
Earnings per share	1.17	1.30	1.01	1.07	1.27	1.35	1.24	1.42
Dividends per share	0.68	0.73	0.76	0.78	0.79	0.81	0.83	0.95
Cash flow per share	3.39	3.42	2.94	3.14	3.43	3.89	3.54	3.85
Price: high	20.2	17.3	14.9	17.0	21.5	21.8	25.7	25.8
low	14.7	8.5	8.7	5.5	15.1	18.1	19.3	21.1

Website: *www.centerpointenergy.com*

GROWTH AND INCOME

Chevron Corporation

Ticker symbol: CVX (NYSE) ❑ S&P rating: AA ❑ Value Line financial strength rating: A++ ❑ Current yield: 4.1% ❑ Dividend raises, past 10 years: 10

Company Profile

Chevron is the world's fourth-largest publicly traded, integrated energy company based on oil-equivalent reserves and production. It is engaged in every aspect of the oil and gas industry, including exploration and production, refining, marketing and transportation, chemicals manufacturing and sales, and power generation.

Active in more than 180 countries, Chevron (formerly ChevronTexaco via the 2001 merger) has reserves of about 6.8 billion barrels of oil and 22 trillion cubic feet of gas, with a production capacity of 2.6 million barrels of oil equivalent and 4 billion cubic feet of gas per day. In addition, it has global refining capacity of more than 1.6 million barrels per day (bpd) and operates more than 16,000 retail outlets around the world. The company also has interests in 30 power projects now operating or being developed. The upstream capacity is concentrated in North America, Africa, Asia, and the Caspian Sea region, with less exposure to the Middle East than some competitors. The company is the leading producer in Kazakhstan, Thailand,

and Indonesia, which rank among the highest-potential and lowest-risk non-U.S. locations.

Although it increased the overall exposure to the 2014 oil price debacle, Chevron is more concentrated in oil (less in gas) than some of its competitors. That said, it is active but not overly concentrated in new shale developments, particularly in gas. The company is a player in new technologies in exploration and production, including "ultra-deep water" and other difficult environments, and, not surprisingly, in the current "fracking" boom in both the typical North American venues and other less obvious places, such as Argentina and Lithuania. Its downstream (refining/retailing) businesses include four refining and marketing units operating in North America, Europe, West Africa, Latin America, Asia, the Middle East, and southern Africa. Downstream also has active global businesses in manufactured products including lubricants, specialty chemicals and additives, specialty refining units for aviation and maritime markets, and various logistics activities, including pipelines, shipping, and a global trading unit.

The company's global refining network comprises 14 wholly owned and joint-venture facilities that process about 2 million barrels of oil per day. Gasoline and diesel fuel are sold through more than 16,600 retail outlets under three well-known consumer brands: Chevron in North America; Texaco in Latin America, Europe, and West Africa; and Caltex in Asia, the Middle East, and southern Africa.

Chevron is the number one jet fuel marketer in the United States and third worldwide, marketing 550,000 barrels per day in 80 countries. The company's fuel and marine marketing business is a leading global supplier and marketer of fuels, lubricants, and coolants to the marine and power markets, with about 500,000 barrels of sales per day.

While the traditional emphasis in oil hurt the company as prices fell almost 60 percent in 2014, and while these changes clearly hurt the bottom line, long term we feel that the emphasis on oil and the diversification through downstream refining and marketing is still the right position, and a recovery in oil and gas prices will only act as a plus going forward.

Financial Highlights, Fiscal Year 2014

Coming off a rather lackluster year in 2013, the rapid shift in energy prices in 2014 clearly hurt the company's performance. Total FY2014 revenues declined some 8 percent, while net earnings dropped some 9.5 percent. Per-share earnings, due mainly to buybacks, dropped a bit less at 9 percent.

The real "hit" is expected in FY2015, with revenues forecast off some

27 percent from FY2014, earnings down almost 54 percent, and per-share earnings, now absent share repurchases as the program was temporarily halted in late 2014, also down 54 percent. Some of this decline, however, comes from asset writedowns, as per-share cash flow is actually expected to stay relatively constant through 2015 and decline only modestly in 2016—a testament to relatively low-cost extraction from wells already in place and the balancing effect of the downstream (refining and marketing) operations. Of course, any rebound in energy prices during late 2015 and into 2016 should dramatically improve overall results.

Reasons to Buy

We had to evaluate all of our energy picks carefully in light of declining prices and worsening industry fundamentals. Not surprisingly, declining product prices, increased inventories and competition, and a relatively fixed cost picture are not features we look for in a *100 Best* pick.

While short-term pain is substantial, we do still like the long term. For exploration and production strength and geographic and technological diversity, few companies exceed Chevron's strengths. The company is most exposed to some of the best sectors and geographies in the business and has established a good brand and track record for discovery, production, and downstream operations. The company has made what we feel are prudent cuts in its exploration activities—which we think could resume successfully as prices rebound—and its expenses in general. Like many in the industry, the company has cut back its refining base a bit too, but will likely remain in the refining business for the long term; we still think that is a good strategy. The company has a solid record of earnings, cash generation, and cash distribution. While share buybacks have been temporarily curtailed, the company expects (and we too expect) a continuation of a persistently strong and growing dividend despite the energy price shifts. We think shareholders will be well rewarded with growing cash returns in the long term—especially as energy prices normalize. Recent purchase prices have been attractive, particularly in light of the steady and likely-to-increase dividend—with a little patience, we think CVX is among the best of a hard-hit and out-of-favor industry.

Reasons for Caution

Of course, recent energy price shifts, which we noted last year as a "risk factor," have put a dent in CVX's universe. Before that, we had some concerns about depleting reserves, which have depleted as they have at many other "majors." But we look at the recent price shifts as an opportunity for some of the wiser—and more cash-rich—players such as Chevron to provide opportunities to rationalize the E&P portfolio and even to acquire productive assets more cheaply. Still, all that said, the Saudis and others appear determined to undermine high-cost oil production—"fracking" in layman's terms; this "growth opportunity" may take a few years to return to the forefront.

SECTOR: Energy ❑ BETA COEFFICIENT: **1.13** ❑ 10-YEAR COMPOUND EARNINGS PER-SHARE GROWTH: **21.0%** ❑ 10-YEAR COMPOUND DIVIDENDS PER-SHARE GROWTH: **9.5%**

	2007	2008	2009	2010	2011	2012	2013	2014
Revenues (bil)	220.9	273.0	172.6	204.9	253.7	241.9	228.8	212.0
Net income (bil)	18.7	23.9	10.5	19.0	26.9	26.2	21.4	8.9
Earnings per share	8.77	11.67	5.24	8.48	13.44	13.32	11.09	10.1
Dividends per share	2.32	2.53	2.66	2.84	3.09	3.51	3.90	4.21
Cash flow per share	12.11	16.69	10.95	15.99	19.98	20.05	18.61	19.1
Price: high	95.5	104.6	79.8	92.4	111.0	118.5	127.8	135.1
low	65.0	55.5	56.1	66.8	102.1	95.7	108.7	100.1

Website: *www.chevron.com*

GROWTH AND INCOME

NEW FOR 2016

Cincinnati Financial Corporation

Ticker symbol: CINF (NASDAQ) ❑ S&P rating: BBB ❑ Value Line financial strength rating: B++ ❑ Current yield: 3.6% ❑ Dividend increases, past 10 years: 10

Company Profile

From time to time we cut a company from our *100 Best Stocks* list when we feel there's a better play in the industry. Sell when there's something better to buy. We didn't really have anything against Cincinnati Financial—they had weathered some stormy weather (literally) early in the decade and emerged a winner especially in 2013, with a 37 percent share price gain for that year. We thought that was pretty good, but decided to switch horses to the larger and more established Allstate, which remains on our 2016 *100 Best* list. But we got to thinking about the basic property/casualty insurer model and how these companies make money not only in profiting from the difference between premiums collected and costs ("underwriting income") but also by being able to invest the "float" over the years for what can be enormous gains (of course, we hold Warren Buffett's Berkshire Hathaway as the obvious paradigm for this model). We think Berkshire is too pricey for the average shareholder, and further, it pays no dividend, but we decided we liked the model well enough to have two choices on our list. So . . . welcome back, Cincinnati Financial.

Cincinnati Financial Corporation (CFC), founded in 1968, is a holding company operating several insurers engaged primarily in property/casualty insurance marketed through independent insurance agents in 39 states. The company, one of the 25 largest property and casualty insurers in the nation, operates in four segments: Commercial Lines Property Casualty Insurance, Personal Lines Property Casualty Insurance, Life Insurance, and Investments. Commercial Lines account for about 66 percent of premium revenues and are sold in 39 states; Personal Lines about 24 percent and are sold in 31 states. All insurance products are sold through independent agencies. Life insurance and other "excess/surplus" lines (specialized niche forms of insurance) are designed to allow the agents to offer a full line and account for the 10 percent remainder.

Cincinnati Financial fully or partially owns a series of subsidiary companies that actually provide and manage the insurance products marketed by the company and its agents. Its standard market property casualty insurance group includes two subsidiaries: the Cincinnati Casualty Company and the Cincinnati Indemnity Company. This group writes a range of business, homeowner, and auto policies. Cincinnati Specialty Underwriters offers the excess/surplus lines and life, disability, and annuity products to complete the insurance product picture.

The two noninsurance subsidiaries of Cincinnati Financial are CSU Producer Resources, which offers insurance brokerage services to CFC's independent agencies so their clients can access CFC's excess and surplus lines insurance products, and CFC Investment Company, which offers commercial leasing and financing services to CFC's agents, their clients, and other customers. Like all property and casualty insurers, CFC earns income from underwriting (premiums collected less casualty payouts) and from investing the vast pool of cash generated through premiums stored up until a loss occurs.

Financial Highlights, Fiscal Year 2014

Results have definitely improved since the Great Recession, which took underwriting income well into the red and put a small dent in investment income as well (that dent was only about 10 percent, showing the resiliency of CINF's investment portfolio). From losing $3.28 per share in underwriting income in 2011, the company brought that back to a positive 78 cents for FY2014 on a 12 percent rise in Premiums Earned (one of two major revenue components). Expenses were down, underwriting margins rose to 3 percent, and investment income ran steady with the total portfolio earning a bit over 4 percent. Currently a soft pricing environment (a funny thing happens in this business: No major catastrophes brings good news on the cost side but makes it harder to raise premiums) has the company backing off the growth rate to something closer to 1 percent for FY2015, with both revenue growth and margin growth revitalizing into FY2016. Projections call for earnings north of $3.00 per share in FY2015 and in the $3.40–3.50 range for FY2016, with continued moderate dividend growth through the period.

Reasons to Buy

CINF enjoys both a loyal customer base and a loyal agency base. It is smaller, more nimble than Allstate, and, unlike Allstate, most business is handled through agencies—with the two companies as choices, you get both ends of the spectrum. Measured by premium volume, the company is ranked as the number one or number two carrier among 75 percent of the agencies that have represented them for the past five years. The company has invested in new pricing and modeling analytics to sharpen its approach to pricing and customer relationships. CINF is on firm financial footing with a dividend covered by investment income and cash flow and a relatively low 11 percent long-term debt as a percentage of total capital. Despite the recent financial storm, dividend payouts have increased slowly and steadily each year. From here forward, the company is uniquely positioned to benefit from interest rate increases, which will help investment income, and underwriting income improving as well.

Reasons for Caution

The current pricing environment is not that favorable; there is a lot of competition in this business, although loyal customers and especially agents will help. Interest rates on the industry's traditional investment instruments could continue to stay weak for some time. A large natural catastrophe could hurt. The stock price has risen with the good news—although we're happy to say not too much during our 2015 "hiatus" year—still, investors should look for good entry points.

SECTOR: **Financials** ❑ BETA COEFFICIENT: **0.79** ❑ 10-YEAR COMPOUND EARNINGS PER-SHARE GROWTH: **2.0%** ❑ 10-YEAR COMPOUND DIVIDENDS PER-SHARE GROWTH: **7.0%**

		2007	2008	2009	2010	2011	2012	2013	2014
Premiums Earned (mil)		3,128	3,010	2,911	2,924	3,029	3,344	3,795	4,242
Net income (mil)		386	344	215	273	121	421	466	454
Earnings per share		3.54	2.10	1.32	1.68	0.74	2.40	2.81	2.86
Dividends per share		1.42	1.53	1.57	1.59	1.60	1.62	1.64	1.74
Underwriting inc. per share		1.83	(0.94)	(2.19)	(1.80)	(3.28)	(0.51)	0.94	0.78
Price:	high	48.4	40.2	29.7	32.3	34.3	41.0	53.7	55.3
	low	36.0	13.7	17.8	25.3	23.7	30.1	39.6	44.0

Website: *www.cinfin.com*

The Clorox Company

Ticker symbol: CLX (NYSE) ❑ S&P rating: BBB+ ❑ Value Line financial strength rating: B++ ❑ Current yield: 2.7% ❑ Dividend raises, past 10 years: 10

Company Profile

A leading manufacturer and marketer of consumer cleaning and other household products, Clorox markets a broad line of highly trusted and recognized brand names, including its namesake bleach, Green Works natural cleaners, Formula 409, Liquid-Plumr, and Pine-Sol cleaning products; Fresh Step and Scoop Away cat litter; Kingsford charcoal; Hidden Valley, KC Masterpiece, and Soy Vay dressings and sauces; Brita water-filtration systems; Glad bags, wraps, and containers; and Burt's Bees natural personal care products. In the U.S., Clorox owns the number one or number two market-share position with over 80 percent of its products, and that continues to be a key part of its long-term strategy.

The company is divided into four segments:

- *Cleaning Products* (32 percent of FY2014 sales, 39 percent of pretax income) includes laundry (10 percent of sales), home-care (17 percent), and professional (5 percent) cleaning products. Home-care products include disinfecting sprays and wipes, toilet bowl cleaners, carpet cleaners, drain openers, floor-mopping systems, toilet and bath cleaning tools, and premoistened towelettes. Professional products are for institutional, janitorial, and foodservice markets and include bleaches, disinfectants, food-storage bags, and bathroom cleaners.
- *Lifestyle* (17 percent, 24 percent) offers Dressings and Sauces (Hidden Valley, Soy Vay, and others: 9 percent), Water Filtration products (Brita: 4 percent), and Natural Personal Care (mainly Burt's Bees: 4 percent).
- *Household Products* (30 percent, 30 percent) includes Bags, Wraps & Containers (Glad and others: 14 percent), Charcoal (Kingsford and MatchLight brands: 10 percent), and Cat Litter (7 percent).
- *International* (21 percent, 7 percent) is set up as a separate entity to market and distribute an assortment of U.S.-made and locally made brands from 39 manufacturing facilities to markets in over 100 countries.

To give an idea how far Clorox has come as a consumer company, it was founded in 1913 as the Electro-Alkaline Company. It has been known as the Clorox Company since 1957, although it was owned by archrival Procter & Gamble from 1957 until 1969 when the FTC forced divestiture to promote competition. The company positions itself not only as a brand leader but also a leader in environmental responsibility and in responding to changing demographics, as exemplified by new formulations and packages specifically targeted to the Hispanic market.

Financial Highlights, Fiscal Year 2014

Clorox rode several crosscurrents of currency fluctuations, especially in key Latin American markets, and strong generic competition in some of its markets. This was offset by a few new products and product packages and strength in professional lines and more recently, the Burt's Bees business— all to a net decrease in sales of just under 1 percent (which the company estimates as a 6 percent gain on a currency-neutral basis). Margins, net, and per-share earnings were largely unchanged; basically the company treaded water with currency effects included. New products, some help from the dollar, and some more help from lower commodity input costs will start to take effect first in profits, which are expected to rise around 5 percent in FY2015 on revenues flat to 1 percent higher; then again another 5 percent in FY2016 on net revenues up in the 3 percent range. The focus will be on driving profitability with new products, lower input prices, and some price increases and cost efficiencies.

Reasons to Buy

Clorox, due to its strong and diverse brand position and market share, has proven to be resilient in the past in all phases of the economic cycle. Their products are standards in the markets they serve. As a personal preference, we especially like the Green Works products, which, unlike many "green" products, seem to actually work and to have become a standard on store shelves.

That said, many consumers have switched away from name-brand products; just how many remains to be seen. Offsetting that, the company seems to be placing more emphasis on innovation, with such new brands as Lightweight Extreme Fresh Step (cat litter), OdorShield Glad Bags (freshened with Hawaiian Aloha Febreze), Burt's Bees Lip Crayons, Clorox Micro-Scrubbers (disinfecting wipes), and so forth.

Clorox has proven itself to be a strong, well-managed, cash-flow and shareholder-oriented defensive player. Dividend raises have been strong and persistent—9 percent in 2014—and the company has reduced share count 40 percent since 2004. The stock has tended to trade in a very tight range even with negative news; with a beta of 0.42 for our *100 Best* portfolio it remains mostly a safety and stability play.

Reasons for Caution

We've seen the lessons of high commodity prices and of dipping too far into the acquisition pool, as was the case in the Burt's Bees acquisition, which, while doing better these days, resulted in a large 2011 write-off. We remain concerned that the company could be tempted again into poor acquisitions to spur growth, as it's pretty challenging to grow demand and market share for bleach, trash bags, and charcoal. Finally, the stock has posted some strong gains in past years, which have finally moderated, but current share prices leave little room for error.

SECTOR: Consumer Staples ❑ **BETA COEFFICIENT: 0.42** ❑ 10-YEAR COMPOUND EARNINGS PER-SHARE GROWTH: **7.5%** ❑ 10-YEAR COMPOUND DIVIDENDS PER-SHARE GROWTH: **11.0%**

	2007	2008	2009	2010	2011	2012	2013	2014
Revenues (mil)	4,847	5,273	5,450	5,534	5,231	5,468	5,623	5,591
Net income (mil)	496	461	537	603	258	543	574	562
Earnings per share	3.23	3.24	3.81	4.24	2.07	4.10	4.31	4.26
Dividends per share	1.31	1.66	1.88	2.05	2.25	2.44	2.63	2.67
Cash flow per share	4.55	4.82	5.22	5.68	3.51	5.56	5.80	5.76
Price: high	69.4	65.3	65.2	69.0	75.4	76.7	96.8	106.4
low	56.2	47.5	59.0	59.0	60.6	66.4	73.5	83.7

Website: *www.clorox.com*

CONSERVATIVE GROWTH

The Coca-Cola Company

Ticker symbol: KO (NYSE) ❑ S&P rating: AA ❑ Value Line financial strength rating: A++ ❑ Current yield: 3.2% ❑ Dividend raises, last 10 years: 10

Company Profile

Changing demographics and new customer preferences have brought us to re-evaluate several "old-line" brands and companies, particularly in the food and beverage industry where such preferences have changed the most and fastest (well, not as fast as smartphone technology or social media, but you get the idea). Simply put, the emerging Millennial generation likes healthier, more customized foods and drinks—and that has not been the "sweet spot" for our larger old-line food and beverage companies. Those of you who prefer Coke over Pepsi (as, full disclosure, we do) will be happy to say that we "pruned the branches" down to one soda company, and, as they like to say, "Coke is it."

This wasn't an easy choice, for PepsiCo is more diverse with its Frito-Lay food business and has put in some more robust growth numbers of late. But we will stick with Coke as the "winner" based on brand, international presence, and a few innovations and initiatives that make us think they might just see where the puck is going with the new generation. Anyway, pour yourself a cold one, and read on . . .

The Coca-Cola Company is the world's largest beverage company. For more than 100 years, the company has mainly produced concentrates and syrups, which it then bottles or cans itself or sells to independent bottlers worldwide. However, it took a big step to "own" the supply chain in 2010 with the acquisition of bottler Coca-Cola Enterprises' North American operations; CCE still handles distribution for Europe. Independent bottlers add water (still or carbonated, depending on the product), sugar, and other (often local) ingredients, then bottle and distribute the products to restaurants, retailers, and other distributors. The company owns the brand and is responsible for consumer brand marketing initiatives, while the distributors handle all downstream merchandising. The company operates in more than 200 countries and markets nearly 500 brands of concentrate and finished beverages. These concentrates are used to produce more than 3,500 different branded products, including Coca-Cola.

The company continues to strive to expand its beverage offerings beyond the traditional carbonated soda drinks. Major brands besides Coke include Minute Maid and Simply Orange juices, Dasani and Evian bottled waters, Powerade and Full Throttle sports beverages, Nestea and Gold Peak Tea and FUZE iced teas, Glaceau vitamin waters, and major brands such as Ayataka Green Tea and I Lohas water in Japan, Del Valle in Latin America, and others similarly local to their markets. The total numbers are staggering: 3,500 products, 500 brands, 20 of which have reached $1 billion in sales, 28.2 billion cases worldwide, which equates to 637 billion servings per year, 1.9 billion beverages consumed per day, and 21,990 servings per second, all processed through more than 250 bottlers serving 200 countries, and all handled through the world's largest beverage distribution system. In terms of unit case volume, 79 percent of all sales are overseas—29 percent in Latin America, 15 percent in Eurasia/Africa, 21 percent in the Pacific, and 14 percent in Europe. In revenue terms, the company counts about 57 percent as overseas sales.

As to whether the company "gets it" in terms of marketing its products to the "new world," we can safely say it has taken some steps, first by buying a 16 percent interest in "K-cup" single-serving beverage maker and marketer Keurig Green Mountain in late 2013 (a homemade one-serving soda beverage called "Keurig Kold" featuring Coke-branded drinks is in the works). Coke then acquired a 17 percent stake interest shortly thereafter in alternative beverage maker Monster Beverage, and now is rumored to be interested in Odwalla and plant-based food and beverage maker WhiteWave Foods. Normally, acquisitions make us nervous, but we see the idea here, and with $18 billion in cash on hand,

Coke has the means. Additionally, their recent innovations resonate well with us. The new "Freestyle" machine found in a growing number of fast-food restaurants allows drinkers to customize their drinks. It's fun, and remember—customization is one of today's biggies. And did you know? It now collects data so that Coke can see what tastes are preferred; what a laboratory! (The dispenser team has its own website—check out *www .coca-colafreestyle.com*). Other innovations include mass-customized cans and bottles with people's names on them, and something we've all awaited: a return to the original Coke bottle shape and format where possible.

Financial Highlights, Fiscal Year 2014

For FY2014, as in FY2013, worldwide unit volumes grew about 2 percent, but with the strong overseas footprint causing dollar headwinds, revenues actually dropped just under 2 percent; earnings and per-share earnings dropped about 2 percent as well. Profit margins, reflecting gradual trends away from traditional soda, dropped just a tiny bit and are projected to drop more in 2015, from 20.0 percent in FY2013 down to 19.1 percent in FY2015, all down from the 22–23 percent range in the company's weak-dollar, strong-overseas-growth, high-calorie heyday (for a company this size still to make 20 percent net profit margin—think about it!). Clearly the mix has changed and the company must respond with new growth in higher-margined products to reverse this minor slide. Prospects for FY2015 aren't too exciting, with flat (sorry!) sales projections and a 3–4 percent drop in net earnings. The fizz starts to return in FY2016 as some of the initiatives we've discussed gain traction (and a weaker dollar maybe); revenues are projected up 2–3 percent with earnings up in the 5–6 percent range as the company adapts to the new mix and cuts costs. Cash returns to investors are decent on both the buyback and dividend front, with high single-digit to 10 percent dividend raises the norm, even with flat performance.

Reasons to Buy

"I like to bet on sure things," Warren Buffett said, on why he'll never sell a single one of the 400 million shares of Coke stock he owns. That pretty much sums it up, and the reasons to buy Coke continue to be solid. The company has category leadership, especially globally, in soft drinks, juices and juice drinks, and ready-to-drink coffees and teas. They're number two globally in sports drinks, and number three in packaged water and energy drinks. In

Coca-Cola, Diet Coke, Sprite, and Fanta, they own four of the top five brands of soft drink in the world.

The Coca-Cola name is probably the most recognized brand in the world and is almost beyond valuation. Indeed, Mr. Buffett once uttered the classic line about brand strength and intangibles in reference to Coke: "If you gave me $100 million and said take away the soft drink leadership in the world from Coke, I'd give it back to you and say it can't be done."

That's all pretty old news now; what's important is that Coke has also shown us, in today's world, that it isn't just going to sit around and go flat while we investors sit around and cry in our beer. We see signs that the company "gets it" and will not only adapt, but eventually has a chance to remain the number one brand even with a full new mix of beverages for the modern world. Coke has traditionally been a steady hedge stock and offers a solid dividend with a constant and recently accelerating track record of dividend growth. The company boasts—quite rightly—about having raised dividends in each of the past 53 years, and returned some $8.5 billion out of $10.5 billion in cash generated to shareholders in 2013. It is also as close to a pure play on international business as you'll find in a U.S. company. Finally, the low beta of 0.49 continues to confirm its low-volatility credentials.

Reasons for Caution

Sales in established markets—the U.S. and Europe, and now Latin America—are still flat or only slightly improving, probably caused in part by interest in health and reducing obesity.

But that's becoming an old story too—for the future, the adaptation and growth strategy could come with some speedbumps. One wonders how the Coke culture will resonate with its newly acquired beverage interests, and one wonders further whether the new-age consumer will adapt well to healthy or fun drinks sold by Coke. The acquisitions and innovations highlighted previously are exciting if the company can carry them to full potential. Therein lies the 64-ounce question: Can they deliver change? Fast enough? Can they get the message out? In time to make a difference as traditional sugary beverages decline? Right now, our bet is "yes."

Overall, this is a slow, steady growth story, which may be too slow for many, with new risks the company didn't face when Mr. Buffett bought in years ago.

SECTOR: **Consumer Staples** ❑ BETA COEFFICIENT: **0.49** ❑ 10-YEAR COMPOUND EARNINGS PER-SHARE GROWTH: **8.0%** ❑ 10-YEAR COMPOUND DIVIDENDS PER-SHARE GROWTH: **9.5%**

		2007	2008	2009	2010	2011	2012	2013	2014
Revenues (mil)		28,857	31,944	30,990	35,123	46,554	48,017	46,854	45,998
Net income (mil)		5,981	7,050	6,824	8,144	8,932	9,019	9,374	9,091
Earnings per share		1.29	1.51	1.47	1.75	1.92	1.97	2.08	2.04
Dividends per share		0.68	0.76	0.82	0.88	0.94	1.02	1.12	1.22
Cash flow per share		1.54	1.79	1.75	2.09	2.41	2.46	2.58	2.53
Price:	high	32.2	32.8	29.7	32.9	35.9	40.7	43.4	45.0
	low	22.8	20.1	18.7	24.7	30.6	33.3	36.5	36.9

Website: *www.coca-cola.com*

CONSERVATIVE GROWTH

Colgate-Palmolive Company

Ticker symbol: CL (NYSE) ❑ S&P rating: AA- ❑ Value Line financial strength rating: A++ ❑ Current yield: 2.2% ❑ Dividend raises, past 10 years: 10

Company Profile

Colgate-Palmolive is the second-largest global producer of detergents, toiletries, and other household products. The company manages its business in two straightforward segments: Oral, Personal, and Home Care; and Pet Nutrition. The Oral, Personal, and Home Care division produces and markets a number of familiar brands and products: Ajax, Palmolive, Irish Spring, Softsoap, Fabuloso, Mennen, and Speed Stick; and Science Diet and Hill's Pet Foods in the Pet Nutrition segment in addition to the familiar Colgate brand of oral care products. These brands are strong with substantial market share in most markets: Colgate owns 46 percent of the worldwide oral care market, 21 percent of personal care, 20 percent of the home care, and 13 percent of the total pet nutrition markets.

Although it hurt during this most recent period of dollar strength, Colgate's real strength is in international consumer products markets, with a presence in more than 200 countries and territories. About 80 percent of its business is international—and more than 50 percent of *that* business is in emerging markets.

Financial Highlights, Fiscal Year 2014

Naturally such a presence in international markets led to a mediocre financial performance once the financials are repatriated to U.S. dollars. Net sales dropped 1 percent to $17.3 billion, but the company estimates that they grew 5 percent organically on a worldwide basis. In Latin America, which makes up 28 percent of sales (and is, by the way, the largest region; the U.S. is at 18 percent), net sales decreased 5 percent on a negative currency effect of 14.5 percent; on an organic basis they actually increased 14.5 percent. So as you can see, a lot has to do with what's going on with the dollar.

Much—but not all—of the company's overseas sales are manufactured locally, so currency doesn't play too much harder into earnings than sales, but even with some cost reduction and global supply chain efficiency measures, which drove operating margins up about 1 percent to 26.4 percent, net earnings still slumped about 3 percent to $2.2 billion. Included in that also was the shutdown of the Venezuela business. A good-sized share buyback kept per-share earnings about constant, and the dividend was raised 6 percent even with the flat overall performance.

Sales through FY2016 should grow modestly but vary in response to currency effects, and are projected to drop as much as 3 percent in FY2015 before rising as much as 5 percent in FY2016. Continued realization of cost savings, greater emphasis on higher-margined personal care lines, and lower input costs should bear fruit in earnings, which, on a per-share basis and helped along by steady 2 percent share buybacks, could grow in the low 20 percent range in FY2015 and another 10 percent in FY2016.

Reasons to Buy

Colgate's brands are market leaders in most of the markets in which they operate, particularly in overseas markets where they are especially strong. They have a 45 percent share of the global toothpaste market and 33 percent of the manual toothbrush market. They're number one or number two with many of their other brands, including Ajax and Softsoap, and have many other well-established brands. The company's "first to market" global strategy has given them a formidable foothold in emerging markets such as China, India, and Latin America. Colgate is in a great position to benefit from the increased acceptance and use of dental care products and other toiletries in these markets.

Colgate is a conservatively run company that prefers slower organic growth over quick (but expensive) acquisitions. They rarely have a downside surprise—they tend to meet or beat their estimates. They plow money back into the company and achieve profitability through operational excellence, rather than paying for gross margins at any price. This is a solid defensive play with a good dividend, real earnings growth, and real earnings predictability. Looking at the bigger picture, Colgate is probably a safer, steadier alternative in the consumer staples marketplace than Procter & Gamble or Clorox (also *100 Best Stocks*), as it is less prone to reach for new, rapidly changing markets, such as cosmetics, and less apt to try to grow through acquisitions. This company is about slow, steady returns with little risk and little market volatility in bad times. The company touts not just ten but *51* consecutive years of dividend increases.

Reasons for Caution

Colgate participates in an increasingly competitive market, requiring more frequent new-product rollouts and related marketing expenses just to keep up. As we've seen, the international exposure brings currency exposure, and sometimes pure and simple business risk, as evidenced by the Venezuela exit. The Colgate business will not stimulate aggressive investors, and it could be that much of the forward good news is already priced into the stock—shop carefully.

SECTOR: **Consumer Staples** ◻ BETA COEFFICIENT: **0.49** ◻ 10-YEAR COMPOUND EARNINGS PER-SHARE GROWTH: **7.5%** ◻ 10-YEAR COMPOUND DIVIDENDS PER-SHARE GROWTH: **12.0%**

		2007	2008	2009	2010	2011	2012	2013	2014
Revenues (mil)		13,790	15,330	15,327	15,564	16,734	17,085	17,420	17,277
Net income (mil)		1,737	1,957	2,291	2,203	2,431	2,472	2,241	2,180
Earnings per share		1.69	1.83	2.19	2.16	2.47	2.58	2.38	2.36
Dividends per share		0.70	0.78	0.86	1.02	1.14	1.22	1.33	1.42
Cash flow per share		2.10	2.27	2.64	2.57	2.97	3.10	2.91	2.89
Price:	high	40.6	41.0	43.7	43.1	47.4	55.5	66.5	71.3
	low	31.9	27.2	27.3	36.6	37.4	43.6	52.6	59.8

Website: *www.colgate.com*

AGGRESSIVE GROWTH

Comcast Corporation

Ticker symbol: CMCSA (NASDAQ) ❑ S&P rating: A- ❑ Value Line financial strength rating: A ❑ Current yield: 1.7% ❑ Dividend raises, past 10 years: 6

Company Profile

Comcast is one of the nation's leading providers of communications services and information and entertainment content passed through those services. The core business is Comcast Cable, the familiar cable TV network that has evolved into a conduit for delivering bundled high-speed Internet services, phone services, and on-demand content. This business has served some 23 million subscribers in 39 states.

The company has been evolving its information and entertainment business gradually through its ownership of regional sports networks and national channels such as the Golf Channel, E! (an entertainment channel), Fandango (a moviegoer's website), and others. The company took a major leap forward as a content provider with the early 2011 closing of the acquisition of 51 percent of NBCUniversal, almost instantly turning the company into not only a connectivity powerhouse but a media powerhouse as well through its ownership of Universal Pictures among other assets. In March 2013, Comcast completed the purchase by acquiring the remaining 49 percent of NBCUniversal from General Electric, the previous parent corporation. With that acquisition, Comcast became the largest integrated content development and distribution business in the United States.

The company has been building its Xfinity Internet portal brand to compete with satellite operators and such offerings as AT&T U-verse and Verizon FiOS. Customers can buy bundles of services including TV, on-demand video, and, as an emerging offering, on-demand TV through the Hulu application. With Xfinity, customers can also get up to 105 mbps Internet service, probably the best service for downloading large chunks of video content. In short, Comcast has evolved from being a lackluster cable TV service to a full-scale communications utility with some of the highest-performance products on the market, using the Xfinity platform to draw customers in for the rest of its service bundle. The company now has nearly as many Internet service customers (22 million) as it does cable subscribers (23 million), with more than 11 million phone service connections thrown in for good measure.

Comcast breaks down its business into two major segments: Cable Communications and NBCUniversal. In FY2014, Cable Communications accounted for 64 percent of total revenues and 79 percent operating income. NBCUniversal, in turn, breaks down into Cable Networks (including the national and regional sports networks), Broadcast Television, Filmed Entertainment, and Theme Parks (the noted "Universal" theme parks in Florida and Hollywood, California). The vast majority of Comcast customers are residential, although the company also offers a business class service, including fiber end-user connections and cloud storage, to meet the needs of small and midsized organizations. That business segment grew some 22 percent on a base of $4 billion, and bears watching. The company also owns the Philadelphia 76ers (NBA basketball) and Flyers (NHL hockey).

In early 2014, the company announced a blockbuster (no pun intended) acquisition of Time Warner Cable for some $35 billion, which would have substantially increased the company's leadership in those markets. Due to intense regulatory pressure and other reasons we may not be privy to, the company dropped this bid. The possibility of acquisitions—either in cable or in adjacent businesses such as content or mobile networks—still looms large as the industry consolidates.

Financial Highlights, Fiscal Year 2014

Continued strength from the NBCUniversal acquisition, stronger consumer subscriber gains (1.7 percent total with a slight shift toward "three-product" from "one-product" customers), expanded per-customer revenue ($139.95 in FY2014 versus $128.38 in FY2013), and continued strength in the Business Services segment created a solid picture again for in FY2014. Total revenues increased 6.4 percent. Positive operating margin trends again in FY2014 led to an 8.8 percent gain in net profits, and share buybacks led to a 14.5 percent gain in per-share earnings. The company bought back another $4 billion in stock and recently authorized the repurchase of $10 billion more.

The picture continues to look good in FY2015 and FY2016 with 4–5 percent revenue increases and per-share earnings increases a still-sharper 10–15 percent.

Reasons to Buy

The addition of Comcast to the 2013 *100 Best* list was one we debated out of concern about cable companies in general. However, it continues to pay off handsomely; the shares have more than doubled since our decision. We like the company's strategic and operational focus—the acquisitions make sense, and the metrics they present truly describe what's important in the business—not just size and volume, but making customer relationships better and more profitable. The different pieces of the company fit together well.

Growth in market dominance, improved branding, and new revenues from the increased adoption of Xfinity all bode well, as does what we think will become the eventual reality of on-demand content as a standard—and profitable—product from suppliers such as Comcast.

Reasons for Caution

Although Comcast is certainly big enough to survive on its own, the trend toward industry consolidation either brings the usual risks associated with an acquisition, or risks that it could be left out and that another player combination overtakes Comcast's leadership position or some of its niches. While recent decisions on net neutrality now look to be a positive, they aren't a done deal, and we could be left with an Internet that can't charge any extra for handling heavy loads, which with the expected expansion of such loads could become a problem.

The company faces extreme competition in most of its markets, although it may have at least a temporary bandwidth advantage at present. It's a lucrative and growing market; there will always be competing technologies and services for what Comcast has to offer.

SECTOR: Telecommunications Services ❑ BETA COEFFICIENT: **1.25** ❑ 10-YEAR COMPOUND EARNINGS PER-SHARE GROWTH: **20.0%** ❑ 5-YEAR COMPOUND DIVIDENDS PER-SHARE GROWTH: **24.0%**

	2007	2008	2009	2010	2011	2012	2013	2014
Revenues (mil)	30,895	34,256	35,756	37,937	55,842	62,570	64,657	68,775
Net income (mil)	2,287	2,701	3,638	3,535	4,377	6,023	6,649	7,418
Earnings per share	0.74	0.91	1.26	1.29	1.58	2.29	2.56	2.93
Dividends per share	—	0.25	0.27	0.38	0.45	0.60	0.78	0.90
Cash flow per share	2.82	3.10	3.57	3.89	4.44	5.26	5.59	6.10
Price: high	29.6	22.5	17.3	21.2	27.2	38.2	52.1	59.3
low	17.3	12.1	10.3	14.3	19.2	24.3	37.2	47.7

Website: *www.comcast.com*

ConocoPhillips Company

Ticker symbol: COP (NYSE) ❑ S&P rating: A ❑ Value Line financial strength rating: A+ ❑ Current yield: 4.3% ❑ Dividend raises, past 10 years: 9

Company Profile

Ouch. When one buys a major integrated energy company, one usually expects steady revenues, steady profits, and a steady business. Such has not been the case recently even with the biggest and the best, including ConocoPhillips and almost everybody else. In 2012, the company split off its refining and marketing units to create a separate company with a familiar name: Phillips 66. That was okay with us; we already had refiners on the *100 Best* list, the pure play Valero as well as a continued interest in refining through Chevron. We opted to retain ConocoPhillips ("COP") to retain a solid and pure play in exploration and production ("E&P"). Then energy prices cratered in 2014, and our once-stable COP went from earning over $6 per share in 2013 to projecting a loss for 2015. Naturally, we weren't expecting this. But we decided that the company is in for the long term and has plenty of wherewithal (and cash flow) to not only endure this "bust" cycle but to maintain and even increase its dividend to boot. So, welcome back, COP—and welcome to you new investors who might be looking for a solid buying opportunity in the oil (and gas) patch.

Although lower oil and gas prices have turned ConocoPhillips from a $54 billion multinational "E&P" company into a $34 billion one (with the refining unit, it was once a $240 billion company), COP is still one of the world's largest E&P enterprises. Headquartered in Houston, TX, the company operates in 30 countries with about 19,100 employees.

The company's E&P operations are geographically diverse, producing most of its resources in the United States, including a large presence in Alaska's Prudhoe Bay. The company also has a large presence in U.S shale "fracking" regions, including Eagle Ford and Permian regions in Texas and the Bakken region in North Dakota. As well, the company produces in Norway, the United Kingdom, western Canada, Australia, offshore Timor-Leste in the Timor Sea, Indonesia, Malaysia, China, Vietnam, Libya, Senegal, Nigeria, Algeria, and Russia.

ConocoPhillips has become a strong natural gas play, with approximately 53 percent of production equivalent in natural gas or natural gas liquids, 39 percent crude oil, and 8 percent bitumen. Production has an unusually high domestic concentration: 27 percent of crude oil production and about 38 percent of natural gas production occur in the Lower 48, with another 32 percent of crude oil production and 1 percent of natural gas coming from Alaska. About 44 percent of total proved reserves are in the Lower 48 or Alaska, with another 28 percent in Canada.

As expected, and as is typical in the industry, COP has scaled back its exploration and capital budgets—in their case, some 33 percent from 2014 levels, more than some of its competitors, from about $16 billion to $11–$12 billion annually. Reductions are occurring across the board and especially in some of the key fracking regions in Eagle Ford, Bakken, and the Permian Basin and in Canada, but the company still projects a full-year growth in production of 2–3 percent. The company has carefully analyzed the effects of each dollar's change in prices on key production areas and is allocating capital accordingly. COP has stated that it is positioning itself for "an extended period of lower, more volatile prices," and has said that "dividend remains a top priority for capital allocation."

Financial Highlights, Fiscal Year 2014

When the unit price of your key product declines from $71.21 (per barrel of oil equivalent) to $36.96 in the last six months of a fiscal year, it is pretty difficult to keep making your numbers. Actually, the negative effects on revenues and earnings don't hit full stride until FY2015. For the record, revenues dropped about 3.5 percent in FY2014; margins and earnings dropped more rapidly with net profit coming in some 22 percent below FY2013 levels, and per-share earnings suffered accordingly. Notably, per-share cash flows only dropped 6 percent. The rubber really hits the road with big skid marks in FY2015, with revenues projected down to $34–$35 billion, a drop of 35 percent. COP, like most others, is predicting a fairly wide range of possible oil prices for FY2015 and beyond, but appears to be basing this forecast on a price for West Texas Intermediate crude (a key U.S. benchmark) of $60 per barrel versus $93 in FY2014, and something closer to $73 for FY2016. The 35 percent drop in revenues for FY2015 correlates directly to that figure, and the 21 percent recovery to $42–$43 billion in FY2016 revenues reflects the $73 price. Naturally, these values are highly volatile, and investors will want to watch crude (and gas) prices carefully. A net loss of $500–$600 million is projected for FY2015, with earnings climbing back to $1.5–$2.0 billion for FY2016. Reduced capital expenditures will steady the cash flows, and those cash flows will sustain the dividend (in fact, it was just increased) but share buybacks are off the table for now.

Reasons to Buy

"Flexible and resilient" is the company's motto and message to shareholders as it enters what it expects to be the "trough" year of 2015. You got that right—at least, we hope. COP is strong enough to sustain itself through these tough times, and management has a good handle on the situation and the various scenarios and risks. We do think oil prices will recover, perhaps a little faster than today's conservative forecasts, as supply and demand naturally correct the current glut. We like the domestic slant on the production mix; it is lower cost and more stable than most, and we don't have to add a measure of geopolitics in to the long list of risk factors. With these factors, plus the sustained and strong dividend yield and solid future prospects, we think 2015 will likely be a good time to drill for some COP shares for 2016 and beyond. As oil price volatility probably won't go away in 2016, that year will probably present buying opportunities as well.

Reasons for Caution

The story of ConocoPhillips has been a story of change over the past three years. The company successfully divested the refining operations to gain focus—only to gain focus on the most volatile part of the business—which has become far more volatile of late. E&P is risky by nature even with a steady oil price (although COP's domestically oriented portfolio reduces this risk); when you add in price volatility it makes for . . . well, a volatile mix. We think that for the most part investors are being compensated for these risks with the high yield and relatively low share prices of late, but if oil drops to $30 as some say it might—or worse, stay below $60 on a sustained basis—even this rock-steady producer will experience some pain.

SECTOR: Energy ❑ BETA COEFFICIENT: **1.29** ❑ 10-YEAR COMPOUND EARNINGS PER-SHARE GROWTH: **5.0%** ❑ 10-YEAR COMPOUND DIVIDENDS PER-SHARE GROWTH: **13.0%**

	2007	2008	2009	2010	2011	2012	2013	2014
Revenues (bil)	187.4	240.8	149.3	189.4	244.8	62.0	54.4	52.5
Net income (bil)	15.1	15.9	4.9	8.8	12.1	7.4	8.0	6.2
Earnings per share	9.14	10.68	3.24	5.92	8.76	5.91	6.43	4.96
Dividends per share	1.64	1.88	1.91	2.16	2.64	2.64	2.70	2.84
Cash flow per share	14.86	16.80	9.58	12.50	15.63	11.47	12.57	11.79
Price: high	90.8	96.0	57.4	68.6	77.4	78.3	74.6	87.1
low	61.6	41.3	34.1	48.5	68.0	50.6	56.4	60.8

Website: *www.conocophillips.com*

AGGRESSIVE GROWTH

Corning Incorporated

Ticker symbol: GLW (NYSE) □ S&P rating: A- □ Value Line financial strength rating: B++ □ Current yield: 2.1% □ Dividend raises, past 10 years: 5

Company Profile

When you think of Corning, you think of glass. All kinds of glass—drinking glasses, glass tableware, and that sort of thing. If you were around in the 1960s, you may remember that well-known white cookware with the little blue flowers on the side.

But things change, and so has Corning. Today's Corning is a premier technology company, more precisely, a technology *materials* company. If you use a smartphone, a tablet, a laptop PC, or a flat-panel television, chances are pretty good that the glass on the screen comes from Corning. A good amount of the data you see on that screen may have come through glass-based fiber-optic materials supplied by—guess who—Corning.

In fact, Corning operates in five segments, all centered on the glass business. Display Technologies (40 percent of FY2014 sales) makes a lot of those screens, actually referred to as "glass substrates for liquid crystal displays." Optical Communications (formerly Telecommunications) (27 percent) makes fiber-optic cable and an assortment of connectivity and other products related to fiber for telecommunications companies, LAN, and data center applications. Specialty Materials (12 percent) provides a wide assortment of high-tech, glass-based materials, including those specialty glass screens for smartphones, tablets, etc., which it has cleverly branded as Corning Gorilla Glass for its endurance characteristics. This product is even gaining traction in automotive and architectural markets. Also out of this division comes a new bendable display substrate known as Willow Glass and a host of glass and ceramic products and formulations used in the semiconductor industry, precision instruments, and even astronomy and ophthalmology. The Environmental Technologies segment (11 percent) makes ceramic substrates and filters for emission control systems, mostly for gasoline and diesel engines. The Life Sciences segment (9 percent) makes laboratory glass and plastic wares

The company competes with a number of suppliers, mostly Japanese, on a variety of fronts, and acquired the remaining 50 percent interest in a joint venture with Samsung (Samsung Corning Precision Materials) during 2014 to make it a wholly owned subsidiary with lower-cost production facilities in Korea. This acquisition drove the Display Technologies unit to 40 percent of the total business, up from 32 percent in FY2013, and added about $1 billion to revenues. Corning also has had a 50–50 joint venture with Dow Chemical for years, known as Dow Corning, a leader in silicon products and technologies producing high-quality sealants, lubricants, etc., from silicon materials. Promising innovations include the adaptation of its "Willow Glass," thinner than a dollar bill, for ultrathin, ultrasensitive touchscreens to improve size and weight characteristics of mobile devices. Eventually this will evolve into bendable, curved, and curvable glass displays, allowing us to literally wear our devices—an exciting prospect. Also noteworthy are the company's new "Dynamic Windows"—architectural glass panels that automatically darken, reducing energy consumption.

Financial Highlights, Fiscal Year 2014

The numbers for FY2014 look especially good with the addition of revenues from Samsung Corning as well as strong TV sales, a shift to larger screen sizes, strong fiber-to-home and data center sales, and new emission regulations in China all driving growth. Gorilla Glass sales were a bit off due to a consolidation in the tablet market, but the new "Gorilla Glass 4" update has been well received. All told, and with approximately $1.8 billion in new revenue from the Samsung joint venture share, FY2014 revenues rose 24 percent, but a more modest 1.2 percent without the joint venture acquisition. Net profits were up 26 percent, again heavily influenced by the joint venture acquisition; this influence runs in multiple directions with operational efficiencies, currency hedges, and one-time adjustments and so is not broken out by the company. Be that as it may, the company expects substantial margin increases through the acquisition and volume scale, up from 32 percent to 36 percent on an operating margin basis, going forward through FY2016—but also with a rise in tax rates. All that settles out to a healthy 6.5 percent advance in revenues in FY2015 followed by 4 percent in FY2016, with a slight decline in total net profit. But with continued strong cash flows and aggressive share repurchases (the company has already retired almost 20 percent of its shares since 2010), per-share earnings should advance to about $1.95 by FY2016, about 13 percent of today's level. With only 13 percent debt to total capitalization, the balance sheet is especially strong for this type of company, and moderate dividend raises look to continue as well.

Reasons to Buy

We like companies that stand to benefit no matter how a market plays out. Our CarMax pick benefits whether Ford or Toyota or Hyundai wins; CarMax sells used cars no matter what. At least for glass displays, Corning is in the same position—whether Samsung or Apple comes out on top of the smartphone contest, Corning wins. Whether tablets or PCs lead the personal computing market, Corning wins. The explosion in smart devices and the new technologies Corning is likely to bring to that space create some excitement down the road. We think the inevitable advent of wearable mobile computing devices, spearheaded by the Apple Watch, will be a big spark for this company. The core businesses aren't too shabby, either. The company endured a huge boom-bust cycle with the first build out of the Internet during the dot-com bubble, and it suffered the consequences. But having a piece of the world's largest fiber-optic supplier and technology leader isn't such a bad thing, either. Across the board, Corning continues to differentiate their products through innovation. The presence of competition, especially Japanese competition, reminds us from time to time that Corning doesn't own the "glass" niche outright, but it is close to owning the innovation in this area; for those who like pure plays in a strong and profitable technology segment, Corning is a good bet.

Finally, this company is profitable, with plenty of cash flow, and is returning plenty of cash to shareholders both in the form of dividends and the share buybacks; the dividend yield is quite decent for this type of company and is growing.

Reasons for Caution

While its product portfolio is broader than it was 15 years ago, supplying well beyond the telecom industry, the company is still subject to business and inventory cycles. Glass, without the right amount of innovation, is a commodity business, and the recent strengthening of Japanese competition through the lower yen continues to present a challenge. If you're concerned that price erosion through competition will outpace innovation and cost savings initiatives, Corning may not be the place to be.

SECTOR: **Information Technology** ❑ BETA COEFFICIENT: **1.63** ❑ 10-YEAR COMPOUND EARNINGS PER-SHARE GROWTH: **34.5%** ❑ 10-YEAR COMPOUND DIVIDENDS PER-SHARE GROWTH: **NM**

	2007	2008	2009	2010	2011	2012	2013	2014
Revenues (mil)	5,860	5,948	5,395	6,632	7,890	8,012	7,819	9,715
Net income (mil)	2,267	2,424	2,114	3,275	2,620	1,728	1,961	2,472
Earnings per share	1.41	1.53	1.35	2.07	1.76	1.15	1.34	1.73
Dividends per share	0.10	0.20	0.20	0.20	0.23	0.32	0.39	0.52
Cash flow per share	1.83	2.01	1.86	2.64	2.49	1.85	2.12	2.79
Price: high	27.3	28.1	19.5	21.1	23.4	14.6	18.1	23.3
low	18.1	7.4	9.0	15.5	11.5	10.6	11.6	17.0

Website: *www.corning.com*

AGGRESSIVE GROWTH

Costco Wholesale Corporation

Ticker symbol: COST (NASDAQ) ❑ S&P rating: A+ ❑ Value Line financial strength rating: A+ ❑ Current yield: 1.1% ❑ Dividend raises, past 10 years: 10

Company Profile

Just about when we think that the retailing behemoth Costco has run its course, has no room to grow, is long in the tooth as a retailing concept, is too small in the margins, too expensive to buy as a stock, and is too "mass" intensive to appeal to today's variety of custom-demanding Millennials, they surprise us with unexpected growth, vitality, and shareholder returns—and as such we'll load up another four-wheel flatbed at Costco for 2016.

Costco Wholesale Corporation operates a multinational chain of membership warehouses, mainly under the Costco Wholesale name, that carry brand-name merchandise at substantially lower prices than are typically found at conventional wholesale or retail sources. The warehouse sales model was designed to help small to medium-sized businesses reduce costs in purchasing for resale and for everyday business use, but as most know, the individual consumer has been their big growth driver. The company capitalizes on size and operational efficiencies, like "cross-docking" shipments directly from manufacturers to stores, to deliver attractive pricing to its customers. Based on sales volume, Costco is the largest membership warehouse club chain and second-largest general retailer in the world.

Costco carries a broad line of product categories, including groceries, appliances, television and media, automotive supplies, toys, hardware, sporting goods, jewelry, cameras, books, housewares, apparel, health and beauty aids, tobacco, furniture, office supplies, and office equipment. The company also operates self-service gasoline stations at a number of its U.S. and Canadian locations. Approximately 56 percent of sales comes from food, beverages, alcohol, sundries, and snacks. Another 16 percent comes from hardlines—electronics, appliances, hardware, automotive, office supplies, and health and beauty aids—and 11 percent from softlines—primarily clothing, housewares, media, jewelry, and domestics. The rest, including gasoline, pharmacy, optical, and other services, form a catchall "other" category. The emergence of Costco as a grocer of choice cannot be missed, and the company reports particular strength in its Fresh Foods lines (meats, produce, deli, and bakery), indicating appeal to the more cost-conscious set of trend-conscious food consumers.

Additionally, Costco Wholesale Industries, a division of the company, operates manufacturing businesses, including special food packaging, optical laboratories, meat processing, and jewelry distribution. A wide and growing variety of products are sold under its "Kirkland" private label.

Costco is open only to members of its tiered membership plan, the higher "Executive" tier at $110 annually gaining access to reward points and other perks and discounts. In all, there are 79 million members, with a 91 percent membership renewal rate in the U.S. and Canada.

As of early 2015 Costco has 671 locations: 474 in the United States and Puerto Rico (up from 461), 89 in Canada (versus 87), 34 in Mexico (from 33), 26 in the U.K. (versus 25), 20 in Japan (versus 18), ten in Taiwan, and 11 in Korea (totaling 41, up from 37 reported for all of Asia), and seven in Australia (versus five). The company also has a significant and growing e-commerce presence at **www.costco.com**. Though it presently accounts for only 3 percent of revenues, it grew 20 percent in FY2014.

Financial Highlights, Fiscal Year 2014

Same-store sales increased about 6 percent in FY2014; that with 30 new stores opened and record per-store revenues both for new stores and all stores together, drove total revenues 7.1 percent higher. Steady operating margins but a higher tax rate led to a 4 percent increase in net income and a comparable increase in per-share income. Share buybacks paused briefly in favor of store openings, keeping the dividend raise rate at about 13 percent. For FY2015 and FY2016, the company expects top-line growth to continue in the 6–7 percent range on comparable same-store sales growth and the addition of 34 new warehouses. They expect an upshift in per-share earnings growth to 10–12 percent in FY2015 and 8–10 percent in FY2016 on a slight margin improvement, in turn brought on by more house brand distribution and growth in more profitable pharmacy, optical, and hearing aid sales.

Membership revenues increased 6 percent to about $2.6 billion annually—an obviously large driver of Costco's $2 billion-plus annual profit.

Reasons to Buy

Costco is in an attractive best-of-both-worlds niche: It is a price leader consistent with the attitudes of today's more frugal consumer, yet it enjoys a reputation for being more upscale than the competition. We've all heard the boast, "I got it at Costco" from even our most affluent and high-minded friends. And of course, there's everybody else.

We also continue to like the international expansion and think the formula will play well overseas—although their ambitious European and Asian plans may be tempered a bit by local preferences for small package sizes and the general lack of residential storage space. Any U.S. resident who has hosted a visitor from abroad knows that Costco is a favored destination during the visit. We expect international expansion will be one of the company's primary growth drivers over the next ten years. We also applaud the recent move to switch exclusive credit card use from American Express to a co-branded Citigroup Visa credit card (in addition to Visa and MasterCard debit cards). This card is less expensive and more accessible to most members, and should broaden sales appeal. Costco also gets high marks for employee pay, satisfaction and loyalty, and for corporate citizenship in general.

In all, the company has a strong brand in a highly competitive sector, is gaining market share, and has a strong management track record. Although the 1.1 percent yield isn't that much of an attraction, the company has raised its dividend consistently in double digits since initiating it in 2004. Share repurchases are still on the table, but may not happen until later in the decade.

Reasons for Caution

One concern is the dependence on low-margin food and sundry lines. With the ramp-up of Walmart and Target groceries and stiff competition else-where, Costco may not always be the food source of choice. That said, food does get customers into the store, and gets them into the store more than once a week. Average sales per visit have been declining as a consequence, but overall the trend is probably favorable; more store traffic means more and more regular store sales overall.

Our biggest concerns continue to be the high share price, low margins, and dependence on membership fees for profitability. All three bring a measure of vulnerability to the stock—a misstep could be costly—and as mentioned at the outset we have wavered the last three years on whether Costco should continue on our *100 Best* list. On the flip side, management has shown its ability to navigate through difficult periods, the brand is strong, and the prospects for a global footprint, above all else, are encouraging for the future. In light of those three items, we're keeping Costco on our shopping list once again.

SECTOR: Retail ◻ BETA COEFFICIENT: 0.53 ◻ 10-YEAR COMPOUND EARNINGS PER-SHARE GROWTH: 10.5% ◻ 10-YEAR COMPOUND DIVIDENDS PER-SHARE GROWTH: 12.5%

	2007	2008	2009	2010	2011	2012	2013	2014
Revenues (mil)	64,400	72,483	71,422	77,946	88,915	99,137	105,156	112,640
Net income (mil)	1,083	1,283	1,086	1,307	1,462	1,741	1,977	2,058
Earnings per share	2.37	2.89	2.57	2.93	3.30	3.97	4.49	4.65
Dividends per share	0.55	0.61	0.68	0.77	0.89	1.03	1.17	1.33
Cash flow per share	4.05	4.48	4.25	4.85	5.34	6.13	6.69	7.05
Price: high	72.7	75.2	61.3	73.2	88.7	106.0	126.1	146.8
low	51.5	43.9	38.2	53.4	69.5	78.8	98.6	109.5

Website: *www.costco.com*

CONSERVATIVE GROWTH

CVS Health Corporation

Ticker symbol: CVS (NYSE) ◻ S&P rating: BBB+ ◻ Value Line financial strength rating: A+ ◻ Current yield: 1.3% ◻ Dividend raises, past 10 years: 10

Company Profile

Stanley and Sid Goldstein were distributing health and beauty products in the early 1960s when they decided to branch out into retailing, opening their first Consumer Value Store in Lowell, MA, in 1963. The CVS chain had grown to 40 outlets by 1969, the year they sold the business to Melville Shoes. Melville underwent a restructuring in the mid-1990s, spinning off CVS and other retail units.

Stan and Sid should be proud. CVS is now the largest pharmacy health-care provider in the United States—and in keeping with its mission, has recently changed its name from "CVS Caremark" to "CVS Health." Its flagship Retail Pharmacy domestic drugstore chain operates 7,822 retail and specialty pharmacy stores in 44 states, the District of Columbia, and now through a small acquisition, Brazil. The company holds the leading market share in 88 of the 100 largest U.S. drugstore markets, more than any other retail drugstore chain. Over time, it has expanded through acquiring other players in the category—Osco, Sav-On, Eckerd, and Longs Drugs. CVS's purchase of Longs Drugs in 2008 vaulted the company into the lead position in the U.S. drug retail market, ahead of Walgreens.

Stores are situated primarily in strip shopping centers or free-standing locations, with a typical store ranging in size from 8,000–13,000 square feet. Most new units being built are based on either a 10,000-square-foot or 12,000-square-foot prototype building that typically includes a drive-thru pharmacy. Proprietary branded products—5,200 of them—now account for just under 20 percent of segment revenues. The company filled 756 million prescriptions in 2014, generating over 70 percent of Retail Pharmacy sales. (The rest: 12.6 percent general merchandise, 11 percent over-the-counter and personal care products, and just under 5 percent beauty and cosmetics.) Retail Pharmacy sales, in turn, makes up about 43 percent of the company's total sales, and is generally more profitable.

The Caremark acquisition in 2007 transformed CVS from strictly a retailer into the nation's leading manager of pharmacy benefits, the middleman between pharmaceutical companies and individuals with drug benefit coverage. The Caremark acquisition forms the core of the company's Pharmacy Benefits Management (PBM) operations, which have some 65,000 pharmacy outlets including hospitals and clinics as well as the previously mentioned retail stores. The company dispenses about a billion prescriptions a year to 65 million plan members, and the Pharmacy Services segment now makes up about 67 percent of sales. This is a low-margin business, with gross profit of 5.4 percent of revenue versus 31.9 percent for the Retail Pharmacy segment. Put differently, just over 80 percent of gross profit is earned in the Retail segment.

Part of the Retail Pharmacy segment, the company's MinuteClinic concept is especially interesting in today's climate of managing health-care costs. CVS now has 971 clinics in 31 states and D.C., offering basic health services like flu shots and such given by 2,200 nurse practitioners and physician's assistants in a convenient retail environment. The company opened 175 new stores in 2014. All but seven of these clinics are located in CVS stores, naturally serving to drive traffic into the stores. Plans are to grow MinuteClinic into 1,500 locations in 35 states by 2017, and the service now has more than 49 major health affiliations—up from 30 just a few years ago. The concept gradually is gaining mainstream acceptance. The company also operates mail order and online pharmacies for regular and chronically ill patients and is working on a "Telehealth" service to accompany its platform of retail health services.

Perhaps as a gesture of thematic and ethical consistency, and clearly as a gesture of leadership in its market, the company discontinued tobacco product sales effective October 2014. The change will adversely affect short-term revenues and profits but generated a considerable amount of positive PR, and several competitors have followed suit.

Financial Highlights, Fiscal Year 2014

Despite the negative effects of discontinued tobacco sales, a less severe flu season, and certain provisions of the Affordable Care Act, and helped along by a few acquisitions, CVS turned in a nice 10 percent gain in the top line for FY2014. One larger acquisition in the Pharmacy Services segment did dilute margins and hence net income, which rose a more moderate 7.2 percent. An aggressive 40 million share buyback, however, drove per-share earnings an even more respectable 12.8 percent ahead of FY2013. Forward projections into FY2015 and FY2016 call for a 7–8 percent growth in revenues annually (this, despite the discontinuance of tobacco!), with per-share earnings growing in the 12–15 percent range. The company is on track to retire all the shares issued since the Caremark acquisition—some 600 million of them—having retired approximately 350 million to date.

Reasons to Buy

CVS is clearly a smartly diversified market leader and knows how to take advantage of that position without alienating customers or key health-care payers. What's more, its "retail" location in the health-care food chain positions it perfectly to capitalize on the initiatives of the Affordable Care Act: more patients getting more and lower-cost services. This, of course, all comes on top of favorable demographics—an aging population; one also ever more willing to pay for convenience, and a growing acceptance of CVS as a local convenience store for needs beyond health and personal care products. We like the fact that the company made a tough decision to discontinue tobacco, and came through with stellar financials anyhow.

These moderate and steady gains have turned into plenty of return for shareholders both in the form of cash dividends, steady and large share buybacks, and resulting share price appreciation, and CVS is one of the surer bets on our list to continue this trend.

Reasons for Caution

The business model is intact and positioned for growth as the ACA becomes standard and as demographics shift in CVS's favor. That, of course, could change dramatically if political forces undermine ACA or force big changes in it. The stock continues to rise steadily, and while we can see the reasons why, it does force new investors to find good entry points. A lot of the good news has already been factored in.

SECTOR: **Retail** ❑ BETA COEFFICIENT: **1.07** ❑ 10-YEAR COMPOUND EARNINGS PER-SHARE GROWTH: **14.5%** ❑ 10-YEAR COMPOUND DIVIDENDS PER-SHARE GROWTH: **19.5%**

	2007	2008	2009	2010	2011	2012	2013	2014
Revenues (mil)	76.3	87.5	98.7	98.0	107.2	123.1	126.7	139.4
Net income (mil)	2,637	3,589	3,803	3,700	3,766	4,394	4,902	5,255
Earnings per share	1.92	2.44	2.63	2.67	2.80	3.43	4.00	4.51
Dividends per share	0.24	0.26	0.30	0.35	0.50	0.65	0.90	1.10
Cash flow per share	2.59	3.37	3.73	3.75	4.10	4.99	5.74	6.30
Price: high	42.6	44.3	38.3	37.8	39.5	49.8	72.0	98.6
low	30.5	23.2	23.7	26.8	31.3	41.0	49.9	64.9

Website: *www.cvs.com*

AGGRESSIVE GROWTH

Daktronics, Inc.

Ticker symbol: DAKT (NASDAQ) ❑ S&P rating: NR ❑ Value Line financial strength rating: B+ ❑ Current yield: 3.6% ❑ Dividend raises, past 10 years: 7

Company Profile

You're driving down the highway. You're thinking about getting rid of a month's worth of grime and dirt and crud from your car. Suddenly, in vivid Technicolor, you see a billboard ahead on your right. Not just any old indifferent and easily ignored billboard displaying the same old thing months on end. It's brightly lit. It flashes an offer. Five Star Car Wash, at this exit, has a "Today Only—25 Percent Off" special. A few minutes ago you passed an electronic sign flashing "Road Work Ahead—Current Delay 30 Minutes." So, you tap the brakes, hit the right lane, and off the interstate you go. A win-win—you have a clean car, and the car wash, having a lighter day than usual and temporarily pricing its services accordingly, gets another unit through their system.

Hockey great Wayne Gretzky made famous the idea of "skating where the puck is going," and it's one of our favorite investing maxims. Like it or not, we think such real-time, highly visual signage is where the puck is going in marketing—real-time visual displays to complement your real-time mobile devices. Give it time, and it will come. Give it time, and there will be real-time visual graphic displays on park benches and subway entrances (there already are, in a few places). Give it time, and there will be "digital street furniture" and such just about everywhere. So how do you invest in this looming megatrend? We just happened to find a small company located literally in the middle of nowhere—Brookings, South Dakota—that makes this stuff. Chances are this company made both of the signs mentioned above. "Digital Street Furniture" is actually one of their product lines. Their core and founding business is really the large multimedia scoreboards in place in a growing number of sports arenas. The company, Daktronics, has a hand in an assortment of places where digital display technology can make a difference in outdoor environments, from $40 million scoreboards to the variable dollars-and-cents-per-gallon digital displays outside your local gas station.

Daktronics is the world's leading supplier of electronic scoreboards, large electronic display systems, digital messaging solutions, and related software and support services for sporting, commercial, and transportation applications. The company offers everything from small signs and scoreboards costing under $1,000 to the large $40 million sports-complex scoreboards just mentioned.

Business segments include Commercial, Live Events, Schools and Theaters, Transportation, and International. These groups are organized around customer segments and are all set up to create and sell unique applications of the core product lines of the company, which include video display systems, scoring and timing systems, digital billboards, digital street furniture, and simpler message displays like price, time, and temperature displays. Most of the company's products are based on LED technology with low to high resolution and embedded digital controllers. Here is a bit more "color" on the five segments:

- Commercial (28 percent of 2014 revenue, 7 percent year-over-year growth) sells a variety of digital signage to auto dealer, restaurant, gaming, retail petroleum (gas stations, mainly), and shopping center markets. Vivid video displays used for architectural or commercial purposes as part of the full building design is another emerging subsegment of this business.
- Live Events (36 percent of revenue, 24 percent growth) produces the traditional and some highly customized scoreboards, as well as signs for

entertainment venues, including programmable displays, parking information signs, and even specialized signs for places of worship.

- Schools and Theaters (11 percent, 10 percent decline). Included here
  are not only digital-age marquis signs for theaters and other venues but
  also for the box office, merchandise sales areas, and others.

- Transportation (10 percent, 25 percent decline). You've seen the freeway
  signs; there is also plenty of digital signage in airports, train stations, and
  other mass transit facilities. Recent large installations were made at Los
  Angeles International Airport and for the New Jersey Turnpike Authority.

- International (15 percent, 13 percent growth) sells all applications into
  international markets.

The company has about 2,300 employees—and, somewhat unusually,
about 400 interns and students on the payroll mostly from the local
South Dakota State University. Retiring cofounder and chairman Aelred
J. Kurtenbach, a PhD electrical engineer and professor at SDSU, owns
5.1 percent of the shares. The website, at *www.daktronics.com*, is a fun and
instructive ride.

We added this company to the 2015 *100 Best Stocks* list in an effort to
inject some small-cap blood into our list, and unfortunately the puck didn't
get to where we thought as fast as we thought it would. But we still think it's
headed in the right direction. Patience, we claim, is one of our virtues, and
the 3.5 percent dividend gives us time, so we're suiting up for Daktronics
once again for 2016.

Financial Highlights, Fiscal Year 2014

Several crosscurrents affected FY2014 performance and appear likely to
remain in place for FY2015. Prices for digital displays, especially the commercial variety (billboards and such) are coming down—bad news for revenue, but eventually, good news for the business as such displays become
more affordable and mainstream. Large sporting venue displays bring large
revenues (and usually lower margins to begin with), but the company ran
into some delays installing them, in part due to severe winter weather, that
negatively affected results. Finally, contractions in highway budgets and an
especially strong 2013 led to a revenue drop as noted in the Transportation
segment. All told, revenues advanced a decent 9 percent, but the business
mix, volume base, and expense base was unfavorable; net earnings suffered
by about 10 percent. FY2015 and FY2016 bring higher backlogs and decent
prospects in all businesses, especially Transportation with the passage of a

new federal highway bill. Revenues are expected to rise in the 10 percent range annually. A new manufacturing expansion, cost reduction measures, and more volume to absorb fixed costs is forecast to bring a 50 percent increase to net profits in FY2015 and a 33 percent increase in FY2016 built on improved operating and net margins and higher throughput. The dividend, already generous for a company of this size, may be in for ongoing 20 percent raises if these earnings numbers materialize; the company has strong cash flows and manages them closely.

Reasons to Buy

Since beaches and surf weren't part of the landscape, like any normal kids growing up in the Midwest we were fascinated with signs of all kinds. Daktronics takes signs to a new level.

We continue to feel that such digital signage is a big part of the future of mass, real-time marketing communications—a "system" including your mobile device plus electronic signage—like it or not. Another positive is the increased adoption and penetration in international markets.

Overall, we like situations where a core technology is applied successfully to an ever-larger number of end markets. Too, we think as such digital signage becomes more mainstream, the company will be able to produce in larger volumes, even mass-produce more of their applications, which should drive down unit costs and increase profitability.

We see advantages in the location, too—a dedicated work force and low cost of doing business. Finally, the company has virtually no debt.

Reasons for Caution

We quote again from the Annual Letter to Shareholders, this time for 2014 and modified only slightly: "Our strategic focus is to be the global dynamic display industry leader in providing value to our customers through understanding their needs and expectations; we leverage our experience and technical knowledge through product innovation to create robust and configurable product platforms that meet or exceed customer expectations in performance, ease of use, quality, and reliability."

While we applaud the concepts, we continue to find it surprisingly reflective of the drippy "say what they all say" business cliché stuff found in much larger, more bureaucratic organizations. We still wonder whether the executives who signed the letter really wrote it—or think this way. We doubt both.

Setting this quip aside, we do see product and price competition in the form of major Japanese firms like Mitsubishi (and if you've been to Tokyo, you know how mainstream digital signage can be). We do also wonder if environmental movements will rise up to quell what could easily become overstimulating visual "pollution," but so far to our knowledge this hasn't happened on a large scale.

More conventionally, Daktronics clearly has a riskier profile than most of our picks. Order flow and timing can vary considerably—as can delivery as we saw in 2014—especially in the sports segment, but we still think the business will smooth out considerably once electronic commercial signage becomes more mainstream.

SECTOR: **Technology** ❑ BETA COEFFICIENT: **1.08** ❑ 10-YEAR COMPOUND EARNINGS PER-SHARE GROWTH: **3.5%** ❑ 10-YEAR COMPOUND DIVIDENDS PER-SHARE GROWTH: **21.0%**

	2007	2008	2009	2010	2011	2012	2013	2014
Revenues (mil)	500	582	393	442	489	518	552	600
Net income (mil)	26.2	26.4	(7.0)	14.2	8.5	22.8	22.2	20.0
Earnings per share	0.63	0.64	(0.17)	0.34	0.20	0.53	0.51	0.50
Dividends per share	0.07	0.09	0.10	0.10	0.22	0.23	0.39	0.40
Cash flow per share	1.17	1.25	0.37	0.81	0.62	0.91	0.85	0.80
Price: high	39.5	23.1	10.5	17.3	16.7	11.9	16.1	15.6
low	19.8	5.7	5.9	7.1	8.0	6.3	9.4	10.8

Website: *www.daktronics.com*

Deere & Company

Ticker symbol: DE (NYSE) ❑ S&P rating: A ❑ Value Line financial strength rating: A++ ❑ Current yield: 2.6% ❑ Dividend raises, past 10 years: 10

Company Profile

Founded in 1837, Deere & Company grew from a one-man blacksmith shop into a worldwide corporation that today does business in more than 160 countries and employs more than 59,000 people around the globe. Deere has a diverse base of operations reporting into three segments: Agriculture and Turf, Construction and Forestry, and Financial Services.

Deere has been the world's premier producer of agricultural equipment for nearly 50 years. The Agriculture and Turf segment produces and distributes tractors, loaders, combines, harvesters, seeding, mowers, hay baling, tilling, crop care and application, and other equipment. If it's used on a farm and requires an engine, Deere likely offers it.

Additionally, over the years, the company has developed and expanded lines of turf and utility equipment, including riding lawn equipment and walk-behind mowers, golf course equipment, utility vehicles, and commercial mowing and snow-removal equipment. Deere also offers a broad line of associated implements, integrated agricultural management systems technology and solutions, precision agricultural irrigation equipment and supplies, landscape and nursery products, and other outdoor power products.

With the Construction and Forestry segment, Deere is also the world's leading manufacturer of forestry equipment and a major manufacturer of heavy construction machines (Caterpillar is still the market leader in this segment). Major lines include construction, earthmoving, material-handling, and timber-harvesting machines including but not limited to backhoe loaders; crawler dozers and loaders; four-wheel-drive loaders; excavators; motor graders; articulated dump trucks; landscape loaders; skid-steer loaders; and log skidders, feller bunchers, log loaders, log forwarders, log harvesters, and related attachments.

As the company reports it, revenue for the Agriculture and Turf segment is about 82 percent of the $33 billion in FY2014 revenue; the Construction and Forestry segment makes up the remainder. The Financial Services segment rolls its revenue into the other segments, and only segment profits are reported, but that segment produces about 20 percent of total net profit.

The Financial Services segment includes John Deere Credit, which is one of the largest equipment finance companies in the United States, with more than 1.8 million accounts, a managed asset portfolio of nearly $40 billion, and a contribution of $630 million in profits. It provides retail, wholesale, and lease financing for agricultural, construction, and forestry equipment; commercial and consumer equipment, including lawn and ground care; and revolving credit for agricultural inputs and services. These services are available in all of Deere's largest markets, including Argentina, Australia, Brazil, Canada, France, and Germany. Overall, international sales continue to account for about 40 percent of the total.

Financial Highlights, Fiscal Year 2014

Farm activity in the drought-recovery year of 2013 made 2014 comparisons difficult; beyond that, strong crop yields in 2014 and into 2015 have dampened U.S. spot farm prices considerably, as much as 20–30 percent for key commodities such as corn, soybeans, and wheat. That means that while more of these crops are being grown, and more machines are being used more of the time to grow them (thus wearing them out faster), revenues in the farm sector are on the decline—so fewer farmers are purchasing new ones.

Adding in the effects of a stronger dollar to boot, FY2014 sales actually decreased 5.8 percent from FY2013. Sales were particularly soft for larger, more profitable machines, so net income dropped a bit over 10 percent, while, aided by buybacks, per-share earnings dropped by a more modest 5 percent.

These trends are expected to continue through 2015, with management now guiding a 15 percent decline in global machinery sales through the year, even with brighter prospects in the Construction and Forestry segment. Agriculture and Turf may experience declines as much as 25 percent. Total sales may drop as much as 14 percent, with per-share earnings down as much as 30 percent. Conservatively, the company forecasts results to level out in FY2016. While it's a sharp decline from 2012–13 results, aggressive buybacks are still keeping per-share results at a higher level than any year before 2011.

Reasons to Buy

Why do we hang on to Deere? For FY2016, Deere has, honestly, been a tough call. As the saying goes, "Everything is a cycle"—and we're placing our bets that this, too, shall pass and the aforementioned heavy use of Deere machinery, coupled with the inevitable long-term growth in agriculture, will put the company back on top of its game in just a few short years. Who can argue about the long-term growth in agriculture, as the global population is predicted to increase 50 percent by 2050 and as global standards of living increase on top of that? Indeed, the company reminds us that global grain demand has already increased 40 percent just from 2000 through 2014. Most of all, Warren Buffett is well known for embracing such facts and figures, and good management teams and strong cash returns as well—indeed, his Berkshire Hathaway has acquired a 5 percent stake in the company. There you have it: our reasons for keeping Deere on our list despite the stumble.

We're also big fans of the brand and historic excellence. "Nothing runs like a Deere" is the company's apt slogan, and as far as industrial companies go, Deere continues to be a poster child for U.S. industrial ingenuity and excellence. It has an outstanding brand (and one of the most popular logos for hats, jackets, and so on, worn by people who have barely seen a farm field!) and reputation in the agriculture industry, and we see the ag industry as strong and strategic far into the future as global living standards improve and emerging markets develop.

Longer term, farm incomes continue to rise worldwide. The company is making good progress in developing markets, particularly in Brazil and India. Too, we think that innovation is a plus—Deere leads its competitors in R&D investment (more than 4 percent of sales), bringing the Internet and GPS to farming and farming machines; new engines also promise greater fuel economy and reduced emissions (although increased costs and prices required for emission controls are a short-term drag).

Beyond its products, Deere has established an almost unassailable brand leadership with its services and customer-centered innovations. Deere, more than others, puts its people in the field (literally) to figure out what agriculture professionals really need, and they work with their customers closely to sell their products through a solid dealer network.

Finally, the company continues to show commitment to shareholders by returning some 50 percent of cash generated over the past ten years to shareholders in the form of dividends and share buybacks.

Reasons for Caution

Clearly, the company is taking a pause from its growth, dividend growth, and share buybacks over this difficult period. The company is, and always will be, vulnerable to cycles in the farm sector. The normal cycle, and in particular indelible memories of 1980s farm difficulties, can cause the farmers who buy this stuff to get cautious pretty quickly. All in all, farming will always be with us, both in the U.S. and overseas, and there will always be a demand for machines and especially smarter, more efficient ones—Deere has an enormous brand and long-term track record.

SECTOR: **Industrials** ❑ BETA COEFFICIENT: **1.21** ❑ 10-YEAR COMPOUND EARNINGS PER-SHARE GROWTH: **18.5%** ❑ 10-YEAR COMPOUND DIVIDENDS PER-SHARE GROWTH: **15.5%**

	2007	2008	2009	2010	2011	2012	2013	2014
Revenues (mil)	21,489	25,804	20,756	23,573	29,466	33,501	34,998	32,961
Net income (mil)	1,822	2,053	1,198	1,865	2,799	3,065	3,533	3,162
Earnings per share	4.01	4.70	2.82	4.35	6.63	7.64	9.08	8.53
Dividends per share	0.91	1.06	1.12	1.16	1.52	1.79	1.99	2.22
Cash flow per share	5.12	6.01	4.05	5.72	8.34	9.56	11.45	11.45
Price: high	93.7	94.9	56.9	84.9	99.8	89.7	95.6	94.9
low	45.1	28.5	24.5	46.3	59.9	69.5	79.5	76.9

Website: *www.deere.com*

GROWTH AND INCOME

E. I. du Pont de Nemours and Company (DuPont)

Ticker symbol: DD (NYSE) ❑ S&P rating: A ❑ Value Line financial strength rating: A++ ❑ Current yield: 2.6% ❑ Dividend raises, past 10 years: 7

Company Profile

The natives are restless. Or in this case, certain activist shareholders are the ones who are restless. As the high-performance material maker DuPont has experienced—and as many other "tired," old-line companies probably should experience—having a few "natives" running for Board seats can shake you up in the right direction, or at least induce you to take a closer look to assure yourself and your investors that you really don't need to change very much. The outcome of the recent self-examination brought on by Trian Fund Management LP for DuPont has been sort of a mix of the two—a "hard look" resulting in some shedding of low-margin, commodity businesses, which already had been underway, a bit of restructuring and restructured thinking about the business, and a reaffirmation that most of what you're doing is right. Indeed, the vote did occur in May of 2015, and the current directorship remained intact, but derived from the vote a mandate to clean things up and to transform the company to better serve and benefit from today's marketplace.

"The miracles of science" is the slogan and rallying cry of this $34 billion-plus science and technology juggernaut originally founded in 1802 to make gunpowder. Although the company is known to many as a cyclical diversified chemical company making a host of lifeless chemical products and ingredients, many by the tank car–load, today's DuPont, with some outside prodding, continues to reawaken as a world leader in science and technology with important end-product ingredients in a range of disciplines, including biotechnology, electronics, materials and science, safety and security, and synthetic fibers. The company has always been a technology leader with such well-known inventions as Nylon and Rayon in earlier years, and Teflon and Kevlar more recently, but at least until lately has been taken in more as a commodity producer than an innovator. We see signs of change in that reputation, toward its own "market-driven science" business vision.

The company began a more deliberate evolution away from more commoditized chemicals and toward more higher-growth, less cyclical technology-based products with the 2012 divestiture of the Performance Coatings Division. In 2013, the company continued the trend by announcing the separation of the Performance Chemicals segment in a $4 billion shareholder spinoff, a transaction just completed in early 2015 into an LLC going by the name of Chemours (our numbers continue to include Chemours). Among other mostly commodity businesses, Chemours took refrigerants and a few other key "legacy" products with it.

Today's DuPont looks at itself as a leader in three fields: Agriculture & Nutrition, Industrial Biosciences, and Advanced Materials. These segments account for 52 percent, 5 percent, and 43 percent of the remaining (after Chemours) business:

- Within the Agriculture & Nutrition segment is the Agriculture business unit itself, accounting for about $11 billion, or about 40 percent of the company's total revenue. Agriculture delivers a portfolio of products and services specifically targeted to achieve gains in crop yields and productivity, including Pioneer brand seed products and well-established brands of insecticides, fungicides, and herbicides. Pioneer develops, produces, and markets corn hybrid and soybean varieties and sells wheat, rice, sunflower, canola, and other seeds under the Pioneer and other brand names. DuPont also sells a line of crop protection products for field and orchard agriculture. The smaller Nutrition and Health unit consists of the recently acquired Danisco's specialty food ingredients business and Solae, a majority-owned venture with Bunge Limited, which is engaged in developing soy-based technologies. The unit provides solutions for specialty food ingredients, health, and safety. Products include cultures, emulsifiers, gums, natural sweeteners, and soy-based food.

- The Industrial Biosciences unit is engaged in developing and manufacturing a wide range of enzymes, the biocatalysts that enable chemical reactions, on a large scale. The segment's enzymes add value and functionality to a broad range of products and processes, such as animal nutrition, detergents, food manufacturing, ethanol production, and industrial applications.

- The Advanced Materials segment is made up of Electronics and Communications, which makes a line of high-tech materials for the semiconductor industry, including ceramic packages and LCD materials. E&C supplies differentiated materials and systems for photovoltaics (solar), consumer electronics, displays, and advanced printing. It also includes the Performance Materials business unit, which supplies high-performance polymers, films, plastics, and substrates to a variety of industries from automotive to aerospace and consumer durable goods manufacturers and many others, and the Safety and Protection unit, maker of protective fibers and clothing, including bulletproof apparel, disinfectants, and protective building surfaces—Tyvek house wrap is one of the bigger brands here.

In 2014, Trian Partners, which is controlled by activist investor Nelson Peltz, approached the company through a detailed memorandum asking for four Board seats, to cut bureaucracy and to break the company into two units, one focused on agriculture and one focused on materials and chemicals. The company, led by CEO Ellen Kullman, vigorously opposed the proposal but agreed to a number of changes, including new focus on higher-margin businesses. Peltz has engaged similarly with other big, old-line companies like PepsiCo, and has mostly succeeded in shaking—rather than breaking—things up, mostly for the better as it turns out. We believe DuPont will take a similar course forward, possibly with some sizeable divestitures, in the aftermath of the shareholder mandate to maintain the existing board.

Financial Highlights, Fiscal Year 2014

The Chemours business accounted for about $6.5 billion, or about 19 percent of the revenues reported, and about 17 percent of pre-tax profits. The figures presented and described here for FY2014 still include Chemours.

We'll review the company's financial performance in view of what has been; what will be still isn't completely clear. FY2014 revenues, already diminished somewhat by the earlier disposal of the Performance Coatings segment, and heavily influenced by currency effects, came in with a largely expected 3 percent sales decline. Some of the net margin improvement from the disposal of that business, plus cost savings initiatives, drove a near 2 percent increase in operating margins—big for a company with 15 percent margins to begin with. This led to a decent 2 percent increase in net earnings, while a moderate buyback led to a 3.4 percent increase in per-share earnings. Figures through FY2016 are a bit difficult to pin down, but the company is looking for revenues in the $36 billion range, which would be a modest 4 percent ahead of today's levels, but a net profit figure 10–12 percent higher than today's figures. Less may be more, and may be more *profits*—just as Mr. Peltz has in mind. We'll soon see.

Reasons to Buy

Even without Mr. Peltz's "help," DuPont had already begun transforming itself (and remarketing itself) as an innovation leader and to capitalize equally on innovation and product leadership in established categories. We think the company is on the right track without a breakup.

The product pipeline continues to be full, individual product margins remain strong, the product mix is improving, and the company's biggest moneymakers still dominate their markets. Slowly but surely, the company is exiting low-margin, cyclical commodity businesses, reducing bureaucracy, and building its brand . . . even without the outside influence.

The company continues to capitalize on "global megatrends"— population growth, alternative energy production, and so forth. The improvement of worldwide food production is at the center of its new growth initiatives. The company has brand leadership in many important categories and is committed to total shareholder returns with a solid dividend track record and an aggressive share buyback program.

Reasons for Caution

The company still needs to overcome the stigma—and some of the behaviors—of a commodity producer. This is part of what the recent proxy fight was about. What is to come may continue to be disruptive, although it appears that management "gets it," and we think the company has weathered this storm pretty well. Too, some of the "new age" businesses like photovoltaic products have been slow to take hold, though that is starting to change. Finally, DuPont's fortunes are tied to hydrocarbon feedstocks and commodity prices in general; while the current picture is favorable particularly with plentiful and cheaper natural gas, this scenario can change quickly.

SECTOR: **Materials** ❑ BETA COEFFICIENT: **1.42** ❑ 10-YEAR COMPOUND EARNINGS PER-SHARE GROWTH: **6.5%** ❑ 10-YEAR COMPOUND DIVIDENDS PER-SHARE GROWTH: **2.5%**

		2007	2008	2009	2010	2011	2012	2013	2014
Revenues (mil)		29,378	30,529	26,109	31,505	37,961	34,812	35,734	34,723
Net income (mil)		3,034	2,477	1,853	3,032	3,698	3,137	3,632	3,703
Earnings per share		3.28	2.73	2.04	3.28	3.93	3.33	3.68	4.01
Dividends per share		1.52	1.64	1.64	1.64	1.64	1.70	1.78	1.84
Cash flow per share		4.89	4.33	3.70	4.80	5.67	5.19	5.65	5.87
Price:	high	53.9	52.5	35.6	50.2	57.0	53.8	65.0	75.8
	low	42.3	21.3	16.0	31.9	37.1	41.9	45.1	59.3

Website: *www.dupont.com*

CONSERVATIVE GROWTH

Eastman Chemical Company

Ticker symbol: EMN (NYSE) ❑ S&P rating: BBB ❑ Value Line financial strength rating: A ❑ Current yield: 2.0% ❑ Dividend raises, past 10 years: 5

Company Profile

Spun off in 1993 from the bankrupted Eastman Kodak, Eastman Chemical is one of those "better living through chemistry" companies with a history of solving problems and providing standard, high-tech, and high-precision materials to industries ranging from food and beverage to toys to medical equipment to computers and electronics. The Eastman mission could be almost be refined into "better living through polymer chemistry"—the chemical building blocks, mostly sourced from petroleum and other feedstocks known as hydrocarbons that turn into all things useful such as plastics, paints, coatings, inks, and the like. Many of their products are "intermediaries," used to manufacture other chemicals and products. When speaking the language of the company you quickly pick up expressions like "olefin cycle" and "phthalate," among the more difficult concepts and spelling challenges, like "ophthalmology," we've encountered in the *100 Best Stocks* space.

The company is organized into five product segments, all of which have something more or less to do with petrochemicals:

- *Advanced Materials* (25 percent of 2014 sales) produces and markets specialty plastics, interlayers, and films, including copolyesters, cellulose esters, and safety glass, plastic, and window film products into the automotive and transportation industries, building materials, LCD and display manufacturing, health and wellness, and durable goods industries.
- *Additives & Functional Products* (19 percent) produces chemical products for the coatings industry and for tires, paints, inks, building materials, durable goods, and consumables markets. Key technology platforms include rubber additives, cellulosic polymers, ketones, coalescents, polyester polymers, olefins, and hydrocarbon resins.
- *Fibers* (15 percent) produces acetate tow, triacetin, and solution-dyed acetate yarns for the apparel, filtration, tobacco (filters), fabric, home furnishings, medical tape, and other industries.
- *Additives & Plasticizers* (14 percent) produces intermediary products, mainly adhesive resins and plasticizers, sold into the consumables, building materials, health and wellness, industrial chemicals, and durable goods markets.
- *Specialty Fluids and Intermediates* (27 percent) is a catchall for other products that don't fall into the other segments, including new or custom-made polymer-based products for key customers. Acetic acid, ethylene, paint and building materials intermediaries, agrichemicals, and aviation hydraulic fluid are among the many products in this group.

Obviously there could be considerably more detail in these descriptions, but it would probably only be meaningful to those with a strong chemistry or materials background. Bottom line: Eastman makes a lot of strategically important materials that support a lot of manufacturing processes for common and fairly high-volume items, such as beer bottles, automotive glass, and LCD displays. Additionally, these materials are used in considerable amounts in overseas manufacturing. Eastman has adapted by setting up plants in 13 countries and driving foreign sales to 57 percent of the total. By region, sales are 46 percent from North America, 27 percent Asia-Pacific, 22 percent EMEA, and 5 percent Latin America.

In 2014, the company remained active in the acquisition market, buying BP plc's aviation turbine oil unit and Belgian water treatment, agriculture, and animal feed products producer Taminco, and solar window film maker Commonwealth Laminating & Coating on top of the larger acquisition of performance materials maker Solutia in 2012. Most of these acquisitions broaden existing product lines or add to market share, but the Taminco acquisition represents a bigger move into agrichemicals and food intermediaries ("people and molecules" was their pre-acquisition slogan) and into international markets.

Financial Highlights, Fiscal Year 2014

Increased global manufacturing activity, and particular strength in the automotive, construction, energy and energy efficiency, and emerging economies, continue to contribute to gradually rising sales results, although with currency headwinds. FY2014 revenues rose about 2 percent after a 15 percent rise in FY2013, although without that acquisition FY2013 revenues would have risen far more modestly. A pension adjustment and acquisition-related adjustments led to a reported 25 percent drop in earnings; pure operating earnings without these adjustments rose about 1.5 percent. The payoff from these acquisitions (and from lower hydrocarbon feedstock costs) will start in FY2015, with a 8–9 percent rise in revenues and a 20–25 percent recovery in net earnings, leading to a 5–8 percent gain in FY2016 revenues and another 20–25 percent gain in earnings. Share counts are flat for the moment as the company absorbs acquisitions and pays down the debt, but dividend increases in the low double digits look likely over the next few years.

Reasons to Buy

Although we often shy away from companies that are aggressive in the acquisition market, we do believe Eastman, as a prominent player in the intermediary niche, knows what it is doing and has used the acquisition tool to broaden its footprint into adjacent markets, sell more higher-margined products, and improve market share and profitability in its existing markets. These acquisitions look "strategic"—not just plays to expand size for the sake of size itself.

Although Eastman lies on the edge of the "buy businesses you understand" test, it's obvious from the numbers and especially the improving margins that the company really does produce things vitally important to manufacturing mainstream and advanced products. Successful product development has always been a key strength for Eastman, but the company has grown margins very steadily over the past few years through careful investments in business restructuring, cost-cutting measures, and additions to its output capacity. Eastman will benefit from the continued strength in domestic manufacturing, although its international operations, particularly in Asia, are also a source of strength. Eastman continues to position itself for continued moderate organic growth with excellent cash flow. The recent acquisition activity and reported earnings drop did hurt the share price and produced one of our poorer performers for the past year (-19.7 percent on a total return basis). It presented a buying opportunity, in our opinion, for 2016 and beyond.

Reasons for Caution

Eastman's fortunes will follow those of the larger manufacturing sector in general and, to a lesser extent, the feedstock (petroleum) market more specifically. Too, their fourth-largest end market by sales volume is tobacco (filter materials) at 15 percent of sales—although it is getting replaced by other product categories, it will be a drag on growth. There is also some concern about the health effects of phthalates, one of their key plasticizer products, although they do sell a line of non-phthalate plasticizers.

Eastman did take on a lot of debt with the Solutia and other acquisitions, but is deploying cash actively to pay down this debt; that said, the debt payments, projected in the billions over the next few years, has taken share repurchases off the table for the time being. We are a bit more concerned with the debt level (at 68 percent of total capital recently) than we were, but projections call for that to be reduced to 46 percent, closer to its long-term norm. The acquisitions nearly doubled the size of the company in five years—such a big bite does produce some management risks in our opinion. That said, Eastman has all the earmarks of a well-managed company.

SECTOR: Materials ◻ **BETA COEFFICIENT: 1.74** ◻ **10-YEAR COMPOUND EARNINGS PER-SHARE GROWTH: 22.0%** ◻ **10-YEAR COMPOUND DIVIDENDS PER-SHARE GROWTH: 3.5%**

		2007	2008	2009	2010	2011	2012	2013	2014
Revenues (mil)		6,830	6,720	5,047	5,842	7,178	8,102	9,350	9,527
Net income (mil)		423	342	265	514	653	802	1,008	751
Earnings per share		2.53	2.25	1.82	3.48	4.56	5.38	6.45	4.95
Dividends per share		0.88	0.88	0.88	0.90	0.99	1.08	1.25	1.40
Cash flow per share		4.71	4.20	3.72	5.62	6.76	7.55	9.45	8.08
Price:	high	39.2	39.1	31.0	42.3	55.4	68.2	83.0	90.6
	low	28.8	12.9	8.9	25.9	32.4	39.2	63.5	70.4

Website: *www.eastman.com*

Empire State Realty Trust

Ticker symbol: ESRT (NYSE) ◻ S&P rating: NR ◻ Value Line financial strength rating: NR Current yield: 1.9% ◻ Dividend raises, past 10 years: 1

Company Profile

Wanna get in on the ground floor? Or close to it, anyway? A ground floor investment in perhaps the most famous office building in the world?

The Empire State Building is a national treasure. Beautifully designed, it is an emblem of New York business known to the world. It is such an emblem that more than 4 million people came to visit it last year, just to go up to the observation deck, almost 60 percent of them from overseas. That observation deck is a $111 million annual icing on the cake for what we think is an exciting new REIT built around the Empire State Building. But is this REIT just the Empire State Building? No—it has diversified to hold 14 office buildings in key locations across the New York area, nine in Manhattan and five others in or near major transportation hubs in White Plains, NY, and Stamford and Norwalk, CT. ESRT also owns six standalone retail properties, four in Manhattan and two in Connecticut. The Empire State Realty Trust is a pure play on real estate in the most dynamic and sought-after real estate market in the world—and it operates a lucrative observation deck business on top of it all (sorry!).

The Empire State Realty Trust was formed in 2011 and went public in October 2013. As a REIT, ESRT is relatively small in comparison to other real estate trusts, but they make up for that in their strengths, which they call out quite clearly in their presentations:

- *Unique, irreplaceable properties.* ESRT is a pure play in the New York area, one of the world's most prized office markets; the cornerstone of their base, the Empire State Building, is one of the most recognized icons in the world. Another concentration of office properties is in the revitalizing 34th Street and Broadway area, home of the Macy's flagship store.
- *Expertise in reconditioning such properties.* The Empire State Building is beautiful, particularly for you fans of classic Art Deco architecture. But it needed a facelift—and got a big one from ESRT. In addition to managing properties, ESRT has a construction arm specializing in reconditioning and repurposing buildings and spaces for tenant use. The Empire State Building got a major energy retrofit in a partnership

with fellow *100 Best* stock Johnson Controls and others; it is a showcase project and is estimated to save some tenants 38 percent and as much as 58 percent on energy costs; it got a new fitness center for tenants also. ESRT will lease you "white box" space—or spaces tailored to your needs. ESRT is performing energy and functionality upgrades to other vintage buildings as well. It is part of their strategy to increase attractiveness . . . and of course, rents.

In area, ESRT owns and manages about 10 million square feet; 74 percent of that is Manhattan office space, 19 percent is Greater New York space, and 7.3 percent is dedicated retail, mostly in Manhattan. The Empire State Building itself is about 2.7 million square feet, or about 27 percent of the rentable space in the trust. The client list is a corporate who's who, with older companies mixed in with latter-day names like LinkedIn. The client base is diverse, with just 18 percent being the "typical" New York financial industry names. About 88 percent of current office space is occupied; 93 percent of retail. Most clients sign long-term leases of ten years or so, and the company is trying to move to large block or entire floor leases.

For 2014, the roughly $590 million in annual revenue breaks down as follows: 58 percent Manhattan office, 12 percent Greater New York Metro office, and 11 percent retail. What about the other 19 percent, you may ask? Look up, please. It's from the Observatory, split between the 86th and 102nd floor of the Empire State Building. We mentioned it at the beginning of this narrative—the Observatory, which had 4.3 million visitors in 2014, brought in $111 million in FY2014, a huge "kicker" to the business most REITs don't have.

Financially, ESRT touts what they refer to as "embedded, derisked growth." The "embedded" part refers to loyal tenants and a carefully managed "laddering" of lease expirations; the company attempts to have 5–10 percent of its lease base expire each year. Those expirations will be renewed at higher rates, not just inflation but also to cover improvements. ESRT estimates that rents will grow overall 20–27 percent per year through 2019 as leases expire. "Derisked" refers to this smooth, steady upward path but also to the location and desirability of the properties they own. They also present "best in class" financial fundamentals, with leasing spreads (roughly comparable to gross margin—lease less mortgage obligations—of 23.4 percent versus 13.8 percent for their peer group, and a "debt to enterprise value" ratio of 25 percent versus 32 percent for peers. Only about 59 percent of the portfolio is encumbered by mortgages at all. Less debt, less leverage, greater profitability.

As investments REITs are typically good income producers, since they are required by law to pay a substantial portion of their cash flow to investors. The accounting rules are different, and REIT investors should focus on Funds From Operations (FFO), which is analogous to operating income; net income figures have depreciation expenses deducted, which can vary in timing and not always be realistic. Funds From Operations (FFO) support the dividends paid to investors.

Financial Highlights, Fiscal Year 2014

As ESRT only went public in the fall of 2013, we do not have a well-developed financial presentation for the company or its financial history. FY2014 results include the execution of 239 new leases with a 20.2 percent increase in rents for those leases; of that total, 181 of those were Manhattan office leases with an average rent increase of 23.4 percent (again, some of that rent increase is "organic," some reflects building improvements). Occupancy rates improved approximately 3.1 percent through the year. Observatory revenue grew 9.5 percent over FY2013, and "signed leases not commenced, or 'SNLC'," a leading indicator of lease revenue and analogous to "backlog," was at $32.5 million at the end of that quarter.

The REIT estimates that it has completed about 85–90 percent of a $700 million spending plan to redevelop and restore its buildings (the largest, of course, being the Empire State Building). The completion of that spend should enhance net income going forward—and in turn, shareholder payouts, since REITs are legally required to pay out 90 percent of reported income.

As yet, we have not been able to obtain projections into FY2015 and FY2016.

Reasons to Buy

ESRT exhibits most of the traits we like to see when we consider buying a real estate investment trust. It has good real estate, yes, but it isn't just the real estate—it's a good business, too. It adds value in the form of redevelopment services, and the observation deck is a nice bonus. We don't depend solely on the rising value of the underlying real estate, and we don't depend too much on increasing the rent. That said, the prime locations they own, and the exclusive focus on the New York area make us pretty sure that the value and rental income from the underlying real estate will do nothing but rise.

And who wouldn't want to own a piece of the Empire State Building? The energy and whole-building retrofit of the Empire State Building has won considerable acclaim with green building advocates and others; a search on "empire state building energy retrofit" gives several angles to this story. The building was once felt to be in an irreversible decline; the retrofit, energy, and publicity around it have returned it to its classic status as a prestige address. ESRT is using it wisely as a brand centerpiece for events, social media, and general marketing.

We think that, as retrofits are completed across the portfolio, ESRT will become a much stronger cash machine, and with REIT rules, that cash will end up in the pockets of shareholders in the not too distant future.

Reasons for Caution

ESRT is new and far less proven than most of our choices, although it has a seasoned management team from its roots as a private equity trust. We can't give you as much historical analysis as we would with most *100 Best* stocks investments. But we thought you might like to get in on the ground floor of what we think will be a strong investment for years to come.

SECTOR: **Real Estate** ❑ BETA COEFFICIENT: **0.60** ❑ 10-YEAR COMPOUND FFO PER-SHARE GROWTH: **NM** ❑ 10-YEAR COMPOUND DIVIDENDS PER-SHARE GROWTH: **NM**

	2007	2008	2009	2010	2011	2012	2013	2014
Revenues (mil)	—	—	—	—	—	—	—	593.2
Net income (mil)	—	—	—	—	—	—	—	26.7
Funds from operations per share	—	—	—	—	—	—	—	0.84
Real estate owned per share	—	—	—	—	—	—	—	8.40
Dividends per share	—	—	—	—	—	—	—	0.34
Price: high	—	—	—	—	—	—	15.6	18.1
low	—	—	—	—	—	—	12.6	14.1

Website: *www.empirestaterealtytrust.com*

Fair Isaac Corporation

Ticker symbol: FICO (NYSE) ❑ S&P rating: NR ❑ Value Line financial strength rating: B++ ❑ Current yield: 0.1% ❑ Dividend raises, past 10 years: 1

Company Profile

"Making Every Decision Count" is the motto of the Fair Isaac Corporation, which provides decision support analytics, software, and solutions to help businesses improve and automate decision-making and risk management. The most well-known and best example of these solutions is the FICO score—an analytic single-figure estimate of a consumer's creditworthiness used in the credit industry and for other purposes such as employment and insurance.

FICO provides its analytic solutions and services to a variety of financial and other service organizations, including banks, credit-reporting agencies, credit card–processing agencies, insurers, telecommunications providers, retailers, marketers, and health-care organizations. It operates in three segments: Applications, Scores, and Tools. The Applications segment provides decision and risk management tools, market targeting and customer analytics tools, and fraud detection tools and associated professional services. (If you've had a credit card fraud alert recently, it probably came from FICO's "Falcon" suite of fraud prediction and protection services.) The Scores segment includes the business-to-business scoring solutions; myFICO solutions, delivering FICO scores for consumers; and associated professional services. The Tools segment provides software products and consulting services to help organizations build their own analytic tools. Many of these analytics and scores are packaged to be available through the "cloud" as "SaaS"—Software as a Service—applications, providing a steady revenue stream tied to their use.

The company actively works with customers in a variety of vertical markets to identify and apply their tools and applications; these analytics go beyond traditional financial applications into marketing and operational optimization. A recent application of the FICO Xpress Optimization Suite to a research arm of the Lawrence Livermore Laboratory to optimize power grids serves as one good example. The company also just announced a partnership with eBay Enterprise to supply marketing and loyalty analytics and analytic services for their e-commerce marketing platform. The company promotes its vertical applications in the grocery, retail, pharmaceutical and life sciences, insurance, financial services, and consumer packaged goods industries.

Financial Highlights, Fiscal Year 2014

FICO is well past the Great Recession crunch, which saw a sharp slackening of demand as financial services firms reduced spending and as credit and loan activity diminished altogether. The demand for traditional credit-scoring products has resumed, and with an increase of lending activity, has almost achieved previous levels, but total revenues still haven't reached the record $826.4 million achieved in 2006.

That said, revenues advanced a healthy 6 percent in FY2014. The largest segment, Applications (at 64 percent of the business) matched this growth rate. The Scores segment, which contributes 24 percent of the business, grew at a more moderate 3 percent rate, while the Tools business, accounting for 12 percent of the business, moved forward at a 14 percent rate. Earnings rose almost in line at 5 percent, but a substantial 8 percent share buyback drove per-share earnings up almost 10 percent.

Going forward into FY2016, strength in the Tools and Applications markets and especially fraud protection (the company recently acquired TONBELLER, a white-collar crime and fraud protection provider) should keep revenues rising in the 6–8 percent range annually, while an uptick in R&D expenses will attenuate bottom-line growth particularly in FY2015. Per-share earnings are projected in the $3.20–$3.30 range for FY2016, a 20 percent advance over today's levels. We should note that the company's apparently "stingy" dividend policy is offset by aggressive share buybacks; the company has reduced share counts some 50 percent since 2005 and has plans to reduce them another 15–20 percent over the next few years. Few companies on our *100 Best Stocks* list have such a deliberate and aggressive share count reduction policy.

Reasons to Buy

"Big data" and related analytics are hot right now as more vertical industries (banking, retail, utilities, pharma, medical devices, health insurers, etc.) learn how to use them more efficiently and effectively to manage different parts of their business. There are a number of companies, large and small, in the analytics business, but few have the brand reputation, product packaging, and leadership enjoyed by FICO. The company is a pure play and is considered to be the gold standard for this type of product. It is more turn-key and easy for customers who don't have advanced mathematicians and software engineering staffs to buy. As a consequence, and with the brand recognition of the FICO score, the company has attained a pretty large moat on its brand and is a good example of how packaging and market definition can be as important as the product.

We also think a stabilizing financial industry with new rules, fewer workers, and a greater recognition for risk and risk management will bode well for the FICO product suite. Financial and other decision-making FICO products offer a good combination of streamlining and sophistication. Long term, we can easily see their modeling approaches being further extended to analyze customer behavior and provide decision support for insurability, employability, acceptance into schools, and even customer behaviors in stores or online, other areas well beyond a consumer's ability to repay extended credit. International demand for FICO's products continues to grow, too, notably in China, where fraud protection is a big business.

The dividend remains inconsequential, but it doesn't take a genius (or analytics) to appreciate the company's policy of providing shareholder returns in the form of cash buybacks.

Reasons for Caution

Although it has perked up a bit lately, the bread-and-butter FICO scoring operation still faces competition. The company recently updated the scoring algorithm to include more factors and make it more plausible (and perhaps more forgiving). We're not sure how this will play out in the marketplace, but the initial results continue to show broad acceptance.

Software companies always run a certain amount of technology risk. The ability to sell in a "cloud" environment and to maintain or increase margins by selling the right mix of products and channels will be key. There is some public concern that scoring models oversimplify lending and insurability decisions and should not be used or relied on so heavily. And, as we've seen, the company is vulnerable to economic downturns.

In all, we feel the company will continue to succeed on the basis of its brand, reputation, and market leadership. But that leads us to our biggest concern at the moment: Investors have figured this out, and bid the stock up some 60 percent in our measurement year. That's a good thing for our *100 Best Stocks* list performance, but we wonder if it's too much given the midrange growth levels and even considering the aggressive buybacks. "Score" your purchases carefully.

SECTOR: **Business Services** ❑ BETA COEFFICIENT: **1.22** ❑ 10-YEAR COMPOUND EARNINGS PER-SHARE GROWTH: **7.0%** ❑ 10-YEAR COMPOUND DIVIDENDS PER-SHARE GROWTH: **0.0%**

		2007	2008	2009	2010	2011	2012	2013	2014
Revenues (mil)		822.2	744.8	630.7	605.6	619.7	676.4	743.4	789.0
Net income (mil)		104.7	81.2	65.1	64.5	71.6	92.0	90.1	94.9
Earnings per share		1.82	1.64	1.34	1.42	1.79	2.55	2.48	2.72
Dividends per share		0.08	0.08	0.08	0.08	0.08	0.08	0.08	0.08
Cash flow per share		3.03	2.49	2.15	2.36	2.58	3.20	3.54	3.98
Price:	high	41.8	32.2	24.5	27.0	38.5	47.9	63.5	74.4
	low	32.1	10.4	9.8	19.5	20.0	34.6	41.3	50.3

Website: *www.fico.com*

FedEx Corporation

Ticker symbol: FDX (NYSE) ❑ S&P rating: BBB ❑ Value Line financial strength rating: A+ ❑ Current yield: 0.5% ❑ Dividend raises, past 10 years: 10

Company Profile

FedEx Corporation is the world's leading provider of guaranteed express delivery services and a major player in the overall small shipment and small package logistics market. The corporation is organized as a holding company, with four individual businesses that compete collectively and operate independently under the FedEx brand, offering a wide range of express delivery services for the time-definite transportation of documents, packages, and freight. The familiar FedEx Express operation offers overnight and deferred air service to 57,000 drop-off locations, operating 650 aircraft and approximately 150,000 ground vehicles to support this business. The company also offers freight services for less time-sensitive items and small or less-than-truckload (LTL) shipments under the FedEx Ground and FedEx Freight brands. FedEx Ground offers overnight service from 500 pickup/delivery terminals for up to 400 miles anywhere in the United States for packages weighing up to 150 pounds, while FedEx Freight offers standard and priority LTL service across North America mainly for business supply-chain operations. Finally, the company has ventured into specialized logistics services with its comprehensive FedEx

Services, which also includes the former Kinko's copy and office centers, now operating under the FedEx/Office brand.

In addition to the 650 aircraft and 150,000 ground vehicles, the company operates an enormous logistics network of over 725 World Service Centers, over 1,750 FedEx Office locations, nearly 6,300 authorized Ship Centers, and more than 38,500 Drop Boxes. The company has about 300,000 "team members"—employees and contractors. They serve over 375 airports in over 220 countries. Except for the number of countries served, all of these figures are slightly attenuated from previous years as the company weeds out unproductive and redundant locations in a drive for efficiency.

In FY2014, the Express segment accounted for 60 percent of revenues, Ground 26 percent, Freight 13 percent, and Services 1 percent, representing another slight annual increase in the overall mix for the Ground and Freight services. The company estimates that over 98 percent of its customers use two or more of these services, attesting to the fact that FedEx's business is increasingly tuned to providing a total and flexible logistics solution.

In a logical effort to expand its footprint into all facets of logistics operations, the company recent acquired "reverse logistics"—returns—specialist GENCO. Clearly, as e-commerce grows, reverse logistics will become greater in strategic importance; GENCO processes some 600 million returns each year. The company is also focusing on expanding its footprint in high-growth markets like Mexico, India, and Eastern Europe.

Financial Highlights, Fiscal Year 2014

FedEx went through a brief soft spot in FY2013, but it has come out of that nicely as global business levels have increased, fuel costs have dropped, and customer companies continue to fine-tune their logistics networks to reduce cost and obsolescence risks. FedEx has achieved solid operating margin improvements, up to 15 percent from the 11–12 percent range through most of the 2000s, delivered by lower fuel costs, pricing and operational adjustments, and cost-cutting measures. Higher volumes and higher margins lead to higher profits, and FedEx has just affirmed its guidance of $8.50–$9.00 per share for FY2015 and a larger increase to as much as $11.00 in FY2016 on revenue growth in the 5 percent range annually. The pace of share buybacks and dividend increases appears to be accelerating as the company deploys its strong cash flows.

Reasons to Buy

FedEx has several tailwinds now—lower fuel costs, the customer-driven logistics fine-tuning just mentioned, and the growth of e-commerce. The company estimates that e-commerce shipments will double to the $1.3 trillion range in the five-year period 2012–2017.

A strong tailwind of e-commerce business and greater need for a complete, economical, and partially time-sensitive logistics mix is the right place to be as American manufacturing activity and local sourcing increase—although this will dampen international shipments, a trend we've already seen. We like the company's partnerships with the U.S. Postal Service. The "SmartPost" service uses the USPS for economical final "last mile" delivery to residences, an attractive route for smaller e-commerce shipments. The company is also a key "wholesale" provider for the USPS express and overnight small package delivery services. Such alliances, or "co-opetition," between archrivals tend to be productive "win-win" arrangements for both carriers and customers as well.

With SmartPost and other business expansions, the Ground segment is approaching a 30 percent market share for such services, a position from which it can start to call the shots in the marketplace for lucrative e-commerce and time-sensitive ground business. Indeed, of late, the company has been able to raise prices while also gaining market share. And for the first time in a few years, overnight shipment volumes have risen, a testimony to the "complete logistics solution" idea and an assurance that Ground isn't simply cannibalizing its air services.

The continued resurgence in the economy and growth in online shopping and delivery will certainly help volumes and pricing, and the continuing shift to e-commerce gives a boost to this recovery. The resumption of strong U.S. exports not only helps volume but also helps fill up planes traveling from the United States. The logistics business is always ripe for innovation, and FedEx has long been an innovator in the transportation and small-package shipment business, not only with new transportation services, but also with new tools to help customers track shipments and manage their supply chains in real time; we expect this to continue.

Reasons for Caution

The company is always vulnerable to economic downturns and fuel prices, particularly if cost increases come faster than they can be recovered in rates and fuel surcharges—as is often the case. While cash flows are strong, this company must occasionally purchase or lease aircraft, and this and other capital expenditures can put a big dent in cash flows. While the company has done a good job of carving out its "full service" niche, it is always vulnerable to competition in both domestic and overseas markets; that said, its size and scale are an advantage in most cases.

To a degree, favorable trends have already been priced into the stock, so investors should be patient as they look for an entry point. We like the fact that the company has raised the dividend every year since starting to pay dividends in 2002, and while payouts are increasing, they are still less than we think they could be.

SECTOR: **Transportation** ❑ BETA COEFFICIENT: **1.23** ❑ 10-YEAR COMPOUND EARNINGS PER-SHARE GROWTH: **7.5%** ❑ 10-YEAR COMPOUND DIVIDENDS PER-SHARE GROWTH: **13.0%**

	2007	2008	2009	2010	2011	2012	2013	2014
Revenues (mil)	35,214	37,953	35,497	34,734	39,204	42,680	44,287	45,567
Net income (mil)	2,073	1,821	1,173	1,184	1,452	2,032	1,561	2,097
Earnings per share	6.67	5.83	3.76	3.76	4.90	6.41	4.91	6.75
Dividends per share	0.37	0.40	0.44	0.44	0.48	0.52	0.56	0.60
Cash flow per share	12.39	12.13	10.09	10.01	11.13	13.08	12.41	16.32
Price: high	121.4	99.5	92.6	97.8	98.7	97.2	144.1	183.5
low	89.5	53.9	34.0	69.8	64.1	82.8	90.6	128.2

Website: *www.fedex.com*

CONSERVATIVE GROWTH

Fresh Del Monte Produce Inc.

Ticker symbol: FPD (NYSE) ❑ S&P rating: NR ❑ Value Line financial strength rating: B++ ❑ Current yield: 1.4% ❑ Dividend raises, past 10 years: 3

Company Profile

Fresh Del Monte Produce is the number one fresh pineapple marketer in the world. Now, we love our pineapple, and we're rather fond of the place where most of this pineapple comes from, the balmy fertile leeward slopes of Hawaii. We like bananas, too, and wouldn't resist forced leisure time in the places where *they* are grown, either. But that's not enough to get a stock on our *100 Best* list, is it? If that's all it took, the *100 Best* list would be littered with beer, pizza, chocolate, and golf club stocks from top to bottom. Don't worry, it isn't enough—and won't be anytime soon.

What brought us to Fresh Del Monte wasn't just the pineapple, or even the bananas. It is their emerging leadership in healthful and especially innovative and modern fresh packaged foods, items we think will play well with today's demographic, who demand fresh, convenient, natural, unique, and customizable foods and "fresh-cut" food packages.

Founded in 1892, Del Monte originated as a brand for coffee packaged for the prestigious Del Monte hotel in Monterey, California. The original firm expanded its business and selected Del Monte as the brand for a new line of canned peaches, and the rest, as they say, is history. The company has grown—in a large part based on acquisitions particularly of tropical fruits and food producers—into one of the largest vertically integrated producers and distributors of fresh and fresh-cut fruits and vegetables, as well as prepared fruits and vegetables, juices, beverages, and snacks, in the world.

The company has 90,000 acres in production, and its products are available in 100 countries. Products include bananas (the largest product line at 46 percent of sales), an all-important "other fresh produce" category (44 percent of sales), and prepared food (10 percent). The "other fresh produce" category deserves further breakout, and in some cases, description:

- Gold pineapples (15 percent)—the branding is "Del Monte Gold Extra Sweet®"
- Fresh-cut produce (10 percent)—this is the category we're most excited about, and is the fastest-growing segment. It offers fresh-cut fruits—pineapples, melons, grapes, citrus, apples, mangos, kiwis, and others—and vegetables for salads packed in convenient, safe, and branded

plastic containers; so far sold only in the U.S., Canada, U.K., Japan, and the Middle East.

- Nontropical fruit (10 percent)—the biggest contributor is avocados, but also includes grapes, apples, pears, peaches, plums, nectarines, cherries, citrus, and kiwis.
- Melons (3 percent)
- Tomatoes (3 percent)
- Vegetables (1 percent)
- Other fruit, products, and services (2 percent)

A big part of why we like Fresh Del Monte is that it's not just a producer but a logistics company specializing in fresh packaging and transport, really for all parts of the fresh-food supply chain from farm to store shelf, including sophisticated refrigerated storage and transport, all the way to helping end-store operators with market research, promotion, display, stocking decisions, and other logistical support. The company owns a fleet of 21 oceangoing refrigerated vessels and manages a network including 4,500 refrigerated containers, refrigerated port facilities, and 28 distribution and "fresh cut" centers. Too, the company has innovated in such areas as Controlled Ripening Technology for bananas, which it licenses to other producers.

As an example of what this brings, for its largest category, bananas, 49 percent of sales are in North America, 21 percent in Europe, 17 percent in Asia, and 11 percent are in the Middle East. In fact, overall sales outside the U.S. account for 46 percent of the business: 19 percent in Europe, 14 percent in the Middle East and Africa, 11 percent in Asia and 2 percent in Latin America. This supply-chain leadership gives the company a distinct advantage and a laboratory within which they can produce and distribute all sorts of new products and packages to a large part of the world, a big advantage over the world's many, many small producers. See a market for fresh fruit snacks in special packages in Japan? Fresh Del Monte can produce it and get it there.

Financial Highlights, Fiscal Year 2014

Historical revenues, profit margins, and profits have been somewhat volatile for Fresh Del Monte, but the increase in scale, diversity of offering, and diversity of market are starting to smooth things out. It is no longer just a banana and pineapple grower and distributor. FY2014 revenues grew about 6.5 percent; operating margins returned to the mid-6 percent range from the mid-5s, producing a 75 percent gain in net income (although most of it just a recovery to more prosperous pre-Recession years). The company bought back about 8 percent of its stock under an authorization issued in May 2013, some three-quarters of that in the final quarter of 2014. Going forward, forecasts call for revenue gains in the 2–3 percent range and net earnings gains in the 3–5 percent range; gradual share count reductions and dividend increases look to follow. We feel that these forecasts are conservative as the fresh-cut product lines gain traction in a widening set of markets.

Reasons to Buy

Many of the attractions of this company have already been mentioned: brand, logistics network, "fresh-cut" opportunities, increased scale, and operating efficiency. We like the vertical integration, which gives it control of its supply chain, and most of all, we like Fresh Del Monte's competitive advantage in distribution, and we see this playing well with what we expect to be a growing demand for smartly packaged fresh and fresh-cut food offerings, which are currently only 10 percent of the business. We think this could take off, and combined with packaged salads and such, become a major category in groceries and mass distributors of food products. People want convenience and variety, and these prepackaged items fit in—and when you take into account storage and spoilage, they actually become cheaper than their unpackaged equivalents. They can be mixed any way the markets want, as we've seen with prepackaged salads. Like pineapples, blueberries, and mangos together? Fresh Del Monte can produce and distribute just such a medley. You don't have to buy a pineapple, cut it up, buy a bag of blueberries; you get the idea.

All of that, plus a helping of financial strength (debt is only 13 percent of total capital) and a bias toward shareholder returns, makes this mid-cap offering a worthwhile recipe to play emerging trends in the food industry.

Reasons for Caution

Past results have been volatile, and the thin margins reflect a company that is more of a "commodity" producer than anything else. We think the "fresh-cut" offerings will grow Fresh Del Monte out of this category. As a logistics company, particularly one with a moderate amount of air cargo in its mix, it is vulnerable to fuel price shocks. There is also strong competition in most parts of this industry.

SECTOR: **Consumer Staples** ◻ BETA COEFFICIENT: **0.36** ◻ 10-YEAR COMPOUND EARNINGS PER-SHARE GROWTH: **3.5%** ◻ 10-YEAR COMPOUND DIVIDENDS PER-SHARE GROWTH: **NM**

	2007	2008	2009	2010	2011	2012	2013	2014
Revenues (mil)	3,365	3,531	3,496	3,552	3,590	3,421	3,684	3,928
Net income (mil)	189	158	144	62	93	143	87	154
Earnings per share	3.22	2.48	2.26	1.02	1.56	2.46	1.54	2.73
Dividends per share	—	—	—	0.05	0.30	0.40	0.50	0.50
Cash flow per share	3.99	3.82	3.58	2.40	2.87	3.69	2.79	4.29
Price: high	38.6	39.8	26.7	25.2	28.6	26.9	30.8	35.0
low	14.4	12.9	12.2	19.2	21.3	21.6	24.7	24.0

Website: *www.freshdelmonte.com*

GROWTH AND INCOME

General Electric Company

Ticker symbol: **GE** (NYSE) ◻ S&P rating: **AA+** ◻ Value Line financial strength rating: **B++** ◻ Current yield: **3.4%** ◻ Dividend raises, past 10 years: **8**

Company Profile

Every now and then, we place our bet on a fallen angel for our *100 Best Stocks* list, a once-excellent company fallen from grace due to bad strategy, bad management, bad luck, or a combination of the three. We place our bet thinking that maybe the company has learned its lesson; maybe it has come to see the light, while its core markets and financials are still strong; maybe it can make the right decisions and get it right this time.

We placed such a bet last year. We placed it on GE, which had been removed from the *100 Best* list in 2010 on account of a variety of ills, its ventures into non-core industries such as television, and the most egregious of all, its ventures into the world of high finance through GE Capital. When those ventures soured in 2008, they almost brought down the company. (One colleague of ours called the company a "hedge fund that also made jet engines.")

GE had started to divest itself of the financial assets—and we liked its other businesses in the present climate more favorable to U.S. heavy industry—when we added it back to the *100 Best* list last year. We didn't get much bang for the buck in 2014; little really changed, and the shares dropped 4.2 percent for the year. Oh well, it'll get better someday, right?

Then, just as we were mulling over "re-upping" GE for 2016, against a backdrop of energy price declines now hurting its recent Dresser Industries acquisition, European woes, currency softness, and the like, lightning struck. The company agreed to divest itself of the GE Capital finance unit, including selling its $26.5 billion real estate portfolio to Blackstone and Wells Fargo, in a sequential deal, which will total $90 billion when completed over the next two to three years.

Voilà! GE the way we wanted it in the first place.

With or without its finance unit, General Electric is colossal. Formed in 1892 as a major producer of all things electric in the wake of the commercial harnessing of electricity, the company evolved over the years into a massive conglomerate producing aircraft engines, power generation, railroad locomotives, household appliances, energy infrastructure, alternative energy equipment, medical imaging equipment, oilfield service equipment, and a vast array of other mostly industrial products—in addition to its soon-to-depart General Electric Capital Services, or "GE Capital" financial arm.

In its remaining total, the company has seven operating segments. By segment and projected percent of FY2015 revenues without GE Capital, they are: Power & Water (23 percent), Oil & Gas (16 percent), Energy Management (7 percent), Aviation (23 percent), Health Care (17 percent), Transportation (5 percent), and Appliances & Lighting (8 percent). GE Capital once produced 30 percent of revenue and a third of profits . . . and a lot of headaches and risks that both management and investors—for the most part—are glad to be rid of.

International sales account for about 53 percent of revenues, a number that is likely to rise with the return to the industrial base. The divestiture, and a refocus on its industrial businesses, will produce an enormous $50 billion share buyback in FY2015 as well as consolidations in other segments. The company, for example, had already announced a divestiture of the majority of its appliance business to Electrolux in 2014, which will further simplify the remaining business mix and change the segment balance previously described. Really, these changes amount to a shakeup of the company and a return to its value "roots"—changes we've felt long to be coming.

Financial Highlights, Fiscal Year 2014

The seas of change make comparisons and forward estimates difficult. The numbers presented below still include the GE Capital unit, so obviously this will change, although the unit was not too "outsized" in its profitability or growth, so percentage changes should track fairly closely. While earnings and revenues will decline sharply into FY2015 and beyond, per-share amounts should remain fairly comparable due mostly to the buybacks in store.

FY2014 revenues advanced a modest 1.7 percent, hemmed in by currency effects, while earnings, hemmed in somewhat by softness in the oil and gas business (which is expected to decline 8 percent in FY2015), remained flat. There's almost no point in describing FY2015 and FY2016 specifics at this time; the company does project its strongest businesses going forward to be Transportation, Appliances & Lighting, Power & Water, and Energy Management, while laggards will include Oil & Gas and to a lesser degree Aviation and Health Care. The company projects that 75 percent of earnings will come from its industrial businesses by 2016 and 90 percent by 2018. Industrial organic revenue gains are estimated in the 5 percent range, while operational efficiencies and other effects from the divestiture should get earnings moving again, especially as the finance arm winds down. Steady and large buybacks and, likely, dividend increases, are clearly in the cards as this happens.

Reasons to Buy

At heart, the company is simplifying, returning to its roots as a colossal industrial infrastructure play. It is downsizing, rightsizing, and trimming businesses all over—not just its financial services arm. We like the fact now that the financial divestiture is happening fast. The value unlocked—not to mention the reduction of risk and the decreased consumption of management bandwidth—should be huge plusses in our view. We should note that the company will keep some of its financial business intact—the part that finances acquisition of GE products—a move that makes a lot of sense to us.

Beyond the finance divestiture, the company continues to tout its "look of a simpler company" goals to downsize HQ operations by 45 percent, reduce the new product introduction cycle time by 30 percent, create 30 percent fewer internal P&Ls, reduce the number of enterprise resource planning (ERP) systems by 80 percent—you get the idea.

All in all, we think the company is getting back to what it does best, and we also think the brand image will improve as well as it retrenches into its core businesses. There is considerable need to replace infrastructure, and GE is right at the heart of this trend. GE is a strong force in its markets, likely to get stronger without the distractions of managing one of the largest financial businesses in the world. Next year, we hope we can devote more of this narrative to describing GE's *businesses*, not its business *change*.

Reasons for Caution

Reasons for caution are plenty, not the least of which is the distraction caused by the divestiture, but we think they will gradually diminish over time. The company is still active in the acquisitions market and is still complex, and now it is more exposed than ever to the vagaries of the oil and gas business—at least a temporary drag on growth and earnings. Finally, one of our biggest concerns has been the gigantic share count—10 billion—one of the biggest we're aware of. It's hard to generate meaningful per-share gains when new sales and profits are divided up into so many little slices. The divestiture and its proceeds should go a long way toward fixing this.

SECTOR: **Industrials** ◻ BETA COEFFICIENT: **1.43** ◻ 10-YEAR COMPOUND EARNINGS PER-SHARE GROWTH: **NM** ◻ 10-YEAR COMPOUND DIVIDENDS PER-SHARE GROWTH: **NM**

		2007	2008	2009	2010	2011	2012	2013	2014
Revenues (bil)		172.7	182.5	156.8	150.2	147.3	147.4	146.0	148.6
Net income (bil)		22.5	18.1	11.4	12.6	14.9	16.1	16.9	16.6
Earnings per share		2.20	1.78	1.03	1.15	1.31	1.52	1.64	1.65
Dividends per share		1.15	1.24	0.61	0.46	0.61	0.70	0.79	0.88
Cash flow per share		3.28	2.81	2.07	2.13	2.28	2.44	2.65	2.60
Price:	high	42.2	38.5	17.5	19.7	21.7	23.2	28.1	27.6
	low	33.9	12.6	5.7	13.8	14.0	18.0	20.7	23.7

Website: *www.ge.com*

General Mills, Inc.

Ticker symbol: GIS (NYSE) ◻ S&P rating: BBB+ ◻ Value Line financial strength rating: A+ ◻ Current yield: 3.1% ◻ Dividend raises, past 10 years: 10

Company Profile

As observed in the Introduction to this year's *100 Best Stocks to Buy*, changing demographics and tastes led us to take a closer look and make some tough choices among old-line mainstays in the food and beverage world and elsewhere. Traditional breakfast cereals are clearly out of favor now; today's

Millennials seek health and uniqueness in addition to convenience. But because of its more diverse product line and slightly better performance to date, General Mills made the cut—and rival Kellogg, a longtime favorite on our list, did not.

General Mills is the second-largest domestic producer of ready-to-eat breakfast cereals and the sixth-largest food company in the world. Sales are broken out into three major segments, organized by channel: U.S. Retail (59 percent of 2014 revenues), International (30 percent), and Convenience Stores and Foodservice (11 percent).

Major cereal brands, most of which bear the Big G label, include Cheerios, Wheaties, Lucky Charms, Total, and Chex (which is as much a snack base as a cereal). The company owns Pillsbury, which it acquired in 2001. Other consumer packaged food products include baking mixes (Betty Crocker and Bisquick); meals (Betty Crocker dry packaged dinner mixes); Progresso soups; Green Giant canned and frozen vegetables; Hamburger Helper; snacks (Pop Secret microwave popcorn, Bugles snacks, and grain and fruit snack products); Pillsbury refrigerated and frozen dough products, including Pillsbury Doughboy, frozen breakfast products, and frozen pizza and snack products; organic foods; and other products, including Nature Valley, Yoplait (which was acquired in 2011 along with Go-Gurt), and Colombo yogurt. The company's holdings include many other brand names, such as Häagen-Dazs ice cream and a host of joint ventures.

In the International sector, General Mills sells numerous local brands, in addition to internationally recognized brands such as Häagen-Dazs ice cream, Old El Paso Mexican foods, and Green Giant vegetables. The company is in a 50–50 joint venture with Nestlé known as Cereal Partners Worldwide. International accounts for about $5.2 billion in sales, or 30 percent of the total, with Europe holding the largest share (41 percent) followed by Canada (22 percent), Latin America at 19 percent, and Asia-Pacific at 18 percent of the International total.

The Convenience Stores and Foodservice sector is mainly a distribution channel targeting convenience stores, hotels, and restaurants, and wholesale and grocery store bakeries with both branded and unbranded products.

The company offers a breakdown of its U.S Retail business by type of product to better understand this relatively diverse food business:

- 22 percent ready-to-eat cereal including the familiar brands
- 17 percent snacks, including Nature Valley, Fiber One, and Chex Mix
- 17 percent baking products including Betty Crocker, Pillsbury, Bisquick, and Gold Medal Flour

- 15 percent frozen foods including Green Giant vegetables, Old El Paso, and Pillsbury Toaster Strudel
- 14 percent meals including Hamburger Helper, Progresso soups, and Betty Crocker side dishes
- 12 percent Yoplait—yogurts, including Go-Gurt and newly popular Greek yogurts
- 3 percent "Small Planet Foods," a new natural and organic foods line including Cascadian Farm and Muir Glen brands

As you can see, General Mills is part of most well-stocked pantries, and they have at least a moderate amount of healthy fare to go with the traditional offerings. We kept this company on the list not just for good financial performance and a better-than-most percentage of healthful offerings, but also for the promise of innovation, with more investment especially in important and relatively more profitable gluten-free foods coming down the line. The company plans to have 90 percent of its Cheerios line gluten-free by 2016. As the company develops new products, it places emphasis not just on the Millennial group, but also the 55-and-over age groups. We like that, too!

Financial Highlights, Fiscal Year 2014

Historically General Mills has been a slow, steady climber producing single-digit business gains with double-digit dividend increases and decent share buybacks—we've liked the combination. FY2014 was a mixed year, with revenue growth of 1 percent and net earnings growth of about 2 percent. Not too exciting, but the company did deliver strong cash flows and an 11 percent dividend increase on top of a 4 percent share buyback. The company faces some headwinds with currency and at the breakfast table, standby cereals—like colas for soda companies—are high-margin components of the mix and lower volumes almost certainly ding profits; overall gross margins have declined the past two years. General Mills follows this model, and reduced cereal sales will throw a blanket on both sales and earnings in FY2015 with flat to slightly negative performances forecast for both. As newer, healthier products take center stage, and achieve critical mass, the company is optimistic to resume revenue and earnings growth by FY2016, and more importantly, in the years beyond. We expect decent dividend growth and share buybacks to continue.

Reasons to Buy

As Chex Mix–crunching 55-and-overs, we can hardly resist General Mills, can we? But more seriously, although the environment—and the customer base—is a challenging moving target, and although GIS almost fell victim to our axe this year, we felt there was enough there in the emerging product base—and strong investor cash returns—to stick with the company. General Mills has a good mix of cash-cow businesses like flour and baking mixes to weather the storm and finance the necessary advancements without depriving shareholders.

The long-term policy aimed at share repurchases has brought the share count down from 758 million in 2004 to 612 million recently; after a pause related to the Yoplait acquisition, sizeable repurchase looks to continue with decent dividend increases adding some icing to the cake. Finally, General Mills continues to be a notably safe and stable defensive play and "sleep at night" stock with a beta of 0.20—among the lowest on our *100 Best Stocks* list.

Reasons for Caution

The shift in consumer preferences is real and here to stay; our long-term commitment to GIS is based on their long-term commitment to avoid soggy cereal and do something about it. While commodity prices have moderated, the company is strongly affected by commodity prices and cycles. A degree of takeover interest more clearly rumored with store shelf neighbor Kellogg has brought the shares up to a new trading range; they aren't the bargain they were a while back. Shop carefully.

SECTOR: **Consumer Staples** ❑ BETA COEFFICIENT: **0.20** ❑ 10-YEAR COMPOUND EARNINGS PER-SHARE GROWTH: **8.5%** ❑ 10-YEAR COMPOUND DIVIDENDS PER-SHARE GROWTH: **9.5%**

	2007	2008	2009	2010	2011	2012	2013	2014
Revenues (mil)	12,442	13,652	14,691	14,796	14,880	16,658	17,774	17,910
Net income (mil)	1,144	1,288	1,367	1,571	1,652	1,707	1,789	1,824
Earnings per share	1.59	1.78	1.99	2.30	2.48	2.56	2.69	2.83
Dividends per share	0.72	0.79	0.86	0.96	1.12	1.22	1.32	1.55
Cash flow per share	2.30	2.50	2.78	3.09	3.29	3.47	3.71	3.94
Price: high	30.8	36.0	36.0	39.0	40.8	41.9	53.1	55.6
low	27.1	25.5	23.2	33.1	34.5	36.6	40.4	46.7

Website: *www.generalmills.com*

W.W. Grainger, Inc.

Ticker symbol: GWW (NYSE) ❑ S&P rating: AA+ ❑ Value Line financial strength rating: A++ ❑ Current yield: 1.8% ❑ Dividend raises, past 10 years: 10

Company Profile

Every now and then, one of our steady performers performs not so steadily, forcing us to take a closer look. Indeed, currency and international business headwinds and a stock price that had left little room for error led to a 5 percent loss on a total return basis for our 2014 measurement year, based on slowing—but not negative—growth. That forced us to re-evaluate as we usually do: Has the core business changed? Should we, after a long and prosperous sequence of "golf clap" gains, change directions on Grainger as the company may have changed directions itself?

You're reading this analysis, so you know the answer—we decided that the core business and its strengths are intact, so here we go for another year . . .

Grainger is North America's largest supplier of maintenance, repair, and operating supply (MRO) products. It sells more than 1.4 million different products from more than 4,500 suppliers through a network of 681 branches (377 in the U.S.), 33 distribution centers (18 in the U.S.), and several websites, with a catalog containing some 570,000 items (a fascinating read if you like this sort of thing). Grainger also offers repair parts, specialized product sourcing, and inventory management supplies. Grainger sells principally to industrial and commercial maintenance departments, contractors, and government customers, but the range of both customers and products is quite broad (see their 2015 Fact Book). The company has nearly 2 million customers, mostly in North America, and achieves overnight delivery to approximately 95 percent of them.

Its Canadian subsidiary is Canada's largest distributor of industrial, fleet, and safety products. It serves its customers through 181 branches and six distribution centers and offers bilingual websites and catalogs. Grainger, S.A. de C.V. is Mexico's leading facilities maintenance supplier, offering customers more than 84,000 products. The company also has important operations, through joint ventures, in Japan, China, and India and does business in 166 countries worldwide.

Grainger's customer base includes government offices at all levels; heavy manufacturing customers (typically textile, lumber, metals, and rubber industries); light manufacturing; transportation (shipbuilding, aerospace, and automotive); hospitals; retail; hospitality; and resellers of Grainger products. Grainger owns a number of trademarks, including Dayton motors, Dem-Kote spray paints, and Westward tools. The top five product categories are Safety and Security (18 percent), Material Handling (12 percent), Metalworking (12 percent), Cleaning and Maintenance (9 percent), and Pumps, Plumbing, and Equipment (8 percent), with 15 categories in all. Although Grainger is the largest single player, the market remains quite fragmented, with Grainger itself claiming only about 6 percent of the total market in North America.

Many of Grainger's customers are corporate account customers, primarily *Fortune* 1000 companies that spend more than $5 million annually on facilities maintenance products. Corporate account customers typically sign multiyear contracts for facilities maintenance products or a specific category of products, such as lighting or safety equipment. The company also helps its customers, large and small, with inventory management, supplying a tool called "Keepstock" to help them manage their MRO inventories. The Grainger strategy is quintessentially multichannel and centered on being easy to do business with. Customers can interact with a direct sales force, with one of the 377 distribution outlets in the United States, or order through an e-commerce website. Released quietly during the dot-com boom, **www.grainger.com** handled some $2.7 billion, or about 36 percent of the company's U.S. business in FY2014, up from 30 percent the previous year, making it the thirteenth largest e-commerce site in the U.S. and Canada. It has plans to perhaps grow e-commerce beyond 50 percent of the total—making it one of the stronger e-commerce success stories out there.

Financial Highlights, Fiscal Year 2014

The U.S. manufacturing sector has been strong, and about 85 percent of Grainger's sales come from it. The company has also successfully gained modest amounts of market share in this fragmented industry. But sales in Canada, Brazil, and China continued soft in FY2014; that and modest negative currency effects held back the revenue increase to 5.6 percent against a projection of 7 percent; that is what has dampened share price performance. Per-share earnings, which had been guided between $12.10 and $12.85, came in at the low end of the range at $12.26—still 6.4 percent ahead of FY2013. Projections now call for another 6–7 percent per-share earnings rise on revenue growth in the 5–6 percent range through FY2015, and a more robust rise to $14.40–$14.50 per share (10 percent) on revenues up another 5–6 percent in FY2016. Share counts continue to be brought down slowly, and are down 25 percent since 2006 and 42 percent since its share repurchase program commenced in 1984, while dividend raises have picked up since 2010, in the upper teens as a percentage in FY2014 and (expected) through FY2016. We should note that the company has raised its dividend 43 consecutive years—these facts all point toward long-term thinking when it comes to shareholder returns.

Reasons to Buy

"For the Ones Who Get It Done" is the subtitle of the company's excellent 2015 Fact Book (available on its Investor Relations webpage), an appropriate title and an informative and fun read, refreshingly clear, and the best of its sort we've found. Grainger is far and away the biggest presence in the MRO world—and we think the story is still intact.

The only broadline competitor is one-quarter its size, and as noted previously the rest of the market is highly fragmented. The company also has the deepest catalog by far. It's estimated that 40 percent of purchases in the MRO market are unplanned, so having the broadest inventory, fastest delivery, and friendliest service—a "one-stop shop"—is a big advantage for Grainger. If you doubt the value of a broad catalog, consider that this is primarily an industrial supplier that skated through the Great Recession practically untouched (just a 10 percent decline in sales).

Even with its size and scope, the small market share still offers a large growth opportunity. The company has minimal debt and outstanding cash flow—it's starting to leverage its footholds in international locations with the purchase of existing distribution chains in Mexico, Brazil, China, Japan, and Korea. Although today's strong "reshoring" of manufacturing is a key success driver, the international opportunity looks very promising for Grainger.

Reasons for Caution

Grainger will always be vulnerable to economic cycles and manufacturing displacement, especially so long as it remains concentrated on U.S. soil. International expansion should help alleviate this concern. Recently, we've also wondered how much Grainger depends on oil exploration, production, and distribution activity, the decline of which could be at least a short-term headwind. We've looked for entry points for years, and it appears that 2015 will provide a few; shop carefully, and your Grainger purchase will come with a measure of Safety and Security right out of their top-selling product line.

SECTOR: **Industrials** ◻ BETA COEFFICIENT: **0.99** ◻ 10-YEAR COMPOUND EARNINGS PER-SHARE GROWTH: **15.5%** ◻ 10-YEAR COMPOUND DIVIDENDS PER-SHARE GROWTH: **17.0%**

	2007	2008	2009	2010	2011	2012	2013	2014
Revenues (mil)	6,418	6,850	6,222	7,182	8,075	8,950	9,438	9,965
Net income (mil)	420	479	402	502	643	690	824	838
Earnings per share	4.94	6.09	5.25	6.81	9.04	9.52	11.52	12.26
Dividends per share	1.40	1.55	1.78	2.08	2.52	3.06	3.59	4.17
Cash flow per share	6.95	8.28	7.60	9.40	11.33	12.22	14.51	15.81
Price: high	98.6	94.0	102.5	139.1	193.2	221.8	276.4	269.7
low	68.8	58.9	59.9	96.1	124.3	172.5	201.5	223.9

Website: *www.grainger.com*

AGGRESSIVE GROWTH

Harman International Industries

Ticker symbol: **HAR** (NYSE) ◻ S&P rating: **BBB-** ◻ Value Line financial strength rating: **B++** ◻ Current yield: **1.0%** ◻ Dividend raises, past 10 years: **3**

Company Profile

When we pick a company for our *100 Best* list, we're usually quite content with a steady incremental gain of, say 10 or 20 percent in the price of its shares, along with the usual signs of shareholder recognition in the form of cash returns and steadily improving business performance to support both. This is our core model for success, and the best we can expect is that most of our "good ideas" deliver this way. But sometimes we find a real gem among our "good ideas," and the results can be exhilarating. It turns out that Harman International was just such a find. It was our number one pick for 2014, rising some 137 percent from $44 to $104 in our one-year measurement period. Then what? We weren't so sure it would continue, but yo!—it tacked on another 26.8 percent ending north of $133, for the 2015 measurement period.

So the question is, once again, now what? Do we take our money and put it elsewhere? Sell when there's something better to buy? We pondered this for the second year in a row for Harman . . . and decided that the same story that got us here in 2014 and 2015 was well positioned to keep on going through 2016 and beyond. "When you find a good horse, keep riding it" is the operative phrase. Harman is a good high-tech "horse"—with strong, customer-minded innovation and a strong, specialized niche providing the legs.

Harman International is one of the world's leading producers of audio and infotainment solutions for an increasingly mobile society. That sounds like marketing copy, but it's a true depiction of this company. Harman, probably more than any other supplier in the world, has made a partner out of its former customer, the automobile manufacturer. How? By selling a branded product in the car. Where there used to be only one logo, one brand, in the interior of an automobile, now there are two—the manufacturer's and brands offered by Harman. It's not unusual to find Infinity, JBL, Mark Levinson, and several other Harman brands front and center on the dashboard of over half of the popular car lines today.

The company divides its business into three segments, which overlap to some degree. The Infotainment business (53 percent of FY2014 revenues) sells built-in, digital, and integrated information and entertainment systems for automobiles, allowing drivers to listen, talk, navigate, and connect to the outside world. Lifestyle (31 percent), more what Harman is known for, manufactures and markets audio components—electronics and speakers, mainly—traditionally for home environments, but now automotive and other "mobile" apps have become a big share of that business, too. Brands range from the high-middle-end JBL, Harman/Kardon, and Infinity to the high-end Mark Levinson, Lexicon, and recently, through license, Bowers & Wilkins. The Professional segment (16 percent) builds loudspeakers and amplifications systems for professional musicians.

Indeed, Harman is really an automotive company, with about 75 percent of sales altogether coming from this business and about 25 million cars on the road today with embedded Harman systems. The company touts itself as the "bridge between Silicon Valley and the automakers." Key customers include most of the major brands: Audi/Volkswagen, BMW, Chrysler, Toyota, Lexus, Porsche, Daimler, GM, Hyundai, Kia, and Honda to name a few—and even Harley-Davidson. New 2014 deals included Toyota, Scion, Suzuki, Yamaha, Jaguar Land Rover, and Chinese automakers Geely (Volvo) and Chang'an.

As you can see, Harman is becoming ubiquitous. Not only is Harman expanding its presence across most brands, it is also penetrating into more mid-market offerings; its infotainment systems are no longer exclusively a "premium" offering suited only for luxury cars. Too, success in the automotive sector has breathed some life into its home entertainment (Lifestyle) brands, with sales in home and multimedia businesses up 24 percent in a year.

In aggregate, design wins have driven current backlog to over $16 billion—almost three years of sales—in early 2015. The company continues to move ahead in integrated digital technologies for automotive applications with a new software engineering center and the acquisition of Interchain Solution, a producer of Android-based infotainment systems, and other small acquisitions to boost the technology portfolio.

Financial Highlights, Fiscal Year 2014

Embedded infotainment systems continue to be the name of the game, with FY2014 sales up some 24 percent in this largest category. Indeed, with complementary performances in other businesses, FY2014 revenues in total rose 24 percent, with a corresponding 21 percent rise in net earnings (after a fairly substantial 3 percent rise in tax rates) and similar rise in per-share earnings. The revenue "volume" will be turned down a bit going forward into FY2016, with revenues estimated (rather conservatively, we think) ahead 13 percent each year, with welcome margin improvements well into the double digits (like most tech companies, scale is a big factor). The company projects $5.65 per share in FY2015 and $6.80–$7.00 in FY2016—sounds pretty good to us.

Reasons to Buy

Harman has virtually created a new market for high-end, integrated automotive systems and has stepped into the automotive market with some of the most respected brands in traditional home electronics creating a nice win-win for themselves and the automakers. More recently, Harman has added a lot of innovation to this thrust. Automotive infotainment and connectivity design is highly specific in its application and is "designed in" from the beginning, and Harman owns a substantial piece of this market. They partner with the auto companies at the design stage to provide infotainment systems—those integrated systems that all work together to provide sound, video, wireless communications, navigation, Internet access, and climate control on demand and in all parts of the vehicle. It's all gaining traction very quickly.

As Harman evolves, the integration of digital automotive electronics with personal digital devices (e.g., the iPod), and now with the "cloud," offers a huge opportunity. The company is also leveraging this idea to "smart" hotel room adaptations, where you can plug in your device to get your music and tap into your chosen personal information, and we expect the company to bring more innovative integrated designs to the home as well. Automobile purchases are strong worldwide, making the scenario one of increasing share in an increasing market with an increasing "value add" brought through innovation and technology—a marketplace triple play that is hard to resist. Financials and cash returns, in the form of a doubling of the dividend plus a $200 million share buyback, are showing strength in lockstep with the marketplace gains.

Reasons for Caution

We can't deny it: There is some risk here. Harman is vulnerable to economic cycles and particularly those in the auto industry, and downturns in discretionary consumer audio purchases will amplify auto industry woes. Audio and infotainment tastes can be fickle, so the company will have to quickly embrace the latest trends. Recent successes have been built into the stock price, but the story remains strong, and we continue to feel that Harman is more than just a one-trick pony.

SECTOR: **Consumer Discretionary** ▢ BETA COEFFICIENT: **1.69** ▢ 10-YEAR COMPOUND EARNINGS PER-SHARE GROWTH: **6.5%** ▢ 10-YEAR COMPOUND DIVIDENDS PER-SHARE GROWTH: **30.0%**

		2007	2008	2009	2010	2011	2012	2013	2014
Revenues (mil)		3,551	4,112	2,891	3,364	3,772	4,364	4,298	5,349
Net income (mil)		25	146	(56)	60	149	211	194	235
Earnings per share		4.14	2.35	(1.01)	0.85	2.08	2.83	2.78	3.36
Dividends per share		0.05	0.05	0.05	0.05	0.05	0.30	0.60	1.20
Cash flow per share		6.17	5.10	1.32	2.70	3.89	4.96	4.74	5.39
Price:	high	125.1	73.8	40.3	53.4	52.5	52.8	85.8	118.6
	low	69.5	9.9	9.2	28.1	25.5	34.1	40.5	79.9

Website: *www.harman.com*

Health Care REIT, Inc.

Ticker symbol: HCN (NYSE) ▫ S&P rating: BBB ▫ Value Line financial strength rating: A++ ▫ Current yield: 4.4% ▫ Dividend raises, past 10 years: 10

Company Profile

Most would expect a large REIT, or real estate investment trust, paying a yield exceeding 5 percent, to be a slow, steady performer in your portfolio. We did too. Only to be delighted—to put it mildly—by a 35 percent total return in our one-year investment period. If we didn't get your attention with this first venture into the REIT space for our 2014 *100 Best* list, surely we have it now.

Health Care REIT, as the name clearly conveys, is a real estate investment trust investing primarily in senior living and medical care properties primarily in the U.S. For 2014, it was our first venture into the REIT space and is still intended as a steady growth plus income investment and to provide some exposure to real estate in our *100 Best Stocks* portfolio. We feel that it not only offers good exposure to a secure and growing segment of the real estate market but it also exhibits qualities of a good business in addition to its core real estate asset holdings. This thesis was extended for the 2015 *100 Best* list with the addition of Public Storage, and for this year's list by the addition of the Empire State Realty Trust. Slow, steady, safe growth, good businesses, good cash returns, and an occasional boost as these REITs become more popular, recover initial investments, and attract more investors—we like it all.

Health Care REIT operates in three primary business segments. The first and largest is referred to as the Seniors Housing "triple-net" segment and is involved primarily in owning senior housing properties, including independent, continuing care, and assisted living facilities, and leasing them to qualified operators like Sunrise Senior Living and Genesis Healthcare in return for a steady income stream. This segment currently owns 666 properties, most in the U.S., in 42 states but is concentrated in high-cost urban areas mostly on the coasts, and contributes about 33 percent of revenues. There are now also 43 facilities in the U.K. and 13 facilities in Canada.

The second and fastest-growing segment is the Seniors Housing Operating segment, which operates some of the facilities owned by the REIT and others owned by third parties. It operates 202 properties in 34 states, 54 in Canada, and 41 in the U.K. and contributes about 43 percent of revenues. The third major segment is Medical Facilities, which operates office space set in 241 facilities for medical purposes, inpatient and outpatient medical centers, and life science laboratories in 33 states, contributing about 14 percent to revenues. The rest comes from an assortment of business and property management services.

The REIT owns and/or operates some 1,328 properties in three countries and operates assisted living, skilled nursing, independent living, and the medical centers just mentioned.

Health Care REIT employs a conscious and stated strategy of being in markets with high barriers to entry and with a more upscale, affluent retiree base—this is part of why we feel it is a good business, not just a real estate play. Markets such as Boston, New Jersey, Seattle, and major coastal California cities are territories for Health Care REIT. The top five markets are New York, Philadelphia, Los Angeles, Boston, and Greater London. The average revenue per occupied room in the Seniors Operating segment is $5,615 per month, some 48 percent higher than the national senior housing industry average. (For the triple-net segment, this figure is $1,213 per bed/unit per month.) In the markets in which HCN operates, the cost of the average single-family home runs 74 percent higher than the national average, and household incomes are 40 percent higher. Seventy-six percent of facilities are in the 31 most affluent U.S. metropolitan areas. Occupancy rates are 87.7 percent in the Seniors Housing triple-net segment, 90.3 percent in the Seniors Housing Operating, and 94.4 percent in the Medical Facilities segments. The facilities are newer, more attractive, and desirable, as a trip through the company's website at *www.hcreit.com* will show.

In 2014 and early 2015, the company made two medium-sized common stock sales, which hurt the stock price temporarily but also funded the acquisition of $3.7 billion in new real estate investments.

REITs, obviously, play on the real estate market, and in this case, in the high-value-add segment of health care. So by investing in such a REIT, you are investing in real estate and in the health-care industry, and with the property mix owned by Health Care REIT, you're investing in the aging population. In this case in particular, you're investing in the willingness of the more affluent segments of the elderly population to spend for a pleasant retirement. REITs are typically good income producers, as they are required by law to pay a substantial portion of their cash flow to investors. The accounting rules are different, and REIT investors should focus on Funds From Operations (FFO), which is analogous to operating income; net income figures have depreciation expenses deducted, which can vary in timing and not always be realistic. Funds From Operations (FFO) support the dividends paid to investors.

Financial Highlights, Fiscal Year 2014

The 2012 acquisition of Sunrise Senior Living added to an already healthy portfolio, and the company has been acquiring properties since, almost 200 in all since we first added HCN to our list two years ago. Net operating income (NOI)—another pure measure of REIT activity—rose 7.3 percent on a same-store basis for the Seniors Housing Operating segment. Per-share Funds From Operations (FFO) rose about 8.7 percent over FY2014, while the dividend was raised about 4 percent. Guidance for FY2015 calls for an FFO of $4.35 per share and $4.60 per share in FY2016 as recent acquisitions and cost efficiencies continue to take root. As the REIT structure implies, those FFO increases should readily turn into similar dividend increases. The company added a modest number of shares again in 2015 to fund acquisitions and to approach a goal of 60 percent equity.

Reasons to Buy

Health Care REIT is a solid way to play the steady growth of the health-care industry and the aging demographic; truly, the idea has outperformed our expectations so far. REITs are a relatively risk-free, income-oriented way to play the steady growth of this intersection of trends. Rents—and rent growth—are better than average, and its income payout is stable and growing. The company estimates that senior housing rent growth will exceed inflation by 1.7 percent, and that the U.S. population over 75 years of age will grow some 86 percent over the next 20 years, and the 85+ population will double —all factors supporting a healthy growth story.

Some 87 percent of revenues are derived from private pay sources, up from 83 percent in 2014. With the concentration on private-pay services, Health Care REIT will avoid some of the exposure to Medicare utilization management initiatives and related cutbacks that many others in the sector are exposed to—and an improving economy will only help further. We like, and most in the industry agree, the expansion into the U.K., which positions them well for other fertile pastures overseas. The company also avoids exposure to debt and interest costs better than most REITs, with a target debt of 40 percent of total capital (they have currently managed this down to 45 percent). That said, we don't generally like it when companies take advantage of high share prices to sell equity into the market; there could be a little of that here.

Reasons for Caution

Because of their differences from ordinary corporations, it may be difficult to understand this investment, particularly the financial performance of

REITs, especially a complex REIT such as this one, which has both traditional property investments and operating company investments. Okay, we'll be more to the point—this company is complex and hard to understand.

One could also question, going forward, whether retirees will be as well-heeled as they are today, with deterioration in retirement savings and increased costs. Finally, while real estate prices have rebounded well since the Great Recession, any hiccup in any sector of real estate is likely to affect this issue.

SECTOR: **Health Care** ❏ BETA COEFFICIENT: **0.43** ❏ 10-YEAR COMPOUND FFO PER-SHARE GROWTH: **20.5%** ❏ 10-YEAR COMPOUND DIVIDENDS PER-SHARE GROWTH: **2.5%**

	2007	2008	2009	2010	2011	2012	2013	2014
Revenues (mil)	486.0	551.2	569.0	680.5	1,421	1,822	2,880	3,344
Net income (mil)	125.2	150.3	161.6	84.4	155.9	294.8	93.3	505.0
Funds from operations per share	3.12	3.38	3.13	3.08	3.41	3.52	3.80	4.13
Real estate owned per share	58.6	55.9	49.3	58.4	72.5	66.9	74.9	69.5
Dividends per share	2.62	2.70	2.72	2.74	2.84	2.96	3.06	3.18
Price: high	48.6	54.0	46.7	52.1	55.2	62.8	80.1	78.2
low	35.1	30.1	25.9	38.4	41.0	52.4	52.4	52.9

Website: *www.hcreit.com*

AGGRESSIVE GROWTH

NEW FOR 2016

Hillenbrand, Inc.

Ticker symbol: HI (NYSE) ❏ S&P rating: BBB- ❏ Value Line financial strength rating: B+ ❏ Current yield: 2.5% ❏ Dividend raises, past 10 years: 6

Company Profile

When the markets have charged ahead as they have, racking up gains year after year to the point where things seem at least fully valued, if not overvalued, we start to look for new ideas in new corners of the market. Mind you, the *100 Best Stocks* list is still going to be comprised mostly of proven ideas, proven brands, and companies with mega-billions in market capitalization.

But as we approach the 2016 list, we're looking under more rocks to find value. We don't want to disappoint you with too many proven but older horses that have already run their race. We'd like a few two-year-olds—or in this case, fresh seven-year-olds—to spruce things up a bit. (We tend to avoid two-year-olds in stock investing; they can lose sight of the finish line rather easily.)

Which brings us to a small town in southeastern Indiana, meriting but one freeway interchange along the trip down I-74 between Indianapolis and Cincinnati. For some, the town of Batesville, Indiana, population 6,250, is known as the first place where you can get world-famous Cincinnati chili as you head southeast, and as the kind of place you'd go cut a Christmas tree if you happen to *live* in Cincinnati. But it is also home to the dominant market player in funeral service products—burial caskets, cremation caskets and urns, and services and supplies for the bereaver and the bereaved: the 131-year-old Batesville Casket Company.

Okay, now you think we've lost our minds. Funeral products? Hardly a growth business. Batesville, Indiana? Hardly a world-class bastion of American industry.

But . . . try to remember how we think as investors. We like value. We like companies with good strategies, solid brands, good positions in their markets, well-managed companies, companies that generate a lot of cash, and companies that return reasonable amounts of it to shareholders.

And we like to take the side roads to reach our destination once in a while. That's where our new pick, Hillenbrand Inc., enters the picture.

Indeed, Hillenbrand owns—and is built around—the Batesville Casket Company. Now a subsidiary, Batesville generates gross margins approaching 39 percent and a lot of cash through the year, but yes, it is declining slightly as the population lives longer and as less profitable cremation products gradually replace the common burial casket. If it were just Batesville Casket in play, we'd have closed the lid early on in our investigation.

As it so happens, around this strong market-share and cash-flow player the management team has set out to design, develop, and acquire its way into position as a "world-class global diversified industrial company." Okay, that's a pretty heady tag line, but what they've done is acquired, integrated, and grown three strong players in the build-to-order industrial equipment business, mostly in dry material handling and processing. Major names in the Process Equipment Group are Coperion, which makes a line of extruders, compounding equipment, pelletizers, and feeders; TerraSource

Global, which also makes conveying, mixing, screening, sorting, and other products; and Rotex, which makes bulk screening equipment. End customers are in the packaged and bulk foods industries, pharmaceuticals, plastics, energy, mineral, petrochemical, and fertilizer industries, among others. Now, such products seem a bit dull and boring, especially on a stock list that includes such high-profile names as Apple, Starbucks, and Costco. But these industrial products are growing, have found overseas markets, and are sold with a fair selection of consumables—screens, extrusion dies, etc.—and services to keep the business strong even amid downturns in the capital investment cycle.

At present, the Process Equipment Group accounts for 60 percent of the business and all of the growth (revenue at Batesville actually declined 5 percent in 2014). Batesville is the financial "foundation"; the Process Equipment Group companies are growing both organically and also by providing ample cross-selling opportunities toward becoming a manufacturer's single source for such dry product–handling equipment. This strategy is playing well in emerging manufacturing markets such as India and China.

Financial Highlights, Fiscal Year 2014

Adding to the 5 percent sales decline for Batesville Casket in 2014 is a 14 percent year-over-year growth in the Process Equipment Group businesses. As previously mentioned, Batesville gross margins approach 40 percent. Process Equipment gross margins grew almost 4 percent to 33.2 percent, but acquisition costs hurt further down toward the bottom line. Thus FY2014 was a good year but not a great one historically with $110 million in net profit, but with operating cash flows up 41 percent over FY2013. For FY2015 and beyond, the acquisition digestion costs go away and operating margins should return to the 20 percent level (they were in the low 20s, not surprisingly, when the business was just Batesville). Such a revived operating margin on a larger business base should produce net profits of about $140 million (up about 28 percent from FY2014) on a business base somewhere close to FY2014's. As the business model kicks into gear, FY2016 profits are forecast ahead in low double digits on a revenue advance in the high single-digit range.

To show its intentions to shareholders, the company has regularly raised its dividend one cent a year, even throughout the recession. This would not excite us much, but the company now indicates that it plans to grow that rate a bit, perhaps to 4 cents per year, and has also done its first share buyback of 16.5 million, or a bit less than 1 percent. It has also indicated plans to pay off most of the $500 million in long-term debt picked up to fund the acquisitions. We expect financial stability and cash returns both to grow.

Reasons to Buy

You probably picked up that the business model—a solid and steady industrial business built on top of an entrenched (sorry) steady cash generator—has not quite matured yet; the biggest acquisitions have come in the past two years and aren't quite fitted into the mix in the marketplace, financially, and management-wise. But we like the company's overall strategy, its style, and its orientation to shareholders; if you tour through the company's materials, it's presented effectively and modestly. Overall, the company has good positions in two completely unrelated niches.

Reasons for Caution

While it is a strong name in the industry and an effective cash cow, nevertheless Hillenbrand is managing a gradually declining business in the Batesville Casket Company. However, this should be more of a drag on revenues than profits going forward. Some of the Process Equipment customer base is in the mining and energy industries—this could be a bit of a drag but not a showstopper. The company is small enough that a sudden shift in the process equipment marketplace could hurt; that said, the funeral products business adds stability. The prudent course for Hillenbrand is to focus on integrating what it already has rather than extending itself into more acquisitions. These, in our view, could be a negative.

SECTOR: **Industrials** ❑ BETA COEFFICIENT: **1.18** ❑ 10-YEAR COMPOUND EARNINGS PER-SHARE GROWTH: **NM** ❑ 10-YEAR COMPOUND DIVIDENDS PER-SHARE GROWTH: **NM**

	2007	2008	2009	2010	2011	2012	2013	2014
Revenues (mil)	667	678	649	749	883	983	1,553	1,667
Net income (mil)	100	105	102	92	106	105	63	110
Earnings per share	1.60	1.68	1.66	1.49	1.71	1.68	1.01	1.72
Dividends per share	0.73	0.73	0.74	0.75	0.76	0.77	0.78	0.79
Cash flow per share	1.90	2.00	1.95	1.93	2.28	2.32	2.42	2.68
Price: high	—	24.8	21.1	26.2	24.2	30.0	35.0	34.9
low	—	13.3	14.6	17.8	16.3	16.8	22.7	26.0

Website: *www.hillenbrand.com*

Honeywell International

Ticker symbol: HON (NYSE) ◻ S&P rating: A ◻ Value Line financial strength rating: A++ ◻ Current yield: 2.2% ◻ Dividend raises, past 10 years: 9

Company Profile

Honeywell is a diversified international technology and manufacturing company operating in four business segments, engaged in the development, manufacturing, and marketing of aerospace products and services; control technologies for buildings, homes, and industry; automotive products; and specialty materials. The company recently regrouped these activities into three segments: Aerospace and Automotive (39 percent of FY2014 sales), Automation and Control Solutions (36 percent), and Performance Materials and Technologies (25 percent). The Aerospace and Automotive segment's aerospace-related businesses include cockpit controls, power generation equipment, and wheels and brakes for commercial and military aircraft and for airports and ground operations. It also makes jet engines for regional and business jet manufacturers. Products include avionics, auxiliary power units (APUs), aircraft lighting, and landing systems. The automotive business consists of a portfolio of parts and supplies for the automotive, railroad, and other industries. Products include cooling system components, turbochargers, and an assortment of other items. In 2014 the company sold its "friction materials" business (mainly brake components) and had sold its retail consumer automotive brands previously to focus on OEM components.

Honeywell's Automation and Control Solutions segment is best known as a maker of home and office climate-control equipment. It also makes home automation systems; thermostats; sensing and combustion controls for heating, A/C, and other environmental controls; lighting controls; security systems and sensing products; and fire alarms. This segment produces most of the components of what is known in the trade and advertising lingo as a "smart building," along with devices that play well with the new "connected" homes, data analytics, and "Internet of Things" concepts. Indeed, the company is looking at itself as ever more a software company and is investing management time, effort, and new hiring in improving the software development cycle. Honeywell estimates that its products are at work in some 150 million homes and 10 million commercial buildings worldwide. This part of the business also produces a number of factory automation products. The company estimates that it holds the number one market-share position in environmental and combustion controls, security and fire protection systems, and industrial safety products and systems.

The Performance Materials and Technologies operation makes a wide assortment of specialty chemicals and fibers, plastics, coatings, and semiconductor and electronics materials, which are sold primarily to the food, pharmaceutical, petroleum refining, and electronic packaging industries. Petroleum-refining catalysts and carbon fiber materials are among the more important and fastest-growing products in this segment.

The company has a considerable international footprint, with technology and manufacturing centers located outside the U.S.; five such centers are located in China along with a similar number in India. The company estimates 54 percent of its business to be done outside the U.S.

Financial Highlights, Fiscal Year 2014

Foreign exchange and softness in its aerospace business, and to a lesser extent its Specialty Materials segment, with its ties to the energy industry, brought in mixed results for FY2014; revenues were up just over 3 percent. Earnings, bolstered by a number of initiatives to cut costs and improve margins (even the aerospace business delivered a 2 percent increase on a 1 percent decline in sales) drove overall operating margins up about 1 percent and net earnings up a healthy 11.5 percent. Energy industry softness and continued dollar strength are expected to hold revenues to less than a 1 percent gain in FY2015, but strong backlogs in all businesses and strength in the commercial aerospace segment are expected to bring revenues gains in the 4–5 percent range in FY2016, with profitability measures continuing net earnings gains in the 9–11 percent range both years. Buybacks are modest, but the company did accelerate its dividend growth with an 11 percent raise in FY2014 and similar raises in store for the near term.

Reasons to Buy

Honeywell is a "best-in-class" producer of a wide variety of business and consumer products with an underlying technology theme—not really "high tech" but using advanced technologies or, in some cases, supporting them. The company shows many of the traditional signs of being well managed, with a strong and strategic focus on profitability, cash flow, and operational efficiency and a healthy respect for transparency, as evidenced by its informative annual reports and other corporate materials.

Honeywell has outlined its key growth vectors as international (globalization), safety and security, energy efficiency, and energy generation. They are now expanding their focus to complete solutions through "connectivity" and "adjacency" opportunities, many being software driven, within many of their platforms. We like this diverse but timely set of focal points. The company also has a valuable distribution network and existing customer base in all of its businesses. The company has a solid balance sheet and participates almost exclusively in high-margin businesses, particularly with the divestiture of the consumer auto and brake lining business.

Reasons for Caution

Many of the industries Honeywell sells to can be cyclical and/or low-growth businesses. However, as we've seen, the focus on profitability will make the most of these businesses. The stock has been on a long run, more than doubling since 2011; new investors are advised to be patient.

SECTOR: **Industrials** ❑ BETA COEFFICIENT: **1.26** ❑ 10-YEAR COMPOUND EARNINGS PER-SHARE GROWTH: **9.0%** ❑ 10-YEAR COMPOUND DIVIDENDS PER-SHARE GROWTH: **7.5%**

	2007	2008	2009	2010	2011	2012	2013	2014
Revenues (mil)	34,589	36,556	30,908	33,370	36,500	37,665	39,055	40,306
Net income (mil)	2,444	2,792	2,153	2,342	2,998	3,552	3,965	4,422
Earnings per share	3.16	3.75	2.85	3.00	3.79	4.48	4.97	5.56
Dividends per share	1.00	1.10	1.21	1.21	1.37	1.53	1.68	1.87
Cash flow per share	4.39	5.03	4.07	4.27	5.11	5.72	6.32	6.83
Price: high	62.3	63.0	41.6	53.7	62.3	64.5	91.6	102.4
low	43.1	23.2	23.1	36.7	41.2	52.2	64.2	82.9

Website: *www.honeywell.com*

CONSERVATIVE GROWTH

International Business Machines

Ticker symbol: IBM (NYSE) ❑ S&P rating: AA- ❑ Value Line financial strength rating: A++ ❑ Current yield: 2.7% ❑ Dividend raises, past 10 years: 10

Company Profile

Ugh. IBM became a charter member of our "vulnerable for 2016" list, with a total return of −14.3 percent for the year. It wasn't the worst on our list; we had a few others, a couple of smaller, riskier new issues and a couple others tied to the energy industry. But IBM? Big Blue? The information technology standard of the world? We had to take a closer look, as they abandoned previously committed $20-per-share earnings targets and dumped upon us four years of slower growth, all with diminished brand prominence with the newer generation (can you say "Millennials?") and what seems an impossible bureaucracy—what's here to like? Ponder we did, and decided there's enough value here to keep them on our list—for another year anyway.

Big Blue is the world's leading provider of computer hardware, software, and services. Really—we should say services, software, and hardware. Get the drift? IBM historically has made a broad range of computers, mainframes, and network servers. But the company has morphed over the years into a software and services company. They continued this trend by selling their low-end server business to Lenovo and their semiconductor business to GlobalFoundries, in part accounting for the revenue drop. As a consequence, fewer folks than ever talk about an "IBM computer" anymore; as we'll see, they talk about an "IBM business solution" or some such.

IBM is divided into four principal business units and a financing unit. The largest, at 38 percent of revenues, the Global Technology Services unit, is really an IT service, offering cloud computing, analytics, and other applications outsourcing. The Global Business Services unit (18 percent) is also a service unit but now provides its service on customer sites through consulting, application design, systems integration, and similar services. The Software unit (32 percent) supplies rather unexciting "middleware" products that make everything in an IT environment work together, but also now, the more interesting "big data" and business analytics is emerging as a leading new offering for the company—as well as an important component of their overall branding and image as exhibited in its recent marketing campaigns.

The Systems and Technology group, which is the unit that most closely harkens back to the "Big Iron" days, is now just 10 percent of the business (was 14 percent in FY2013 and 17 percent in FY2012). Finally, the Financing unit (2 percent) helps the company market it all. Overseas sales make up about 55 percent of revenues—down from 65 percent fairly recently but still significant especially in today's strong dollar climate.

The company has kept "strategic" (as opposed to commoditized) large systems but little else; it is now offering cloud-based and integrated hardware/software/service solutions for diverse needs such as business analytics and data security. The company, more than most in the industry, lives up to a common industry promise to provide "solutions," not just products.

The most promising recent news comes in the form of a new campaign to essentially double down on what it sees as its "new" core strategic areas, investing $4 billion in cloud and mobile computing, analytics, and what could be a real dark horse—information security. If it hadn't been for this "doubling down" in what we feel is the right direction for the company—and for the fact that it's buying up gobs of its own stock, almost 6 percent of its float last year—the company's position on our *100 Best* list would be in serious doubt.

Financial Highlights, Fiscal Year 2014

With its fairly sizeable divestitures and heavy currency impacts, one must take a closer look at the 7 percent revenue drop reported for FY2014. All factors included, the true drop was still a moderate 2–3 percent, with hardware revenues down 12 percent in all. If the goal was to shift the business mix from less profitable hardware to more profitable services, it is certainly in progress, although the rate of net income decline was almost the same as the revenue decline. The bright spot was per-share earnings, which rose 14 percent on the back of 65 million shares repurchased, and cash flow per share, which also rose about 2 percent.

Less may be more going forward—at least we hope. Revenues—again including currency and divestitures—for FY2015 are expected to drop 9–10 percent, but stabilize or even increase slightly for FY2016. Some say the devil is in the details, but in this case we see a few possible angels: The company projects that by FY2018, the strategic areas of analytics, security, and cloud will account for some 40 percent of revenues (up from 27 percent today)—an important transition. Overall, revenues should advance at a low single-digit pace once this transition matures, with a similar to slightly better advance in earnings. Once again, per-share earnings will be the highlight for the next few years, with a long-range forecast of $15.75–$16.00 in FY2016 and higher going forward. The company, quite simply, has not achieved scale in these new core businesses. On the shareholder return front, IBM will have retired almost 40 percent of its shares and raised its dividend from $1.10 to $4.75 in a ten-year period if current estimates hold.

Reasons to Buy

Once viewed as a teetering giant of the computer industry with a massive intellectual property portfolio but an uncertain product strategy, IBM has, over the past decade, tried to reinvent itself as a go-to new-age solutions powerhouse. First came consulting, then outsourcing, and now, leading-edge analytics, security, and cloud services. We think this is the right direction; this, not "big iron" in the data center, nor big consulting teams and contracts, will define the IBM brand, and make it more profitable along the way.

The company needs to stick to the strategy and stick to the message. Despite the revenue softness, the company is very tenacious about its goals and strategies, as we've observed in the exit of its mainstay hardware businesses. Not too long ago they promised $20 per share in earnings for FY2015; this goal is gone, but we like such goals with strategies to achieve them, and we're cautiously optimistic that IBM is now aiming more squarely in the right direction. And one cannot possibly ignore the cash returns generated for shareholders over the past few years, a trend which is likely to continue.

Reasons for Caution

Strong dollar, diminished hardware sales, large investments to catch up with major IT trends—these all stand in the way of growth at IBM. But one factor we feel others haven't considered is the diminished brand reputation in the eyes of today's IT decision-makers—the Millennials—who didn't grow up thinking you "could never be fired for buying IBM." Indeed, we think one of the company's biggest challenges is regaining that Top Dog brand reputation in today's IT-buying demographic.

IBM does have a larger exposure to governments and government contracts than many of its competitors. While this can be stabilizing in hard times, this time we feel that a massive and widespread public-sector belt tightening could hurt the company. Finally, IBM has a reputation, somewhat deserved, of being big, bureaucratic, laden with headcount, and not very nimble, which can be a serious negative in the tech world—but unlike many big, unwieldy tech companies, IBM has demonstrated a clear go-forward strategy. Now more than ever they need to execute on it, and perhaps even more importantly, need to make it part of a "new" IBM brand, acceptable, even desirable, to those of us born after 1982. The early steps look promising, but there's work to do.

SECTOR: **Information Technology** ❑ BETA COEFFICIENT: **0.63** ❑ 10-YEAR COMPOUND EARN-INGS PER-SHARE GROWTH: **13.0%** ❑ 10-YEAR COMPOUND DIVIDENDS PER-SHARE GROWTH: **19.5%**

	2007	2008	2009	2010	2011	2012	2013	2014
Revenues (bil)	98.8	103.6	95.8	99.9	106.9	104.5	99.8	92.8
Net income (bil)	10.4	12.3	13.4	14.8	15.9	16.6	16.5	15.7
Earnings per share	7.18	8.93	10.01	11.52	13.06	14.37	14.94	15.59
Dividends per share	1.50	1.90	2.15	2.50	2.90	3.30	3.70	4.25
Cash flow per share	11.28	13.28	14.11	16.01	17.77	19.04	20.07	20.44
Price: high	121.5	130.9	132.3	147.5	194.9	211.8	215.9	199.2
low	88.8	69.5	81.8	116.0	146.6	177.3	172.2	150.5

Website: *www.ibm.com*

CONSERVATIVE GROWTH

Illinois Tool Works Inc.

Ticker symbol: ITW (NYSE) ❑ S&P rating: A+ ❑ Value Line financial strength rating: A++ ❑ Current yield: 2.0% ❑ Dividend raises, past 10 years: 10

Company Profile

Illinois Tool Works is a longstanding multinational conglomerate involved in the manufacture of a diversified range of industrial products, mainly components, fasteners, and other "ingredients" for manufacturers. Customers include the automotive, machinery, construction, food and beverage, and general industrial markets. The company currently operates some 90 divisions in 57 countries, employing approximately 49,000. Some of the products are branded and familiar, like Wolf and Hobart kitchen equipment and Paslode air power tools; most are obscure and only known to others in their industries. Overseas sales account for about 57 percent of the total.

In 2014 the company spun off its Industrial Packaging segment to the private equity firm Carlyle Group for $3.2 billion. That operation accounted for some 14 percent of revenues in FY2012, hence the apparent downdraft in sales, profits, and briefly, per-share earnings. The company deployed much of the cash received to buy back about 45 million of its common shares—a bit over 10 percent of its float at the time—roughly in line with the size of the divestiture, so per-share earnings are largely comparable going forward.

The remaining segments are presented here with approximate figures for percentages of total 2014 ITW revenues post-divestiture:

- *Automotive OEM* (18 percent) includes transportation-related components, fasteners, and polymers, as well as truck remanufacturing and related parts and service for the automotive manufacturer market. Important brands include Drawform ("high volume, highly toleranced deep drawn metal stampings") and Deltar, which makes things like interior door handles.

- *Test & Measurement and Electronics* (15 percent) supplies equipment and software for testing and measuring of materials and structures, solder, and other materials for PC board manufacturing and microelectronics assembly. Brands include Brooks Instrument, Buehler, Chemtronics, Instron, Magnaflux, and Speedline Technologies.

- *Polymers & Fluids* (13 percent) businesses produce adhesives, sealants, lubrication and cutting fluids, and hygiene products for an assortment of markets. Their primary brands include Futura, Krafft, Devcon, Rocol, and Permatex and such brands as Rain-X and Wynn's for the automotive aftermarket.

- *Food Equipment* (12 percent) produces commercial food equipment and related services, including professional kitchen ovens, refrigeration, mixers, and exhaust and ventilation systems. Major brands include Hobart, Traulsen, Vulcan, and Wolf.

- *Construction Products* (12 percent) concentrates on tools, fasteners, and other products for construction applications. Their major end markets are residential, commercial, and renovation construction. Brands include Ramset, Paslode, Buildex, Proline, and others.

- *The Welding segment* (13 percent of revenues) produces equipment and consumables associated with specialty power conversion, metallurgy, and electronics. Their primary products include arc-welding equipment and consumables, solder materials, equipment and services for electronics assembly, and airport ground support equipment. Primary brands include AXA Power, Hobart, and Weldcraft.

- *Specialty Products* (14 percent) is a hodgepodge of brands and businesses that includes Diagraph (industrial marking and coding systems), Fastex (engineered components for the appliance industry), and ZipPak reclosable plastic packaging.

In 2012, the company embarked on a five-year "Enterprise Strategy" program aimed at simplifying the business and applying sound customer-driven operating principles to fine-tune its base of customers, markets, products, facilities, and supply chains. Emphasis is placed on removing customer pain points, reducing complexity by applying the "80-20" rule (focusing on the 20 percent of customers, products, and processes that deliver 80 percent of the results), and by fine-tuning the relationships between headquarters and the operating entities. Improving margins is the chief business objective. We normally don't bring too many such strategic initiatives to light, but we will in this case because (1) it's working, as gross margins have improved from the 19–21 percent range to a projected 25 percent in FY2016; and (2) such focus is needed in a company with such size and operating complexity; otherwise, it quickly becomes an uncoordinated conglomerate jumble, as many others before it have. We appreciate ITW's efforts to recognize the opportunities and deal with them successfully.

Financial Highlights, Fiscal Year 2014

The Industrial Packaging divestiture clouds the comparison somewhat, but in every way ITW continues to enjoy both a recovery in the economy and in U.S. manufacturing activity. Comparable revenues continued to rise about 2.5 percent in FY2014, driven by strength across the board and particularly in the Automotive OEM segment (+8.7 percent) and Food Equipment (+6.4 percent). Laggards included Polymers & Fluids (-3.2 percent) and Construction Products (-0.4 percent), in case you're interested. Net earnings, driven in part by the margin improvements previsouly mentioned, moved nicely ahead 16 percent, while per-share earnings, which cannot be reasonably measured against the FY2013 base due to the spinoff, are ahead 14 percent from FY2012.

For FY2015 and beyond, the company is more committed to profits than just gross revenue per se and expects the auto boom to play out a bit and for currency effects to take a bite as well. Revenues are projected down a little over 1 percent in FY2015, but then up a more robust 4–5 percent in FY2016. Per-share earnings, helped along by better margins and buybacks, are the real story here, rising 10–12 percent in each of the two years.

Reasons to Buy

Buying shares of ITW continues to be like buying a mutual fund of medium-sized manufacturing businesses you've probably never heard of but would definitely like to own. Indeed, think of it as the Berkshire Hathaway of manufacturing companies if you will—we do. We enjoy doing this presentation every year; it's a good tour through how to run a modern conglomerate effectively, and they present themselves well to investors.

ITW is well diversified and serves many markets, some with end products, some with components, some in cyclical industries such as automotive and construction, some in steady-state industries like food processing. The company has solid models for making acquisitions and seems to do better than most conglomerates historically in choosing candidates and then managing them once they're in the fold. Especially with the new "Enterprise" initiative, the company does a good job of turning opportunity into cash flow and using that cash flow to enhance shareholder returns. The balance sheet is strong and net profit margins are projected to rise quite nicely for this type of business. Too, the company appears to be slowing down its acquisitions, which should reduce distractions and costs in absorbing new businesses.

Reasons for Caution

ITW is by nature tied to some of the more volatile elements of the business cycle, so it may not be the best pick for investors living in fear of the next downturn. In particular, we worry a bit about the Automotive segment going forward. Conglomerates are notoriously difficult to manage (it's hard enough to manage one business, let alone 90 of them); that said, the company is working to streamline management structure and is also putting fewer new acquisitions on its plate.

SECTOR: **Industrials** ❑ BETA COEFFICIENT: **1.25** ❑ 10-YEAR COMPOUND EARNINGS PER-SHARE
GROWTH: **10.0%** ❑ 10-YEAR COMPOUND DIVIDENDS PER-SHARE GROWTH: **12.0%**

		2007	2008	2009	2010	2011	2012	2013	2014
Revenues (mil)		16,169	15,869	13,876	15,870	17,787	17,924	14,135	14,484
Net income (mil)		1,826	1,583	969	1,527	1,852	1,921	1,629	1,890
Earnings per share		3.36	3.05	1.93	3.03	3.74	4.06	3.63	4.67
Dividends per share		0.91	1.15	1.24	1.27	1.38	1.46	1.60	1.75
Cash flow per share		4.44	4.56	3.27	4.17	5.06	5.55	5.20	6.25
Price:	high	60.0	55.6	51.2	52.7	59.3	63.3	84.3	97.8
	low	45.6	28.5	25.6	40.3	39.1	47.4	59.7	76.3

Website: *www.itwinc.com*

NEW FOR 2016

International Flavors & Fragrances, Inc.

Ticker symbol: IFF (NYSE) □ S&P rating: BBB+ □ Value Line financial strength rating: A+ □ Current yield: 1.6% □ Dividend raises, past 10 years: 10

Company Profile

Some of you more cynical readers may have come to suppose that even the ticker symbol becomes a factor in choosing our companies. For those of you in this vein, we present one of this year's new picks: International Flavors & Fragrances, ticker symbol "IFF." IFF only this stock would rise 20 percent during 2016.

IFF and only if.

Actually, IFF as a company has passed many of our smell tests for years, and believe it or not, the ticker symbol didn't even enter our collective olfactory. The company is a leading manufacturer of natural and artificial flavoring and fragrance chemicals for the food and beverage and consumer products industry, including cosmetics, perfumes, soap and detergents, hair care, pharmaceuticals, and a wide variety of other products. Fragrances accounted for about 53 percent of 2014 sales; flavorings the other 47 percent.

Not surprisingly, the company's value proposition and strategy is to create a differentiated and high value add for its customers by providing critical, unique, and highly researched ingredients. Many of the thousands of flavorings and fragrances are custom-made for clients. For the food and beverage industry, the company estimates that its flavorings cost only 1–5 percent of the product's total cost, but generate 45 percent of the motivation to purchase it and to purchase it repeatedly.

The company is truly "international," with 78 percent of sales originating outside the U.S.; in fact, 50 percent of sales originate in emerging markets. Recognizing that flavor and fragrance preferences are very local in nature, the company has established an operational presence in 32 countries and lab facilities in 13 of them, including the U.S. Still, they estimate only a 16 percent share of the global flavorings and fragrances market and hold the number two position behind Swiss flavorings maker Givaudan. For U.S. investors, they are by far the largest pure play available in this niche.

Research and development is a big part of what IFF does—researching consumer tastes and preferences, how flavors and aromas work and hold up in different environments, and how to manufacture their products and develop the best delivery system to make them work over the desired life cycle. Research includes things like study of the "psychophysics of sensory perception" and the genetic basis for preferences in flavor and fragrance. New products and concepts include a proprietary encapsulation technology, which coats individual fragrance droplets with a polymeric shell to enhance life-cycle performance, and a product called "PolyIFF"—a solid-fragrance technology embedding scent into molded plastic. The company collaborates with chefs, fashion designers, filmmakers, and other trendsetters to evolve new ideas. R&D accounted for 8.2 percent of sales in 2014.

Financial Highlights, Fiscal Year 2014

IFF projects that the $18 billion market for flavors and fragrances will grow about 3–4 percent annually, with fully 75 percent of the growth coming from emerging markets, as taste and aroma become a more important product component in China, Latin America, Africa, and the Middle East. FY2014 revenues rose almost 5 percent, which would have been at least 2 percent higher without currency effects. Margins grew nicely with moderating ingredient costs and reduced expenses; the net profit margin advanced a full percentage point to a record 13.5 percent, and total earnings advanced 19 percent as a consequence. Revenue gains in the 4–6 percent annual range are expected going forward in FY2015, with continued profitability improvements delivering earnings gains in the 5–7 percent range. If the dollar weakens, these figures could be much stronger due to the international strength.

IFF has accelerated its dividend increases into the low double-digit range annually, although is not reducing share count at present. They do make small acquisitions—such as the 2014 acquisition of Israeli aroma chemicals specialist Aromor—and pay for them with debt, which they pay down pretty quickly afterwards. Their capital is allocated primarily for this purpose, capital expenditures, and for dividend increases.

Reasons to Buy

IFF we had only put this company on our list a few years ago when we first considered it . . . but we can't make a big stink about that now. We like this company a lot. It has a strong niche and produces elements critical in differentiating products in the fairly undifferentiated food and consumer products businesses. That should play better over time as people's tastes become more trained and more demanding—both in the rich world and especially in developing nations, which is an important trend right now. Not only does the company produce many of the world's leading flavorings and fragrances, it also has the market research and know-how to give it a competitive advantage—a moat—both with its customer insights and knowing how to make and deliver the stuff. We also like the relatively recession-proof nature of this business; we doubt that they will take the flavoring out of your favorite foods anytime soon, although we suppose that a greater uptake of generic products, such as cleaning products, could put a bit of a dent in this business. But remember, flavorings only account for 1–5 percent of the cost of your favorite beverage, and we Coke drinkers all know what happens when a company monkeys with that.

Reasons for Caution

The cost and availability of key ingredients like vanilla (a large portion of which comes from unstable regions in West Africa) can affect IFF adversely. The strong overseas footprint is probably an advantage most of the time, but today's strong dollar attenuates that advantage; also, it's hard to keep up with changing consumer tastes in so many places. Intellectual property protection is also a challenge; many try and some succeed in reverse engineering key ingredients. Finally, the share price has almost doubled since we became interested in this issue three years ago. Buying at the wrong price could leave you with a bad taste in your mouth.

SECTOR: Consumer Staples ❑ BETA COEFFICIENT: **0.83** ❑ 10-YEAR COMPOUND EARNINGS PER-SHARE GROWTH: **8.0%** ❑ 10-YEAR COMPOUND DIVIDENDS PER-SHARE GROWTH: **8.0%**

	2007	2008	2009	2010	2011	2012	2013	2014
Revenues (mil)	2,277	2,389	2,326	2,623	2,788	2,821	2,953	3,089
Net income (mil)	237	221	214	264	306	328	368	416
Earnings per share	2.70	2.76	2.69	3.26	3.74	3.98	4.47	5.08
Dividends per share	0.88	0.96	1.00	1.04	1.16	1.30	1.46	1.72
Cash flow per share	3.94	3.77	3.70	4.27	4.71	4.95	5.54	6.25
Price: high	54.8	48.0	42.6	56.1	66.3	67.8	90.3	105.8
low	45.7	24.7	25.0	39.3	51.2	52.1	67.5	82.9

Website: *www.iff.com*

`AGGRESSIVE GROWTH`

Itron, Inc.

Ticker symbol: ITRI (NASDAQ) ❑ S&P rating: NR ❑ Value Line financial strength rating: B+ ❑ Current yield: Nil ❑ Dividend raises, past 10 years: NA

Company Profile

Patience can be a virtue. That's a fact, whether it be in love, marriage, business, or investing.

What do we mean? It may be hard to articulate, but we're the sort who like to explain things by example. Itron offers a good one.

Those of you who read our book every year may recall Itron being our worst performer on the 2014 *100 Best Stocks* list. It lost 25 percent and to boot, doesn't pay a dividend. Good memory, for those who remember; good information, for the rest of you. This year, no recovery—performance has been pretty much flat.

So why another year on the list? Why do we even deal with this difficult teenager who seems to fall short—year after year—of what he or she is capable of? In short, it's because we still believe Itron is a fine company in a good market, and maybe *this* will be the year. Itron is the world's largest provider of standard and intelligent metering systems for residential and commercial gas, electric, and water usage, primarily to the utility industry. Intelligent meters, in addition to tracking raw usage over time, can also measure at the point of use operating parameters such as pressure, temperature, voltage, phase, etc. This information can be extremely valuable to the supplying utility but has in the past been difficult and expensive to obtain.

Itron supplies a range of products from basic meters that are read manually to meters that act as network devices and transmit their data in real time to the managing utility and/or to the consuming customer. Products and systems are produced and sold in three groupings:

- Standard metering—basic meters that measure electricity, gas, or water flow by electrical or mechanical means, with displays but no built-in remote reading or transmission capability.
- Advanced metering—these units, depending on the country and the communications technologies available—transmit usage data remotely through telephone, cellular, radio frequency (RF), Ethernet, or power line carrier paths. Among other value adds, these meters transmit usage

data for billing, thereby eliminating the need for onsite meter reading—
a big savings for utility companies.

■ Smart metering—smart meters collect and store interval data and
other detailed info, receive commands, and interface with other devices
through assorted communication paths to thermostats, smart appliances, and home network and other advanced control systems.

Itron also sells a range of software platforms for utilities and building
managers for the management of the installed base and the analysis and
optimization of usage, and it is active in developing so-called "smart grid"
solutions for utilities and utility networks. The company also markets
advanced metering initiative (AMI) contracts to utilities, where it installs
devices and monitors and optimizes power usage for a utility.

At present, electric meters represent about 40 percent of the business,
gas meters about 30 percent, and water meters the remaining 30 percent. The
company has about 8,000 customers in 130 countries, and about 55 percent
of the business comes from outside the U.S. and Canada. The company has
become a major player in the emerging "Smart City" energy use concept,
and won the Frost & Sullivan 2014 North American Smart City Company
of the Year Award. Itron products are also frequently mentioned in "Internet
of Things" circles.

Pretty smart stuff, don't you think? Now the question is—can they
make money?

Financial Highlights, Fiscal Year 2014

Through 2013–2014 the company suffered through several ailments, chiefly
the completion of some lucrative contracts without sustaining new business,
an accompanying drop in relatively more profitable smart metering sales,
and malaise in the utility industry due to higher fuel and environmental
compliance costs, gas-fired plant conversions, and other capital needs. At
last, as FY2015 and FY2016 unfold, the company has overcome some of
these issues (the strong dollar is still a problem) and is now forecasting a
business recovery through the period.

FY2014 revenues and profits were largely consistent with FY2013 at
$1.97 billion in sales and $13.7 million in profits, respectively. These figures
suggest a company that's a better idea than it is a business. But good industry
fundamentals and a resumed interest among utilities to cut costs (another
new trend—low-cost leased individual solar systems—are a contributing

factor) have caused a resumption in demand to what the company expects to be a 5 percent annual revenue growth rate and possibly higher through the remainder of the decade. Indeed, bookings were up 22 percent in 2014 and year-end backlog was a full 39 percent ahead of the previous year. Efficiency improvements are expected to drive earnings from a paltry 35 cents per share in 2014 to $1.30 in 2015, close to $2.00 in 2016, and above $3.00 by the end of the decade. The company also authorized a third consecutive $50 million share buyback in early 2015—a substantial commitment for a company with a $1.4 billion market capitalization.

Reasons to Buy

Can you picture a day when you might manage your energy consumption, device by device, in your home using your smartphone? Even if you're away from the home? And the day when utilities can monitor usage in real time to shift supply of a resource such as electricity that virtually cannot be stored? A day when you (or your apps) work together with your utility to optimize energy use from all sources at all times of the day? A day when solar energy generated from one locale on a sunny day is moved to another with clouds and rain?

If you believe that the need for managed energy efficiency will only grow in the future, Itron is a good place to be. As utilities modernize, reduce costs, and replace infrastructure, Itron products and networks will be in the sweet spot. Internationally, utilities are adding infrastructure, as well as replacing it, and Itron is positioned well for that, too. Public policy will provide some tailwinds too, as the European Union is committed to reduce energy use by 2020. Recent droughts will probably bode well for water conservation and smart metering as well. Worldwide, only about 12 percent of 2.5 billion meters are "smart" or "advanced."

These are great concepts; the question for investors is obvious: Can they make money? Itron has guided optimistically before and missed. But what they suggest now makes more sense in a better economy with growing and unmet needs for energy and water conservation. We'll bet with them—one more time.

Reasons for Caution

Needless to say, Itron is one of our more risky picks—but in today's markets, we feel there's more risk than usual in a lot of stocks; might as well pick one that has already suffered the bad news and can be had at a relatively low price, right? For sure, companies that sell good ideas don't always grow, particularly if the size of their markets is limited or they are particularly conservative about spending money; that might describe the utility industry, which has been spending money on a lot of other things lately, including new gas-fired plants. Energy credits and subsidies are always subject to change. The next two years will be a test of whether the company can size its business properly to the conditions, bring more good ideas to more markets successfully, and execute in general.

If not—out to the woodshed we go.

SECTOR: **Information Technology** ❑ BETA COEFFICIENT: **1.79** ❑ 10-YEAR COMPOUND EARN-INGS PER-SHARE GROWTH: **6.0%** ❑ 10-YEAR COMPOUND DIVIDENDS PER-SHARE GROWTH: **NA**

		2007	2008	2009	2010	2011	2012	2013	2014
Revenues (mil)		1,464	1,909	1,687	2,259	2,434	2,178	1,949	1,971
Net income (mil)		87.3	117.6	44.3	133.9	156.3	128.5	15.0	13.7
Earnings per share		2.78	3.36	1.15	3.27	3.85	2.71	0.36	0.35
Dividends per share		—	—	—	—	—	—	—	—
Cash flow per share		4.24	4.96	2.53	4.85	5.56	4.84	2.60	2.93
Price:	high	112.9	109.3	69.5	81.9	64.4	50.3	48.4	43.7
	low	51.2	34.3	40.1	52.0	26.9	33.3	37.0	32.3

Website: *www.itron.com*

GROWTH AND INCOME

The J.M. Smucker Company

Ticker symbol: SJM (NYSE) ❑ S&P rating: NR ❑ Value Line financial strength rating: A++ ❑ Current yield: 2.2% ❑ Dividend raises, past 10 years: 10

Company Profile

"With a name like Smucker's, it has to be good!" This ad copy says it all about this eastern Ohio–based firm, a leading manufacturer of jams, jellies, and other processed foods for years. Thanks in part to divestitures from the Procter & Gamble food division and other companies, it has grown itself into a premier player in the packaged food industry.

Smucker manufactures and markets products under its own name, as well as under a number of other household names such as Crisco, Folgers, Millstone, Knudsen, Hungry Jack, Eagle, Carnation, Pillsbury, Jif (why not sell the peanut butter if they sell the jelly?), and naturally, Goober (a combination of peanut butter and jelly in a single jar), and Uncrustables (why not just sell the whole sandwich?). The company also produces and distributes Dunkin' Donuts coffee and produces an assortment of cooking oils, toppings, juices, and baking ingredients. The company has revitalized such brands as Folgers and Jif through improved marketing, channel relationships, and better focus on the packaging and delivery of these brands to the customer. In the coffee business, for example, for custom blends, K-Cup offerings, etc., "Coffee Served Your Way" is their motto, and there are new convenience packages for peanut butter, jelly, and other spreads as well. Organic brands, most of which have been around for a while, include Santa Cruz Organic, Smucker's Natural, Laura Scudder's, and a handful of others; they also produce a line of sugar-free, reduced sugar, and sugar alternative products. Overall, the company aims to sell the number one brand in the various markets it serves.

The company is currently organized into three reporting segments: Retail Coffee (38 percent of revenues, 54 percent of profits), Retail Consumer Foods (39 percent revenues, 34 percent profits), and International, Foodservice, and Natural Foods (which contributes the remaining 23 percent of revenues and 12 percent of profits). Operations are centered in the United States, Canada, and Europe, with about 10 percent of sales coming from overseas.

In early 2015 the company completed the $5.8 billion acquisition of pet food and snack maker Big Heart Pet Brands, known more for their brands than the company name itself, including Meow Mix, Milk Bone, 9Lives, and others. The acquisition is sizeable, growing the total business by more than a third. The strategy is to add another premium brand portfolio in the more rapidly advancing pet food market. The estimated "future" portfolio is 38 percent food, 32 percent coffee, and 30 percent pet food.

Even as a nearly $6 billion a year enterprise, the company still retains the feel of a family business, with brothers Tim and Richard Smucker sharing the CEO responsibilities as chairman and president respectively. Their annual report is the only one we've come across that has recipes in it. Last but not least, the J.M. Smucker Company Store and Café located just outside of Orrville, Ohio, is a national treasure and a classic case study in branding and brand image.

Financial Highlights, Fiscal Year 2014

Headwinds in the form of high coffee prices and intense competition in that market, and to a degree, competition everywhere lead to a relatively poor performance in FY2014, with revenues down about 3 percent and net earnings down a heftier 8 percent. Against a backdrop of changing consumer tastes and competition that isn't going away anytime soon, these figures would have caused considerable concern. But brand strength is brand strength, and execution is execution: The large acquisition adds more to what is already shaping up as a turnaround year in FY2015 with pre-acquisition revenues projected up about 4 percent with net earnings unchanged. Profits gain speed in FY2016 with revenues projected up about 3 percent (on a larger base) and net income up 11–12 percent. In actual numbers, the acquisition adds $2.3 billion to the top line and about $160–170 million to the bottom line. The company is issuing nearly 20 million shares to finance the acquisition (which is usually how it finances such acquisitions), but per-share earnings actually march well ahead of the total profit advance indicating some financial leverage. Per-share earnings projections are up 9 percent in FY2015 and 11–12 percent in FY2016.

Reasons to Buy

This is a very well-managed company with an excellent and lasting reputation in its markets. In recent years, it has a proven track record in buying and revitalizing key brands, the most prominent being former Procter & Gamble food brands, Sara Lee food-service coffee and beverage brands, and a few International Multifoods brands. We expect this trend to continue. The company's aggressive moves into coffee and other beverages were well timed and have provided a boost to the bottom line; we hope that story is repeated with the Big Heart acquisition.

The base for steady growth in cash flows and investor returns is well established over the long term. Steady and safe, Smucker is the ever-improving peanut butter and jelly sandwich of the investing landscape.

Reasons for Caution

The prepared-food business is very sensitive in the short term to commodity and energy costs. As the company relies more and more on coffee products for earnings growth, it will find itself exposed to instability in the cost of raw materials and transportation and to changes in consumer tastes; both have provided headwinds in the near term. Yes, these are costs that also affect all of their competitors, but Smucker is in competition with a number of low-margin brands and has customers (such as Walmart) that have enormous buying power. Smucker will need to rely on brand strength and breadth should the economy slow again. And we do respect changing consumer tastes and the emergence of the Millennial generation, and hope the company can extend its healthy and wholesome image into this group, too.

We do wonder if the company has strayed just a bit outside of its traditional feel-good, relatively healthy or at least wholesome, peanut-butter-and-jelly base. While you can't grow a business much on peanut butter and jelly alone, ventures into pet foods, donut-shop coffee, and the like may not be such a good fit with what has made Smucker's taste so good up to now. We had the same question about its relatively recent additions in coffee—pet food adds another question but also some diversity and growth to the mix.

SECTOR: Consumer Staples ❑ **BETA COEFFICIENT: 0.61** ❑ **10-YEAR COMPOUND EARNINGS PER-SHARE GROWTH: 10.0%** ❑ **10-YEAR COMPOUND DIVIDENDS PER-SHARE GROWTH: 10.0%**

	2007	2008	2009	2010	2011	2012	2013	2014
Revenues (mil)	2,525	3,758	4,605	4,826	5,526	5,897	5,611	5,450
Net income (mil)	178.9	321.4	520.3	566.5	535.6	584	588	540
Earnings per share	3.15	3.77	4.15	4.79	4.73	5.37	5.64	5.30
Dividends per share	1.22	1.31	1.40	1.68	1.88	2.06	2.32	2.50
Cash flow per share	4.42	3.73	5.60	7.06	6.75	7.85	8.30	7.75
Price: high	64.3	56.7	62.7	66.3	80.3	89.4	114.7	107.1
low	46.6	37.2	34.1	53.3	61.2	70.5	86.5	87.1

Website: *www.smuckers.com*

Johnson & Johnson

Ticker symbol: JNJ (NYSE) □ S&P rating: AAA □ Value Line financial strength rating: A++ □ Current yield: 2.8 percent □ Dividend raises, past 10 years: 10

Company Profile

"Caring for the world, one person at a time" is the slogan of Johnson & Johnson, one of the largest and most comprehensive health-care "family of companies" in the world. JNJ offers a broad line of consumer products, over-the-counter drugs, and various other medical devices and diagnostic equipment.

With total FY2014 sales of over $74 billion, the company has three reporting segments: Consumer Health Care ($145 billion in FY2014 sales), Medical Devices and Diagnostics ($27.5 billion), and Pharmaceuticals ($32.3 billion). In those segments, Johnson & Johnson has more than 250 operating companies in 60 countries, selling some 50,000 products in more than 175 countries. Among Johnson & Johnson's premier assets are its well-entrenched brand names, which are widely known in the United States as well as abroad. As a marketer, JNJ's reputation for quality has enabled it to build strong ties to commercial health-care providers.

In the Consumer segment, the company's vast portfolio of well-known trade names includes Band-Aid adhesive bandages; Tylenol; Stayfree, Carefree, and Sure & Natural feminine hygiene products; Mylanta; Pepcid AC; Motrin; Sudafed; Zyrtec; Neosporin; Neutrogena; Johnson's baby powder, shampoo, and oil; Listerine; and Reach toothbrushes. Names in the Pharmaceuticals segment are less well-known but include major entries in the areas of antiseptics, antipsychotics, gastroenterology, immunology, neurology, hematology, contraceptives, oncology, pain management, and many others distributed both through consumer and health-care professional channels. Medical Devices and Diagnostics products include professionally used cardiovascular, orthopedic, diabetic, neurologic, and surgical products among others.

The company is typically fairly active with acquisitions, acquiring small niche players to strengthen its overall product offering.

Financial Highlights, Fiscal Year 2014

Johnson & Johnson continues to own a dominant and stable franchise in a secure and lucrative industry. We like the model of steady, recurring income from solid consumer brands such as Tylenol combined with more aggressive and lucrative ventures into pharmaceuticals and surgical products. Small acquisitions, new drug releases (especially a new Hepatitis C drug), and increased emphasis on biopharmaceuticals led to a 14.9 percent FY2014 advance in the Pharmaceuticals business, while modest organic growth in the other two segments was for the most part offset by currency effects.

In total, FY2014 revenues grew just over 4 percent (the company suggests it would have been just over 6 percent without currency effects) and earnings grew a more robust 7.7 percent, reflecting a more profitable mix and efficiency improvements. Persistent and moderate share buybacks and dividend increases gave shareholders their fair share of these advances. However, future guidance, always conservative for J & J, now calls for slight decreases in both revenues and earnings for FY2015, as currency effects bite hard, and with no major drug releases on the near-term horizon. The company suggests that, due especially to the Pharma business success in FY2014, comparisons will be tougher going forward. That all said, after a lackluster FY2015, the company expects to resume a mid-single–digits growth pace for both revenues and earnings in FY2016, with corresponding benefits paid to shareholders.

Reasons to Buy

A term we don't hear much anymore in the investment arena is "blue chip." A name taken from the highest-value poker chip on the table, it was used to describe a stock into which you could put your money without fear. A blue-chip stock was where you put money that you would normally put in a bank, if banks would only pay dividends and occasionally offer you more than a toaster as an incentive to stick around. Johnson & Johnson has been a blue chip for as long as there have been blue chips.

JNJ continues to be a conservatively run company whose growth prospects are on the lower end of this book's scale, but clearly the company has great appeal in the investment community. Even if it's more often unexciting for the growth and momentum investor, JNJ's business model reminds us of the blue chips—steady earnings and cash flow combined with a healthy dividend and share repurchases, leading to very gratifying total shareholder returns. It's a "sleep at night" stock with a decent track record for shareholder "raises."

Reasons for Caution

While we still think JNJ is a good, steady horse for a relatively long race, it has picked up some speed of late, increasing the chance of getting winded somewhere along the way. The P/E, a figure we don't rely on heavily but do look at, has expanded from 14–15 to the 16–17 range, adding a bit of downside risk to the mix. It's still a good horse, but some investors might want to wait for better odds—a lower price point—before making a bet. Too, we worry that the company could get a little more "acquisition-happy" to fuel growth. That all said, this company should fare better than most on a "sloppy track" market downturn.

SECTOR: **Health Care** ▫ BETA COEFFICIENT: **0.55** ▫ 10-YEAR COMPOUND EARNINGS PER-SHARE GROWTH: **8.5%** ▫ 10-YEAR COMPOUND DIVIDENDS PER-SHARE GROWTH: **11.5%**

	2007	2008	2009	2010	2011	2012	2013	2014
Revenues (mil)	61,095	63,747	61,897	61,587	65,030	67,224	71,312	74,311
Net income (mil)	10,576	12,949	12,906	13,279	13,867	14,345	15,576	17,105
Earnings per share	4.15	4.57	4.63	4.76	5.00	5.10	5.52	5.97
Dividends per share	1.62	1.80	1.93	2.11	2.25	2.40	2.59	2.76
Cash flow per share	5.23	5.70	5.69	5.90	6.25	6.45	7.10	7.90
Price: high	68.8	72.8	65.9	66.2	66.3	72.7	96.0	106.5
low	59.7	52.1	61.9	56.9	64.3	61.7	70.3	96.1

Website: *www.jnj.com*

CONSERVATIVE GROWTH

Johnson Controls Inc.

Ticker symbol: JCI (NYSE) ▫ S&P rating: vBBB+ ▫ Value Line financial strength rating: A ▫ Current yield: 2.1% ▫ Dividend raises, past 10 years: 9

Company Profile

The name may only describe a portion of the business, but Johnson Controls is a large manufacturer of automotive parts and subassemblies, heating, ventilation, and air conditioning (HVAC) and other energy controls, and an assortment of battery technologies and products. Its products are found in more than 12 million homes, 1 million commercial buildings, and are installed in more than 50 million new vehicles every year. The company operates in four segments: Automotive Experience, Building Efficiency, Global WorkPlace Solutions, and Power Solutions.

Automotive Experience (51 percent of FY2014 revenues, 31 percent of profits) is one of the world's largest automotive suppliers, providing seating and overhead systems, door and instrument panels, and floor consoles. Customers include virtually every major automaker in the world, including newer startups and plants in China and U.S plants operated by foreign automakers. The business, including affiliates, has 240 plants and produces automotive interior systems for original equipment manufacturers (OEMs) and operates in 33 countries worldwide. Additionally, the business has partially owned affiliates in Asia, Europe, North America, and South America—in all supplying the manufacture of more than 50 million cars each year.

Building Efficiency (33 percent of revenues, 32 percent of profits) is the original business at its founding in 1900 and the source of the company's name. The unit is a global leader in delivering integrated control systems, mechanical equipment, services, and solutions designed to improve the comfort, safety, and energy efficiency of nonresidential buildings and residential properties with operations in more than 150 countries. Revenues come from new construction, technical services, and the replacement and upgrade of controls and/or HVAC mechanical equipment in the existing buildings and "smart buildings" market.

The Global WorkPlace Solutions business, still a part of the Building Efficiency segment for financial reporting purposes, provides integrated facility energy management services for many of the world's largest companies. The operation manages 1.8 billion square feet of facility space in 75 countries.

The Power Solutions business (15 percent of revenues, 37 percent of profits) produces traditional lead-acid automotive batteries as well as more advanced metal hydride and lithium-ion batteries for "Start-Stop," electric, and hybrid vehicles, and battery recycling services. The segment serves both automotive OEM and the general vehicle battery aftermarket.

Johnson has been active in acquisitions and in the forming of partnerships: In 2014 it acquired ventilation products provider Air Distribution Technologies; in early 2015 it announced a global joint venture with Japan's Hitachi, which will expand the product offering and geographic footprint in HVAC and refrigeration product lines. The company expects a $3 billion revenue boost from the venture.

The company is also driving a major energy-saving retrofit of the Empire State Building—a major project in its own right, not only reducing energy costs 38 percent for its owners, the Empire State Realty Trust, (a new

100 Best stock this year), but also providing a valuable showcase for other building retrofits.

Financial Highlights, Fiscal Year 2014

In the past few years, all three of JCI's businesses have come into favor. The automotive industry and its aftermarket have recovered nicely, and most of the geographies supported by its building equipment and management businesses have done well, although Europe lags in the automotive business, Asia lags somewhat in the construction business, and the strong dollar remains in the way.

FY2014 revenues flattened a bit due to the divestiture of an automotive interior electronics business early in the year, and growth percentages suffered from strong compares to the FY2011–2013 period as the auto market regained traction during those years. Reported revenues advanced less that 1 percent, but the real story was profitability—margin improvements due to volume, operational, and pricing improvements, especially in the Building Efficiency business, led to a healthy 17.5 percent gain in net earnings. Revenues look to be flat to slightly down due to currency effects and a continued "topping" in the auto business through FY2016, but operating margin gains in the 1–2 percent range, substantial on a 7.5 percent base, look to move earnings forward more than 10 percent each year. The profitability gains appear to be across all parts of the business—a good sign. Dividends have been raised at an expanding rate, and the company continues to retire shares at a 1–2 percent annual rate.

Reasons to Buy

JCI was one of the great recovery stories coming out of the Great Recession and continues to be well positioned for the auto industry and building industry recoveries worldwide. While cyclical, its place in the auto industry supply chain is secure, and we like the worldwide footprint. We also think JCI is a strong long-term play in energy efficiency, with leadership both in building energy controls and in batteries and battery technologies—these should do well in the long term. Too, we like the company's more solid positioning in the operating portion of building management—not just selling equipment, but a steady revenue and income-producing service. And one more thing: The company seems to be overcoming a slight difficulty in creating a strong brand and image for itself; its use of the Empire State Building project as a marketing reference signals better times ahead for its marketing and branding efforts. Overall, the company is well managed, with an ever-greater portion of its success dropping to the bottom line—and on to shareholders.

Reasons for Caution

A significant portion of JCI's success continues to be tied to the automotive industry. Currently the domestic auto industry is selling 16–17 million cars a year, but if this drops back to the 12 million pace experienced during the Great Recession or anything close, this company (and many others) will suffer. In addition, many of these business lines are low margin, as evidenced by the portion of revenues and profits they represent, as shared. JCI's business has a strong cyclical component, both in domestic and foreign markets.

SECTOR: **Industrials** ❑ BETA COEFFICIENT: **1.68** ❑ 10-YEAR COMPOUND EARNINGS PER-SHARE GROWTH: **8.5%** ❑ 10-YEAR COMPOUND DIVIDENDS PER-SHARE GROWTH: **12.0%**

	2007	2008	2009	2010	2011	2012	2013	2014
Revenues (mil)	34,624	38,062	28,497	34,305	40,833	41,995	42,730	42,828
Net income (mil)	1,252	1,400	281	1,365	1,665	1,749	1,833	2,153
Earnings per share	2.09	2.33	0.47	2.00	2.42	2.54	2.66	3.19
Dividends per share	0.44	0.52	0.52	0.52	0.72	0.74	0.76	0.88
Cash flow per share	3.34	3.63	1.48	3.00	3.45	3.68	4.07	4.67
Price: high	44.5	36.5	28.3	40.2	42.9	35.9	51.9	52.5
low	28.1	13.6	8.4	25.6	24.3	23.4	30.3	38.6

Website: *www.johnsoncontrols.com*

Kimberly-Clark Corporation

Ticker symbol: KMB (NYSE) ▫ S&P rating: A ▫ Value Line financial strength rating: A++ ▫ Current yield: 3.3% ▫ Dividend raises, past 10 years: 10

Company Profile

Kimberly-Clark develops, manufactures, and markets a full line of personal care products, mostly based on paper and paper technologies. Well-known for its ubiquitous Kleenex brand tissues, KMB also is a strong player in bath tissue, diapers, feminine products, incontinence products, industrial and professional—all primarily paper-based cleaning and sanitation products. The company was founded in 1872 and is headquartered today near Dallas, TX, with a historical, technology, and manufacturing base in the Fox River Valley in Wisconsin. There are manufacturing facilities in 38 countries serving customers in 175 countries; about 53 percent of the company's sales originate outside North America.

After a major spinoff described shortly, the company now operates in three segments: Personal Care, Consumer Tissue, and K-C Professional & Other. The Personal Care segment (now 49 percent of FY2014 revenues) provides disposable diapers, training and youth pants, and swim pants; baby wipes; and feminine and incontinence care products, and related products. Brand names include Huggies, Pull-Ups, Little Swimmers, GoodNites, Kotex, Kotex Lightdays, Depend, and Poise. Baby care is the single largest business category with $6 billion in revenues—about 28 percent of the business—mostly sold under the Huggies brand. The diaper brands, including adult versions Poise and Depend, are among the faster-growing businesses.

The Consumer Tissue segment (now 34 percent) offers facial and bathroom tissue, paper towels, napkins, and related products for household use under the Kleenex, Scott, Cottonelle, Viva, Andrex, Scottex, Hakle, and Page brands. Ah (choo), there's Kleenex, a $2 billion business in itself, almost 10 percent of the total. But Scott is no softie either, accounting for another 10 percent.

The K-C Professional & Other segment (17 percent) provides paper products for the away-from-home, that is, commercial/institutional marketplace under Kimberly-Clark, Kleenex, Scott, WypAll, Kimtech, KleenGuard, Kimcare, and Jackson brand names.

On October 31, 2014, the company completed the spinoff of what was the fourth segment of the business: the Health Care segment, which became a separate new company called Halyard Health. Halyard offers KMB's former lines of disposable health-care products, such as surgical drapes and gowns, infection control products, face masks, exam gloves, respiratory products, pain management products, and other disposable medical products. This segment accounted for about 8 percent of Kimberly-Clark's FY2013 business and some 16,500 of 57,000 employees. The spinoff allows KMB to focus on more core and more manufacturing-oriented businesses.

On the innovation front, KMB is working on personalized "MyKleenex" tissue packaging (yes, you can create your own Kleenex boxes with your name, pictures, and designs), fast-dissolving Scott toilet tissue, and new Huggies sun care lotions and dispensers for "little swimmers."

Financial Highlights, Fiscal Year 2014

The Halyard spinoff and continued currency headwinds made meaningful comparisons challenging for FY2014. Halyard accounted for about $1.7 billion in revenue, so if you add that back into the $19.7 billion reported for FY2014, that would give total FY2014 adjusted revenues of $21.4 billion—about 1.3 percent ahead of FY2013, about 2 percent without currency effects. Net income was hit by a $462 million balance sheet writedown due to currency devaluation in Venezuela as well as about $166 million in restructuring charges and a loss of only about $50 million in net income from the Halyard spinoff; add these back, and you get $2,154 million in net income, up less than 1 percent from FY2013 on a roughly comparable basis.

New product developments, international expansion, and a highly successful cost reduction and restructuring program known as "FORCE" will be with us through FY2016, although its biggest costs savings, some $500 million, may now be past. FY2015 sales, deeply impacted by currency, are projected to fall some 3–5 percent, but earnings, helped along by FORCE and lower commodity prices, are expected to rise 5 percent but not back to 2013 levels; revenues return to the growth track, approaching $20 billion in FY2016 with profits slightly ahead of FY2015. Again, the full net effects of the Halyard spinoff make these comparisons more difficult.

Cash returns to investors should continue to grow, perhaps at a higher rate into FY2016. The company will probably repurchase $1 billion in stock this year; together with the spinoff, which reduced share count some 60 million, share counts will have dropped some 35 percent in the past ten years and should continue to decline.

Reasons to Buy

Kimberly-Clark has shown itself to be a steady and solid business and investment performer in all kinds of economic climates. The Health Care segment spinoff looks to be a successful disposition of a low-margin business with different end markets; the remaining business should be more focused and easier to manage. The relatively high yield and strong track record of raising dividends and buying back shares is a definite plus. Strong cash flow has financed strategic business investments, including international expansion in emerging markets, product innovations, and strategic marketing. The company continues to be rock solid, with a microscopic beta of 0.20 and with shareholder interests a consistent priority.

The company has stellar brands and should do well expanding them into overseas markets. Also, compared to some peers, especially Procter & Gamble, the company is less inclined to go for "glamour" markets such as cosmetics, choosing instead to add to margins through operating efficiencies and scale. Safety-oriented investors may find this approach preferable, and the company gets top ratings for financial strength and price stability.

Reasons for Caution

While the paper products business is steady, it isn't too easy to see where additional growth will come from, even with more innovation and brand-strengthening activity. The company, rightly so, is targeting international expansion, but competition and currency fluctuation make the results far from certain. The cost of pulp and paper raw materials will always be volatile. Companies like KMB have sometimes come to rely on acquisitions for growth; KMB has, so far, largely resisted this temptation but that could change. Finally, investors and the markets have recognized KMB's consistent excellence and continue to bid up the share price in response to all the good earnings news.

SECTOR: **Consumer Staples** ◻ BETA COEFFICIENT: **0.20** ◻ 10-YEAR COMPOUND EARNINGS PER-SHARE GROWTH: **3.0%** ◻ 10-YEAR COMPOUND DIVIDENDS PER-SHARE GROWTH: **8.5%**

		2007	2008	2009	2010	2011	2012	2013	2014
Revenues (mil)		18,266	19,415	19,115	19,746	20,846	21,063	21,182	19,724
Net income (mil)		1,862	1,698	1,884	1,843	1,591	1,750	2,142	1,476
Earnings per share		4.25	4.14	4.52	4.45	3.99	4.42	5.53	3.91
Dividends per share		2.08	2.27	2.38	2.58	2.76	2.92	3.24	3.36
Cash flow per share		6.34	5.98	6.40	6.53	6.78	6.70	7.89	6.40
Price:	high	72.8	69.7	67.0	67.2	74.1	88.3	111.7	118.8
	low	63.8	50.3	43.1	58.3	61.0	70.5	83.9	102.8

Website: *www.kimberly-clark.com*

The Kroger Company

Ticker symbol: KR (NYSE) ❑ S&P rating: BBB ❑ Value Line financial strength rating: A ❑ Current yield: 1.0% ❑ Dividend raises, past 10 years: 8

Company Profile

We thought we were cruising down the right aisle with our pick of the Kroger Company, first for the *100 Best Stocks* 2014 list. But to pick a grocery-based retailer and have it come in third place overall on the 2015 *100 Best* gainers list with a 77.3 percent total return for the year? Never would have guessed a trip to the butcher counter would have wrapped up one like that to take home. In a word, wow—now the question is, what could possibly be in store for 2016?

Kroger is the nation's largest retail grocery store operator, with about 2,625 supermarkets and multidepartment stores, 782 convenience stores, and 326 specialty jewelry stores operated around the country. Supermarket operations account for about 94 percent of total revenue and are located in 34 states with a concentration in the Midwest (where it was founded) and in the South and West, where it grew mostly by acquisition. The company is dominant in the markets it serves, with a number one or two market-share position in 36 of its 44 major markets.

Kroger operates through a series of store brands many of you will be familiar with but probably did not associate with the Kroger name, including King Soopers, City Market, Fred Meyer, Fry's, Ralphs, Dillons, Smith's, Baker's, Food 4 Less, and an assortment of others totaling about two dozen business names. In 2014 the company completed its merger with Harris Teeter, a large supermarket chain mainly in the Mid-Atlantic and Southeast regions.

The typical Kroger supermarket is full service and well appointed with higher-margin specialty departments such as health foods, seafood, floral, and other perishables. The Fred Meyer stores carry a large assortment of general merchandise in addition to groceries, turning them into modern-era big-box department stores; the company has 128 stores in all that meet this format, mostly in the West. There are also 146 "warehouse" stores under the Food 4 Less brand and 78 "marketplace" stores with expanded offerings similar to Fred Meyer to complement the supermarkets. About 1,330 "supermarket fuel centers" and 1,950 pharmacies round out the supermarket picture. Finally, the company has a considerable presence in manufacturing its own store-branded food items, with 38 such plants located around the country and estimates that just over 25 percent of revenues and 40 percent of unit volumes come from in-house brands. The company also plays well in the organic subsegment, growing natural and organic sales roughly 15 percent annually compared to an overall growth of 10 percent in this market U.S. wide. Kroger is also a leader in applying the latest smartphone technologies to the grocery shopping experience; they estimate that their shoppers spend 43 percent more time on their mobile apps than other grocery shoppers.

The company's appealingly simple operating philosophy is summed up in three words: "Simple. Consistent. Differentiator." The mantra continues: "Products I want, plus a little. Great people. Good prices. 'I want to return.'" We usually don't go too far with slogans and mantras found on websites and investor presentations, but we liked this one a lot.

Financial Highlights, Fiscal Year 2014

Kroger boasts that same-store supermarket sales have grown for 41 consecutive quarters, and this is a good track record particularly in light of the Great Recession and more recently, heightened competition from the likes of Wal-Mart, Target, and others. Same-store sales grew about 5.2 percent in FY2014, a healthy jump from FY2013's 3 percent. Revenues in total advanced a very healthy 10.3 percent—and for once, we can chuck the line "hurt by currency headwinds"—Kroger is 100 percent U.S. based. Operational efficiencies, critical mass, more house brand sales, and a leveling off of commodity food prices gave strength to gross, operating, and net margins. Net profit rose an even better 18 percent, with per-share earnings, helped along by a 4 percent buyback, up a full 23 percent. The company projects a continued same-store sales increase in the 3–4 percent range, a slight expansion in operating margins, and net per share in the $3.80–$3.90 range, up another 11 percent from current levels, on a 3 percent total sales gain (implying not too much store expansion). Although per-share earnings gains are expected to slow a bit into 2016, current trends look largely to continue, a positive sign for a $110 billion company. Kroger's own shares continue to top its shopping list; they have now retired a third of their float since 2005. The dividend, which commenced in 2006, should also continue to rise, perhaps a bit faster as the company slows its share repurchases in 2016.

Reasons to Buy

Kroger has done a good job in a tough market. Major discount retailers like Wal-Mart and Target have stepped into the grocery business with a fairly significant price advantage, yet so far Kroger has been able to fend them off by focusing on product breadth, the shopping experience, and strategic price reductions.

We also like the Fred Meyer quality grocery-plus-department-store format, a more pleasant and balanced shopping experience than either Walmart or Target and a format that Kroger would do well to roll out nationwide. The company also has a good toehold on the low-price warehouse food business with Food 4 Less.

This success has finally been recognized in the share price, which too has been helped along by the dramatic share buybacks. Kroger has surprised us by becoming something of a momentum stock in today's market. All told, this is a well-managed company that continues to dominate its niches.

Reasons for Caution

You can't think "full-service grocer" without raising the fear of competition from discounters, and the recent recession trained a lot of shoppers to look for the lowest possible prices, even if they had to go to two or three stores to complete a week's shopping. If the conventional grocery store format is condemned to the dustbin of retail history, Kroger could be vulnerable, but we feel it has enough clout and experience in new formats to adapt. The razor-thin 1.5 percent profit margins characteristic of this industry leave little room for error, though they did tick up to 1.6 percent in 2014. The fact that the stock market has finally recognized Kroger's success makes the shares more volatile and less of a bargain—shop carefully.

SECTOR: **Retail** ❑ BETA COEFFICIENT: **0.79** ❑ 10-YEAR COMPOUND EARNINGS PER-SHARE
GROWTH: **9.0%** ❑ 10-YEAR COMPOUND DIVIDENDS PER-SHARE GROWTH: **10.5%**

	2007	2008	2009	2010	2011	2012	2013	2014
Revenues (bil)	70.2	76.0	76.7	82.1	90.4	96.7	98.5	108.5
Net income (mil)	1,181	1,249	1,122	1,118	1,192	1,423	1,445	1,757
Earnings per share	1.69	1.90	1.73	1.74	2.00	2.63	2.85	3.52
Dividends per share	0.30	0.36	0.37	0.40	0.44	0.53	0.63	0.70
Cash flow per share	3.83	4.15	4.12	4.38	5.05	5.98	6.10	7.63
Price: high	31.9	31.0	26.9	24.1	25.8	27.1	43.8	65.0
low	22.9	22.3	19.4	19.1	21.1	21.0	25.2	35.1

Website: *www.kroger.com*

`AGGRESSIVE GROWTH`

Macy's, Inc.

Ticker symbol: M (NYSE) □ S&P rating: BBB+ □ Value Line financial strength rating: B++ □ Current yield: 1.9% □ Dividend raises, past 10 years: 7

Company Profile

Macy's is now by far the largest operator of department stores in the U.S. The company operates mainly under two brand names, Macy's and Bloomingdale's, and operates, after a recent closure of 22 stores, about 823 stores in 45 states, Puerto Rico, and Guam. Macy's has been assembled over the years from a large assortment of famed department store predecessors including Marshall Field, May, and a portfolio of names once under ownership of Federated Department Stores, including Lazarus, Weinstocks, Dillard, Abraham & Straus, I. Magnin, and others. The company, in current form, was assembled after Federated emerged from bankruptcy in 1992.

In addition to department stores, Macy's operates its own credit card operations and an internal merchandising group that, among other things, develops or licenses and markets a number of familiar proprietary brands such as Charter Club, Club Room, Hotel Collection, Tommy Hilfiger, Ellen Tracy, the Martha Stewart Collection, and more recently, Finish Line activewear. Private-label brands continue to account for 20 percent of sales. The company has also embarked on a deliberate strategy to target the "Millennial" age group (born between 1982 and 2001) with selected styles and brands—an important growth strategy as the department store demographic typically leaves this group out. Macy's has unabashedly declared that it is focused on an "upscale niche," with greater emphasis on the "hottest" brands and special "customer amenities" such as personal shoppers, "outstanding" fitting rooms and lounges, and international visitors centers.

The company also operates 90 specialty stores including outlets and furniture stores. The sales mix for Macy's and Bloomingdale's is approximately 23 percent feminine apparel; 38 percent feminine shoes, cosmetics, intimate apparel and accessories; 23 percent men's and children's; and 16 percent home and miscellaneous. Macy's acquired luxury beauty products and spa retail chain Bluemercury, with 62 outlets, in early 2015. International expansion is also a growth vector, with a Bloomingdale's store in Dubai and more to come in that region; Macy's online ships to 100 countries.

The online presence, macys.com, continues to grow and is strategically more integrated with the sales process, what it calls "omnichannel" shopping.

It's easy to shop online, then see the product, pick it up, and importantly, pay the online price at the store. Such store pickups are thought to lead to more sales when at the store picking up merchandise. Also, omnichannel shopping expands available stock, colors, and sizes and produces logistical and supply-chain efficiencies, as orders can be flexibly filled from nearby stores if that makes sense; all stores support each other and the online channel, too.

Financial Highlights, Fiscal Year 2014

Macy's continues to ride a combination of economic recovery and a series of internal operational improvements to find a successful new growth tra-jectory in a business that many had given up on. Same-store sales ticked upward about 1.4 percent, which combined with the aforementioned store closures to produce an 0.8 percent increase in sales. Better news was found in operating margins, which ticked up from 13.6 percent to a ten-year high of 14.0 percent, in part reflecting operational improvements. That led to an earnings gain of 3.4 percent; a substantial 6 percent share buyback drove per-share earnings forward 10 percent. The story will be much the same through FY2016, with 7–10 percent annual per-share earnings increases on the back of relatively modest 1–2 percent sales gains.

Reasons to Buy

Justifiably perhaps, most investors would perceive Macy's and the depart-ment store business to be yesterday's news, as big-box retailers and the Internet have taken over. True, those players have snatched important parts of the retail business, but the department store idea has made a comeback with more affluent, brand-conscious, and experience-conscious shoppers. The stores have been upgraded, merchandise assortments made more exciting and targeted to younger buyers, and service has improved. Merchandise assortments have been localized and are now more exciting and edgier and more aimed at the younger set. Department stores aren't just for grandma any longer; more and more they're being tuned for the Millennial generation. The company has managed its image and product well and has turned the new interest and a more scientific approach to management and execution into solid bottom-line results.

The integration of online and physical stores into a unified experience is one of the best such efforts we've seen. New technologies, such as large-screen digital displays and tablets in the hands of store personnel, are expanding the sales experience. We think the merchandise localization efforts (referred to by the company as "My Macy's") are working well, as is the "omnichannel" integration of inventories across the physical and online systems. The company has learned a lot from the past seven years of experimentation with both initiatives, and is starting to reap the rewards as all stores and store inventories are now online with the omnichannel strategy. In sum, we find a lot to like about the company's strategy and, more recently, its execution. It has been quite successful in garnering more profit out of a low-growth business. Cash flow continues to almost double reported per-share earnings and, through dividend increases and large share buybacks, Macy's continues to lure investors through its front doors.

Reasons for Caution

The economy, of course, is always a risk, and any return to higher levels of unemployment, foreclosures, taxes, or any other factors that would make customers feel less flush will hurt. Macy's still relies heavily on promotional discounts and special sale events, which have probably become habitual shopping practice among many customers; we suspect that relatively few customers actually pay full price for most of what they buy. That, of course, puts a limit on achievable top-line growth. While Macy's is increasing its appeal to the younger set, the Internet is still a big contender here, although the growth in macys.com is encouraging.

SECTOR: **Retail** ◻ BETA COEFFICIENT: **0.89** ◻ 10-YEAR COMPOUND EARNINGS PER-SHARE GROWTH: **8.0%** ◻ 10-YEAR COMPOUND DIVIDENDS PER-SHARE GROWTH: **13.0%**

	2007	2008	2009	2010	2011	2012	2013	2014
Revenues (mil)	26,313	24,892	23,489	25,003	26,405	27,686	27,931	28,105
Net income (mil)	970	543	595	867	1,238	1,410	1,539	1,591
Earnings per share	2.18	1.29	1.41	2.03	2.88	3.45	4.00	4.40
Dividends per share	0.53	0.20	0.20	0.20	0.35	0.80	0.90	1.13
Cash flow per share	5.42	4.33	4.29	4.77	5.61	6.34	7.01	7.71
Price: high	46.7	28.5	20.6	26.3	33.3	42.2	54.1	66.6
low	24.7	5.1	6.3	15.3	21.7	32.3	36.3	50.1

Website: *www.macys.com*

McCormick & Company, Inc.

Ticker symbol: MKC (NYSE) ❑ S&P rating: A- ❑ Value Line financial strength rating: A+ ❑ Current yield: 2.1% ❑ Dividend raises, past 10 years: 10

Company Profile

As you've probably noted in this year's Introduction and company reviews, we took a hard look at food companies. We probably had too many on our list to begin with, and we now see a sea change in demographics and tastes that are leaving such items as sodas and breakfast cereals on the table. People—especially the emerging Millennial generation—want fresh and healthy, unique and interesting, and customizable. So as we go through our 2016 *100 Best* list, we're keeping the companies that follow these themes the best and that have relatively stronger niches in the industry—as well as the usual strong marketplace and financial performance and solid investor returns—and spicemaker McCormick & Company fills the bill on all counts.

McCormick manufactures, markets, and distributes spices, herbs, seasonings, flavors, and flavor enhancers to consumers and to the global food industry. It is the largest such supplier in the world. Customers range from retail outlets and food manufacturers to foodservice businesses.

McCormick's U.S. Consumer business (about 40 percent of sales), its oldest and largest, manufactures consumer spices, herbs, extracts, proprietary seasoning blends, sauces, and marinades. Spices are sold under an assortment of recognizable brand names: McCormick, Lawry's, Zatarain's, Thai Kitchen, Simply Asia, Club House, Billy Bee, Produce Partners, Golden Dipt, Old Bay, and Mojave. The company estimates its retail market share to be four times the nearest competitor.

Industrial customers include foodservice, food-processing businesses, and retail outlets. The Industrial segment was responsible for 38 percent of sales.

Many of the spices and herbs purchased by the company, such as black pepper, vanilla beans, cinnamon, and herbs and seeds, must be imported from countries such as India, Indonesia, Malaysia, Brazil, and the Malagasy Republic. Other ingredients such as paprika, dehydrated vegetables, onion, garlic, and food ingredients other than spices and herbs originate in the United States.

The company was founded in 1889 and has approximately 10,000 full-time employees in facilities located around the world. Major sales, distribution, and production facilities are located in North America and Europe. Additional facilities are based in Mexico, Central America, Australia, China, Singapore, Thailand, and South Africa. There are innovation centers in 12 countries. The biggest sales components are Americas Consumer (40 percent), Americas Industrial (25 percent), EMEA Consumer (14 percent), EMEA Industrial (8 percent), and Asia-Pacific Consumer (8 percent). The company's products reach consumers in 125 countries. Emerging markets accounted for 17 percent of sales, up from 10 percent three years ago. China is now the number three country, thanks to the 2013 acquisition of Wuhan Asia-Pacific Condiments (WAPC). The recent acquisition of Italian spicemaker Drogheria & Alimentari serves to both expand its international footprint and to bring a few more interesting flavors into the domestic market.

McCormick has been innovating both on the product and on web and media fronts, including more informative print and web content with recipes and other information to spur cooking with spices. Last year, the company reported a 94 percent increase in recipe views on its U.S. website and a 24 percent increase in Europe. They also have an initiative to map your spice tastes by giving you a personalized "FlavorPrint"—then e-mailing you weekly recipes with spice recommendations tailored to that map. Flavor and flavor trend innovations include a new packaging initiative—called Recipe Inspirations—to sell prepackaged spices set to cook a particular meal. Too, they have a place on their website to enter in a singular spice, one that you might like and/or have an abundance of in your pantry; they shoot back recipes for that spice (something we amateur hash slingers have longed for in cookbooks; give me a selection of recipes that use allspice, my favorite spice, for instance). All of these initiatives broaden the market to reach the millions of plain folks like us who weren't born with a wooden spoon. For those who were born with such a spoon, or who acquired one through years of training and experience, there is also a "McCormick for Chefs" page. In short, we like this recipe: dominant brand, effective digital marketing to spice it up. McCormick is one of the best examples we've seen.

Financial Highlights, Fiscal Year 2014

Overall, business continues to respond nicely to new trends for more interesting foods and to a greater likelihood of eating at home after the recession.

Growth has slowed somewhat, but the company reported a 6 percent gain in net earnings on a 3 percent gain in sales, and, helped along by buybacks, per-share earnings rose almost 8 percent. Strong international demand and continuation of current trends should bring similar results in FY2015 with a slight uptick in FY2016; projections call for earnings in the $3.70–$3.80 range per share in FY2016, about 11 percent ahead of today's levels. Dividend increases, which have occurred for 29 straight years now, should continue.

Reasons to Buy

As a strong pure play in the seasonings business, McCormick is the largest branded producer of seasonings in North America, and the largest private-label producer of seasonings as well, giving the company a substantial level of price protection. McCormick is not just a producer, it is also an innovator and a marketer, and we feel they've done the right things to build interest in their products and in their brand. They also do well in specialized niche markets, like Mexico and China. We think they're in the right place as new, fresher, and more tailored, customized, interesting, and international food trends all emerge.

On the consumer side, as amateur cooks ourselves we continue to feel that people would use more spices if they only knew how to use them. The website and its recipe offerings and the prepackaged Recipe Inspirations meal kits will get the less-experienced cooks using spices more effectively in their own cooking. Doesn't that prepackaged Country Herb Chicken & Dumplings, which deploys six prepackaged McCormick spices, sound good? In our view, these initiatives, combined with continuing growth in the health-conscious segment by learning to replace fat flavoring with spice flavoring, will add to a solid business base for the company.

McCormick estimates the spice market to be growing at 6 percent annually, and with their 22 percent share of the global market, there is plenty of opportunity. That mixes well with the profitability, stability, and defensive nature of the company; it continues to present an attractive combination for investors.

Reasons for Caution

Downsides include the rising cost of ingredients and the sourcing of many of these ingredients in geopolitically unstable regions. Top-line growth is likely to remain moderate except by acquisition, and projections seem muted in contrast to their view of global spice market growth (maybe they're just being conservative?). While earnings and share-price growth have been steady, they don't add a lot of "spice" to an aggressive portfolio; too, in the past three years the price of the stock has been spiced up a bit by its success. All that said, we don't see people's tastes in taste diminishing anytime soon.

SECTOR: **Consumer Staples** ❑ BETA COEFFICIENT: **0.58** ❑ 10-YEAR COMPOUND EARNINGS PER-SHARE GROWTH: **8.5%** ❑ 10-YEAR COMPOUND DIVIDENDS PER-SHARE GROWTH: **11.0%**

		2007	2008	2009	2010	2011	2012	2013	2014
Revenues (mil)		2,916	3,177	3,192	3,339	3,650	4,014	4,123	4,243
Net income (mil)		230	282	311	356.3	380	408	418	442
Earnings per share		1.92	2.14	2.35	2.65	2.80	3.04	3.13	3.37
Dividends per share		0.80	0.88	0.96	1.04	1.12	1.24	1.36	1.48
Cash flow per share		2.64	2.83	3.08	3.39	3.55	3.85	4.00	4.24
Price:	high	39.7	42.1	36.8	47.8	51.3	66.4	75.3	77.1
	low	33.9	28.2	28.1	35.4	43.4	49.9	60.8	52.6

Website: *www.mccormick.com*

CONSERVATIVE GROWTH

McKesson Corporation

Ticker symbol: **MCK (NYSE)** ❑ S&P rating: **BBB+** ❑ Value Line financial strength rating: **A++** ❑ Current yield: **0.4%** ❑ Dividend raises, past 10 years: **6**

Company Profile

McKesson Corporation is America's oldest and largest health-care services company and engages in two distinct businesses to support the health-care industry. Pharmaceutical and medical-surgical supply distribution is the first and by far the largest business: The company is the largest such distributor in North America, delivering about a third of all medications used daily. The company delivers to approximately 40,000 pharmaceutical outlets as well as hospitals and clinics throughout North America from 28 domestic and 17 Canadian distribution facilities, and has just added a major distribution stronghold for Europe.

Second, and not to be ignored, is a technology solutions business that provides clinical systems, analytics, clinical decision support, medical necessity and utilization management tools, electronic medical records, physical and financial supply-chain management, and connectivity solutions to hospitals, pharmacies, and an assortment of health-care providers. While the 2014 Celesio acquisition bumped the distribution segment portion of the whole up a percentage point to 98 percent, the strategically important information technology business is a $3.2 billion business all by itself. McKesson's software and hardware IT solutions are installed in some 76 percent of the nation's hospitals with more than 200 beds and 52 percent of hospitals overall.

The company offers products and services covering most aspects of pharmacy and drug distribution, including not only physical distribution and supply-chain services but also a line of proprietary generics and automated dispensing systems, record-keeping systems, and outsourcing services used in retail and hospital pharmacy operations. The central strategies are to provide a one-stop distribution solution for pharmaceuticals, generics, and surgical supplies, and to provide technology solutions to deliver higher-quality and more cost-effective care at the hospital and clinical levels.

In line with those strategies, McKesson continues along the path of acquiring significant health-care businesses—large and small—to add to its core offering and to expand globally. All are good fits in our opinion. In late 2010, the company completed a $2.16 billion acquisition of U.S. Oncology, a distributor of products targeted at the cancer-care industry. With that acquisition, McKesson became the leading supplier of materials, technology, and operational platforms to the oncological community, and that acquisition has performed well. In early 2012, the company acquired the Katz Group, a major distributor supplying more than 1,000 Canadian pharmacies, and medical supplies distributor PSS World Medical during FY2013. Finally, in early 2014, the company completed the acquisition of German pharmaceutical distributor Celesio, gaining a strong entry into the international wholesale, retail, and generic distribution markets, particularly in Europe.

Financial Highlights, Fiscal Year 2014

The Celesio acquisition added significantly to the top and bottom line at McKesson. With annual revenues of $28 billion for this subsidiary alone, total revenues advanced some 30 percent; backing Celesio out still gives a healthy 10 percent top-line increase. Operational performance remains strong, and the company continues to enjoy the slightly higher net profit margins, at 1.4 percent, it built up with process improvements and market-share strength in the early part of the decade. Net earnings rose 18.7 percent, driven too by the acquisition and pricing strength in the distribution business. Going forward, the company projects 2015 as a period to digest the new businesses, with revenues advancing a modest 3 percent and earnings a more modest, but still robust 10 percent, in part due to acquisition synergies. For FY2016, the company expects a stronger sales gain, in the 8 percent range, and a similar rise in earnings. The company will continue with moderate dividend increases and share buybacks, and has retired 25 percent of its shares in the past ten years.

Reasons to Buy

The distribution business continues to be solid and relatively recession-proof. Demographics and the addition of millions to the insured health-care rolls will keep demand moving in the right direction, and acquisitions have strengthened that position in domestic and especially international markets. McKesson dominates its niches and is a go-to provider of much of what hospitals and clinics need to operate. It holds market leader position in several important market categories, including number one in pharmaceutical distribution in the U.S. and Canada, number one in generic pharmaceutical distribution, number one in medical management software and services to payers—you get the idea.

Additionally, hospitals and other health-care providers are starting to get the memo that it is time to improve utilization and operational efficiency, and McKesson's technology solutions are hard to ignore, although many might do so at first glance, as they are only 3 percent of the business. As most distributors do, McKesson operates on very thin margins; the expansion of technology services and generic-equivalent drugs should eventually become a growth driver as efficiency measures continue to catch on. The company has a strong track record of stability and operational excellence and is well managed; the stock has many of the characteristics of a true long-term equity holding, and indeed has done well in the five years we've had it on the *100 Best* list.

Reasons for Caution

Acquisitions can increase risk, and notably Standard & Poor's dropped McKesson's bond rating a notch with the Celesio acquisition. Additionally, the company does operate on thin margins and as such has a low tolerance for mistakes or major changes in the health-care space, changes that could be brought on by legislation or regulation. While we applaud the aggressive buyback strategy, we'd like to see a bit more return to shareholders in the form of cash dividends; that said, the company has quintupled the indicated dividend since 2007 and appears to be poised to continue on that path. Finally, the strong and persistent price appreciation makes it necessary to select entry points carefully.

SECTOR: **Health Care** ❑ BETA COEFFICIENT: **0.70** ❑ 10-YEAR COMPOUND EARNINGS PER-SHARE GROWTH: **14.0%** ❑ 10-YEAR COMPOUND DIVIDENDS PER-SHARE GROWTH: **13.0%**

	2007	2008	2009	2010	2011	2012	2013	2014
Revenues (bil)	101.7	106.8	106.7	112.1	122.7	122.5	137.6	179.5
Net income (mil)	1,021	1,194	1,251	1,316	1,463	1,516	1,947	2,300
Earnings per share	3.43	4.28	4.58	5.00	6.05	6.33	8.35	10.10
Dividends per share	0.24	0.48	0.48	0.72	0.76	0.80	0.88	1.04
Cash flow per share	5.03	6.03	6.37	7.18	8.40	9.30	11.50	13.40
Price: high	68.4	68.4	65.0	71.5	87.3	100.0	166.6	214.4
low	50.5	28.3	33.1	57.2	66.6	74.9	96.7	96.7

Website: *www.mckesson.com*

Medtronic plc

Ticker symbol: MDT (NYSE) ❑ S&P rating: A ❑ Value Line financial strength rating: A++ ❑ Current yield: 1.6% ❑ Dividend raises, past 10 years: 10

Company Profile
Medtronic is the world's largest manufacturer of implantable medical devices and is a leading medical technology company, providing lifelong solutions to "alleviate pain, restore health, and extend life," primarily for people with chronic diseases.

The company is organized into two broad product groups—Cardiovascular and Restorative Therapies and a third smaller segment focused on diabetes treatment. The Cardiovascular Group accounts for 52 percent of FY2014 revenues (pre-Covidien), the Restorative Therapies Group accounts for 38 percent, and the smaller Diabetes Group accounts for the remaining 10 percent.

The two larger groups each have four and three major businesses, respectively. First, the Cardiovascular Group's four segments:

- *Cardiac Rhythm Disease Management* (29 percent of FY2014 sales) develops products that restore and regulate a patient's heart rhythm as well as improve the heart's pumping function. This segment markets implantable pacemakers, defibrillators, Internet and non-Internet–based monitoring and diagnostic devices, and cardiac resynchronization devices. A new implantable cardiac monitor about a third the size of an AAA battery and 80 percent smaller than competing products was recently approved by the FDA, exemplifying the company's R&D leadership in this industry, as do new efforts to automate remote monitoring and management of heart rhythm patients, a promising expansion of the "Internet of Things" concept into health care.
- *The Coronary segment* (10 percent) includes therapies to treat coronary artery disease and hypertension, including balloon angioplasty catheters, guide catheters, diagnostic catheters, guidewires, and accessories.
- *The Structural Heart segment* (7 percent) produces a line of products and therapies to treat heart valve disorders and to repair and replace heart valves, some through catheters without chest incisions. The unit also markets tools to assist heart surgeons during surgery, including circulatory support systems, heart positioners and tissue stabilizers, and ablation tools.
- *The Endovascular segment* (5 percent) produces stent graft and angioplasty systems to treat various heart and arterial conditions.

The Restorative Therapies Group's three segments include:

- *Spine* (18 percent) develops and manufactures products that treat a variety of disorders of the cranium and spine, including traumatically induced conditions, deformities, herniated discs and other disc diseases, osteoporosis, and tumors. Within the Spine segment, the Biologicsbusiness is the global leader in biologics regeneration and pain therapies across a variety of musculoskeletal applications including spine, orthopedic trauma, and dental.
- *Neuromodulation* (11 percent) employs many technologies used in heart electrical stimulation to treat diseases of the central nervous system. It offers therapies for movement disorders; chronic pain; urological and gastroenterological disorders, including incontinence, benign prostatic

hyperplasia (BPH), enlarged prostate, and gastroesophageal reflux disease (GERD); and psychological diseases.

■ *Surgical Technologies* (9 percent) develops and markets products and therapies for ear, nose, and throat–related diseases and certain neurological disorders; among them are precision image-guided surgical systems.

The Diabetes Group offers advanced diabetes management solutions, including insulin pump therapy, glucose monitoring systems, and treatment management software.

The pre-Covidien company operated in 140 countries, with about 46 percent of revenues coming from outside the U.S. and 11 percent from emerging markets. Research and Development expenses are about 9 percent of sales.

In 2014 Medtronic made a massive $49.9 billion acquisition of Irish medical device and global health-care product provider Covidien, which not only gained share with three complementary Covidien product lines—Surgical Solutions, Vascular Therapies, and Respiratory & Monitoring Solutions—but it also acquired a headquarters in Dublin, Ireland, in a somewhat controversial move to lower overall corporate tax rates. For now, the combined company is located in Ireland, and has been renamed "Medtronic plc."

"Creating meaningful change together" is the slogan of the combined entity. Indeed, Covidien will expand international reach to about 150 countries including an additional $1.6 billion in annual sales in emerging markets, and add "number one" market positions in minimally invasive surgery, peripheral vascular, neurovascular, respiratory and monitoring, and medical supplies in the United States. The combined entity will be stronger with larger market share in some of the former Medtronic's smaller subsegments, giving a more evenly spread presence across the various businesses.

Financial Highlights, Fiscal Year 2014

The Covidien acquisition, begun in mid-2014 and completed in early 2015, will on an annual basis add something north of $10 billion to net revenues and $2 billion to annual net income, plus or minus tax effects and eventual acquisition synergies. For FY2014, Covidien added approximately $3 billion in sales and an undetermined amount of additional net income; we estimate that "organic" growth without the acquisition was in the mid-single digits in both revenues and earnings prior to the acquisition. The company expects substantial synergies—almost $1 billion annually in a few years—to evolve from the merger, and projects a more aggressive sales growth in FY2016 of 11 percent and 7 percent on the bottom line (synergies will come a bit more gradually) as the combined company expands its emerging-market footprint and grows market share.

Reasons to Buy

The name Medtronic continues to be synonymous with medical technology; the company remains one of the pure plays in the health-care technology space. The company was already a "best in class" player in the markets and technologies it was engaged in, and over time its technologies have become more mainstream. Too, we are big supporters of its investments in remote medicine and its investments in emerging markets, and new products and breakthroughs especially in neuromodulation and diabetes management. Finally, while the merger adds some acquisition risk and long-term debt, the company has a strong track record for share buybacks and dividends; we expect this to continue as the company has reaffirmed its commitment to return 50 percent of its annual free cash flow to shareholders.

Reasons for Caution

Our previous concerns had to do with exposure to new trends in health-care cost containment and utilization, particularly in the U.S. Adding Covidien's geographic and product line diversity tempers these concerns somewhat. Still, Covidien is an aggressive move, and carries with it some acquisition risk in size, complexities, and unknown outcomes particularly with the Ireland relocation. The company's presentations to date are less clear than they could be about the future of the combined company; this itself adds some risk in our view. Public and U.S. government pressure to "repatriate" some of the tax savings might become an issue as well. That said, Medtronic still appears to be a strong, entrenched leader in medical technology, and well positioned to get stronger still.

SECTOR: **Health Care** ❑ BETA COEFFICIENT: **1.09** ❑ 10-YEAR COMPOUND EARNINGS PER-SHARE GROWTH: **10.0%** ❑ 10-YEAR COMPOUND DIVIDENDS PER-SHARE GROWTH: **15.5%**

	2007	2008	2009	2010	2011	2012	2013	2014
Revenues (mil)	13,515	14,599	15,817	15,933	16,184	16,590	17,005	19,950
Net income (mil)	2,984	3,282	3,576	3,647	3,447	3,857	3,878	4,175
Earnings per share	2.41	2.61	2.92	3.22	3.46	3.75	3.82	4.20
Dividends per share	0.47	0.63	0.82	0.90	0.97	1.04	1.12	1.22
Cash flow per share	3.22	3.45	3.96	4.16	4.13	4.60	4.73	5.15
Price: high	58.0	57.0	44.9	46.7	43.3	44.6	58.8	75.7
low	44.9	28.3	24.1	30.8	30.2	35.7	41.2	53.3

Website: *www.medtronic.com*

Microchip Technology, Inc.

Ticker symbol: MCHP (NASDAQ) □ S&P rating: BBB+ □ Value Line financial strength rating: A □ Current yield: 2.9% □ Dividend raises, past 10 years: 10

Company Profile

Your washing machine senses the load, adjusts the wash time and temperature accordingly, and tells you when it's done. Your refrigerator expands or contracts its power cycle according to outside temperature and the time of day to save on peak power costs. Your car shows you what it's about to back up into and may even prevent such a collision in the first place. Security systems show you what's happening in all parts of your home—and in other homes, such as that of your aging elders. Asset monitors keep track of inventory and key business equipment. It's all connected, always on, all the time.

Ready or not, this "Internet of Things," this Star Wars world of all of our stuff connected to all our other stuff and doing our thinking for us, is really coming. In many ways, it's already here. Your car talks to you and tells you when you're about to back into a light pole. Your phone (for better or for worse) senses where you are and sends that information everywhere. Wave your hands the right way and the force will be with you, or perhaps a Microchip Technology–powered sensor will turn the lights on for you. We don't know for sure if your washing machine will ever talk directly to your refrigerator, but that aside, the application possibilities are almost endless.

Microchip Technology is a leading manufacturer and supplier of specialized semiconductor products primarily embedded as controllers, processors, or memory into products, mostly products other than computers. The company's devices, many of which are customizable, custom-made, or programmable, sense motion, temperature, touch, proximity, and other environmental conditions, process the information, and control the device accordingly. Applications number literally in the thousands but are concentrated in automotive, communications, consumer product, appliance, lighting, medical, safety and security, and power and energy management products. Microchip products are typically small in size (the smallest is 1.5 × 2.5 millimeters), low power, low cost, and capable of operating reliably in extreme conditions. The company offers a full suite of design assistance, tools, and consulting services to help customers, usually OEM manufacturers, develop the best applications. They position these services as "low-risk product development" resources for their customers.

Microchip owns most of its manufacturing capability in four plants: two in Arizona, one in Oregon, and one in Thailand, as part of a deliberate strategy to increase process yields and shorten cycle times (the list of facilities will grow somewhat at least short term with acquisitions—see the following). Most but not all products are shipped "off the shelf" with short cycle times or as a scheduled production. R&D accounts for about 16 percent of revenues. As the company sells primarily to other OEM electronic product manufacturers, about 84 percent of sales are to international customers; about 29 percent are to China. Technology licensing accounts for about 5 percent of revenues.

Microchip has more clearly aligned itself and its branding behind the concept of embedded control solutions, and now calls itself "The Embedded Control Solutions Company"—a clear and well-defined business position. The company was fairly active on the acquisition front in 2014 and early 2015, the largest of which was for Taiwan-based ISSC, a provider of semiconductors and solutions for the Bluetooth and wireless markets. The company also acquired Supertex, a medical and industrial lighting products company, and Belgian high-speed data and video transceiver maker EqcoLogic.

Financial Highlights, Fiscal Year 2014

Design wins, market-share gains, and a general uptick in the manufacturing economy resulted in an 11 percent revenue gain in FY2014, a more pure and less acquisition-influenced gain than the 15.8 percent gain recorded the previous year. Net income rose a little faster, up about 12 percent, while a modest share count increase held per-share gains to about 8 percent. Backlogs were up about 25 percent from the previous year. Going forward into 2015 and 2016, again not counting acquisitions, the company projects revenue growth in the 7 percent range for both years, with net income gains approaching 10 percent. The company is issuing shares to fund acquisitions, so per-share earnings will be slightly less, but on the other hand, the dividend is solid and considerably more generous than many in the industry.

Reasons to Buy

The Internet of things is upon us. One doesn't have to look hard to find "smart" products; they're almost everywhere. Not just your smartphone,

but your appliances, car, climate control system, alarm system, in elevators, airplanes, airports, hospitals—you name it. And as their functionality
improves, they will become a standard part of daily life, just as compact
discs, Bluetooth, flat-screen TVs, smartphones—heck, the Internet—have
all become in the past few decades. Manufacturers will have to embrace
these new technologies and build them in just to stay in the market.

We like companies that make the things that make things work, and
Microchip seems well positioned as a leading supplier of all this intelligence
as "smart" moves far beyond the "smartphone." We were hesitant to include
a semiconductor company on our list, but we made our first entry last year.
Development and manufacturing costs are high, especially if a company
owns its own "fabs"—manufacturing facilities—and product cycles are
short. There is plenty of competition everywhere for most products, much
of it from lower-cost producers in Asia. Inventory cycles can also play havoc
with semiconductor producers, who do best by producing in large quantities.
Microchip, in our view, has overcome a lot of that by choosing high-value-
add niches and by offering plenty of design and technical support "value
add" to go along with the product.

All that said—and for many of these reasons—it has also become a
tradition for capital-intensive semiconductor companies to not pay dividends
or much else in the way of cash returns to shareholders. Capital is gobbled
up internally for what seems to be endless new investments in fab capacity,
design tools, and ever more expensive materials and supplies. Microchip has
bucked that trend—how many semiconductor firms have paid a dividend,
let alone raised it, for ten consecutive years?

In all, we're happy with the pick, and it will remain "embedded" in our
2016 *100 Best Stocks* list.

Reasons for Caution

Despite what we just said, semiconductor makers will always endure the
burdens of high capital requirements, short product cycles, inventory cycles
of OEMs and distributors, and to no small degree the economy as a whole.
Competition, especially from low-cost foreign suppliers, is keen in all semiconductor markets. Unfortunately, that competition includes at least a measure
of "illegal" competition through pirated or reverse-engineered technologies,
which the company vigorously fights. To address all forms of competition,
Microchip has worked hard to make its offering more "whole" with design
assistance and short lead times, both of which have pleased its customers.

SECTOR: **Technology** ◻ BETA COEFFICIENT: **1.07** ◻ 10-YEAR COMPOUND EARNINGS PER-SHARE GROWTH: **12.5%** ◻ 10-YEAR COMPOUND DIVIDENDS PER-SHARE GROWTH: **4.0%**

	2007	2008	2009	2010	2011	2012	2013	2014
Revenues (mil)	1,036	903	948	1,487	1,383	1,606	1,920	2,150
Net income (mil)	304	206	213	430	337	389	531	595
Earnings per share	1.43	1.11	1.14	2.21	1.65	1.89	2.45	2.65
Dividends per share	1.21	1.35	1.36	1.37	1.39	1.41	1.42	1.43
Cash flow per share	2.19	1.66	1.63	2.83	2.26	3.02	3.60	4.30
Price: high	42.5	38.4	29.6	36.4	41.5	38.9	44.9	50.0
low	27.5	16.3	16.2	25.5	29.3	28.9	32.4	36.9

Website: *www.microchip.com*

AGGRESSIVE GROWTH

Monsanto Company

Ticker symbol: MON (NYSE) ◻ S&P rating: BBB+ ◻ Value Line financial strength rating: A+ ◻ Current yield: 1.6% ◻ Dividend raises, past 10 years: 9

Company Profile

Monsanto was once a major chemical company with a broad pedigree ranging from saccharine to sulfuric acid to Agent Orange and DDT. Monsanto was absorbed into Pharmacia & Upjohn in 2000, which kept its pharmaceutical products and spun off the agricultural products business into a "new" Monsanto in 2002. Today's Monsanto provides a set of leading-edge, technology-based agricultural products for use in farming in the United States and overseas. The company broadly views its business as providing a system of seeds, biotechnology trait products, herbicides, and now, data, mainly to farmers to produce better-quality and healthier foods and animal feedstocks while expanding yields and reducing the costs of farming.

The company has two primary business segments: Seeds and Genomics, and Agricultural Productivity. The Seeds and Genomics segment (68 percent of FY2014 revenues) produces seeds for a host of crops, most importantly corn and soybeans, but also canola, cotton, and a variety of vegetable and fruit seeds. Most of the seed products are bioengineered to provide greater yields and to be more resistant to insects and weeds. Familiar to many consumers, especially those who travel in the Midwest, is the DeKalb seed brand, but there are many others.

The Agricultural Productivity segment (32 percent) offers glyphosate-based herbicides, known as Roundup to most of us, for agricultural, industrial, and residential lawn and garden applications. Beyond this market-leading product, the division also offers other selective herbicides for control of pre-emergent annual grass and small-seeded broadleaf weeds in corn and other crops. Monsanto owns many of the major brands in both seed and herbicide markets.

In recent years, the company underwent some upheaval as patents on its flagship Roundup herbicide system expired, almost immediately followed by reports that certain weeds were developing immunity to it anyhow, and cheaper foreign competitors were starting to invade its garden. Beyond that, Monsanto alienated some of its farmer base with pricing and marketing practices for its seed and herbicide systems. These reports and a sag in earnings brought the share price from the 70s to the mid-40s in mid-2010. Since then, the company has taken steps to modernize its herbicide offerings and become less dependent on them, to develop the core seed businesses further especially in soybeans and cotton, and to focus on developing markets like Latin America and China, making it less dependent on the "one-trick" Roundup pony. That said, it has introduced new and more effective (and more profitable) versions of this product, choosing not to rely on its expired patent base and technology laurels here, either. Among the many positive moves, the company also diversified into the agricultural consulting, analytics, and decision support business by acquiring The Climate Corporation. We continue to applaud these moves.

But the biggest news is happening as we review Monsanto for 2016: the company is attempting to acquire global agribusiness giant Syngenta AG (based in Switzerland) for $42 billion. Syngenta, a leader in agrochemicals, pesticides, and seed and itself involved in agricultural biotechnology and research, was formed in 2000 as a combination of two European agricultural firms, Novartis Agribusiness and Zeneca Agrochemicals. Syngenta annual sales are about $15 billion, which would roughly double Monsanto's global sales. Syngenta is thought to complement Monsanto's offering well, as they specialize in pesticides and herbicides for pests and problems not well fended off by Monsanto's current genetically modified seeds and specialty chemicals. Too, Syngenta has a strong global footprint, with almost 50 percent of sales coming from emerging markets. Obviously this is a huge step for Monsanto, and merits analysis and follow-up beyond what we can provide here.

Financial Highlights, Fiscal Year 2014

Three years past the major U.S. drought of 2012, the farming business suffers from weaker farm incomes but also a glut in agricultural production. Demand for farm products in the rest of the world continues to increase. As such, U.S. farmers seek Monsanto solutions to reduce costs and produce efficiently, and more farmers in more regions of the world are adopting Monsanto solutions as demand for farm products increases.

All of that led to another strong year in FY2014, with overall revenues up 6.7 percent even with a 1 percent currency headwind. New Roundup products and the incorporation of the new analytics and consulting business led to a 5 percent volume increase and a 10 percent price increase across the Agricultural Productivity segment—leading to a 13 percent revenue gain in this smaller share of the business. Net income rose 11.3 percent for the year, and per-share earnings, on the back of a substantial 8.5 percent share reduction, rose 14.3 percent, a pretty good year down on the farm all in all.

The company expects soft farm incomes, competition, and currency headwinds to keep revenues and earnings largely flat through FY2015, with new products and stronger pricing leading to growth in revenues and earnings in the 10 percent range for FY2016. Cash flows, dividend raises, and share buybacks all look to advance at moderate rates for the next few years. All of this, of course, does not consider the Syngenta AG acquisition.

Reasons to Buy

Monsanto will provide business schools with an excellent case study in becoming too dependent on one product and watching that product decline—and responding by retrenching back to its core strengths for a resurgence. The company continues to lead in innovation and technology applied to agricultural use and continues to advance in biotech applications in its Seeds and Genomics segment while advancing its products in the Agricultural Productivity segment with glyphosate-related products and analytics and consulting services as well. All of this is working in the backdrop of growing food demand from growing middle classes on a growing global scale. Monsanto doesn't own the "agriculture tech" space outright but clearly plays a leadership role; the company has stated a goal to double corn, soybean, cotton, and canola yields by 2030, thus becoming a leading agent of efficiency and change. When that formula is also profitable, great things can happen, and they have up to now—revenues, margins earnings, cash flow, and dividends are all moving in the right direction at an accelerating pace.

Reasons for Caution

Not everyone—including its customer base of farmers—is happy with Monsanto. Many have been outspoken for years about the power and practices of the company, and some of that angst has turned into possible legal headwinds. More recently—and a bit more concerning—is the global movement against "GMO" foods, that is, genetically modified food products. The movement has strengthened markets for organically grown products and created an upswell of negative perceptions about the Monsanto system (and those of competitors as well). Adding fuel to the fire, the World Health Organization released a study listing glyphosate as a "category 2A" probable carcinogen, although many outside agencies have questioned this report.

To date, these issues collectively are presenting little more than a PR challenge for the company, which has started to incorporate "health" into its research and marketing messages, but it all bears watching. Aside from that, of course, the Syngenta acquisition presents some risks and challenges. We had thought Monsanto was pretty comfortable in its niche and with its products; the quest for Syngenta suggests there may be some doubts about the company's potential with its current product base. Stay tuned.

SECTOR: **Industrials** ◻ BETA COEFFICIENT: **1.39** ◻ 10-YEAR COMPOUND EARNINGS PER-SHARE GROWTH: **20.5%** ◻ 10-YEAR COMPOUND DIVIDENDS PER-SHARE GROWTH: **20.0%**

	2007	2008	2009	2010	2011	2012	2013	2014
Revenues (mil)	8,563	11,365	11,724	10,502	11,822	13,516	14,861	15,855
Net income (mil)	1,027	1,895	2,448	1,327	1,615	1,997	2,450	2,787
Earnings per share	1.98	3.39	4.41	2.41	2.93	3.70	4.54	5.19
Dividends per share	0.55	0.83	1.01	1.08	1.14	1.28	1.56	1.78
Cash flow per share	2.85	4.50	5.49	3.57	4.07	4.90	5.79	7.06
Price: high	116.3	145.8	93.4	87.1	78.7	94.8	116.8	128.8
low	49.1	63.5	66.6	44.6	58.9	69.7	94.0	104.1

Website: *www.monsanto.com*

Mosaic Company

Ticker symbol: MOS (NYSE) ❏ S&P rating: BBB ❏ Value Line financial strength rating: A ❏ Current yield: 2.4% ❏ Dividend raises, past 10 years: 3

Company Profile

We generally shy away from commodities producers. Why? Because it's hard to establish a brand or a competitive advantage. Typically the business becomes a race to the bottom, where the low-cost producer wins. But if you're the low-cost producer, you probably aren't making much money—and you probably won't stay the low-cost producer for long.

We prefer companies that have other routes to establishing—and maintaining—a competitive advantage. But there are commodities, and then there are *strategic* commodities. What do we mean by that? Well, some commodities are more important—and in more constrained supply—than others. If a company can invest itself wholly in these commodities, can own the largest and most efficient mines and establish a dominant market share and position, it will establish a competitive advantage. With that idea in mind, we introduce the Mosaic Company. "Helping the World Grow the Food it Needs" is the website headline for plant nutrient miner and producer Mosaic Company.

Formed in 2004 through a merger of Cargill's fertilizer operations with IMC Global, Mosaic is the dominant world producer in the so-called "P+K" market—that's phosphorus and potassium, for those of you who shied away from high school chemistry. And in case you're not clear on why P and K are important, they are vital fertilizer ingredients and hence essential to most of the world's agriculture production. Plants require more potassium than any other nutrient besides nitrogen, and it is important to root-system development and many processes that form plant starch and proteins. Potassium is mined and sold in its oxide form known more popularly as potash. Phosphorus is a vital component of photosynthesis for plant metabolism and growth.

Mosaic is the largest combined—and among the most efficient—P+K producers in the world. About two-thirds of the business is phosphorus and a third potash. Both minerals are produced commercially in a limited number of places in the world. Mosaic has interests in the important locations in North and South America, notably Florida phosphorus mines and potash mines in Saskatchewan, Michigan, New Mexico, and Peru. Through a network of processing and packaging plants in several countries, the company sells its product in approximately 40 countries. As a percentage of FY2014 sales, North America accounted for 51 percent, Asia 31 percent, Latin America 15 percent, and the rest 3 percent. The company is particularly enthused about growth in Brazil, and recently acquired a fertilizer distribution business there from Archer Daniels Midland (another *100 Best* stock).

The "strategic commodity" idea introduced previously got tarnished a bit by a market disruption in 2013, but we think the markets have stabilized and are generally on the road to recovery. In 2013 Russia's Uralkali, a major producer, got into a tiff with Belarus's Belaruskali, another major producer, and broke their cartel agreement. Uralkali announced a new business strategy emphasizing volume over price, leading to stiff 25–40 percent declines in world potash prices, undercutting Mosaic. (Actually Mosaic's own potash cartel formed with Potash Corp. of Saskatchewan and Agrium known as "Canpotex.") Anyway, the new strategy not only disrupted prices but also lured away lucrative long-term contracts particularly in Asia, causing a 20 percent dent in Mosaic's stock price at the time, putting it near the bottom of our performance list, and casting some doubt about the future. It's taken a bit longer than expected, but commodity prices have recovered somewhat, and as a low-cost producer, Mosaic has learned to survive, even thrive, in this lower-priced environment, which was also affected by 2014's decline in oil prices and commodity prices in general. We think global potash markets will eventually recover, although not to 2007–2008 levels where potash approached $1,000 a ton (versus today's $325), as higher-cost producers take product off the market and as Uralkali re-evaluates its strategy.

Financial Highlights, Fiscal Year 2014

As expected, the 2013 market disruption affected FY2014 results significantly. But other fundamentals have improved for Mosaic. World food demand is up, crop production is up (although prices still aren't), and inventory stockpiles are down, all of which have led to a slight uptick in global prices, and production has nearly reached previous levels.

FY2014 revenues dropped almost 9 percent after a 10 percent drop the year before. Operating margins contracted a bit with the lower prices and volumes, and net profits were some 40 percent lower than FY2013; most of the profit decline from the market disruption occurred in FY2014. Per-share earnings, aided by a large share buyback of $2 billion in shares held by the Cargill family from the original formation of the company, dropped about 35 percent.

Although P+K prices remain fairly low at the time of this analysis, what really counts is what happens from here. As mentioned, the market is regaining equilibrium, inventories have declined, demand has strengthened somewhat, and Mosaic has traditionally been one of the most efficient producers. All of that leads to a cautiously optimistic forecasted 8 percent revenue rise for FY2015 leading to a 9–10 percent gain for FY2016. Operating efficiencies and reduced share counts are projected to drive per-share earnings up close to 15 percent for FY2015 and another 12–15 percent in FY2016. Mosaic raised its dividend 10 percent in early 2015.

Reasons to Buy

Particularly for those interested in investing in commodities, we think this is some of the most fertile ground on which to stand. Demand for food will only increase over time, and Mosaic is the largest of ten world producers of P+K. The combination of prime mining sites, size, and operational efficiency in its processing and distribution operations should lead to at least maintaining, if not expanding, market share. We enthusiastically applaud the dividend hikes and the dedication to returning cash to shareholders in general, whatever form that may take.

Reasons for Caution

Commodity markets and commodity producers are inherently volatile, and any reduction in planting or backup in inventory, not to mention overall global economic weakness or short-term droughts as experienced in the U.S. in 2012, can drive prices down in a heartbeat. Low crop prices, while often driven by larger plantings (using more fertilizer), also strain farm budgets; this mixed effect is hard to predict and can cause short-term inventory disruptions. Worse, a commodity volume and price war such as the one that erupted during FY2013 can be particularly damaging if it blows the assumptions of the most carefully laid business plans and strategies. We think the Uralkali disruption will eventually go away (with Mosaic having learned a lot from it), and the natural economics of world food demand and supply will take over; Mosaic is a long-term story as well as an opportunity for short-term investment success if and when market conditions improve.

SECTOR: **Materials** ❑ BETA COEFFICIENT: **1.40** ❑ 10-YEAR COMPOUND EARNINGS PER-SHARE
GROWTH: **19.0%** ❑ 10-YEAR COMPOUND DIVIDENDS PER-SHARE GROWTH: **NM**

	2007	2008	2009	2010	2011	2012	2013	2014
Revenues (mil)	5,774	9,812	10,298	6,759	9,937	11,108	9,974	9,056
Net income (mil)	342.5	1,962.2	1,909.7	862.8	1,942.2	1,930	1,744	1,029
Earnings per share	0.80	4.38	4.28	1.93	4.34	4.42	4.09	2.68
Dividends per share	—	—	0.20	0.20	0.20	0.28	1.00	1.00
Cash flow per share	1.67	5.20	5.11	2.94	5.35	5.73	5.51	4.64
Price: high	97.6	103.3	62.5	76.9	59.5	62.0	64.6	51.3
low	19.5	21.9	31.2	37.7	44.9	44.4	39.8	40.3

Website: *www.mosaicco.com*

GROWTH AND INCOME

NextEra Energy, Inc.

Ticker symbol: NEE (NYSE) ❑ S&P rating: A- ❑ Value Line financial strength rating: A ❑ Current
yield: 3.1% ❑ Dividend raises, past 10 years: 10

Company Profile

NextEra is a full-service utility, power-generating unit, and utility services
provider built around the utility stalwart Florida Power & Light, which for-
mally changed its name to NextEra in 2010. NextEra not only represents an
evolution in name but also a hint about how the company does business and
expects to do business in the future as a leading user and innovator in clean
and large-scale alternative energy sourcing for the power market.

Headquartered in Juno Beach, FL, FPL Group's principal operating
subsidiaries are NextEra Energy Resources, LLC, and the original Florida
Power & Light Company, one of the largest rate-regulated electric utilities
in the country. FP&L serves 8.9 million people and 4.7 million customer
accounts in eastern and southern Florida. Through its subsidiaries, NextEra
collectively operates the third-largest U.S. nuclear power generation fleet
and has a significant presence in solar and wind generation markets. NEE is
the world's largest user of wind and sun resources to generate electricity. As
proof that such leadership works, customer electricity rates in its operating
territories are 25 percent below the national average.

As a nonregulated subsidiary, NextEra Energy Resources, LLC (or "NEER"), is a wholesale energy provider and a leader in producing electricity from clean and renewable fuels and, unlike many other alternative-energy-driven businesses, is a viable standalone business entity. It has 4,700 employees at 115 facilities in 26 states and has solar and wind farms, nuclear energy facilities, and gas infrastructure operations not just in Florida but in 22 states and Canada. NEER's energy-producing portfolio includes 9,277 wind turbines on 100 farms in 19 states and four Canadian provinces, which is estimated to comprise 17 percent of the entire wind power–generating capacity in the U.S., 14 percent of utility-scale solar power production, and 6 percent of total U.S. nuclear power production. All told, the combined fuel mix of alternative energy and natural gas not only reduces fuel costs (33 percent of revenues, compared to 40s and 50s in much of the industry), but it also produces levels of sulfur dioxide (the cause of acid rain) some 96 percent below the average for the U.S. electric industry, a nitrous oxide emission rate 82 percent below the industry, and a carbon dioxide (CO_2) emission rate 53 percent below industry averages—these numbers have all significantly improved over the years, too. The NEER subsidiary accounts for nearly a third of NextEra's total revenue—and nearly half of its profits—a healthy return for an alternative energy–based operation.

The company has a few small but promising nonregulated subsidiaries, offering design and consulting services for other alternative and conventional utility providers. Its FPL FiberNet subsidiary specializes in high-bandwidth data transmission from telecommunications locations to cell phone towers, mainly in Florida, Texas, and other areas in the South.

NextEra is a regular winner of awards for most green, most ethical, and most admired companies—in fact, it made a Top 10 position on 2015 *Fortune*'s list of World's Most Admired Companies.

Finally, in December 2014 the company announced an agreement to acquire the electric- generating business of Hawaiian Electric for about $4.3 billion. Hawaiian Electric faces more challenges than most from individual solar panel installation; the merger appears to be an attempt to lead the development of a "new era" for electric utilities integrating individual with centralized generation. NEE will likely set a path for optimized, integrated grids while also satisfying the state's desire to move to alternative energy platforms. Stay tuned—this should be an interesting show of NEE's global leadership in the electric industry.

Financial Highlights, Fiscal Year 2014

The strong economic recovery and the addition of new alternative energy production to sell to other utility providers led to a boom in 2014, with revenues up some 12.3 percent from FY2013—a significant jump for a utility business indeed. Per-share earnings did even better, up 15.3 percent over the period—even with a slight uptick in share counts as NEE, like others in the industry, deleveraged some by issuing stock. After the banner year in 2014, revenues are expected to flatten in FY2015, then grow a more typical 4 percent into FY2016. Earnings will continue on a moderate upward path, and are projected in the $5.75–$6.25 range for FY2016. Dividends should continue to grow in the high single-digit range annually.

Reasons to Buy

Every year we look forward to evaluating and writing about NextEra; they are leading so many initiatives in what's really a pretty boring industry otherwise, and their website and presentation materials do a good job describing them.

For those who believe that alternative energy is the future for large-scale power generation, NextEra continues to be the best play available. The company continues to grow alternative energy capacity on all fronts, particularly wind and solar, and continues to make money on these efforts. All of this adds to the solid and traditional FP&L regulated utility base; this company has the steady feel of a traditional utility with a bit more interest in the form of alternative energy plays and leading-edge power utility technology. As previously mentioned, NEE will lead the way into figuring out the grid of the future, utilizing an optimized mix of centralized and distributed alternative and conventional generating resources. Cash flow is very strong and supports both hearty dividend increases and continued investments in alternative energy production but hasn't been used to reduce share counts.

Reasons for Caution

The company's FP&L subsidiary is still a regulated utility and may not always receive the most accommodating treatment. Additionally, alternative energy tax credits may diminish over time. Alternative energy innovations and nuclear power carry some risk, and NEE may have trouble optimizing the grid as mentioned due to regulatory and other constraints. The dividend yield, while still healthy for a company with future growth prospects in an up-and-coming industry, is still a little low by current utility standards—reflecting in part the fact that investors have already put a lot of energy into this stock, and the price accounts for its prospects. This is a dynamic, growth-oriented utility company, but buyers should continue to look for good entry points—a $100 utility stock is unusual to say the least.

SECTOR: **Utilities** ❑ BETA COEFFICIENT: **0.32** ❑ 10-YEAR COMPOUND EARNINGS PER-SHARE
GROWTH: **7.5%** ❑ 10-YEAR COMPOUND DIVIDENDS PER-SHARE GROWTH: **7.5%**

	2007	2008	2009	2010	2011	2012	2013	2014
Revenues (mil)	15,263	16,410	15,646	15,317	15,341	14,256	15,136	17,021
Net income (mil)	1,312	1,639	1,615	1,957	2,021	1,911	2,062	2,469
Earnings per share	3.27	4.07	3.97	4.74	4.82	4.56	4.83	5.60
Dividends per share	1.64	1.78	1.89	2.00	2.20	2.40	2.64	2.90
Cash flow per share	6.85	8.03	8.75	9.60	9.29	8.70	10.65	12.10
Price: high	72.8	73.8	60.6	56.3	61.2	72.2	89.8	110.8
low	53.7	33.8	41.5	45.3	49.0	58.6	69.8	84.0

Website: *www.nexteraenergy.com*

AGGRESSIVE GROWTH

Nike, Inc.

Ticker symbol: **NKE** (NYSE) ❑ S&P rating: **AA-** ❑ Value Line financial strength rating: **A++** ❑ Current yield: **1.1%** ❑ Dividend raises, past 10 years: **10**

Company Profile

Nike's principal business activity is the design, development, and worldwide marketing of footwear, apparel, equipment, and accessory products. Nike is the largest seller of athletic footwear and athletic apparel in the world, but a big part of the story is how it is extending beyond traditional footwear and apparel. Its products are sold through retail accounts, Nike-owned retail outlets (of which there are 322 in the U.S. and 536 overseas), its website, and a mix of independent distributors and licensees in more than 190 countries around the world. Recently, the company has experimented with specialized destination "Running Stores" and has expanded reach with more "Direct-to-Consumer," or DTC or "factory" outlets, carrying its traditionally strong product innovation to the channel and retail marketplace.

Nike does no manufacturing—virtually all of its footwear and apparel items are fashioned by independent contractors outside the United States, while equipment products are produced both in the United States and abroad.

Nike's shoes are designed primarily for athletic use, although a large percentage of them are worn for casual or leisure purposes. Shoes are designed for men, women, and children for running, training, basketball, and soccer use, although the company also carries brands for casual wear.

Nike sells apparel and accessories for most of the sports addressed by its shoe lines, as well as athletic bags and accessory items. Nike apparel and accessories are designed to complement its athletic footwear products, feature the same trademarks, and are sold through the same marketing and distribution channels. The new buzzword is "athleisure," and Nike is there front and center. All Nike-branded products are marketed with the familiar "swoosh" logo, one of the most recognized and successful branding images in history.

Nike has a number of wholly owned subsidiaries, or "affiliate brands," including Converse, Hurley, Jordan, and Nike Golf, which variously design, distribute, and license dress, athletic, and casual footwear, sports apparel, and accessories.

Of the total $26 billion in 2014 Nike-branded revenues (excluding subsidiaries), about 62 percent of it comes from footwear, 31 percent from apparel, and the remainder from equipment. Footwear remains the fastest-growing segment of the business at 12 percent, although the much smaller Converse subsidiary grew at 16 percent for the year albeit only representing 7 percent of total revenues. Approximately 46 percent of sales come from North America, 18 percent from Western Europe, 9.5 percent from China (down from 11 percent in FY2013), 9 percent from Central and Eastern Europe, 3 percent from Japan, and 14 percent from other emerging markets. FY2014 growth was strongest in Western Europe (19 percent), North America (10 percent), and Central and Eastern Europe (13 percent), while China slowed to 5 percent growth, emerging markets slowed to 3 percent, and Japan actually dipped 12 percent. This pattern reversed the trend seen in the previous few years, although there are signs that China growth will restart after some retail strategy changes. Strength in Europe is real and reflects increasing market share over local favorites Adidas and Puma, and is particularly impressive, given currency effects.

Financial Highlights, Fiscal Year 2014

FY2014 revenues headed down the track another 10 percent to just under $27.8 billion, a pretty strong kick considering currency effects. While labor and material costs rose again, the company also leveraged newer, higher-margined products, firm pricing, DTC sales, and some operating efficiencies into another 0.5 percent increase in operating margins (to 15.1 percent) to cross the finish line with a 9.3 percent gain in net income. That and a healthy 2.7 percent share buyback combined to strengthen per-share earnings by 10.4 percent over FY2013, after a 13.5 percent gain for that year.

Direct-to-consumer channels—mainly factory stores and online—continue to be a strong story, with growth in that category of about 22 percent to $5.3 billion, or almost 20 percent of the business. Online sales, now conducted in 18 languages, jumped 42 percent in the first quarter of FY2015.

The company stands in good position with recent gains in the U.S. and Europe and an expected turnaround in its Asia markets. Overall Nike manages for a high single-digit growth rate long term for revenues and a mid-double–digit growth in per-share earnings, and buybacks should continue at a moderate pace. Per-share earnings are forecast to sprint ahead in the $3.50–$3.60 range in FY2015—a 19 percent gain, tiring a bit to 8–9 percent for FY2016, with revenues setting the pace at 5–10 percent each year.

Reasons to Buy

Why buy Nike? In a word, brand. The Nike brand and its corresponding swoosh continue to be one of the most recognized—and sought after—brands in the world. It is a lesson in simplicity and image congruence with the product behind it. Nike doesn't sit still with it; rather, the company is learning to leverage it into more products outside the traditional athletic wear circuit—golf clubs, golf balls, even a new line of GPS watches and apps to find, say, a new route for your run and to track your performance right on your phone. The company continues to invest in innovation in all of its segments, including new fabrics, colors, uniform materials, and digital linkages to make active lifestyles more productive and fun—and it is now extending this innovation further into marketing and retail. As well, Nike doesn't just limit the brand appeal to athletes: Slogans like "Just Do It" and "If you have a body, you're an athlete" emphasize the appeal and lifestyle across all segments of the population. We continue to think this is drop-dead smart.

Of course, solid brand and brand reputation lead to category leadership and, hence, higher profitability, and Nike has finished far ahead of the pack in this area, too. We think the latest turn in the business toward strength in Europe and North America only suggests even better days when Asian and emerging markets resume stronger growth. The brand and the moat created by the brand seem to have nowhere to go but forward, and improved manufacturing efficiencies, strong channel relationships, and international exposure all keep the company moving faster in the right direction. Despite its size, the company continues to deliver double-digit earnings, cash flow, and dividend growth. We continue to like the combination of protected profitability through brand excellence, operational excellence, and a clean, conservative balance sheet, all providing a good combination of safety and growth potential—and we like the fact that the company is returning more of the proceeds to shareholders.

Reasons for Caution

A few things could put hurdles in Nike's path. The first is higher labor and commodity input prices. Second, the company has occasionally been in the news—and the rumor mill—for unfair labor practices and child labor violations in some of its foreign manufacturing plants. The company doesn't actually own or operate these plants, but the rumors can stick nonetheless. Too, we think Nike gets today's more trendy, fashion-conscious, variety-seeking consumer, but we have also noticed what we feel is a degradation in value to achieve variety and offer lots of bright colors. We hope the company doesn't steer too far off the track to be "trendy." As well, while we think its image and marketing extend well into a direct-to-consumer selling strategy, the potential for conflict with existing channels is always a cause for concern. Finally, the stock price has also risen at full speed lately; we'd recommend looking for good entry points before getting into the starting blocks on this one.

SECTOR: **Consumer Discretionary** ❑ BETA COEFFICIENT: **0.77** ❑ 10-YEAR COMPOUND EARNINGS PER-SHARE GROWTH: **14.0%** ❑ 10-YEAR COMPOUND DIVIDENDS PER-SHARE GROWTH: **18.5%**

		2007	2008	2009	2010	2011	2012	2013	2014
Revenues (mil)		16,326	18,627	19,176	19,014	20,862	24,128	25,313	27,799
Net income (mil)		1,458	1,734	1,727	1,907	2,133	2,223	2,464	2,693
Earnings per share		1.43	1.72	1.76	1.93	2.20	2.37	2.69	2.97
Dividends per share		0.36	0.44	0.49	0.53	0.60	0.70	0.81	0.93
Cash flow per share		1.72	2.07	2.12	2.23	2.60	2.83	3.25	3.69
Price:	high	34.0	35.3	33.3	46.2	49.1	57.4	80.3	99.8
	low	23.7	21.3	16.1	30.4	34.7	42.6	51.4	69.9

Website: *www.nikeinc.com*

Norfolk Southern Corporation

Ticker symbol: NSC (NYSE) ❑ S&P rating: BBB+ ❑ Value Line financial strength rating: A ❑ Current yield: 2.2% ❑ Dividend raises, past 10 years: 10

Company Profile

Norfolk Southern Corp. was formed in 1982 as a holding company when the Norfolk & Western Railway merged with the Southern Railway. Including lines received in the split takeover (with CSX) of Conrail, the current railroad operates 20,000 route-miles of track in 22 eastern and southern states. It serves every major port on the East Coast of the United States and has the most extensive intermodal network in the east.

Company business in FY2014 was about 17 percent coal (down from the low 20s in previous years), 33 percent carload industrial products, and 50 percent intermodal. Major gateways include ports in the eastern half of the U.S., Great Lakes ports, and major interchange points with the two major Western systems, Union Pacific (another *100 Best* stock) and Burlington Northern Santa Fe. The company estimates that its networks reach 65 percent of U.S. manufacturing and 55 percent of U.S. energy consumption. In the late 1990s, the company split the acquisition of northeastern rail heavyweight Conrail with rival CSX Corporation, so it has considerable operations in the Northeast and Midwest in addition to its traditional southeastern base. The heaviest traffic corridors are New York–Chicago; Chicago–Atlanta; Appalachian coalfields to the port of Norfolk, VA, and Sandusky, OH; and Cleveland–Kansas City. The company has a diverse base of large Midwestern factories and large and smaller southern factories and basic materials producers in the coal, chemical, automotive, and lumber industry, giving a well-diversified traffic base.

The company has been an innovator in the intermodal business, that is, combining trucking and rail services—with its Triple Crown services, centered on the Roadrailer, a train of coupled-together highway vans on special wheelsets. At the terminal, a cab simply backs up to the van and drives it off.

The company provides a number of logistics services and has substantial traffic to and from ports and overseas destinations. The recent disruptions in West Coast port facilities, and the opening of the widened Panama Canal appear poised to give some lift to southern and East Coast ports, which NSC serves well. The company has an active program to attract lineside customers to build freight volumes.

Financial Highlights, Fiscal Year 2014

It's common knowledge that the recent oil and gas boom has caused a major shift in energy markets. In particular, cheaper and more plentiful natural gas and a continued shift in basic metals manufacturing have to a degree derailed the lucrative coal traffic enjoyed by the railroads; Norfolk Southern with its geography has been front and center in this shift. As a portion of the company's revenues, coal dropped from 31 percent in FY2011 to 26 percent in FY2012, 23 percent in FY2013, and now 17 percent in FY2014. Although this loss has been partially offset by the oil boom and tank-train shipments to East Coast and southern refineries, the real story is the broadening of the traffic mix especially into intermodal—and a continued benefit from a forward-looking series of improvements in infrastructure all begun years ago. For FY2014, there was good news both on the top and bottom line. Reduced coal shipments had caused revenues to flatten over the 2011–2013 period, but the improved economy, stronger pricing, higher volumes, and increased oil shipments drove revenues 3.4 percent higher. The better news was in profits. First, the key "operating ratio" measure—the ratio of variable to total costs—dropped to 69.2 from 71.0 percent in FY2013 (and 71.7 and 75.4 in FY2012 and FY2011 respectively), indicating the reaping of rewards from prior physical plant improvements, lower fuel prices, and general operating improvements. Net income rose a healthy 5.8 percent.

The next headwind for FY2015 is a decline in export traffic due to the strong dollar, particularly coal traffic for export; as such the company is guiding a 1 percent revenue increase but with a stronger net income increase of 8 percent. Share count reductions of roughly 2 percent per year help per-share earnings still more.

Reasons to Buy

NSC and its competitors have all been hurt by the coal slowdown, but there are some silver linings, both short and long term. For the short term, increased exploration and production of crude oil in places like North Dakota have changed around oil supply chains in the U.S., and since there are no pipelines to serve the need, trainloads of oil are moving from this and a few other booming regions to eastern refineries. The boom has also brought new business moving other commodities used in the new fracking extraction process. The recent drop in oil prices adds a question mark, but most companies continue to operate wells already drilled and financed; volumes have yet to be affected in a major way. While the stronger dollar and weaker export market are short-term drags, the ports NSC serves will clearly benefit from the Panama Canal widening, as customers will opt for longer sea and shorter land passages. The recent West Coast port strike pushed more traffic this way short term, but most industry analysts suggest that at least some of this traffic will continue to avoid the less dependable West Coast port system.

Norfolk Southern continues to do an excellent job sizing its physical plant and managing costs, as evidenced by the operating ratio mentioned earlier. NSC has proven over the past 30 years that it can compete effectively for long-haul truck business with its intermodal offerings and has some of the most competitive service and terminal structures in the business. It has gained market share from trucks, and general merchandise volume increased dramatically, fully 8 percent for intermodal in FY2014, with more than 62 percent of merchandise traffic originating on its own lines.

Additionally, NSC serves some of the more dynamic and up-and-coming manufacturing markets in the United States, namely, Asian and other foreign-owned manufacturing facilities found particularly in the Southeast. The company has created a Heartland Corridor time freight and double-stack container routing between Chicago and the East Coast, reducing distance by 250 miles and, more importantly, transit times from four to three days. Similar improvements have occurred on its Crescent Corridor between Louisiana and New Jersey. Such innovations will further assert the company's leadership. Additionally, we like the strength and diversity coming from serving the domestic and especially the foreign-owned auto industry—the company serves plants for (in alphabetical order) BMW, Chrysler, Ford, General Motors, Honda, Isuzu, Mazda, Mercedes-Benz, Mitsubishi, Nissan, Subaru, Suzuki, and Toyota.

Finally, cash flow continues to be strong, dividend raises are consistent, and the company continues down the share repurchase track.

Reasons for Caution

The decline in coal traffic, which mostly supports electric utilities, also exposes the company more to general economic downturns as the remaining mix is more economically sensitive. Oil-related traffic may come into question if energy prices stay low—it's too soon to tell. Too, increased oil shipments expose the company to headline risk and accidents, and NSC hasn't escaped this risk with a 2014 headline accident in Lynchburg, VA.

Finally, in the railroad industry, as in other capital-intensive, high–fixed cost industries, it's hard to have just the right amount of capacity. Too much volume can actually be a bad thing as it overtaxes physical plant and causes service disruptions. The tendency is to overreact and spend too much on capital improvements—then the next recession hits. While NSC has proven capable and fairly agile in managing such swings, they always pose a risk.

SECTOR: **Transportation** ❑ BETA COEFFICIENT: **1.11** ❑ 10-YEAR COMPOUND EARNINGS PER-SHARE GROWTH: **14.0%** ❑ 10-YEAR COMPOUND DIVIDENDS PER-SHARE GROWTH: **21.0%**

		2007	2008	2009	2010	2011	2012	2013	2014
Revenues (mil)		9,432	10,661	7,969	9,516	11,172	11,040	11,245	11,624
Net income (mil)		1,464	1,716	1,034	1,498	1,853	1,749	1,850	2,000
Earnings per share		3.68	4.52	2.76	4.00	5.27	5.37	5.85	6.39
Dividends per share		0.96	1.22	1.36	1.40	1.68	1.94	2.04	2.22
Cash flow per share		5.90	6.88	5.07	6.48	8.22	8.49	8.96	9.57
Price:	high	59.6	75.5	54.8	63.7	78.4	78.5	93.2	117.6
	low	45.4	41.4	26.7	46.2	57.6	56.1	62.7	87.1

Website: *www.nscorp.com*

AGGRESSIVE GROWTH

Novo Nordisk A/S

Ticker symbol: NVO (NYSE) ❑ S&P rating: AA- ❑ Value Line financial strength rating: A++ ❑ Current yield: 1.4% ❑ Dividend raises, past 10 years: 10

Company Profile

In our search for new companies for the 2016 *100 Best Stocks* list, we sought to add a pharmaceutical firm to replace Allergan, which was acquired during 2015, and to replace Philips N.V. as a strong non-U.S. player because that company had faltered and engaged in restructuring plans we, frankly, didn't quite get. So, in seeking a replacement ("sell when there's something better to buy"), naturally, we could fill the bill with a large, growing, non-U.S. pharmaceutical company that we could easily embrace and understand. (We may be good, but we don't claim to understand most pharma, nor do we claim to understand most big overseas companies and their presentations as well as we should.) Could we find a compelling pharma story out there with a strong international footprint that we could get our arms around for 2016? Turns out, we could—in the form of Danish diabetes-care specialist Novo Nordisk A/S.

Diabetes, of course, is huge and is growing as more people around the world live to an older age and, unfortunately, eat higher-calorie diets. Novo Nordisk, which started out in the early 1920s as two separate diabetes medicine producers, merged in 1989 and now garners almost 80 percent of its current $15 billion in revenues supplying diabetes medicine and care products. The company estimates that it owns 47 percent of the world market and 36 percent of the U.S. market for insulin, and 27 percent of the worldwide diabetes care market overall.

And, unfortunately, diabetes as a disease continues to grow. Although diabetes is a complex disease for which the many treatments aren't easy to understand, it does break down into two "types" (really, three, if you include the rarer gestational diabetes occurring only in pregnant women): Type 1, where the pancreas fails to produce enough insulin (and regular insulin supplements are required) and Type 2, a condition where cells fail to absorb insulin properly, often called "adult onset" diabetes. NVO estimates that 387 million people (about 5 percent of the world population) have diabetes of one type or another—and that only about half of them have been diagnosed. On top of that, NVO estimates that 600 million live with obesity, which has a tendency to bring on diabetes. The company estimates that its products are used by about 25 million people worldwide today, and plans to grow this to 40 million by 2020.

Major products include traditional human-based insulin and protein-related products for Type 1 diabetes treatment, which are being replaced by higher-performance "modern" and "new generation" insulins. The company is now rolling out a new-generation insulin called *Tresiba*, which lasts 42 hours or more; this rollout has recently happened in the U.S. after a delay in approval. The rollout is already complete in 23 countries and has reached a 26 percent insulin market share in those countries. Another treatment called *Ryzodeg* for both Type 1 and Type 2 diabetes is manufactured artificially. It is absorbed faster and lasts longer than traditional human insulin and has been approved in Mexico and selected other markets, and another called *Xultophy* for Type 2 diabetes and hypoglycemia treatment, which has been rolled out in Europe, awaits FDA approval. Another new treatment called *Saxenda* has just been approved in the U.S. as a treatment for obesity and overweight adults with Type 2 diabetes or cardiovascular problems. You can see the pattern: The company develops new, more effective formulas and delivery systems (including new oral delivery systems) and typically gets them approved in non-FDA-controlled markets first. By the time they hit the U.S., they are both proven and more profitable.

We shouldn't ignore the 20 percent of Novo Nordisk devoted to diseases outside the diabetes space. The Biopharmaceuticals segment targets hemophilia and other bleeding disorders, hormone replacement therapies, and human growth hormone markets. The model is similar—pioneering approvals outside the U.S., then migrating them into U.S. markets. The company spends about 15 percent of revenues on R&D; about 49 percent of sales in total come from the U.S., which the company indicates is currently responsible for 61 percent of its top-line growth.

Financial Highlights, Fiscal Year 2014

As you'll note from the following figures (especially the ten-year compounded growth) Novo Nordisk clearly qualifies as an "aggressive growth" player. The company hit a flat spot in 2014 with a 13 percent depreciation of the Danish crown against the U.S. dollar; that of course bit into both revenues and earnings for the year. Without that factor, revenues actually increased about 6 percent for the year (versus a 6 percent reported decline) and net earnings increased 5 percent (against a 7 percent reported drop). The year was still a bit soft as the newly approved products hadn't hit full stride. For FY2015, the company expects strong adoption of new products and a moderation of currency effects to drive revenues up 15–20 percent, while the growth and shift to newer products will help margins a bit and bring net earnings up about 12 percent. New products and growth in existing markets should tack another 10 percent onto sales and 15–20 percent onto net earnings for FY2016. Meanwhile, NVO has plans to retire about 10 percent of its shares over the next few years and grow the dividend at something around 10 percent. Also worth noting: the company has zero long-term debt and, since domiciled outside the U.S., enjoys a tax rate in the low 20s versus low 30s for most U.S.-based corporations.

Reasons to Buy

Novo Nordisk appears to be an excellent growth story in what is, unfortunately, a health-care market that is only going to grow over time. It is the closest thing to a "pure play" in this market. Steady revenues and profits from a traditional insulin treatment base fund new research and releases of more effective, more tailored, easier-to-use diabetes treatments. We feel this is exactly the right course, and the strong international footprint allows them to gain regulatory and market acceptance long before they enter the prized U.S. market. Financials, too, are excellent.

Reasons for Caution

Taking all this growth into account, shares sell for a premium to earnings that may make some investors uncomfortable; it is more a growth story and less of a cash return story than most stocks on our list. We do feel, however, that the cash returns will catch up. Naturally, we are concerned about regulatory approvals, attempts to control prescription drug costs, and the potential aggressiveness of competitors, who could want their bigger slice of this lucrative market. Finally, even though Novo presents itself well, it is in a complex business on a complex international stage; it pushes our "buy businesses you understand" mantra to its limits.

SECTOR: **Health Care** ❑ BETA COEFFICIENT: **0.94** ❑ 10-YEAR COMPOUND EARNINGS PER-SHARE GROWTH: **22.5%** ❑ 10-YEAR COMPOUND DIVIDENDS PER-SHARE GROWTH: **28.5%**

	2007	2008	2009	2010	2011	2012	2013	2014
Revenues (mil)	8,251	8,629	9,842	10,814	11,559	13,384	15,435	14,511
Net income (mil)	1,681	1,827	2,075	2,563	2,979	3,800	4,651	4,326
Earnings per share	0.53	0.59	0.69	0.88	1.04	1.38	1.73	1.65
Dividends per share	0.12	0.19	0.22	0.27	0.38	0.50	0.62	0.83
Cash flow per share	0.73	0.75	0.87	1.05	1.24	1.58	1.95	1.88
Price: high	13.7	14.7	14.0	22.8	26.6	34.1	38.9	49.1
low	7.8	8.4	8.3	12.8	18.9	22.8	29.9	36.6

Website: *www.novonordisk.com*

AGGRESSIVE GROWTH

Oracle Corporation

Ticker symbol: ORCL (NYSE) ◻ S&P rating: AA- ◻ Value Line financial strength rating: A++ ◻ Current yield: 1.4% ◻ Dividend raises, past 10 years: 4

Company Profile

Oracle Corporation is best known as the producer and marketer of . . . the Oracle database. Why rename your company after your mainline product? Well, with the possible exception of Coca-Cola, maybe no single product has meant as much to one company as this database has meant to Oracle. It put the company on the map and fueled all of its growth for the first three decades of its existence.

Led by tech pioneer Larry Ellison, who still owns 26 percent of the company, Oracle is a global provider of database and applications software, "engineered systems" (Oracle hardware preconfigured with Oracle software), and services. Software licenses, renewals, and support constitute roughly 75 percent of revenue, with nearly 56 percent of revenue coming from outside the United States. In detail: New software licenses account for 28 percent of FY2014 revenue, software license updates and product support 48 percent, hardware systems (see next) 8 percent, and services 6 percent.

The acquisition of Sun Microsystems in 2010 brought with it what was to become Oracle's first hardware products. These were basically little more than standard Sun servers with Oracle software installed. These product lines have now been pared down and customized into Oracle's "Exadata" machines, which are very large standalone installations with enormous storage capacity.

In the enterprise world, Oracle is ubiquitous. Its database, middleware, and applications, which include everything from sales to accounting to supply-chain to human resources management products, hold the top spots in retail, banking, manufacturing, financial services, the public sector, and several other industry segments. Increasingly, the company is offering its customers a full choice of deployment models: These products and services are being delivered through the "cloud" as SaaS (Software as a Service) and PaaS (Platform as a Service) offerings. Too, the company has acquired over 100 companies in the past decade; perhaps the most visible is the 2004 acquisition of applications software provider PeopleSoft. The ad refrain "More Enterprise SaaS Applications Than Any Other Cloud Services Provider" pretty much sums up where the company's head is at the moment.

In addition, the company spent over $5 billion—almost 14 percent of revenues—on R&D.

Financial Highlights, Fiscal Year 2014

FY2014 total revenues were up just under 3 percent to $38.3 billion and would have been up about 6 percent on a constant currency basis. Software and Cloud revenues were up 5 percent, with Cloud SaaS and PaaS revenues up almost 30 percent, while Hardware systems were flat, and Services actually declined 5 percent. Earnings rose 2 percent in total, while per-share earnings, on the back of a substantial 300 million share buyback (more on this follows), rose about 7 percent. Currency and some business shifts will keep revenue growth largely flat in FY2015, with continued SaaS/PaaS strength leading to a 4–5 percent top-line growth rate for FY2016, with a similar trajectory in per-share earnings. We should note that, although net earnings growth is modest, the net profit margin is fully 33 percent—software is a very profitable business.

Reasons to Buy

For many years people viewed Oracle as a company that just didn't get it. Why design and market an Exadata machine for a data center when no one builds their own data center anymore? Why not just use Amazon Web Services? Why continue to market a giant database that requires a large staff of expensive professionals to configure? Everybody knew the sexy part of the market is in small, targeted application software.

These were valid questions and would have been reasons for concern if Oracle were just now getting into the business, but the simple truth is there are over 300,000 Oracle database customers, including nearly all of the *Fortune* 100. Oracle database support and licensing revenues were, and continue to be, a massive cash cow. This large installed base brings with it a large population of very skilled practitioners, people who have made their entire careers out of installing, configuring, and supporting this software. Understanding that, the company continues to update its namesake product with new capabilities.

However, Oracle also came to recognize the trend among small and midsized companies toward lower capital investment in data services, which has now migrated into larger enterprises. Many startups and even mature companies are moving to cloud service schemes such as SaaS and PaaS. Oracle has responded with a dual approach of internal development programs and targeted acquisitions. As a result, Oracle is now the second-largest (by revenue) SaaS vendor in the world.

We like Oracle's financials, its steady share price growth, and its wallet—if you plan to grow by acquisition, it's good to have $44 billion in cash. Share price increases have not been stellar over the years, but through share buybacks (which have totaled 16 million shares or so *per month* recently) the company expects to have reduced share counts by a billion shares—about 20 percent—in a 12-year period ending in 2015, and could reduce the share count by another 500 million in the next five years. The company also instituted a dividend in 2009, which has grown steadily since.

Reasons for Caution

In spite of Oracle's history of steady, if not spectacular, share price increases, questions about its future growth—and profitability—remain: Can Oracle compete effectively in an increasingly mobile and cloud-based computing environment? Is it too dependent on its cash-cow database products? Are the company's acquisitions hitting the right segments, and is it buying at the right price? Is it moving fast enough in the cloud and SaaS space? Oracle seems to be at an inflection point: Will it dominate the cloud as it has dominated the data center? Initial prospects are encouraging, but there are a lot of nimble competitors out there, and the technology changes rapidly.

SECTOR: **Information Technology** ▫ BETA COEFFICIENT: **1.42** ▫ 10-YEAR
COMPOUND EARNINGS PER-SHARE GROWTH: **20.0%** ▫ 10-YEAR COMPOUND
DIVIDENDS PER-SHARE GROWTH: **NM**

		2007	2008	2009	2010	2011	2012	2013	2014
Revenues (mil)		18,208	22,609	23,495	27,034	35,850	37,221	37,253	38,305
Net income (mil)		5,295	6,799	7,393	6,494	11,385	12,520	12,958	13,214
Earnings per share		1.01	1.30	1.44	1.67	2.22	2.46	2.68	2.87
Dividends per share		—	—	0.05	0.20	0.20	0.24	0.30	0.48
Cash flow per share		1.09	1.37	1.53	1.75	2.32	2.65	2.91	3.10
Price:	high	23.3	23.6	25.1	32.3	36.5	34.3	38.3	46.7
	low	16.0	15.0	13.8	21.2	24.7	25.3	29.9	35.4

Website: *www.oracle.com*

Otter Tail Corporation

Ticker symbol: OTTR (NASDAQ) ❑ S&P rating: BBB ❑ Value Line financial strength rating: B+ ❑ Current yield: 3.8% ❑ Dividend raises, past 10 years: 4

Company Profile

Otter Tail Corporation is a holding company and a mini-conglomerate operating primarily in the upper Midwest. The conglomerate is centered on and stabilized by the Otter Tail Power Company, a regulated utility serving about 130,000 customers in rural western Minnesota, the eastern half of North Dakota, and the eastern quarter of South Dakota. (In case you're wondering, these areas just miss the vast energy exploration territories of western North Dakota.) About 50 percent of electric revenues come from Minnesota; 42 percent from North Dakota, and 8 percent from South Dakota. After some 2014 divestitures primarily in the electric utility construction business, the utility accounted for about 51 percent of the total business in FY2014, while the Manufacturing & Infrastructure unit, a group of five businesses engaged in metal parts, plastic pipe, and infrastructure products manufacturing and infrastructure construction services, make up the other 49 percent; these non-utility businesses are further described in the following bullets.

Extensive use of wind generation and hydro power, and lower grades of coal available in the region, have driven fuel costs down to 16.6 percent of revenues, a very low figure for the industry. (By comparison, Xcel Energy, which supplies electricity to surrounding areas in North Dakota and Minnesota as well as other Great Plains locations, Colorado, and Texas, spends 50 percent of revenues on fuel, and most conventional utilities run in the 35–50 percent range.) Approximately 15 percent of power generation is from wind power sources; another 1 percent comes from hydro, and the company has made its first investments in solar to meet a Minnesota state requirement by 2020.

Beyond the utility, the company has sold seven fairly good-sized businesses in the past three years in order to sharpen its focus. The remaining five businesses within its Manufacturing & Infrastructure segment include:

■ BTD Manufacturing is a metal-stamping, fabricating, and laser-cutting shop supplying custom parts for agriculture, lawn care, health and fitness, and the RV industry.

- T.O. Plastics supplies thermoformed packaging and handling products for the horticultural, medical, food, electronics, and other consumer industries, including medical device packaging, plastic trays, housings and enclosures, and food and plant containers.
- Northern Pipe Products produces PVC water and sewer pipes up to 24 inches in diameter for pressurized applications and drainage.
- VinylTech, a producer of a similar line of utility-grade PVC products in Arizona, serves more of a southwestern geography.
- The Foley Company is a specialty contractor involved in industrial power, water and wastewater, and other complex construction projects.

The company takes a very hands-off approach to managing its Manufacturing & Infrastructure subsidiaries; in fact, each has its own unique website with links within the Otter Tail Corporation site. In total, the company has 1,893 employees, and most operations are centered in the upper Midwest, VinylTech being the exception.

Financial Highlights, Fiscal Year 2014

Because of the divestitures over the years, sequential numbers are difficult to compare. The company "pruned" more than 10 percent off its revenues; yet as an affirmation of its strategy, reported a greater than 10 percent gain in net earnings. This was helped along in part by cost recovery from recent utility plant upgrades and lower input costs for some of its infrastructure materials lines—although about two-thirds of operating income is derived from the electric utility operations.

For FY2015 and FY2016, the company expects healthy revenue gains, first 13–15 percent in FY2015, then another 5–6 percent in FY2016, as growth trends in its remaining businesses look healthy. Profitability looks to be on the rise in all businesses, and profit growth in the 15 percent range is expected in both years. Like many utilities, the company has been issuing a few shares to "deleverage," probably a smart move with impending interest rate increases, but earnings and cash-flow improvements will support a solid and steadily growing dividend, something we weren't sure about when Otter Tail first came to our *100 Best* list.

Reasons to Buy

When we first added Otter Tail to the 2012 *100 Best Stocks* list, admittedly we were taken by its Berkshire Hathaway–like construct of a basic business around a steady core, the electric utility. We also liked its commitment to the wind energy business. However, aside from reducing energy input costs to the utility, the wind power construction business wasn't working well, and the other businesses may have been a bit too far-flung to manage effectively—so the company retrenched, trimmed the branches, so to speak, first with windmill construction and transportation, then with other businesses that didn't fit so well. After the pruning, the company is still more or less constructed around this diverse and well-anchored model. The non-utility core is centered on infrastructure construction and materials—which we like—and is managed much in the Berkshire Hathaway style of hands-off, autonomous, you-supply-the-management-not-us style, which we also like.

Otter Tail still appears to be a good way to participate in several well-managed businesses while getting a decent current return with solid cash flows and dividends. It remains a "small town" company in contrast to "big city" corporate America.

Reasons for Caution

The utility is stable but not likely to be helped along by population growth, and the manufacturing and construction businesses are cyclical. The company is on much more solid footing than it was a few years ago, but it still doesn't have the reserve strength of larger companies. We compared Otter Tail to Berkshire Hathaway but should note that Berkshire is more diversified and has much larger anchor businesses.

SECTOR: **Utilities/Industrials** ❑ BETA COEFFICIENT: **1.00** ❑ 10-YEAR COMPOUND EARNINGS PER-SHARE GROWTH: **-2.0%** ❑ 10-YEAR COMPOUND DIVIDENDS PER-SHARE GROWTH: **1.0%**

		2007	2008	2009	2010	2011	2012	2013	2014
Revenues (mil)		1,239	1,311	1,040	1,118	1,078	859	893	799
Net income (mil)		54.0	35.1	26.0	13.6	16.4	39.0	50.2	56.9
Earnings per share		1.78	1.09	0.71	0.38	0.45	1.05	1.37	1.55
Dividends per share		1.17	1.19	1.19	1.19	1.19	1.19	1.19	1.21
Cash flow per share		3.55	2.81	2.76	2.82	2.39	2.71	3.03	3.09
Price:	high	39.4	46.2	25.4	25.4	23.5	25.3	31.9	32.7
	low	29.0	15.0	18.5	18.2	17.5	20.7	25.2	26.5

Website: *www.ottertail.com*

AGGRESSIVE GROWTH

Pall Corporation

Ticker symbol: PLL (NYSE) ◻ S&P rating: BBB+ ◻ Value Line financial strength rating: A+ ◻ Current yield: 1.2% ◻ Dividend raises, past 10 years: 10

Company Profile

Pall Corporation supplies filtration, separation, and purification technologies for the removal of solid, liquid, and gaseous contaminants from a variety of liquids and gases. Its products are used in thousands of industrial and clinical settings: removal of contaminants from gas reagents in every semiconductor production facility in the world, removal of bacteria and virus spores from water in hospitals and other clinical settings, and detection of bacteria in blood samples. Its products range in scale from simple inline filters, sold 100 to the carton, to entire graywater treatment systems with capacities up to 150,000 gallons/day. The company holds a market-leading position in most of its filtration, separation, and purification markets and is often called the "original clean technology company" by industry cohorts.

Pall's product and customers fall into two broad categories each making up about half of the business: Life Sciences and Industrial. The Life Sciences category breaks down further into Biopharma (33 percent of FY2014 revenues), Blood/Medical (8 percent), and Food & Beverage (7 percent). The company's Life Sciences technologies are used in the research laboratory, pharmaceutical and biotechnology industries, in blood centers, and in hospitals at the point of patient care. Certain medical products improve the safety of the use of blood products in patient care and help control the spread of infections in hospitals. Pall's separation systems and disposable filtration and purification technologies are critical to the development and commercialization of chemically synthesized and biologically derived drugs and vaccines.

The Industrial segment includes Process Technologies (21 percent of FY2014 sales), Aerospace and Transportation (8 percent), and Microelectronics (11 percent). Industrial markets include, but aren't limited to, consumer electronics, municipal and industrial water, fuels, chemicals, energy, pulp and paper, automotive, and food and beverage markets. Using food and beverage as an example, Pall sells filtration solutions to wine, beer, soft drink, bottled water, and food ingredient producers. Additionally, the company sells filtration and fluid monitoring equipment to the aerospace industry for use on commercial and military aircraft, ships, and land-based military vehicles to help protect critical systems and components. Pall also sells filtration and purification technologies for the semiconductor, data storage, fiber-optic, advanced display, and materials markets, and a line of contamination-control products for an assortment of industries.

Pall is the leader in almost all of these markets. International sales account for 68 percent of the total. Increasingly, the company looks at itself as a supplier of single-use and automated filtration or chemical analysis *systems*, such as a new product called AcroPrep that can filter 24 syringe samples simultaneously, and *consumables*: the filters and substrates used across all applications. Looking at Pall in this light, Life Sciences consumables account for 46 percent of sales, Industrial consumables 41 percent, Industrial systems 9 percent, and Life Sciences systems 4 percent.

Financial Highlights, Fiscal Year 2014

Total revenues advanced 5.3 percent in FY2014, although 2.5 percent of that was due to three modestly sized acquisitions. Currency headwinds took about 1 percent out of the top line, a figure we found surprisingly small given the large international sales footprint. Of the two major business segments, Life Sciences, driven by the acquisitions but also a strong biopharma business, grew about 10 percent, while the Industrial business was roughly flat. The takeaway is that "bio" is hot, while the industrial segments suffer a bit from lagging capital investment and cost-cutting efforts on the part of major customers. Technology advances in their "systems" lines will be important going forward, and these lines are also running well ahead of the company-wide growth curve.

Sales, margins, and net profits are projected roughly flat through FY2015, although a regular annual $260 million buyback (translating into a bit less than 3 percent of the share count) will help per-share earnings advance about 5 percent in FY2015. FY2016 looks a bit stronger with a 9–10 percent advance in earnings on a 3–4 percent advance in the top line.

Reasons to Buy

As the company puts it, "sophisticated filters are rarely discretionary." We like companies with a strong niche, a diversified customer base, and a strong and ongoing base of repeat business. Pall delivers on all three principles. The company sells into the medical, biopharma, energy, and water-process technologies; aerospace; and microelectronics spaces, among others. These sectors will continue to show consistency and strength over time. Further, Pall's products are consumables used consistently within the lab and manufacturing processes they sell into. Some 87 percent of Pall's sales are repeat-purchased consumables; this establishes the company as the slow, steady performer it has been and gives it a line of defense in a poor economy. Too, the company has shown a good track record in increasing the profitability from these ongoing sales; net profit margins have advanced from the 7–8 percent range ten years ago to 13 percent recently. Finally, the company has a good track record for returning some of these profits to shareholders, although we'd like to see a bit more on the dividend front.

Reasons for Caution

While its presence in the consumables side of the business attenuates the effects of economic cycles somewhat, the company is still sensitive to economic downturns. Recent acquisitions have been well targeted and modest; we hope the company doesn't embark on a larger acquisition campaign just to reach for growth. The recent success in the biopharma market is generally a good thing, but may be more volatile and less dependable than its other businesses. Finally, the share price has run in line with the company's success and leaves less room for growth than we'd like particularly with the modest dividend—choose entry points carefully.

SECTOR: **Industrials** ❑ BETA COEFFICIENT: **1.46** ❑ 10-YEAR COMPOUND EARNINGS PER-SHARE GROWTH: **11.5%** ❑ 10-YEAR COMPOUND DIVIDENDS PER-SHARE GROWTH: **9.5%**

		2007	2008	2009	2010	2011	2012	2013	2014
Revenues (mil)		2,250	2,572	2,392	2,402	2,741	2,672	2,658	2,789
Net income (mil)		128	217	196	241	315	319	330	364
Earnings per share		1.02	1.76	1.64	2.03	2.67	2.71	2.89	3.25
Dividends per share		0.48	0.51	0.58	0.64	0.70	0.88	1.03	1.10
Cash flow per share		1.81	2.60	2.44	2.90	3.60	3.77	3.90	4.37
Price:	high	49.0	43.2	37.3	44.7	59.5	65.8	85.6	102.7
	low	33.2	21.6	18.2	31.8	39.8	50.0	61.3	76.6

Website: *www.pall.com*

Patterson Companies, Inc.

Ticker symbol: PDCO (NASDAQ) ❑ S&P rating: NR ❑ Value Line financial strength rating: A ❑ Current yield: 1.7% ❑ Dividend raises, past 10 years: 5

Company Profile

Patterson Companies is a value-added distributor operating in three segments—Dental Supply, Veterinary Supply, and Medical Supply. Dental Supply (about 59 percent of sales) provides a complete range of consumable dental products, equipment, and software; turnkey digital solutions; office design and setup; and value-added services to dentists and dental laboratories primarily for the North American market. Veterinary Supply (29 percent) is the nation's second-largest distributor of consumable veterinary supplies, equipment, diagnostic products, vaccines, and pharmaceuticals to companion-pet veterinary clinics. This segment grew considerably from 21 percent in FY2012, in part due to an acquisition, and is Patterson's most rapidly growing business. Medical Supply (12 percent) distributes medical supplies and assistive products, primarily for rehabilitation and sports medicine, globally to hospitals, long-term-care facilities, clinics, and dealers.

Patterson has one-third of the North American dental supply market. Its main competitors are HSIC (Henry Schein), which also has about a one-third share, and Dentsply (a former *100 Best* stock). The remaining share is fragmented among a number of smaller players. Sales in the dental market break down as follows: 56 percent consumables, 33 percent total equipment, 11 percent technical services and other.

As one of the lead dogs, Patterson has the clout to negotiate a number of exclusive distribution deals. It is sole distributor for the industry's most popular line of dental chairs and also has an exclusive on the CEREC 3D dental restorative system, an increasingly popular alternative to traditional dental crowns. Patterson is also the leading provider of digital radiography systems, which create instant images of dental work, superior to the images generated by traditional x-ray equipment. The company also supplies and supports dental practice financial and supply-chain management software and offers physical and system design and consulting services to dentists seeking to build or remodel dental offices. The company positions itself as a one-stop shop for its customer dentists and dental clinics, and identifies "Digital Dentistry" as a key trend in its marketing presentations and product mix.

Financial Highlights, Fiscal Year 2014

We've been talking about "dental lag" for several years now—the natural human tendency to delay elective and semi-elective dental procedures for as long as possible. The soft economy gave patients plenty of reasons (and excuses) to defer elective and even not-so-elective procedures, and their dentists, as a result, drew down their inventories and delayed capital purchases for things like dental chairs and digital imaging systems. The effects of "dental lag" lingered into the recovery, but we think now we can finally stop talking about dental lag—and start talking about how Patterson will do increasingly better as their market comes down off its dose of novocaine.

Patience typically pays off, and top-line growth has resumed into the 8–9 percent range for both FY2013 and FY2014. It may moderate some back to the 4–5 percent range for FY2015 through FY2016, but these are still healthy sales gains on top of stronger years in the previous two. Per-share earnings is the real story; aggressive buybacks (Patterson estimates it will have bought back a third of its shares in the ten-year period 2006–2015) and steady profit gains have led to steady 7–8 percent per-share earnings increases for quite some time, and more than 60 percent over that same ten-year period. The only glitch has been in the slow, steady slide in profit margins from the 7 percent range down to around 5 percent, led in part by recession weakness. If the company is able to bring them back into the 7 percent range from economic strength and a higher margin mix—as it projects—the future may bring an even brighter smile.

Reasons to Buy

We think the end of "dental lag" could bring better-than-expected results, as the population has grown older, in addition to the dental ailments already put off. Dental procedures, capital investment, and inventory replenishment will all return to more normal levels—and perhaps then some. When this happens, it may not be too much to expect a "hockey stick"-shaped trajectory for sales, earnings, cash flow, and yes, the stock price—although some would probably prefer to avoid using the hockey stick analogy to describe a dental supply stock!

While there have been some improvements in the art of long-term dental care, such as more widespread fluoride use, we also see a growing need for more expensive procedures, including replacement crowns as well as more expensive and material-intensive implant restorations continuing, if not growing, as the population ages and as dental care becomes a bigger industry overseas.

The aforementioned CEREC 3D is an imaging and milling system that allows the dentist to take an image of the area to be restored and in less than 30 minutes produce a crown, inlay, or other device that is then fitted to the patient's existing dental structure. It's a compelling proposition for high-volume offices where patient throughput is at a premium and the equipment can be fully utilized. Sales of this high-ticket item have been very good and generate ongoing supplies revenue. Patterson's exclusive license for this product is a powerful foot in the door for new accounts. In general, we like the company's initiatives in "Digital Dentistry"—although reluctant to use another hockey analogy, we do feel this is where the puck is going in dentistry. Digital imaging, digital craftwork and analysis, digital records, and digital offices are being embraced by dentists and patients alike. Not everyone will want to watch a root canal as it's being performed, but you get the idea.

The company's moves into the companion-pet veterinary and rehabilitative markets, both of which are driven by a growing and profitable demographic, are an added plus. The company estimates that 68 percent of households own a pet, compared to 56 percent in 1988, another of several favorable demographic trends.

Today the company is primarily focused on the North American market, with promised 24- to 48-hour delivery for most items. International growth presents another large opportunity, with recent acquisitions gaining a foothold in Western Europe, especially in the veterinary business.

As we mentioned, Patterson continues to aggressively return cash to its investors, making significant share repurchases and now, larger dividend increases. Patterson is one of a small handful of mid-cap companies on our *100 Best Stocks* list, so it may be of interest to investors looking for something in that size range to complement our mostly large-cap-dominated list.

Reasons for Caution

Competition in this arena is strong, and the company will have to stay sharp to take advantage as dental lag subsides; otherwise, it could lose share to competitors. We believe that the number of companies offering good dental insurance is declining, and any factor that makes dental procedures more "elective" will likely work against Patterson. Some of the expected recovery from dental lag may already be priced into the stock; rosier times may require some patience and entry points should be chosen carefully. While the wait may be long, we also believe this stock has less downside than most.

SECTOR: **Health Care** ❑ BETA COEFFICIENT: **0.75** ❑ 10-YEAR COMPOUND EARNINGS PER-
SHARE GROWTH: **8.5%** ❑ 10-YEAR COMPOUND DIVIDENDS PER-SHARE GROWTH: **NM**

		2007	2008	2009	2010	2011	2012	2013	2014
Revenues (mil)		2,998	3,094	3,237	3,415	3,536	3,637	4,064	4,400
Net income (mil)		208	200	212	225	213	210	214	220
Earnings per share		1.69	1.70	1.78	1.91	1.92	2.03	2.10	2.25
Dividends per share		—	—	0.10	0.42	0.50	0.58	0.68	0.74
Cash flow per share		1.88	2.00	2.04	2.20	2.31	2.43	2.54	2.85
Price:	high	40.1	37.8	28.3	32.8	39.9	37.6	44.4	49.5
	low	28.3	15.8	16.1	24.1	26.2	29.0	34.3	37.0

Website: *www.pattersoncompanies.com*

AGGRESSIVE GROWTH

Paychex, Inc.

Ticker symbol: PAYX (NASDAQ) ❑ S&P rating: NR ❑ Value Line financial strength rating:
A ❑ Current yield: 3.1% ❑ Dividend raises, past 10 years: 8

Company Profile

Paychex, Inc. provides payroll, human resource, and benefits outsourcing
solutions for small- to medium-sized businesses with 10–200 employees.
Founded in 1971, the company has more than 100 offices and serves over
580,000 clients in the United States as well as about 2,000 clients in Germany and a new base through a partnership in Brazil. Some 85 percent of its
customers are the small- to medium-sized businesses previously mentioned.
The company has two sources of revenue: service revenue, paid by clients for
services, and interest income on the funds held by Paychex for clients.

Paychex offers a one-stop shop portfolio of services and products (and
consequently, employees), including:

- Payroll processing
- Payroll tax administration services
- Employee payment services, including expense reporting, reimburse-
  ments, etc.

- Regulatory compliance services (new-hire reporting and garnishment processing)
- Comprehensive human resource outsourcing services
- Retirement services administration
- Workers' compensation insurance services
- Health and benefits services
- Time and attendance solutions
- Medical deduction, state unemployment, and other HR services and products

The company's products are marketed primarily through its direct sales force, the bulk of which is focused on payroll products. In addition to the direct sales force, the company uses its relationships with existing clients, CPAs, and banks for new client referrals. Approximately two-thirds of its new clients come via these referral sources.

Larger clients can choose to outsource their payroll and HR functions or to run them in-house using a Paychex platform. For those clients, the company offers what it calls "Major Market Services" (MMS) products, which can be run locally or on a web-hosted, SaaS environment.

In addition to traditional payroll services, Paychex offers full-service HR outsourcing solutions; custom-built solutions including payroll, compliance, HR, and employee benefits sourcing and administration; outsourcing management; and even professionally trained onsite HR representatives. The company also manages retirement plans and other benefits, including pretax "cafeteria" plans, and has a subsidiary insurance agency offering property and casualty, workers' comp, health, and auto policies to an employer's employee base. About 28,000 of the 580,000 clients use the full Human Resource Services offering, with a total employee count of 770,000, and it accounts for about 35 percent of Paychex's revenues. The company has recently made a push to implement web-based and mobile versions of its key products, adding to convenience and reducing paperwork for its clients, and has devoted a lot of resources lately to assisting with compliance with the Affordable Care Act.

The company has increased its R&D budget approximately 80 percent in six years to fund the development of new online user interfaces and SaaS (Software as a Service) client delivery. The company acquires small companies both vertically to offer new services and horizontally to expand market presence, and now, to buy a small Canadian supplier of cloud accounting software called Kashoo. The company has also expanded its presence in Germany through another small acquisition, and now has a joint venture in Brazil.

Financial Highlights, Fiscal Year 2014

As the global economy continues to strengthen after the Great Recession, employment expansion helps Paychex's business, and the company has done well expanding the breadth of its services, too. The payroll base expanded only 2 percent in FY2014, but the HR services employee base expanded by 14 percent, retirement service plan base expanded 6 percent, and the health and benefits services base expanded 3 percent. All of that combined into an 8.3 percent top-line gain for FY2014, and a slightly more profitable business mix and the additional volume led to a 10.4 percent gain in net earnings. Results would have been better if short-term interest rates on deposits were higher than last year's 1 percent—and it's anybody's guess when this might actually happen going forward. For FY2015 and FY2016 (we do expect some increase in interest rates by 2016!) revenues should advance in the 7–8 percent range, with earnings up 9–11 percent. Revenue and earnings gains should be at the top end of that scale—or better—if short-term interest rates do pick up.

Reasons to Buy

A bet on Paychex is a bet on two things: continued improvement in the economy and an eventual increase on interest rates (so they can make money on the float). In the meantime, you get a decent yield and little downside risk if you own the stock.

Paychex's primary market is companies with fewer than 100 employees. This is one of the primary reasons that Paychex lost clients—many small businesses, being undercapitalized, went under during the Great Recession. That trend has turned around with the economy; in fact, small business is leading the way while larger businesses are focused on reducing costs, which also helps Paychex as a provider of outsourced services. Beyond that, the cost of switching and a generally good client relationship has made for a loyal client base. We continue to think the trend to outsource payroll and HR activities will not only continue but accelerate as easier Internet-based solutions come more into favor.

The company is conservatively run, well managed, and well financed. Margins are significantly higher than its closest competitor, Automated Data Processing (ADP). It carries no long-term debt—zero—and should have little difficulty funding the generous dividend, even at its current payout level of 80 percent of earnings. Fragmentation in the market and Paychex's extremely strong financial position will allow the company to continue to grow market share through acquisition. The company is also expanding, somewhat cautiously for the moment, in Europe and in South America, a move that could blossom into more business down the road. Finally, sooner or later short-term interest rates must tick upward; when that happens the company will once again be able to profit from the float (the company has $3–$4 billion of its customers' money held for payroll at any given time). Such an increase in interest income would likely fund greater dividend increases and share repurchases; this is one of the few stocks on our list that can tangibly benefit from *moderate* interest rate increases. We like that defensive characteristic.

Reasons for Caution

This company will always be vulnerable to economic swings, such as those brought on by large interest rate increases. The company's acquisition strategy makes sense, as those acquisitions will increase market share, but they do come with costs and risks.

SECTOR: **Information Technology** ❏ BETA COEFFICIENT: **0.95** ❏ 10-YEAR COMPOUND EARNINGS PER-SHARE GROWTH: **7.5%** ❏ 10-YEAR COMPOUND DIVIDENDS PER-SHARE GROWTH: **12.5%**

		2007	2008	2009	2010	2011	2012	2013	2014
Revenues (mil)		1,887	2,066	2,083	2,001	2,084	2,230	2,326	2,519
Net income (mil)		515	576	534	477	516	548	569	678
Earnings per share		1.35	1.56	1.48	1.32	1.42	1.51	1.56	1.71
Dividends per share		0.79	1.20	1.24	1.24	1.24	1.27	1.31	1.40
Cash flow per share		1.54	1.82	1.72	1.56	1.67	1.78	1.83	2.02
Price:	high	47.1	37.5	32.9	32.8	33.9	34.7	45.9	48.2
	low	36.1	23.2	20.3	24.7	25.1	29.1	31.5	39.8

Website: *www.paychex.com*

Perrigo Company

Ticker symbol: PRGO (NASDAQ) ❑ S&P rating: BB+ ❑ Value Line financial strength rating: A ❑ Current yield: 0.3% ❑ Dividend raises, past 10 years: 10

Company Profile

Perrigo is the world's largest manufacturer of over-the-counter pharmaceutical products for the store-brand market. They also manufacture generic prescription pharmaceuticals, nutritional products, and active pharmaceutical ingredients (APIs).

Consolidation is the name of the game in the pharmaceutical business and especially in the lucrative generics segment. In 2014, Perrigo acquired Elan, an Irish maker of mostly prescription pharmaceuticals, broadening their offering in this subsegment and acquiring an Irish headquarters base for tax advantages. The company also added another generic marketer to its portfolio—Omega Pharma—mostly to build the generics business in European markets and 35 countries in all.

While digesting these acquisitions, Perrigo received an offer of $205 per share from rival Mylan, and at the time of this analysis, there are rumors circulating around the acquisition of Mylan by former *100 Best* list participant Teva Pharmaceuticals or another firm. While we can't predict the outcome of these acquisition attempts, we feel that they illustrate the value of the niche in which companies such as Perrigo operate, so we'll keep Perrigo on our *100 Best* list for now and discuss the company as it presently exists.

Perrigo operates in four segments: Consumer Healthcare, Nutritionals, Rx Pharmaceuticals, and API. With Elan blended in, but Omega not quite yet, Consumer Healthcare is by far the largest segment, generating about 54 percent of Perrigo's FY2014 revenue, while Nutritionals brings in 13 percent, Rx Pharma 23 percent, and APIs 4 percent. The Omega acquisition is estimated to shift this mix back toward generics in a major way, to roughly 77 percent Consumer Healthcare and Nutritionals, now taken together, 16 percent Rx Pharma, 4 percent APIs, and 3 percent from a royalty stream for the licensed Rx multiple sclerosis drug Tysabri.

The company's success depends on its ability to manufacture and quickly market generic equivalents to branded products. It employs internal R&D resources to develop product formulations and manufacture in quantity for its customers. It also develops retail packaging specific to the customers' needs. The company expects a greater percentage of medicines to become available over the counter (versus Rx) as has Allegra and similar medications in recent years. The company estimates that 72 percent of educated consumers choose store brands, and 91 percent of them stay with them once chosen.

If you have bought a store-branded over-the-counter medication such as ibuprofen, acetaminophen, skin remedies, or cough medicine at a store like Target or Walmart in the past year, there's a good chance (a 75 percent chance, in fact) that it was made by Perrigo. The company's Consumer Healthcare business produces and markets over 2,700 store-brand products in 18,000 individual SKUs to approximately 1,000 customers, including Wal-Mart, CVS, Walgreens, Kroger, Target, Safeway, Dollar General, Costco, and other national and regional drugstores, supermarkets, and mass merchandisers. Wal-Mart is its single largest customer and accounts for 19 percent of Perrigo's net sales. It's a good deal, because it's a steady cash stream, and Perrigo doesn't really have to invest in marketing.

The Nutritionals segment is relatively new as a standalone segment and includes store-brand infant formula, vitamins, and minerals. The segment distributes 900 store-brand products in 3,400 SKUs to more than 150 customers.

Enlarged by the Elan acquisition, the Rx Pharma operations produce generic prescription drugs (in contrast to the over-the-counter drugs produced in the Consumer Healthcare segment), obviously benefitting when key patented drugs run past their patent protection. Rx Pharma markets approximately 800 generic prescription products, many of them topicals and creams, with over 1,300 SKUs, to approximately 350 customers, while the API division markets an assortment of active ingredients to other drug manufacturers as well as providing them for the company's own products, including a number of active ingredients that we'd have trouble spelling correctly, so we won't even try. The company's products are manufactured in nine facilities around the world. Its major markets are in North America, Mexico, the UK, and China. About 33 percent of sales are overseas.

Financial Highlights, Fiscal Year 2014

With so much happening on the acquisition front, the numbers are a bit hard to follow, and what's discussed here includes Elan but does not include Omega; and obviously doesn't include the other acquisitions, which are only at the discussion stage.

FY2014 revenues were ahead 15 percent including the acquisition, not bad but nothing to write home about. However, the acquisition brought a step function increase in operating margins—from the low 20s as a percent to the low-to-mid 30s—consequently posted net profits rose a stellar 67 percent for FY2014.

The company financed most of the Elan purchase by issuing shares, which will certainly not put it on this year's "buyback achievers" list. As a consequence of that, FY2014 per-share earnings rose a more modest but still respectable 39 percent. Going forward, the company projects a continued 15 percent annual revenue increase (7–11 percent without acquisitions), continued gains in operating margins, and per-share earnings in the $7.25–$7.60 range by the end of FY2015, rising to $8.10–$8.40 in FY2016. That would represent a doubling of FY2013 per-share earnings even with the issuance of shares for acquisitions—little wonder Perrigo is an attractive acquisition candidate!

Reasons to Buy

Perrigo is a real success story of solid niche dominance (store-branded medications) with a couple of high-growth, high-margin businesses mixed in. Steady growth in sales combined with a steady growth in margins has a multiplicative effect, and the company has enjoyed well-above-average profit growth in this industry. Frankly, we had some doubts about the Elan merger and whether it would dilute Perrigo's focus on its core niche businesses, but we've been fans of this company and its management team for a while and have more trust than usual that things will come out right. The Omega Pharma acquisition extends this formula to new markets, and we think that will work as well.

Not only does Perrigo currently dominate a niche, it is a growing niche. The company calls it "Quality Affordable Healthcare Products." People are becoming more sensitive to their own health-care costs and spending in general and are opting more often for the store brand; after all, 200 mg of ibuprofen is 200 mg of ibuprofen. This all sits on top of the demographic tailwind of the aging population and the institutional tailwind of doing what's necessary to rein in costs.

Reasons for Caution

Perrigo broke most of our rules in making a major acquisition of a complex business, then moving to another country where accounting standards make business evaluation more difficult. Normally we would have dropped the company right then and there, but again, we like its track record and niche dominance. If anything, the confusion around the merger provided a buying opportunity in FY2014. Now—with the acquisition "sharks" in the waters, the price of Perrigo's stock has been driven skyward. And naturally, we're not too thrilled with the company's cash returns to investors and rapidly increasing share counts. All in all we're not sure about the right price to buy, but the stock is an excellent one to own—there is more opportunity albeit with more risk than in years past.

SECTOR: Health Care ❏ BETA COEFFICIENT: **0.80** ❏ 10-YEAR COMPOUND EARNINGS PER-SHARE GROWTH: **21.0%** ❏ 10-YEAR COMPOUND DIVIDENDS PER-SHARE GROWTH: **19.5%**

	2007	2008	2009	2010	2011	2012	2013	2014
Revenues (mil)	1,447	1,822	2,007	2,269	2,765	3,173	3,540	4,081
Net income (mil)	78.6	150	176	263	341	411	442	739.5
Earnings per share	0.84	1.58	1.87	2.83	3.64	4.37	4.68	6.39
Dividends per share	0.18	0.21	0.22	0.25	0.27	0.32	0.35	0.39
Cash flow per share	1.46	2.35	2.67	3.69	4.78	5.84	6.41	8.21
Price: high	36.9	43.1	61.4	67.5	104.7	120.8	157.5	171.6
low	16.1	27.7	18.5	37.5	62.3	90.2	98.6	125.4

Website: *www.perrigo.com*

CONSERVATIVE GROWTH

Praxair, Inc.

Ticker symbol: PX (NYSE) ❏ S&P rating: A ❏ Value Line financial strength rating: A ❏ Current yield: 2.3% ❏ Dividend raises, past 10 years: 10

Company Profile

Praxair, Inc. is the second-largest supplier of industrial gases in the world. The company, which was spun off to Union Carbide shareholders in June 1992, supplies a broad range of atmospheric, process, and specialty gases; high-performance coatings; and related services and technologies.

Praxair's primary products are atmospheric gases—oxygen, nitrogen, argon, and rare gases (produced when atmospheric air is purified, compressed, cooled, distilled, and condensed) and process and specialty gases—carbon dioxide, helium, hydrogen, and acetylene (produced as by-products of chemical production or recovered from natural gas). Customers include makers of primary metals, metal fabricators, petroleum refiners, and producers of chemicals, health-care products, pharmaceuticals, biotech, food and beverage, electronics, glass, pulp and paper, and environmental products. By end market, manufacturing, metals, and energy producers account for 55 percent of sales; chemicals, electronics, and aerospace another 20 percent; and health care and food/beverage the next 16 percent, with the remaining 9 percent to "other" industries.

The gas products are sold into the packaged-gas market and the merchant market. In the packaged-gas market, bulk gases are packaged into high-pressure cylinders and either delivered to the customer or to distributors. In the merchant market, bulk gases are liquefied and transported by truck to the customer's facility.

The company also designs, engineers, and constructs cryogenic and noncryogenic gas supply systems for customers who choose to produce their own atmospheric gases onsite. This is obviously a capital-intensive delivery solution for Praxair but results in lower delivered cost to the customer and higher returns for Praxair, as all operational costs are paid by the customer. Contracts for these installations can run to 20 years.

Praxair Surface Technologies is a subsidiary that applies wear-, corrosion-, and thermal-resistant metallic and ceramic coatings and powders to metal surfaces in order to resist wear, high temperatures, and corrosion. Aircraft engines are a primary market, but it serves others, including the printing, textile, chemical, and primary metals markets, and provides aircraft engine and airframe component overhaul services. About 48 percent of Praxair's sales come from outside North America.

Financial Highlights, Fiscal Year 2014

After a strong FY2013, revenues for FY2014 flattened out a bit to $12.3 billion, a modest 2.9 percent ahead of FY2013, and will likely flatten further to a 1 percent gain in FY2015 mostly due to the headwinds of a strong dollar. Despite the dollar and a concentration in the now-declining energy industry, the company expects new plant construction, especially in international markets and in some of the smaller sectors like health care and food and beverage, to boost the top line more substantially in FY2016, as much as 6.5 percent. Earnings took a bit of a vacation in FY2014 as well, but lower input prices, cost efficiencies, and moderate share buybacks are projected to drive a 12 percent gain in per-share earnings in FY2015 and another 9–11 percent gain in FY2016—this improvement in profitability and a steadily increasing return to shareholders is more compelling than business growth per se. The company specifically targets to return about half of its cash flow to shareholders while investing the other half in the business.

Reasons to Buy

Although Praxair has missed a few putts in the top and bottom lines in the past few years, it's nice to own a few "golf clap" stocks in companies that show high margins, steady growth, and few to no surprises. Par, par, birdie, par, maybe a bogey every now and then—not a bad round, and Praxair continues to be the sort of company that can deliver that.

Praxair is the largest gas provider in the emerging markets of China, India, Brazil, Mexico, and Korea and continues to invest heavily in plants in these regions. In general, the international presence is more balanced and diversified than most of its competitors, and it is not as dependent upon growth in China. The company is a big player in the petroleum industry and especially the heavy crude segment; equally if not more importantly, the company is a strong and pure play in the re-emergence of U.S. manufacturing.

We especially like the company's high margins (31 percent and growing) and cash-flow generation—and the willingness to share it with shareholders.

Reasons for Caution

Competitors are strong, and getting stronger with the recent Air Products–Airgas merger and a consolidation of smaller players in the industry. As hydrocarbon energy products are feedstock for many of Praxair's products, the company is sensitive to increases in energy prices, and the price of natural gas in particular, an important feedstock, has fluctuated considerably while being historically low; of course recent trends are favorable. Currently energy is a two-edged sword—lower input prices, yes, but also a looming drop in one of its larger customer segments (the energy industry accounts for 14 percent of sales), especially those producers of heavy crudes we just mentioned.

The strong international presence means that results are sensitive to currency headwinds, but those headwinds may subside or even turn into tailwinds; we expect a little help on that front in FY2016 too. Finally, the markets have recognized Praxair's recent scorecard and are still giving a low handicap in the form of a high share price continuing at 22 times earnings, difficult to sustain for a high single-digit growth rate—new investors should thus look for favorable entry points. That said, this has been one of the more dependable performers on our scorecard.

SECTOR: **Materials** ❑ BETA COEFFICIENT: **0.83** ❑ 10-YEAR COMPOUND EARNINGS PER-SHARE GROWTH: **13.0%** ❑ 10-YEAR COMPOUND DIVIDENDS PER-SHARE GROWTH: **19.0%**

	2007	**2008**	**2009**	**2010**	**2011**	**2012**	**2013**	**2014**
Revenues (mil)	9,402	10,796	8,956	10,118	11,252	11,224	11,925	12,273
Net income (mil)	1,177	1,335	1,254	1,195	1,672	1,692	1,755	1,694
Earnings per share	3.62	4.19	4.01	3.84	5.45	5.61	5.87	5.73
Dividends per share	1.20	1.50	1.60	1.80	2.00	2.20	2.40	2.60
Cash flow per share	6.18	8.63	6.85	6.95	8.95	9.10	9.70	10.35
Price: high	92.1	77.6	86.1	96.3	111.7	116.9	130.5	135.2
low	58.0	53.3	53.3	72.7	88.6	100.0	107.7	117.3

Website: *www.praxair.com*

The Procter & Gamble Company

Ticker symbol: PG (NYSE) ❑ S&P rating: AA- Value Line financial strength rating: A++ ❑ Current yield: 3.1% ❑ Dividend raises, past 10 years: 10

Company Profile

Procter & Gamble dates back to 1837, when William Procter and James Gamble began making soap and candles from surplus animal fat from the stockyards in Cincinnati, OH. The company's first major product introduction took place in 1879 when it launched Ivory soap. Since then, P&G has continually created a host of blockbuster products, added some key acquisitions, exited the food business and a few others, and, in total, has some of the strongest, most recognizable consumer brands in the world.

P&G is a uniquely diversified consumer products company with a strong global presence. P&G markets its broad line of products to nearly 5 billion consumers in more than 180 countries.

The company is a recognized leader in the development, manufacturing, and marketing of quality laundry, cleaning, paper, personal care, and health-care products.

To understand Procter, it's worth a look at how the company is organized. The business mix was realigned again in FY2014:

- *Beauty, Hair, and Personal Care* (24 percent of FY2014 sales, 23 percent of profits) includes shampoo, skin care, deodorant, hair care and color, and bar soap products, including such traditional brands as Head & Shoulders, Ivory soap, Safeguard, Secret, Pantene, Vidal Sassoon, Cover Girl, and Old Spice, and some newer and edgier brands like Olay, Hugo Boss, SK-II, James Bond 007 men's fragrances, Gucci, and Dolce & Gabbana, and a handful of professional brands. There are 36 brands in all.
- *Grooming* (10 percent, 17 percent) includes razors, blades, pre- and post-shave products, and other shaving products, including Gillette, Fusion, Mach3, and Prestobarba brands.
- *Health Care* (9 percent, 9 percent) is made up of two subunits, Personal Health Care and Oral Care. Personal Health Care in turn includes gastrointestinal, respiratory, rapid diagnostics, and vitamins/minerals/supplements, and includes such brands as Vicks, Metamucil, Prilosec, and Pepto-Bismol. Oral Care includes the familiar Crest, Scope, Fixodent, and Oral-B brands among others.
- *Fabric and Home Care* (32 percent, 26 percent) covers many of the familiar laundry and cleaning brands—Tide, Cheer, Dawn, Febreze, Downy, Bounce, Era, Mr. Clean, and a handful created for international markets—34 brands in all.
- *Baby, Feminine, and Family Care* (25 percent, 15 percent) markets mostly paper products like Puffs, Charmin, Pampers, Bounty, Always, and Tampax into baby care, feminine care, adult incontinence, and family care markets.

Procter has always been a hallmark example of brand management and building intrinsic brand strength—that is, strength not from the company name but through the brand's own name and reputation. It is described as a "house of brands," not a "branded house," although we're starting to see the "P&G" name more prominently in its marketing and advertising. The company tells us that its 50 "Leadership Brands" are some of the world's most well-known household names, that 90 percent of its business comes from these 50 brands, and that 25 of them are billion-dollar businesses.

The company has a strong and growing international presence, with 65 percent of sales originating outside the U.S., up from 61 percent in FY2013. The company also manufactures locally in its largest international markets.

The company has recently stepped up an aggressive "spring cleaning" campaign. First is the previously mentioned realignment of brands into five separate segments (it was four segments plus an "international" business unit previously). Second is a widely announced campaign to shed as many as 100 brands, mostly smaller ones, to increase focus on the larger, more successful brands. Third, and related to the second, is a continued effort to sell larger brands that don't align well with the others, like its food brands (Jif, Duncan Hines, Folgers, etc., in recent years); the company sold its Duracell battery brand, acquired in the 2005 Gillette acquisition, to Warren Buffett's Berkshire Hathaway. We expect more moves in all three of these areas.

Financial Highlights, Fiscal Year 2014

The previously mentioned housecleaning and currency effects were the big stories for FY2014. The concentration of overseas business pushed net revenues down about 4 percent for the year, despite the fact that a favorable product mix and some price increases brought a base "organic" 2 percent growth for the period. However, continued manufacturing cost savings and other efficiencies (they've been outsourcing major manufacturing operations for years, even bringing outside operators onto their own factory sites), and lower commodity costs brought a decent 3 percent gain in total earnings; that, combined with a 30 million share buyback, brought a 4.2 percent rise in per-share earnings.

The picture through FY2016 is mixed. Brand divestitures and continued currency headwinds are projected to diminish revenues as much as 6 percent in FY2015, with a 2 percent recovery into FY2016 assuming some reversal of recent currency effects. The bottom line, too, will decrease in total even as operating and net margins improve modestly; net profit is projected down a bit over 5 percent in FY2015, recovering to near FY2014 levels (on the smaller revenue base) in FY2016. Most analysts see an acceleration of both revenues and profits as the "housecleaning" winds down; share repurchases and dividend increases should continue throughout the period.

Reasons to Buy

Regardless of developments in the world economy, people will continue to shave, bathe, do laundry, and care for their babies, and P&G is the global leader in baby care, feminine care, fabric care, and shaving products. Everyone should consider at least one defensive play in their portfolio, and P&G continues to deserve a spot at the top of the list.

P&G is extending its reach to capture share in channels and markets currently underserved. Developing markets are a huge opportunity, representing 86 percent of the world's population, and P&G feels it can be a leader in many product categories. Emerging markets now represent 39 percent of their FY2014 revenue, up from 32 percent in 2011 and 20 percent in 2002. P&G is also broadening its distribution channels to pursue opportunities in drug and pharmacy outlets, convenience stores, export operations, and even e-commerce.

As the company continues to evolve its organizational structure, it has departed from its traditional model of managing brands as wholly separate businesses with brand-specific advertising budgets, product research labs, and so forth. Synergies from combining ads and ad strategies alone should reduce total costs across the company's many portfolios. While we will miss some of the brands they are likely to cut, the business won't miss them all that much; focus, critical mass, and profitability appear to be their strategic mainstays moving forward.

In short, we continue to like the brand, marketplace, and financial strength; sure and steady dividend growth (the company has raised its dividend 59 straight years); and short- and long-term prospects.

Reasons for Caution

Revenue growth remains a key challenge—although the company seems to be taking the right steps to prosper in a low-growth environment. The recent recession made consumers much more price conscious, and many switched to generics. That switch has reversed to a degree, but not everyone is coming back on board. While commodity prices are favorable today, rising commodity costs can affect P&G, and the emphasis on the health and beauty business brings more exposure to often-fickle consumer tastes and shorter brand life than the company may be used to. Finally, we think the steady stream of change is a distraction and makes the future a bit harder to predict than for other players in this business.

SECTOR: **Consumer Staples** ▫ BETA COEFFICIENT: **0.46** ▫ 10-YEAR COMPOUND EARNINGS PER-SHARE GROWTH: **7.0%** ▫ 10-YEAR COMPOUND DIVIDENDS PER-SHARE GROWTH: **10.5%**

	2007	2008	2009	2010	2011	2012	2013	2014
Revenues (mil)	76,476	83,503	79,029	78,938	82,559	83,680	85,500	83,062
Net income (mil)	10,340	12,075	11,293	10,946	11,797	11,344	11,869	12,220
Earnings per share	3.04	3.64	3.58	3.53	3.93	3.85	4.05	4.22
Dividends per share	1.28	1.45	1.64	1.80	1.97	2.14	2.29	2.45
Cash flow per share	4.25	4.97	4.65	4.87	5.21	5.20	5.33	5.57
Price: high	75.2	73.8	63.5	65.3	67.7	71.0	85.8	93.9
low	60.4	54.9	43.9	39.4	57.6	59.1	68.4	75.3

Website: *www.pg.com*

GROWTH AND INCOME

Public Storage

Ticker symbol: PSA (NYSE) ▫ S&P rating: A ▫ Value Line financial strength rating: A+ ▫ Current yield: 3.0% ▫ Dividend raises, past 10 years: 8

Company Profile

You have stuff. We have stuff. We all have stuff. Stuff to store somewhere. Stuff from our families, stuff from our kids, stuff from our past. Boats, RVs, and extra vehicles. And we all need to store that stuff. But where? As more of us live in houses with smaller yards and devoid of basements, where? As more of us choose to rent rather than buy, where? As more of us, especially the younger "Millennials" among us, choose to live closer to the centers of larger cities, where? As the retirees among us downsize, where? As the elderly give up their primary residences, where?

You get the idea. There is more personal stuff for most of us to store, and less space to do it. That's where Public Storage comes in.

Public Storage is a real estate investment trust owning and operating 2,250 self-storage properties in 38 states and another 192 facilities in seven countries in Europe. The company has a 49 percent interest in Europe's Shurgard, and also owns a 42 percent interest in another trust called PS Business Parks, which owns 103 rentable properties in eight states. The company points out that, based on the number of tenants, it is one of the world's largest landlords.

Most are probably familiar with the format—small, unfinished, generally not-climate-controlled lockers rentable on a month-to-month basis for personal and business use. They range in size from 25–400 square feet, and there are typically 350–750 storage spaces in each facility. Some include covered parking for vehicle, boat, and RV storage. On average the company nets about $1 per square foot per month—a rather handsome sum considering these units do not come with any of the finish or comfort of an apartment, which may rent for something similar per square foot depending on the market.

Not surprisingly, the largest concentrations are in California, Texas, and Florida, (since these are centers for retirees and homes with no basements) and most are near a major U.S. or European city. The three largest markets are New York, San Francisco, and Los Angeles. Branding in the U.S. is "Public Storage;" in Europe it is "Shurgard."

The key strategies are revenue and cost optimization, market share growth in major markets, and building brand recognition. The company has a centralized call center and a website to help market its product and facilitate transactions. Acquisitions are also an important part of the strategy; the current market is fragmented with PSA only owning 10–20 percent of the market at most, and good properties come up regularly. The company acquired 50 such properties in 2014 and expects to grow its property base a steady 1–2 percent annually.

Public Storage represents our second *100 Best* venture into the REIT market; the first was Health Care REIT two years ago. Our principle here remains the same: We're not looking for just real estate—we want to own a good business that *just happens* to own a lot of real estate. REITs are typically good income producers, as they are required by law to pay a substantial portion of their cash flow to investors. The accounting rules are different, and REIT investors should focus on Funds From Operations (FFO), which is analogous to operating income; net income figures have depreciation expenses deducted, which can vary in timing and not always be realistic. FFO supports the dividends paid to investors.

Financial Highlights, Fiscal Year 2014

FY2014 was another strong and steady year. Occupancy rates ran at 93.5 percent for the year, and realized rents rose almost 5 percent. Revenues grew almost 11 percent in all, while the core self-storage business grew 5.4 percent on a same-store basis. With some adjustments added in, net income grew 35 percent; on a "same-store" basis it grew about 6.7 percent. The key funds from operations (FFO) figure increased just over 6 percent on a per-share basis, as the company has been adding a few more shares following an industry-wide trend toward deleveraging its balance sheet (more equity, less debt).

For FY2015 and FY2016, the company projects revenue growth, aided but not as much by acquisitions, in the 3–4 percent range for each year, with per-share FFO growth in the 6–9 percent range annually.

Reasons to Buy

As previously stated, our emphasis is more on the business and less on real estate, and with Public Storage, we feel we've found a good business that happens to be based on real estate. PSA has the best brand and highest operating efficiency in the business, and the core business model and need for its product is sustained and growing. No matter how easy it is to sell stuff on Craigslist, it's also too easy to acquire stuff, and we don't see people getting out of that habit anytime soon. At the same time, real estate is trending away from large suburban McMansions with extra space and more toward city digs, patio homes, cluster homes, and the like. All point to strong, steady business prospects for providers of flexible storage solutions, and as PSA strengthens its brand and market-share foothold, more of that business will go its way. The dividend has risen substantially in recent years and is well funded; too, there is less debt than typically found in a real estate investment business.

Reasons for Caution

Real estate is real estate, and is more subject to ups and downs than was once thought. Increased dividends and general strength of this business have continued to store away some pretty healthy gains for the stock—unlock the door and enter carefully.

SECTOR: Real Estate ▫ BETA COEFFICIENT: 0.63 ▫ 10-year compound FFO per-share growth: 8.5% ▫ 10-YEAR COMPOUND DIVIDENDS PER-SHARE GROWTH: 11.5%

	2007	2008	2009	2010	2011	2012	2013	2014
Revenues (mil)	1,616	1,746	1,628	1,647	1,752	1,826	1,982	2,195
Net income (mil)	457	636	835	672	824	670	845	1,144
Funds from operations per share	4.74	5.17	5.03	5.22	5.93	6.31	7.53	7.98
Real estate owned per share	56.61	46.48	46.48	44.51	43.35	42.71	47.97	49.20
Dividends per share	2.00	2.20	2.20	3.05	3.65	4.40	5.15	5.80
Price: high	117.2	102.5	85.1	106.1	136.7	152.7	176.7	190.2
low	68.1	52.5	45.3	74.7	100.0	129.0	144.4	148.0

Website: *www.publicstorage.com*

AGGRESSIVE GROWTH

Quest Diagnostics Inc.

Ticker symbol: DGX (NYSE) ▫ S&P rating: BBB+ ▫ Value Line financial strength rating: B++ ▫ Current yield: 2.0% ▫ Dividend raises, past 10 years: 5

Company Profile

If you have gone for any kind of medical test, either at the recommendation of a doctor or as required by an employer or insurance company, chances are you got that test in a lab operated by Quest Diagnostics. Quest is the world's leading provider of diagnostic testing, information, and services to support doctors, hospitals, and the care-giving process.

The company operates more than 2,200 labs and patient service centers including about 150 smaller "rapid-response" labs in the U.S., and has facilities in India, Mexico, the U.K., Ireland, and Sweden. It provides about 150 million lab test results a year and serves physicians, hospitals, employers, life and health-care insurers, and other health facilities. The company has a logistics network including 3,000 courier vehicles and 20 aircraft, and has some 20 *billion* test results from the past decade on its databases, a rich source for medical research data. Quest estimates that it serves more than half the hospitals and physicians in the United States.

The company offers diagnostic testing services covering pretty much the gamut of medical necessity in its testing facilities. It also offers a line of diagnostic kits, reagents, and devices to support its own labs, home and remote testing, and other labs. The company offers a series of "wellness and risk management services," including tests, exams, and record services for the insurance industry. The company also does tests and provides other support for clinical research and trials, and finally, through its information technology segment, offers a Care360 platform to help physicians maintain charts and access data through its network, which has about 200,000 physicians enrolled. Mobile technology is another innovation front; the company has developed a mobile solution within Care360 known as "MyQuest" to help patients keep track of test results, schedule appointments and medications, and share information with physicians and other care providers. The company is also innovating with its 200,000-square-foot "lab of the future" prototype in Marlborough, MA.

The company has begun to provide "insourced" solutions to hospitals that formerly ran their own labs. More progressive hospitals and hospital systems have been trying to cut costs and are starting to look at independent labs to run some of their in-house functions. The company recently acquired parts of the UMass Memorial Medical Center and California's Dignity Health's (formerly Catholic Healthcare West) "outreach" lab business, that is, labs located off hospital premises.

The company has also been a leader in developing so-called "moderate complexity" direct molecular testing procedures, where more complex diagnostic tests can be performed in "moderate complexity" environments— i.e., a "retail" lab format such as Quest operates. Such a new test for encephalitis was cleared by the FDA in March 2014—a first, and a strong endorsement of this type of procedure delivery. The company is also a leader in "gene-based" and "esoteric" testing and has launched an assortment of molecular genetics tests supporting new trends in the health industry toward individualized medicine—medicine based on a patient's own unique gene makeup and characteristics.

Financial Highlights, Fiscal Year 2014

Medicare cutbacks and competition in the lab diagnostic business softened results through FY2012 and FY2013; things began to recover in FY2014 especially on the revenue front. As we predicted, patient volumes increased due to expanded coverage through the Affordable Care Act and from out-sourcing/insourcing arrangements. Reimbursement levels, however, are still a headwind; the resulting small margin dip drove a flat earnings performance for FY2014. The company expects continued volume expansion in FY2015 and FY2016, with revenues up in the 2–3 percent range both years. But also a stronger value-add component with complex testing and better scale for outsourced operations lead to a healthy gain in net margins, leading in turn to profit increases of as much as 15 percent in FY2015 and 8 percent in FY2016. That, with small share buybacks, should bring per-share earnings into the $5–$5.25 range in FY2016. The company appears to be poised to deliver double-digit dividend increases through this period.

Reasons to Buy

Granted, increased utilization initiatives, particularly on the Medi-care front, have softened results. But going forward and especially into FY2016, we think the company will continue to benefit from the Afford-able Care Act as 30 million more patients get access to subsidized health care. Additionally, an ever-greater emphasis on wellness and preventative care is likely to send more people for routine checkups, particularly if insurance carriers offer benefits (like free tests or lower coinsurance) to motivate such preventative care.

Even more, we're excited about the innovative new tests performed at the retail lab level for molecular-level and gene-based diagnostics, which bode well for the future; the company is advancing to higher, more profitable levels of the diagnostic food chain. When the company announced FDA approval of the encephalitis test, it woke the stock up to a 12 percent gain that day and garnered a considerable amount of positive attention in the markets and marketplace.

We're also fans of the ancillary businesses—clinical trials, insurance qualifications, employer testing, and IT services—which all should do well in an environment favoring greater cost control and outsourcing of distinct services as Quest provides. The company is a leader in its industry and has a beta of 0.67 indicating relative safety. Finally, shareholder returns have become considerably more attractive in the past few years. Cash returns to investors— and increases to those cash returns—have been healthy; Quest has retired more than 25 percent of its shares in the past ten years.

Several factors in the ongoing evolution of health care and health-care cost management seem to line up right for this company, and the cash returns give us a decent cushion if we turn out to be wrong.

Reasons for Caution

While the ACA and recent Medicare adjustments do enhance Quest's patient volumes, continued pressure to contain costs may bring some malaise over the next few years. Offsetting that is the placement of more emphasis on preventative care, a Quest sweet spot. To a degree, the company has been forced to reach for growth through acquisitions, which don't always work out—but again, better volumes through ACA and new testing should mitigate this trend. New hospital partnerships can lead to some revenue sharing and thus pressure on margins. The company may also face more competition as large-group physician practices get larger and bring some of their lab operations in-house—although that trend may be countered by hospitals and other large organizations getting out of this relatively easily outsourced business. In all, it's a complex and ever-changing environment with a lot of moving parts. It gives management and investors more to worry about than in a lot of industries; we think management is up to the task, but Quest is not one of our steady-as-she-goes, "golf clap" companies.

SECTOR: **Health Care** ❑ BETA COEFFICIENT: **0.67** ❑ 10-YEAR COMPOUND EARNINGS PER-
SHARE GROWTH: **11.0%** ❑ 10-YEAR COMPOUND DIVIDENDS PER-SHARE GROWTH: **13.5%**

		2007	2008	2009	2010	2011	2012	2013	2014
Revenues (mil)		6,705	7,249	7,455	7,400	7,511	7,468	7,146	7,435
Net income (mil)		553.8	640.0	730.3	720.9	728.7	700.0	612.0	587.0
Earnings per share		2.84	3.27	3.88	4.05	4.53	4.43	4.00	4.10
Dividends per share		0.40	0.40	0.40	0.40	0.47	0.81	1.20	1.29
Cash flow per share		4.08	4.75	5.52	5.00	6.42	6.23	6.22	6.21
Price:	high	58.6	59.9	62.8	61.7	61.2	64.9	64.1	68.5
	low	48.0	38.7	42.4	40.8	45.1	53.3	52.5	50.5

Website: *www.questdiagnostics.com*

AGGRESSIVE GROWTH

Ralph Lauren Corporation

Ticker symbol: RL (NYSE) ❑ S&P rating: A ❑ Value Line financial strength rating: A+ ❑ Current
yield: 1.5% ❑ Dividend raises, past 10 years: 6

Company Profile

Sometimes, it's all about the timing.

Last year we added premier clothing maker and brand Ralph Lauren to our *100 Best Stocks* list. The stock proceeded to open up 2015 with a soft revenue and earnings report, and the stock slumped 25 percent, making it one of our biggest losers for our measurement year. As is our practice, we asked ourselves: Have the fundamentals changed? Did the business really change, or did it suffer from currency effects and other temporary ills or adjustments, creating a ripe opportunity for a bounceback? More to the point, we asked ourselves whether RL is falling victim to changes in demographics and tastes we've reported on throughout the book—translation, Millennials—who now hold the keys to the kingdom, and that kingdom neither drives Dad's old Cadillac nor wears his old pony-emblazoned Polo shirts.

We came very close to eliminating RL from our list, which is something we long-term thinkers don't like to do after carrying a new pick for only one year, but we'll do it when we have to. Yes, we have some doubts whether RL will endure the Millennial shift, and we're not so sure that bringing out more variety in ever-wilder flash-in-the-pan colors as we're seeing Nike and others do plays to RL's strengths. On top of that, there seems to be a "clothing glut" everywhere we look. Nevertheless, we see enough strength in RL's core business, its traditions, its qualities, its management style to feel that it will endure through this rough patch (they've done it before), and management's recent dividend raises, if nothing else, seconds the motion. So we'll keep this pony yet for at least another year and hope the 2015 dip is nothing more than a great trip to the markdown table.

Ralph Lauren Corporation is a leader in the design, marketing, and distribution of premium lifestyle products in four categories: apparel, home, accessories, and fragrances. Since 1967, the year it was founded by Ralph Lauren himself (who is still the President, Chairman, and CEO of the company), Ralph Lauren's reputation and distinctive image have been consistently developed across an expanding number of products, brands, and international markets. The company's brand names, which include Polo Ralph Lauren, Ralph Lauren Collection, Ralph Lauren Purple Label, Black Label, Blue Label, Lauren by Ralph LaurenRRL, RLX, Ralph Lauren Childrenswear, Denim & Supply, Ralph Lauren, Chaps, and Polo Sport, constitute one of the world's most widely recognized families of consumer brands.

The brands reflect a lifestyle of luxury, understated elegance, distinct design, and quality, widely available to but aspirational for most consumer segments. Typical designs are understated but colorful, traditional but somewhat attention getting, well made, and well fit. When you see someone wearing a Polo or other Ralph Lauren product, you recognize it right away. It's the sort of fashion you can wear days in a row almost anywhere.

The company is divided into three segments: Wholesale, Retail, and Licensing. The Wholesale segment is the "traditional" sales channel, selling primarily to more than 13,000 department stores and other retail shops worldwide, representing 46 percent of FY2013 revenues. The Retail segment (52 percent) operates approximately 680 standalone stores and 536 concession-based "shop-within-shop" outlets primarily in North America, Europe, and Asia, some through licensed partners. The Licensing unit allows third parties, such as makers of sunglasses and fragrances, the right to RL trademarks, and accounts for 2 percent of revenues. The company also sells directly through ralphlauren.com.

About 37 percent of the business originates outside the U.S., and the Lauren family owns some 83 percent of voting power through ownership of a Class B stock. Ralph Lauren himself is still involved in product design along with an internal design staff; much of the marketing and advertising material is also generated internally.

Financial Highlights, Fiscal Year 2014

Total net revenues for the year 2014 (which the company calls FY2015 as it ends in February 2015) were 2.3 percent higher than 2013 and 4.6 percent higher on a constant currency basis. Wholesale growth was a mixed bag, strong in the Americas but weak in the rest of the world due to currency effects. Sales in the retail segment were relatively strong compared to other groups as this segment is relatively more concentrated in the U.S. The company ran into some headwinds particularly in late 2014 and early 2015, with currency effects, an oversupply in clothing, stiff competition and discounting, and high advertising costs all hitting at the same time. On a constant currency basis, 2014 year-end quarter sales were off 2 percent with a decline in margins leading to 6 percent decline in earnings. Including currency, the drop was closer to 5 percent.

Projections for FY2015 are similarly weak, as currency will still be a drag, and a restructuring will add a bit to that drag. Projections call for flat sales and operating margins still stuck in a range about 2 percent lower than the previous two years; earnings could drop as much as 10 percent. Turnaround and growth strategies include expanding the international presence, increasing "omnichannel" capability (mixing the channels together, including online) to improve the customer experience and tap new markets, negotiating lower costs with suppliers, and adjusting the price mix in some markets. The restructuring will reduce some SKUs (a good idea, we thought they were reaching too far with some lines) and a centralization of some operations. Dividend increases should continue in the 10 percent range along with moderate share buybacks. For FY2016, revenues are projected to recover and advance into the $8–$8.2 billion range, 6–7 percent ahead of FY2014, with per-share earnings only recovering to FY2012 levels. The company expects a real return to growth and advancing profitability beyond FY2016.

Reasons to Buy

The Ralph Lauren story continues to be about brand and all about the enduring taste and quality that support that brand. As it's supposed to, the brand makes a promise of tradition and quality, and it delivers. Over and over. We still think, all in all, people of almost all walks of life, around the world, covet the brand; the only question is whether they want to pay for it and whether they want to substitute something more trendy. Ralph Lauren is our first, and admittedly rather conservative, venture into the often-fickle fashion industry—which we'll admit we don't on the whole really understand—but we do understand this brand and the products and images that go with it. And we like the growing shareholder returns—and what we see as an attractive share markdown into the $130s as we write this narrative.

Reasons for Caution

Fashion is fashion, and tastes do change—and now we have the Millennials and their tastes for variety, individualism, and change. On a personal level, we see products that might be a little too bright and colorful at least for our doughty tastes; if they work in today's markets, fine, but we don't want to see too many leftover RL products in our Ross Stores (another *100 Best* pick). We're putting some faith and trust in fashion, something we don't have much faith and trust in, but RL has developed one of the steadiest and most enduring approaches to running any business—fashion or otherwise. Fierce competition in the fashion industry could knock RL off its "full-price" horse into discounting mode; once that starts it's hard to stop. Needless to say, there are risks here, but we invest for the long term, and if they get their short-term issues resolved and long-term fashion trends carry the day, we'll be good. If not, well, we'll put this pony back in the barn and look for a "hot pink" choice for next year.

SECTOR: Consumer Discretionary ❑ **BETA COEFFICIENT: 1.26** ❑ **10-YEAR COMPOUND EARNINGS PER-SHARE GROWTH: 16.0%** ❑ **10-YEAR COMPOUND DIVIDENDS PER-SHARE GROWTH: 24.0%**

		2007	2008	2009	2010	2011	2012	2013	2014
Revenues (mil)		4,880	5,018	4,980	5,660	6,859	6,944	7,450	7,600
Net income (mil)		420	406	479	568	681	762	776	700
Earnings per share		3.99	4.01	4.73	5.75	7.13	8.13	8.43	7.80
Dividends per share		0.20	.020	0.30	0.60	0.80	1.60	1.70	1.85
Cash flow per share		6.24	5.95	6.73	8.06	9.78	10.94	11.66	11.05
Price:	high	102.6	82.0	83.5	115.3	164.5	182.5	192.0	187.5
	low	60.4	31.2	31.6	71.1	102.3	134.3	149.3	141.9

Website: *www.ralphlauren.com*

ResMed, Inc.

Ticker symbol: RMD (NYSE) □ S&P rating: NR □ Value Line financial strength rating: A □ Current yield: 1.7% □ Dividend raises, past 10 years: 2

Company Profile

Sleep disorders are a big deal among adult populations. Reading the clinical description of sleep disorders and their myriad causes could for some be a cure for such disorders, but suffice it to say (as ResMed does in its market analysis) that 26 percent of U.S. adults age 30–70, or about 46 million people, have some form of sleep apnea. That's where the story of ResMed begins.

Perhaps you know someone using a "CPAP" (continuous positive airway pressure) machine to alleviate "SDB" (sleep-disordered breathing) or "OSA" (obstructive sleep apnea). As we age and tend to gain weight, these devices are becoming a more mainstream way for folks (and their partners) to get some much-needed sleep.

Formed in 1989, ResMed develops, manufactures, and distributes medical equipment for treating, diagnosing, and managing sleep-disordered breathing and other respiratory disorders. Products include diagnostic products, airflow generators, headgear, and other accessories. The original and still largest product line of CPAP machines delivers pressurized air through a mask during sleep to prevent collapse of tissue in the upper airway, a condition common in people with narrow upper airways and poor muscle tone—in many cases, people who are older and overweight. A great many of the estimated 46 million with sleep apnea, who exhibit the typical symptoms of daytime sleepiness, snoring, hypertension, and irritability, have yet to be diagnosed.

CPAP machines and their cousins VPAP (variable positive airway pressure) and others were at one time massive, clunky machines restricting movement and very difficult to travel with. No more: The new machines are smaller, lighter, cheaper, and easier to use. We don't like solutions that are worse than the problem, and ResMed has turned the corner on that with the new machines; they're becoming more acceptable, less expensive, and more mainstream. We think the company's four-pronged strategy is a good one—make the machines easier to deal with (and afford), increase clinical awareness and the rate of diagnosis, expand into new applications including stroke and congestive heart failure treatment, and expand internationally. The company has executed effectively on all fronts.

The company markets its products in 100 countries, makes them in in the U.S. and five countries abroad, and invests about 8 percent of revenues in R&D.

Financial Highlights, Fiscal Year 2014

For FY2014, net revenues slowed to a 3 percent increase, a figure dampened in roughly equal parts by the onset of competition, primarily in North America, and currency effects. More recently, sales have advanced at something closer to an 8 percent annualized rate due to the introduction of new flow generator products, and the company projects forward to an 8 percent rise in revenues through FY2015 and a slightly larger increase in FY2016. Supply-chain improvements and a more favorable product mix led FY2014 earnings some 12 percent higher. With these improvements already realized, the company projects FY2015 earnings to attenuate to 3 percent higher than FY2014, with a rise back in the 7 percent range by FY2016. However, aggressive share buybacks should bring per-share earnings forward 8–10 percent in both years. These figures could go higher as new sleep mask innovations take hold in the market—sleep masks are more profitable and a more repeatable sale.

Reasons to Buy

We believe that the company's four-pronged strategy, previously outlined, is right on. As these machines, and the diagnosis of the condition they're designed for, become more mainstream, we expect more people in the market, lower prices, and reduced inconvenience should open up larger and larger slices of the market for the company. Demographics are a plus, too— as people get older and heavier, these machines will find more potential users. It's a niche business, and ResMed dominates the niche and is the only company solely focused on this market. While we tend not to rely on this in our selections, we feel the company has the earmarks of a good acquisition candidate for a larger provider of health-care technology products. Unlike most emerging companies in the health-care technology sector, the dividend is substantial and share buybacks have already been a healthy source of shareholder return. Outstanding shares are projected to drop to 133 million in FY2016 from 152 million in 2011. Upon examining recent share purchases, the company appears to wait for favorable prices to repurchase shares—another plus.

Reasons for Caution

One of the bigger issues facing CPAP and related technologies is the eligibility for reimbursement or coverage through Medicare/Medicaid and through private insurers. The current landscape is a mixed bag: Many non-Medicare health insurance plans do not cover the machines (which range from about $600–$1,900 in price), and Medicare has driven payment rates down through competitive bidding and across-the-board cuts.

Too, the market is becoming more competitive; and there have been a few legal contests on intellectual property—most of which have gone ResMed's way so far. We feel that ResMed's technology leadership (as exemplified by a new wireless control for one of its major devices), full-line offering, and experience in this market will prevail.

SECTOR: **Health Care** ❑ BETA COEFFICIENT: **0.77** ❑ 10-YEAR COMPOUND EARNINGS PER-SHARE GROWTH: **20.0%** ❑ 10-YEAR COMPOUND DIVIDENDS PER-SHARE GROWTH: **NM**

	2007	2008	2009	2010	2011	2012	2013	2014
Revenues (mil)	716	835	921	1,092	1,243	1,368	1,514	1,555
Net income (mil)	108.1	114.1	146.4	190.1	227.0	254.9	307.1	345.4
Earnings per share	0.69	0.73	0.95	1.23	1.44	1.71	2.10	2.39
Dividends per share	—	—	—	—	—	—	0.68	1.00
Cash flow per share	1.01	1.14	1.33	1.66	1.96	2.40	2.71	2.99
Price: high	28.1	26.2	26.7	35.9	35.4	42.9	57.3	57.6
low	19.2	14.5	15.7	25.0	23.4	24.4	42.0	41.5

Website: *www.resmed.com*

AGGRESSIVE GROWTH

Ross Stores, Inc.

Ticker symbol: ROST (NASDAQ) □ S&P rating: A- □ Value Line financial strength rating: A □ Current yield: 0.9% □ Dividend raises, past 10 years: 10

Company Profile

"Always a Great Bargain" is the motto of Ross Stores, the second-largest off-price retailer in the United States. Ross and its subsidiaries operate two chains of apparel and home accessories stores. As of 2014 the company operated a total of 1,362 stores, up from 1,125 in 2011, of which 1,210 were Ross Dress for Less locations in 33 states, D.C., and Guam and 152 were dd's DISCOUNTS stores in four states. Just under half the company's stores are located in three states—California, Florida, and Texas.

Both chains target value-conscious women and men between the ages of 18 and 54. Ross's target customers are primarily from middle-income households, while dd's DISCOUNTS target customers are typically from lower- to middle-income households. Merchandising, purchasing, pricing, and the locations of the stores are all aimed at these customer bases. Ross and dd's DISCOUNTS both offer first-quality, in-season, name-brand and designer apparel, accessories, and footwear for the family at savings typically in the 20–60 percent range off department store prices (at Ross) or 20–70 percent off (at dd's DISCOUNTS). The stores also offer discounted home fashions and housewares, educational toys and games, furniture and furniture accents, luggage, cookware, and at some stores jewelry.

Sales break down by category roughly as follows: 29 percent Ladies', 24 percent Home Accents, Bed and Bath, 13 percent each for Men's, Accessories, Lingerie, Jewelry and Fragrances, and 8 percent Children's. The shopping demographic is 75–80 percent female, shopping for herself or other family members; the core customer averages about three store visits a month, a number that surprised us a bit (as, personally, we average about 3 clothes shopping trips per year!) They also suggest that the average customer "wants"—not "needs"—a bargain; these are frugal but fairly well-heeled customers looking for a brand at a price.

Ross's strategy is to offer competitive values to target customers by offering a well-managed mix of inventory with a strong percentage of department store name brands and items of local and seasonal interest at attractive prices.

Financial Highlights, Fiscal Year 2014

The Great Recession was nothing but good news for this company, bringing in newly cost-conscious customers by the busload. The question was—what would happen after that? Would people feel they were on more solid footing and abandon Ross in droves for more fully priced favorites? The answer, so far, continues in a large measure to be no.

The main growth vector is store base expansions, which continue at a healthy clip; Ross added 84 new stores in FY2014 onto a 1,276 store base, and has long-term plans to reach 2,500 stores (2,000 Ross, 500 dd's DISCOUNTS). Revenues advanced about 8 percent, slightly ahead of the 6.7 percent advance in the store base. Operating margins grew sequentially about a half a percent mostly on supply-chain efficiency initiatives to 15.6 percent; net income rang up a nice 10.3 percent gain, and a 3 percent share buyback helped per-share earnings to a 13.3 percent gain for the year. As efficiency improvements won't recur, operating margins will likely flatten out in FY2015 and beyond; revenues look to grow in the 5–6 percent range (again, mainly due to store expansion) while earnings should grow just a bit faster: 6–7 percent on a total basis and 7–8 percent on a per-share basis. Cash flows are strong, and we do believe the company will step up the dividend more quickly and continue moderate share buybacks.

Reasons to Buy

We had become a little tired of this story—which really got a boost from the now-fading Great Recession years. We saw revenue growth being driven mainly by store expansion, and profit growth attenuating. Did we also see that, with more disposable income, consumers may wander away? Did we see signs of too many stores? All might be warning signs of future trouble, and it got us to take another look. But we stayed on this horse for one big reason: profitability. Net profit margins—after taxes and everything else—run in the 8–9 percent range. And they've been steadily improving over the years. Where else can you find that in the retail world? Answer: nowhere—at least on as sustained a business as Ross Stores. So, welcome once again, Ross, to the 2016 *100 Best Stocks* list. We're sorry we doubted you guys.

The recession apparently helped Ross gain mainstream appeal across a wider set of customers. While some of those customers defected back to full-price retail stores as things improved, a greater number have shown that they will continue to shop at the stores. At the same time, the company was successful with operational changes begun in 2009 to improve merchandising and inventory management, which led to better stocking of a more favorable mix of goods and better inventory turnover. The higher store count has increased operating leverage as well—more volume through the same infrastructure and cost base. These marketplace and operational changes have led to the financial success one would expect and then some, and the company continues to improve its inventory management. Nothing is mentioned about international expansion, but we wonder if there too lies an opportunity.

Moderate expansion, operational excellence, sustained shareholder returns; it's an attractive formula—bottom line, we like this model and moreover, we like how this company is managed. And one more thing: We like how they present all of this to shareholders; their Investor Relations materials are far better than average.

Reasons for Caution

One concern is that the company is dependent on the actions of others—mainly first-line apparel retailers—for its success. Currently there is a glut of supply in the clothing business as more "trendy" styles and colors hit department store shelves only to be changed out more frequently, presenting opportunity to Ross. This may or may not continue as tastes change or as department stores become fed up trying to chase these trends and changes. This inventory cycle may present some challenges for Ross. We also remain concerned that the company still depends to a degree on store expansion, which carries its own risks, and could make supply bubbles and constraints hurt even more.

SECTOR: **Retail** ❑ BETA COEFFICIENT: **0.76** ❑ 10-YEAR COMPOUND EARNINGS PER-SHARE GROWTH: **19.5%** ❑ 10-YEAR COMPOUND DIVIDENDS PER-SHARE GROWTH: **26.5%**

		2007	2008	2009	2010	2011	2012	2013	2014
Revenues (mil)		5,975	6,486	7,184	7,866	8,608	9,721	10,230	11,042
Net income (mil)		261	305	443	555	657	787	837	925
Earnings per share		0.95	1.77	1.77	2.32	2.84	3.53	3.88	4.42
Dividends per share		0.16	0.20	0.25	0.35	0.47	0.59	0.71	0.80
Cash flow per share		1.42	1.76	2.45	3.03	3.65	4.42	4.89	5.58
Price:	high	17.6	20.8	25.3	33.3	49.2	70.8	82.0	96.2
	low	12.2	10.6	14.0	21.2	30.1	47.1	53.0	61.8

Website: *www.rossstores.com*

RPM International Inc.

Ticker symbol: RPM (NYSE) ❑ S&P rating: BBB- ❑ Value Line financial strength rating: B+ ❑ Current yield: 2.1% ❑ Dividend raises, past 10 years: 10

Company Profile

Have you ever finished a piece of furniture or a wood floor with Varathane? Stained it with Watco? Caulked a bathtub or leaky sink with DAP? Spray-painted a rusty gate with Rust-Oleum? Primed bathroom walls with Zinsser primers before painting it? Glued a model airplane together with Testors? We have—and it seems like every time we do those little weekend warrior tasks around the house, we're using one of these products.

So we wondered, who makes and markets this stuff? Where do these well-established brands that seem to show up in every hardware store and home improvement center we go into come from? How did they become household names, even category-defining names like Kleenex? After a little digging, we came up with a company we'd never heard of. Sometimes, that's a really good sign. A "house of brands," each with its own strength, image, and loyal following, can have more staying and growing power than a "branded house." Just ask anyone on the marketing team at Procter & Gamble.

Anyway, the company we found is in all likelihood one you've never heard of, based in Medina, Ohio—a town you've probably never heard of, either. The company is RPM International. RPM International makes and markets an assortment of specialty chemicals and coatings, targeted mostly to repair, maintenance, and replacement, for consumer and industrial markets.

Industrial markets? Indeed, only about a third (37 percent, actually) of RPM's sales come from the aforementioned "consumer" brands found in Home Depot and the like. The company also makes and markets a vast line of brands for industrial and construction use—sealants, chemicals, roofing systems, corrosion control coatings, marine paints and coatings, fluorescent pigments (you've probably heard of DayGlo, their line of fluorescent paints), powder coatings, fire coatings, and concrete waterproofing and repair products. There are 48 industrial brands in all, and if you take a tour of their well-organized and informal website, which includes brands such as Increte Systems, a maker of textured stamped concrete systems, or USL bridge care solutions, or Dryvit insulation solutions, you'll get the idea. The Industrial segment makes many products aimed at the preservation and corrosion protection of existing structures, which makes the company a strong play in the infrastructure reinvestment market. About 60 percent of Industrial segment business comes from repair and maintenance, and about 40 percent comes from new construction. The Industrial segment accounts for 67 percent of the business, and many of its brands are made and sold in foreign markets. In fact, about 50 percent of Industrial business is overseas, while 85 percent of the consumer business originates in North America.

Not to beat the brand thing to death, but Rust-Oleum, Varathane, DAP, and Zinssr on the consumer side own number one positions in their respective markets, while eight industrial brands, including DayGlo of course, own number one positions in their markets.

Financial Highlights, Fiscal Year 2014

We like the products and the brand strength, but we also like the improving financials of this company. After years of lackluster performance, strong performance in Europe and encouraging sales into the construction and especially infrastructure maintenance sectors woke the business up; FY2014 revenues rose a bit over 7 percent, a trajectory that should continue into the next few years. Reduced input costs and improved efficiency and scale brought stronger margins—the net profit margin was 6.7 percent compared to 4s and 5s for the past five years. Net earnings increased 20 percent in FY2014 and should continue to outpace sales increases, with 10–15 percent increases each year into FY2016. Cash flows are strong and dividend increases have been increasing as well.

Reasons to Buy

We always like premier brands in relatively simple, well-managed businesses, and RPM International seems to fit the model. The company presents itself well—its website is one of the best and most informative we've encountered (maybe this goes hand in hand with a relatively straightforward business; anyway, kudos to management or to the web designer). These factors alone wouldn't be enough to land RPM on our *100 Best* list, however, we also take notice when financials improve, especially when they improve at an accelerating rate. We also take notice of a company that has raised its dividend 41 straight years, and we like the defensive nature of its repeat-purchase, mainly maintenance and repair, product lines. We think other investors—large and small—are beginning to refinish their portfolios with some RPM shares, too.

Reasons for Caution

Such "refinishing" of investor portfolios has made RPM's share price "rev up" very fast recently. While we were impressed with the breadth of the RPM brand universe and the depth and strength of a few of them, we wonder if the business is stretched a bit too thin and if consolidating some of those brands to make stronger brands might make sense. That said, the way these brands are presented on the website leads us to believe that a Berkshire Hathaway model is in effect here: Let the business leaders of those business units do things as they see fit without undue influence from headquarters. RPM would also be somewhat exposed to price increases in petrochemical inputs.

RPM is also not on as solid a financial footing as other companies on our *100 Best* list, with a debt to total capital ratio of almost 50 percent. That explains why the company isn't doing buybacks and why it will probably increase share counts slightly over the next few years—to reduce debt and improve this ratio. We agree with this direction, particularly in light of the increasing cash dividends.

SECTOR: **Basic Materials** ❏ BETA COEFFICIENT: **1.34** ❏ 10-YEAR COMPOUND EARNINGS PER-SHARE GROWTH: **5.5%** ❏ 10-YEAR COMPOUND DIVIDENDS PER-SHARE GROWTH: **5.5%**

	2007	2008	2009	2010	2011	2012	2013	2014
Revenues (mil)	3,334	3,644	3,368	3,413	3,382	3,777	4,081	4,376
Net income (mil)	199	233	135	188	189	215	241	292
Earnings per share	1.57	1.81	1.05	1.45	1.45	1.65	1.83	2.18
Dividends per share	0.69	0.75	0.79	0.82	0.84	0.86	0.89	0.95
Cash flow per share	2.32	2.60	1.71	2.10	2.01	2.20	2.45	2.86
Price: high	25.7	25.2	21.0	22.9	26.0	29.6	41.6	52.0
low	17.3	10.0	9.1	16.1	17.2	23.0	29.1	37.6

Website: *www.rpminc.com*

AGGRESSIVE GROWTH

Schlumberger Limited

Ticker symbol: SLB (NYSE) ❑ S&P rating: AA- ❑ Value Line financial strength rating: A++ ❑ Current yield: 2.2% ❑ Dividend raises, past 10 years: 9

Company Profile

Schlumberger Limited is the world's leading oilfield services company. It provides technology, information solutions, and integrated project management services with the goal of optimizing reservoir performance for its customers in the oil and gas industry. Founded in 1926, today the company has a large international footprint, employing more than 115,000 people in 85 countries, with 67 percent of revenue generated outside of North America. The company operates in three primary business segments:

- The Reservoir Characterization Group (24 percent of FY2014 revenues, 34 percent of pretax income) is mostly a consulting service, applying many digital and other technologies toward finding, defining, and characterizing hydrocarbon deposits. Interestingly, the company compares the electronic characterization of a hydrocarbon-producing zone to the imaging of a human body, using an assortment of technologies (for example, a technology referred to as a "Saturn 3D radial fluid sampling probe") to identify what you can't see directly.
- Not surprisingly, the Drilling Group (37 percent of revenues, 35 percent of pretax income) does the actual drilling and creation of wells for production, both in onshore and offshore environments. Again, a number of new drilling, drill bit, and drilling fluid technologies are in play, and naturally, so-called "fracking" is an important new part of the product offering.
- The Reservoir Production Group (39 percent of revenues, 32 percent of pretax income) completes and services the well for production, maintaining and enhancing productivity through its life.

Throughout the petroleum production process, the company not only provides physical onsite services but also substantial consulting, modeling, information management, total cost, yield, and general project management around these activities. In short, SLB offers a full outsourced supply chain for oil and gas field development and production.

Schlumberger manages its business through 28 GeoMarket regions, which are grouped into four geographic areas: North America (29 percent); Latin America (21 percent); Europe, Commonwealth of Independent States, and Africa (22 percent); and Middle East and Asia (28 percent). The company made the big-ticket acquisition of oil services giant Smith International, which was integrated into the operations and financials during FY2011.

You might have expected that such an oil field services company, dependent on the now-attenuated production plans of oil "E&P" producers worldwide suffering from the 40 percent drop in oil prices in 2014, might have been cut from our *100 Best* list, Obviously, we didn't. The question, of course and as always, is whether or not the market changes represented a fundamental and irreversible negative shift in the business. In the end, we determined that the changed markets present a challenge to the company, but not an irreversible one.

First, SLB is the largest and most well-established player in the business. That, in itself, doesn't merit retention any more than GM's size in the car business would have years ago. But the company knows where it stands and is making the appropriate adjustments. The company presentation explains well; here is a synopsis: First, the reason for the oil price crash stems largely from the changed balance of production from the Middle East and OPEC to new extraction in the Americas driven by the new fracking boom—the OPEC folks chose to fight this by pumping more oil to preserve market share. And SLB, with its strong international and especially Middle Eastern footprint, will prosper as the OPEC countries ramp up production. Second, as the fracking boom came on line, the role of "swing producer" has shifted to the U.S. When supplies are tight, the U.S. will ramp up (as OPEC did in the past); when supplies are abundant, the U.S. will ramp down. That's what's happening now, and it has indeed cut into SLB's North American operations (and the company has announced plans to cut 20,000 jobs as a result). But the company maintains, probably correctly, that U.S. producers will have to lower costs, and thus apply SLB technologies and know-how to producing shale oil and gas at a cost economical to a $70 or $80 oil price. In the company's view, these two factors, plus a strong financial base to weather a downturn and business shift and the inevitable long-term growth in world oil consumption, will get them by and position them well for recovery, probably starting in 2016 and strengthening beyond that year.

We agree—for now at least.

Financial Highlights, Fiscal Year 2014

Not surprisingly, the financial picture is mixed, especially going forward into 2015 and 2016 as customers reduce rig counts. As SLB put it, "near-term visibility remains poor." As the business is largely contract driven, the effects of the downturn, with layoffs and asset writedowns, hit profits more than revenues in 2014. Revenues rose just over 7 percent, but the initial downsizing ate into profits to the tune of 9 percent, although cash flows were up, buybacks were maintained, and the dividend was raised again to a $2.00 per-share rate, a 25 percent increase. FY2015 will be the "dry hole" year, with revenues projected down in the 15–17 percent range and earnings projected down 12–13 percent. For FY2016 Schlumberger doesn't project a full recovery. Revenues could rise 8–10 percent from depressed FY2015 levels; earnings are projected up in the 10–12 percent range—but again, "lack of visibility" is the key word. Share buybacks will take a pause, although dividend increases in the low double digits still look possible. The company projects a return to full health—and likely beyond as weaker hands in the industry decline—in the 2017–2018 timeframe.

Reasons to Buy

"Accelerating the Pace of Technology Innovation" is Schlumberger's new annual report headline (the old one was "The Age of Easy Oil is Over"). Such represents the dynamic shift occurring in the oil service business. SLB brings the largest, most complete, and most technically advanced offering to the oil patch, and as the supply geography shifts first toward OPEC, then back to the most efficient producers in the U.S., it isn't lost on us—nor on SLB—that major producers still have to replace depleted reserves, and that world oil demand will continue to grow, albeit slowly, in the longer term. SLB is well positioned, with its size, present geography, and expertise, to move with these shifts. The company appears to be embracing these cross-currents and is applying its competitive advantages in technology and size strategically. Too, SLB appears committed to keeping shareholder returns moving forward despite the short-term weakness.

In the long term, we agree that SLB could come out of this shift stronger than ever as the oil service industry and the U.S. producer landscape both consolidate.

Reasons for Caution

The shifts and uncertainties caused by the oil market disruption could get larger, and that plus cutthroat competition could put a bigger dent in the oil service industry. The fortunes of SLB are inevitably tied to the price of oil, and nobody is predicting with any great certainty where that price will end up by 2016—although most agree that it will be north of the low-$40s low experienced in January 2015. The company will always face the traditional risks of oil drilling—particularly offshore drilling—that culminated in the BP Deepwater Horizon disaster of 2010.

SECTOR: **Energy** ❑ BETA COEFFICIENT: **1.64** ❑ 10-YEAR COMPOUND EARNINGS PER-SHARE GROWTH: **18.5%** ❑ 10-YEAR COMPOUND DIVIDENDS PER-SHARE GROWTH: **13.5%**

	2007	2008	2009	2010	2011	2012	2013	2014
Revenues (mil)	23,277	27,163	22,702	27,447	39,540	42,149	45,266	48,580
Net income (mil)	5,177	5,397	3,142	3,408	3,954	5,439	6,210	5,643
Earnings per share	4.18	4.42	2.61	2.70	3.51	4.06	4.70	4.32
Dividends per share	0.70	0.81	0.84	0.84	0.96	1.06	1.25	1.60
Cash flow per share	5.94	6.42	4.70	4.55	6.05	6.73	7.55	7.64
Price: high	114.8	112.0	71.1	84.1	95.6	80.8	94.9	118.8
low	56.3	37.1	35.1	54.7	54.8	59.1	69.1	78.5

Website: *www.slb.com*

AGGRESSIVE GROWTH

Schnitzer Steel Industries, Inc.

Ticker symbol: SCHN (NASDAQ) ❑ S&P rating: NR ❑ Value Line financial strength rating: B ❑ Current yield: 4.9% ❑ Dividend raises, past 10 years: 3

Company Profile

Ugh. A swing and a miss. A loss of some 45 percent for this 2015 newcomer to the *100 Best* list. A crisis? Kick it out after only one year? We've done that with some companies, but it doesn't happen often because we take a longer-term view. What are we thinking? Maybe that commodity prices will recover. Maybe that Schnitzer has a more unique niche in the business and is well positioned to recover in a rebound. Maybe we're just a couple of typical stubborn "guy" investors. Maybe a combination of the three. Remember though—where we come from, it takes three strikes to make an out, unless something fundamentally and permanently changes in the business.

We knew taking this company on was a bit risky. It posted a loss for 2013 (mostly on paper, cash flows remained solid). But unfortunately, things did not get better in FY2014 and through most of FY2015, as steel prices (and thus steel *scrap* prices) and competing iron ore prices in particular became even more depressed. China end-user demand slowed down even more, among other things causing cheap imported steel to flood U.S. markets. And to add to the troubles, a West Coast port strike to snarl export scrap shipments and a strong dollar . . . what's to like here?

Truth of the matter is, while we don't like companies that are too vulnerable to economic cycles, we *do* like companies that know how to make the best of them. And we like companies in commodity industries that occupy niches in their industries and add relatively more value than their larger competitors.

We also like companies that are innovative, that are good citizens, and that think shareholders are important and who return lots of cash to them. Finally, we wanted to offer another "small-cap" stock for those who might like to feel as if they own a bigger part of a smaller but successful and dynamic business.

Founded in 1946, Schnitzer Steel is mainly a collector and recycler of ferrous and non-ferrous scrap, with smaller operations that collect, dismantle, and market auto and truck parts and a steel mill "mini mill" finished steel product business. The Metals Recycling business (75 percent of FY2014 revenues) collects, recycles, processes, and brokers scrap steel and non-ferrous metals to domestic and foreign markets. Larger scrap mills are located in Oregon; Washington; Oakland, CA; and Massachusetts, with smaller mills in Rhode Island, Puerto Rico, Hawaii, and Alaska, all with adjacent deep-water ports, correctly suggesting an orientation toward international export of scrap metal for foreign mills. Indeed, that is true—some 50 percent of ferrous shipments go to Asia, 25 percent to Europe/Africa/Middle East, and 25 percent to U.S. steel mills (this means—for this part of the business, anyway—that it doesn't matter who wins the current trade wars in steel). The company operates 60 metals recycling facilities ("scrapyards," in popular vernacular) in 15 states, mostly on the coasts and in the South, seven in Canada, and five in Puerto Rico. The operation adds value in part by sorting and shredding input scrap into homogenous materials well suited to the needs of downstream customers.

The Auto Parts business (12 percent of revenues) operates 61 self-serve locations and remarketing centers, some co-located with Metals Recycling facilities, in 16 states with a concentration in California. Some of these centers operated under the "Pick-n-Pull" franchise. This operation processes about 350,000 cars per year. Inventories of scrapped autos and common parts from those autos are posted online and updated as new inventory is received.

The Steel Manufacturing business (13 percent of revenues) operates an electric arc furnace mini mill in McMinnville, Oregon, producing rebar, wire rod, merchant bar, and other specialty products, of course from scrap steel available from the company's own Metals Recycling facilities.

The numbers for the whole operation are fascinating. Recently reported figures include 4 million tons of ferrous metal and 530 million pounds of non-ferrous metal shipped, 900 million pounds of metal from crushed auto bodies, 9.6 million pounds of catalytic converters, 1.2 million gallons of fuel, 800,000 gallons of motor oil, 7.5 million pounds of batteries, and 838,000 tires and wheels from all those cars. What would happen to all this stuff without Schnitzer Steel?

Appropriately, "Recycling for Value" is the company's slogan, and the synergies between the three businesses are obvious; the company is also thought to have some of the better locations and especially port facilities in the industry.

Schnitzer's strong and respected management team is exemplified by its selection by the Ethisphere Institute as a 2015 World's Most Ethical Company, recognizing its "culture of ethics and transparency at every level of the company"—a nice honor for a steel company. Perhaps most telling is the fact that President and CEO Tamara Lundgren also serves as board chairman for the United States Chamber of Commerce.

Financial Highlights, Fiscal Year 2014

The late-2014 commodity price and oil price collapse, shrinking China end-user demand, soft Europe, and the strong dollar were negatives that accelerated through the year. The only real bright spots were firming domestic finished steel demand and the realization of productivity improvements started earlier. Without delving too far into the specifics, iron ore prices declined 40 percent for the year, which naturally drove down scrap prices; other metals prices were also weak. The company's "average inventory cost" accounting policy means that costs declines lag sales and selling price declines, naturally hurting FY2014 and probable FY2015 full-year results.

Revenues dipped 3 percent in FY2014, with reported earnings just a bit higher than FY2013 because of an acquisition writedown, but off more than 80 percent from the previous comparable year. Ouch. FY2015 bakes in the productivity improvements and a modest 5 percent revenue increase with a gradual recovery in earnings and domestic steel sales to improve margins a bit, to end up with per-share earnings in the 50-cent range. We aim to keep this stock for FY2016, when firming worldwide prices and demand should bring per-share earnings north of $1.00. We do not expect per-share cash flows to diminish below $3.00 per share; thus we feel (and the company indicates) that the dividend is secure for now.

Reasons to Buy

Clearly we're betting on a turnaround in steel and especially steel scrap prices as demand improves and competing iron ore supplies dwindle, which could happen quickly as major world iron ore producers finally throw in the towel. Scrap and recycled material businesses are flexible and less capital intensive than mining, can respond more quickly to market changes, and are likely to ramp up volumes more quickly when the market turns and prices head higher. We don't believe the fundamental recycling-based business model is by any means broken.

There are a lot of mom-and-pop scrap dealers around the world, but few have the size, operating leverage, and remarketing abilities of Schnitzer. The company is a strong and recognized brand in a fragmented and unbranded industry, offering advantages both on the sales and operational side. When prices and markets are soft, the company loses a little, but as we saw particularly in 2008, when markets are strong, the company does really, really well. And, whether steel is made domestically or imported, Schnitzer wins as a universal supplier. Schnitzer is well managed, adds a lot of value in a relatively non-value-add industry, and keeps its shareholders in mind.

Reasons for Caution

We could be very, very wrong, but we don't feel there's much to lose from here. More generally, Schnitzer is very sensitive to global steel and non-ferrous metals markets and the ups and downs of pricing. While its size and marketing advantages serve it well in tough times, inventory is inventory, and the company can get caught with a lot of it purchased at higher prices if the markets don't move to its advantage. It does okay in bad economic climates, but the company is really a bet on recycling value add and on good times in global manufacturing. If you buy in, you'll want to watch global steel and other metals prices. Too, while the company has a good track record, there are always some environmental risks and costs in this sort of business. The high beta of 1.93 reflects some of this risk and the volatility inherent in the relatively low share count.

SECTOR: **Industrials** ❑ BETA COEFFICIENT: **1.93** ❑ 10-YEAR COMPOUND EARNINGS PER-SHARE GROWTH: **-14.0%** ❑ 10-YEAR COMPOUND DIVIDENDS PER-SHARE GROWTH: **25.0%**

	2007	2008	2009	2010	2011	2012	2013	2014
Revenues (mil)	2,572	3,641	1,900	2,301	3,459	3,341	2,621	2,544
Net income (mil)	131	249	(32.2)	67	119	30	(2.0)	5.1
Earnings per share	4.32	8.61	(1.14)	2.86	4.24	1.10	(0.07)	0.19
Dividends per share	—	0.10	0.20	0.20	0.20	0.41	0.75	0.75
Cash flow per share	6.02	10.74	1.03	4.75	7.08	4.28	3.05	3.19
Price: high	77.9	118.5	64.0	66.9	69.4	47.4	33.0	22.8
low	33.3	16.5	23.3	37.0	32.8	22.8	23.1	21.4

Website: *www.schnitzersteel.com*

GROWTH AND INCOME

The Scotts Miracle-Gro Company

Ticker symbol: SMG (NYSE) ❑ S&P rating: BB+ ❑ Value Line financial strength rating: B++ ❑ Current yield: 2.8% ❑ Dividend raises, past 10 years: 6

Company Profile

Scotts Miracle-Gro, formerly Scotts Co., formerly O.M. Scott & Sons, is a 147-year-old provider of mostly packaged lawn- and garden-care products for consumer markets. Originally it was a seed company; today lawn-care products include packaged, pre-mixed fertilizers and combination fertilizer, weed- and pest-control products marketed mainly under the Scotts and Turf Builder brand names. The company also markets packaged grass seed and a line of individually packaged pest- and disease-control products mainly under the Ortho brand, acquired in 1997, and a line of specialty garden fertilizers and pest-control products under the Miracle-Gro name, acquired in 1995. The company also markets a line of home protection pest-control products, and also distributes the Roundup brand (from Monsanto, another *100 Best* stock in the U.S and five other countries. Through a series of small acquisitions, the company has entered the lawn service business, which now operates out of 26 company-operated and 93 franchised locations. Consumer businesses account for about 90 percent of revenues, Lawn Service another 9 percent.

Scotts is a study in branding in an otherwise highly fragmented market. The attractive core brands of Scotts, Turf Builder, Miracle-Gro, and Ortho are being leveraged into other businesses such as lawn service under the Scotts LawnService brand and home pest control under the Ortho brand. The company acquired Action Pest Control in FY2014 to add to this line.

The vision is interesting: "To help people of all ages express themselves on their own piece of the earth." While this sounds pretty groovy, it also connotes the possibilities to expand markets. Further trendy elements in this business include an ongoing demographic shift—more returning to cities—different styles of gardening, more specialty products—a shift that may prove positive but will take some work. The company has created a dedicated team to address this segment. People are also seeking organic gardening products in consumer packages; Scotts is testing a new line of organic Miracle-Gro products to address this trend. Innovations also include new packaging to simplify the measurement and application and improve the safety of key products. Recently the company has embarked on some internal restructuring to simplify the organization structure and to become more nimble going forward.

Financial Highlights, Fiscal Year 2014

Scotts has endured its second straight year of subpar spring weather conditions, which tends to dampen sales for the remainder of the year; FY2014 revenues were just 1 percent ahead of FY2013 (1–2 percent before currency effects). Some cost-savings efforts and a lower ingredient cost for fertilizer products resulted in a 2.5 percent earnings increase, a good result after a strong 42 percent increase in earnings in FY2013; profitability in general continues to be on the upswing. The dividend was raised another 25 percent on top of a 15 percent increase in FY2013.

Although small acquisitions play a part, and assuming a good growing season, revenues are predicted to rise about 5 percent in FY2015 and another 3–4 percent in FY2016. The real story will once again be in profits, which the company now projects could rise some 33 percent again in FY2015 moderating to 7 percent in FY2016. Per-share earnings will rise similarly;

share repurchases are modest in favor of "plenty of green for shareholders" in the form of double-digit dividend increases, which should continue.

Reasons to Buy

Scotts Miracle-Gro is increasingly leveraging its brand strength both in the U.S. and abroad. Beyond focus and increased prominence of core brands, there continue to be several tailwinds that should help the company. First on the list is the economy and resurgence in housing: People are spending more on their homes. We see more emphasis on quality landscapes over quantity and size of lawn, which should help Scotts. Too, we see help coming from changing demographics and aging clientele with disposable income and physical limitations who want easier, more complete solutions like Scotts LawnService and similar services we think will take root. The company has seen some recent market-share gains in its core products and is a mainstay at key channel partners like Home Depot, Lowe's, and Wal-Mart. The set of brands remain strong and trusted, and we expect to see it in more places and connected to higher-margined services; Ortho pest-control services is but one example. It wouldn't surprise us to see a branded Scotts "store within a store" like Apple's stores in consumer electronics retailers or Ralph Lauren's Polo shops within major department stores. Fresh marketing and advertising are also a plus; we like the new Scotsman "Feed Your Lawn Now—Feed It!" campaigns.

We also think there will be some opportunity in the international sector for these same reasons and with the growing middle classes and urban gardening formats that could become mainstream in emerging-market regions. Finally, cash returns for investors have provided a solid base for investors awaiting future extension of brands and expansion of profitability.

Reasons for Caution

Scotts isn't the only brand in town, and the company does face some competition from less expensive house brands such as those sold at Ace Hardware, Home Depot, Lowe's, and elsewhere. Lawn and garden spend is naturally sensitive to sluggish economies, but we do think that there is a baseline level people will drop to and remain at; they want to maintain their lawns and provide pleasant stay-at-home environments if they can't do much else. Finally, the demographic shifts away from the suburbs noted previously, including downsizing and increases in renting versus owning, could hurt the traditional bagged fertilizer and lawn goods business; that's where the new products and services in new niches will come into play.

SECTOR: **Materials** ❑ BETA COEFFICIENT: **0.90** ❑ 10-YEAR COMPOUND EARNINGS PER-SHARE GROWTH: **4.0%** ❑ 10-YEAR COMPOUND DIVIDENDS PER-SHARE GROWTH: **30.0%**

	2007	2008	2009	2010	2011	2012	2013	2014
Revenues (mil)	2,672	2,983	3,141	3,139	2,835	2,826	2,819	2,841
Net income (mil)	113.4	(10.9)	153.3	212.4	121.9	113.2	161.2	165.4
Earnings per share	1.69	(0.17)	2.32	3.14	1.84	1.62	2.58	2.64
Dividends per share	0.50	0.50	0.50	0.63	1.05	1.23	1.41	1.76
Cash flow per share	2.82	0.91	3.23	4.07	3.00	2.86	3.67	3.74
Price: high	57.4	40.7	44.3	55.0	60.8	55.9	62.6	64.0
low	33.5	16.1	24.9	37.5	40.0	35.5	42.0	52.4

Website: *www.scotts.com*

AGGRESSIVE GROWTH

Seagate Technology

Ticker symbol: STX (NASDAQ) ❑ S&P rating: BBB- ❑ Value Line financial strength rating: B+ ❑ Current yield: 3.9% ❑ Dividend raises, past 10 years: 9

Company Profile

About 30 years ago, you could buy a 5-megabyte hard disk drive from a major computer manufacturer like IBM or HP. It was about the size of a washing machine, cost several thousand dollars, and made little grunting noises that would have driven R2-D2 into a frenzy.

Today, you can store about 200,000 times the information—1 terabyte—on an inexpensive hard drive measuring about 2.5" × 3", about 7mm thick, that makes no noise whatsoever, retrieves information almost instantly, and never breaks. These hard drives fit into laptops, netbooksor even smaller devices, and you scarcely know they're even there. Or they can be assembled into racks and arrays to provide huge storage capability for enterprise servers and data centers—and most importantly, major and minor hubs in the cloud.

And now, you can store 12 gigabytes on ultrafast and indestructible solid state drives (SSD) about the size of credit cards. One of these will support an advanced personal system; a few hundred of these plug 'n' play units in a rack, and you've got yourself a data center.

At the heart of this evolution, as well as a dominant force in producing these devices today, is Seagate Technology—the world's largest producer of computer hard disk drives, SSDs, and related storage media. Seagate offers a range of internal (that is, built-in) and external (packaged standalone) drive devices for high-performance enterprise, cloud, client, networked, and noncomputer environments, such as DVRs, video game consoles, and the like.

Computer hard disk drives have become a high-volume commodity. Seagate shipped around 220 million drives in FY2014, with an average capacity of 915 gigabytes (compared to 307 GB in 2009). By unit volume, roughly two-thirds continue to be for client applications—PCs, notebooks, external storage for PCs, workstations, and similar. About 20 percent are for the noncomputer market—DVRs, video game consoles, and so forth, and 13 percent currently are for enterprise storage applications.

The biggest factor driving long-term profitability is the in-progress change in the computing landscape toward cloud computing. The cloud is part of a larger computing ecosystem linking an assortment of architectures including mobile, consumer products and the "Internet of Things," content storage, and delivery including vast amounts of data for such things as video-on-demand, big data and analytics, and information security.

Not surprisingly, data storage—and fast network access—are at the heart of these converging architectures, and Seagate is at the heart of storage. And it's growing fast.

True, while the cloud may temper client demand somewhat for client storage devices like common and more commoditized hard drives, cloud server centers will need huge amounts of larger, more efficient, cooler running—and more profitable-storage devices. Consumers and businesses, large and small, are adopting the cloud as their storage solution, and this extends storage makers' reach far beyond the PC ecosystem, as tablet devices, smartphones, etc., will produce and consume images, video, music, etc., all stored somewhere in the cloud. According to estimates, data creation rises some 35 percent per year, projected to end up at 44 zettabytes (a zettabyte is a trillion gigabytes) in 2020, and storage capacity will rise in the 20–25 percent range yearly to accommodate (obviously, this assumes that some data is deleted). Seagate estimates that 13 new zettabytes will need to be stored annually by then, and given current capacity expansion trends, only 6.5 zettabytes will be available; thus, there will be growth upon growth to keep up and accelerate storage capacity. Incidentally, Seagate estimates that by 2020, some 60 percent of storage will be delivered to the cloud compared to 25 percent recently.

Operationally, the largest concentrations of manufacturing capacity continue to be in Thailand, Singapore, and China, respectively, and not surprisingly, as Asia is the locus of PC and other computer manufacturing, and about 58 percent of sales are to Asian customers.

The company has been fairly active on the acquisition front, buying a couple of semiconductor operations in the flash components business from component maker Avago and storage technology developer Xyratex; larger and more interesting is a recently announced strategic partnership with memory maker Micron Technology to collaborate on solid state drives for enterprise markets.

Financial Highlights, Fiscal Year 2014

As companies such as Seagate advance along the technology curve, price erosion in core product lines is natural; companies like Seagate make up for it by (1) increasing shipment volumes, (2) driving down costs, and (3) improving the product mix and selling upward in their product lines. These strategies did not quite pan out for FY2014—a moderate slowing of shipment volume combined with natural price erosion resulted in a moderate 4.5 percent decline in revenues. Although gross margins improved slightly from 27 to 28 percent, operating expenses and slightly higher tax rates reduced net margins, and net profit slowed accordingly, off about 14 percent from FY2013—although 2013 was a tough compare because it was a recovery year from the supply-chain-battered FY2012, where flooding in Thailand disrupted both supply and shipments. Such are the cycles in the tech business.

Future projections are driven by a variety of crosscurrents, including moderated enterprise investment, soft Europe demand, the strong dollar, and a few supply constraints. Currently the company is projecting an FY2015 recovery of 4–5 percent on the top line lost in FY2014 with fairly flat revenues in to FY2016. A recovery in operating and net margins by FY2016 will likely drive net profits in the 10–12 percent range higher for that year after a relatively flat FY2015. The better news is in cash flow and returns, which are still substantial and growing; after a 20 percent dividend raise in FY2014 projections call for another increase as much as 30 percent for FY2015. Share buybacks will slow, but the company has repurchased almost half of its outstanding shares since 2006.

Reasons to Buy

Seagate is one of the more volatile and aggressive stocks on our *100 Best* list, but we think the future is bright and probably more stable. We've already shared most of the "buy side" story—a shift to a suppliers' market with Seagate and Western Digital in charge, larger long-term contracts, higher-value-add technology, and most of all, an evolving computing and network ecosystem that requires enormous amounts of new storage capacity should drive more high-value demand. The company seems to be capitalizing on these trends well, is improving its technology, and over time will achieve a healthy and profitable steady state. In the meantime, it continues to return substantial cash to shareholders both through dividends and buybacks.

Reasons for Caution

The biggest concern—and it's clearly reflected in the numbers—is whether the cloud and enterprise storage markets will grow fast enough to compensate for the inevitable decline of the PC business and pricing and margins in general. We think it will, but wish the cloud ramp-up would come a little faster! No matter what the device, data will have to be stored in ever-increasing volumes with greater miniaturization—Seagate will play well no matter where this puck goes.

This industry is noted for its "dreaded diamonds"—where scant supply triggers over-ordering, which eventually triggers overproduction into a softening market; on top of that, the excess orders get cancelled, supply balloons, and prices drop. All in all, this will, by nature, be a more volatile play than most on the *100 Best Stocks* list (the beta of 2.65 serves as evidence), but we still do think that volatility will decline from years past and is compensated for by the strong cash flows paid to investors.

SECTOR: **Information Technology** ❑ BETA COEFFICIENT: **2.65** ❑ 10-YEAR COMPOUND
EARNINGS PER-SHARE GROWTH: **20.0%** ❑ 10-YEAR COMPOUND DIVIDENDS
PER-SHARE GROWTH: **31.5%**

		2007	2008	2009	2010	2011	2012	2013	2014
Revenues (mil)		11,380	12,708	9,805	11,395	10,971	14,939	14,351	13,724
Net income (mil)		822	1,415	(231)	1,609	578	2,977	2,028	1,751
Earnings per share		1.40	2.63	(0.47)	3.14	1.09	6.75	5.31	5.04
Dividends per share		0.40	0.42	0.27	—	0.18	0.86	1.40	1.67
Cash flow per share		3.13	4.63	1.42	5.08	3.14	9.57	8.01	8.05
Price:	high	28.9	25.8	18.5	21.6	18.5	35.7	57.1	69.4
	low	20.1	3.7	3.0	9.8	9.0	16.2	30.3	48.2

Website: **www.seagate.com**

AGGRESSIVE GROWTH

Southwest Airlines Co.

Ticker symbol: LUV (NYSE) ▫ S&P rating: BBB ▫ Value Line financial strength rating: B+ ▫ Current yield: 0.5% ▫ Dividend raises, past 10 years: 4

Company Profile

We were long critical of the airline industry for its inability to control prices because of intense competition and costs that largely are comprised of fuel, airport, and unionized labor. Lack of profitability and inability to control these factors made airlines into poster children for the kinds of stocks we tend to avoid.

Not so much, anymore. Fuel costs have gone down and look to stay there for a while. Most airlines have, by design or by default, rationalized their route structures and capacity, necessitated by once-high fuel costs, airport constraints, and the Great Recession. So, with this rationalized capacity, they are better able to control both prices and costs, and their outlooks are much brighter.

We're still not sold on the idea that all airlines are well managed. But we'll stick with our favorite; one that is far better managed than most and in fact has scored us a quintupling in price since we added it to the *100 Best* list for 2012. That fave: Southwest Airlines.

Southwest Airlines provides passenger air transport mainly in the United States, all within North America. In early 2015, the company served 94 cities in 41 states, and with the acquisition of AirTran it also serves Mexico, Central America, and the Caribbean with point-to-point, rather than hub-and-spoke, service. The company serves these markets almost exclusively with 680 Boeing 737 aircraft. Southwest continues to be the largest domestic air carrier in the United States, as measured by the number of domestic-originating passengers boarded. This should give an idea of their business model—low cost, shorter flights, and maximum passenger loads.

The business model is one of simplicity—no-frills aircraft, no first-class passenger cabin, limited interchange with other carriers, no onboard meals, simple boarding and seat assignment practices, direct sales over the Internet (over 80 percent of sales processed online), no baggage fees—all designed to provide steady and reliable transportation, with one of the best on-time performances in the industry, and to maximize asset utilization with minimal downtime, crew disruptions, and other upward influences on operating costs. The company has long used secondary airports—such as Providence, RI, and Manchester, NH, to serve Boston and the New England area; Allentown, PA, and East Islip, NY, to serve the New York/New Jersey area (though it now serves LaGuardia, too, if you want that choice); and Chicago Midway to reduce delays and costs. This strategy has worked well.

Most of what we have just said reflects the business of the original Southwest Airlines. In 2012 the company acquired AirTran Holdings, a medium-sized, Florida-based discount carrier. With 140 aircraft, again mostly 737s, service expanded to mainstream eastern airports, particularly Atlanta, Orlando, LaGuardia, Washington National, and Mexico and the Caribbean. December 28, 2014, was "sunset day" for the AirTran brand. Southwest has successfully implemented a few initiatives to squeeze out some extra revenue without alienating the core passenger group, mostly business travelers. One such initiative is Business Select, which offers priority boarding, priority security, bonus frequent flyer credit, and a free beverage for an upgrade fee. The company also sells early boarding for a small fee. They're also tinkering with baggage fees, raising fees for overweight or excess bags, though leaving the basic two-bag limit free for now (we continue to applaud that move). Southwest also produces about $600 million in revenue annually from its Rapid Rewards loyalty point program through partnerships and sales of points. The program routinely wins "best of" awards in the industry.

Financial Highlights, Fiscal Year 2014

Southwest had been taxiing into position for takeoff for the two years on our *100 Best* list prior to 2014, with operational improvements, capacity rationalization, the AirTran acquisition, and other market and efficiency gains. Events in FY2014, most prominently the 50 percent drop in oil prices, put Southwest in position for takeoff, and take off it did.

Revenues advanced a moderate 5 percent during the year, while the fuel prices and other operational improvements led to a whopping 40 percent gain in operating and net profit margins, all told leading to a 50 percent gain in net earnings on top of a 79 percent gain in FY2013. Not only did fuel prices help, but so did strong gains in revenue seat miles. The load factor hit a record 82 (percentage of seats paid for and occupied—*that's* why their planes have been so crowded lately!), and that combined with more available seat miles and longer average trips really helped the top line; the aforementioned fuel cost declines and efficiencies owing to a gradual fleet replacement with more efficient versions of its Boeing 737 aircraft all contributed to solid 2014 results.

These trends are likely to continue in FY2015 and FY2016: The company sees top-line growth in the 4 percent range in FY2015 and almost 7 percent in FY2016; profits on the other hand will take another steep ascent, almost 80 percent ahead in FY2015. Fuel prices won't go down forever; earnings growth is expected to moderate in line with revenue growth in FY2016. But the reality—*any* gain in earnings after the stellar three years is by all means a good thing.

Reasons to Buy

Southwest continues to be the best player in an industry whose fundamentals have dramatically improved. The company continues to be the "envy" value proposition of the industry, and we continue to be surprised that no one else has been able to emulate it successfully—but at this point, even if they do, Southwest has a decades-long first mover advantage.

The airline "gets it" that what customers want is no-hassle transportation at best-possible prices—and yes, no bag fees—and has been able to do that better than anyone else for years, and is now extending its value proposition further for business travelers, who increasingly book their own fares and respond well to $15 priority boarding upgrades and other offers. Good management, efficient operation, and excellent marketing make it all possible. Larger market share in a geographically larger and financially stronger market—we like the whole story.

Reasons for Caution

Fuel prices are a big part of the recent success but are still—and will always be—a wild card. The company has shown in the past that it can use hedges to manage fuel price shocks, and we're guessing they're putting their hedges in place now.

We hope the company doesn't become complacent with its recent success, assume low fuel prices will last forever, and start flying 747s to London or some such. The recession forced all airlines, even Southwest, to "fly smart," and we hope this continues.

Generally we fear anything that would move Southwest away from its core competencies—complacency in the short run, acquisitions in the longer term. The AirTran acquisition story appears to have a happy ending but was probably also a challenge—different practices, processes, and cultures. The longer Southwest can stay Southwest, and avoid looking like other airlines, the better.

Finally, much of the good news may have already been priced into the stock's steep ascent; it may be time to level off at cruising altitude for just a bit.

SECTOR: **Transportation** ❑ BETA COEFFICIENT: **0.91** ❑ 10-YEAR COMPOUND EARNINGS PER-SHARE GROWTH: **12.5%** ❑ 10-YEAR COMPOUND DIVIDENDS PER-SHARE GROWTH: **22.0%**

		2007	2008	2009	2010	2011	2012	2013	2014
Revenues (mil)		9,861	11,023	10,350	12,104	15,658	17,088	17,699	18,605
Net income (mil)		471	294	140	550	330	421	754	1,136
Earnings per share		0.81	0.40	0.19	0.73	0.42	0.58	1.05	1.64
Dividends per share		0.02	0.02	0.02	0.02	0.03	0.04	0.10	0.22
Cash flow per share		1.40	1.41	1.21	1.02	1.35	1.73	2.35	3.07
Price:	high	17.0	16.8	11.8	14.3	13.9	10.6	19.0	43.2
	low	12.1	7.1	4.0	10.4	7.1	7.8	10.4	18.8

Website: *www.southwest.com*

AGGRESSIVE GROWTH

St. Jude Medical, Inc.

Ticker symbol: STJ (NYSE) ❑ S&P rating: A ❑ Value Line financial strength rating: A ❑ Current yield: 1.7% ❑ Dividend raises, past 10 years: 4

Company Profile

St. Jude Medical, Inc. designs, manufactures, and distributes cardiovascular medical devices for cardiology and cardiovascular surgery, including pacemakers, implantable cardioverter defibrillators (ICDs), vascular closure devices, catheters, neuromodulation devices, and heart valves. The company has four main business segments:

■ The Cardiac Rhythm Management (CRM) portfolio (responsible for about 52 percent of sales) includes products for treating heart rhythm disorders as well as heart failure. Its products include ICDs, pacemaker systems, and a variety of diagnostic and therapeutic electrophysiology catheters. The company also develops catheter technologies for the Cardiology/Vascular Access therapy area. Those products include hemostasis introducers, catheters, and a market-leading vascular closure device. Many products in this portfolio use RF (radio frequency) and other leading technologies for rhythm management, ablation, and other advanced cardiovascular problems.

- The Cardiovascular segment (24 percent) has been the leader in structural heart and mechanical heart valve technology for more than 25 years. St. Jude Medical also develops a line of tissue valves, intravascular imaging systems, vascular closures, and valve-repair products for various cardiac surgery procedures.

- The company's Neuromodulation segment (8 percent) produces implantable stimulation devices and drug delivery systems for use primarily in chronic pain management and in treatment for certain symptoms of Parkinson's disease and epilepsy.

- The Atrial Fibrillation business (16 percent) markets a series of products designed to map and treat atrial fibrillation and other heart rhythm problems.

St. Jude Medical products are sold in a highly targeted niche market in more than 100 countries. International sales account for about 53 percent of the total; R&D investment is also substantial at more than 12 percent of sales. The company just introduced a new treatment system known as "CardioMEMs" designed to wirelessly measure and monitor pulmonary artery pressure, thus reducing readmission rates for patients with heart failure. In today's environment of increased scrutiny of readmissions and capitated care payments for various conditions, such a product has good business prospects going forward and exemplifies the kinds of technology applications and niche markets St. Jude is involved with.

Financial Highlights, Fiscal Year 2014

The cardiac care business is by nature really two business. The cardiac surgery business is critical and almost completely immune to economic cycles; when you need it, you need it. The largest segment, Cardiac Rhythm Management, which essentially makes pacemakers and related products, is a bit more discretionary and vulnerable to expense cuts on the part of patients and care providers and contractions in the inventory pipeline.

With the effects of the Great Recession on the wane, St. Jude, like many others in the industry, enjoyed a mild uptick in its business, helped along too by strength in its Atrial Defibrillation business. But currency effects wiped out much of the gain, and year to year the company reported a 2.2 percent increase in revenues after a 3–4 percent currency effect. Total earnings, again attenuated by currency effects, advanced a relatively healthier 5.4 percent, and, aided by a 2 percent share repurchase, per-share earnings advanced closer to 6 percent. Continued dollar strength and trends toward streamlined health care will keep both revenues and profits pretty much on a flat line through FY2015, beyond which the company projects a return to 6 percent earnings growth on slightly better margins and on a 4–5 percent growth in revenue. The company appears to be growing cash returns to investors at a higher pace, close to 8 percent growth per year for dividends (dividends have already gone from zero to $1.16 indicated per share in a four-year period) with a steady 2–3 percent annual share repurchase.

Reasons to Buy

St. Jude continues to be a market leader in the heart rhythm and vascular surgery niche, a solid position in the health-care industry. Both the Neuro-modulation and Atrial Fibrillation segments have grown rapidly and seem well positioned for growth in at least the 15 percent range. The techniques employed in neuromodulation are growing quickly in the field as a preferred treatment for long-term pain management. St. Jude (and others) see this as a disruptive technology, potentially replacing drug and physical therapy regimens and offering improved lifestyle at a reduced cost. These two busi-nesses, while small, serve as solid growth kickers, complementing the flatter CRM and Cardiovascular segments.

As part of a bigger picture, St. Jude is an innovation leader, and its innovations are starting to pay off. We like the combination of innovation-led growth and willingness (and ability) to share the proceeds with investors.

Reasons for Caution

We almost jumped off the bandwagon in 2014 due to flat performance and cost moderation trends in the industry, but it is one of the steadier hands in a solid industry with a good innovation track record; we couldn't find anything better to buy. Too, the market seems to like these features as well, and has driven the stock price up a bit faster than these fundamentals might support; it would be prudent to buy on pullbacks. For those who thrive on momentum, this stock will not get your heart beating very fast.

SECTOR: **Health Care** ◻ BETA COEFFICIENT: **1.32** ◻ 10-YEAR COMPOUND EARNINGS
PER-SHARE GROWTH: **16.5%** ◻ 10-YEAR COMPOUND DIVIDENDS PER-SHARE GROWTH: **NM**

	2007	2008	2009	2010	2011	2012	2013	2014
Revenues (mil)	3,779	4,363	4,681	5,165	5,612	5,503	5,501	5,622
Net income (mil)	652	807	838	995	1,074	1,095	1,094	1,153
Earnings per share	1.85	2.31	2.43	3.01	3.28	3.48	3.76	3.98
Dividends per share	—	—	—	—	0.84	0.92	1.00	1.08
Cash flow per share	2.48	2.92	3.24	3.70	4.35	4.50	4.79	5.00
Price: high	48.1	48.5	42.0	43.0	54.2	44.8	63.2	71.9
low	34.9	25.0	28.9	34.0	32.1	30.3	36.1	54.8

Website: *www.sjm.com*

AGGRESSIVE GROWTH

Starbucks Corporation

Ticker symbol: SBUX (NASDAQ) ◻ S&P rating: A- ◻ Value Line financial strength rating: A++ ◻ Current yield: 1.4% ◻ Dividend raises, past 10 years: 5

Company Profile

Starbucks Corporation, formed in 1985, is the leading retailer, roaster, and brand of specialty coffee in the world. The company sells whole-bean coffees through its retailers, its specialty sales group, and supermarkets. After a brief pause in the aftermath of the Great Recession, the company footprint is expanding once again, with 8,462 company-owned stores in the Americas (8,105 at the end of 2013) and 3,391 in international markets (2,187 at the end of 2013), in addition to 10,025 licensed stores worldwide (8,892 at the end of 2013). Retail coffee shop sales constitute about 89 percent of its revenue, up from 86 percent in 2012. About 79 percent of revenue originates in company-operated stores. Unlike many in the restaurant sector, the company does not franchise its stores—all are either company owned or operated by licensees in special venues such as airports, college campuses, and other places where access is restricted, and in foreign markets where it is necessary or advantageous.

The company continues to expand overseas, usually at first through partnerships and joint ventures; sometimes it buys out the partner as it did in China in 2011. The FY2014 sales breakdown: 73 percent Americas, 8 percent Europe/Middle East/Africa, 7 percent China/Asia-Pacific, and 12 percent other segments and "channel development," which is largely made up of branded product sales through non-Starbucks retailers. The company now operates in 62 countries in total; the China and Asia-Pacific segment, which now includes active stores in Vietnam and India, not surprisingly is the fastest-growing segment growing revenues, with company store base up some 28 percent and revenues up some 23 percent in FY2014.

The company is gradually expanding beyond its traditional coffee base, opening a new Teavana Fine Teas Bar in New York and adding Teavana tea-related items into its traditional stores as a consequence of its recent acquisition of that company. Evolution Fresh juices are now widely available, and the company has done well with its food menu, including its "La Boulange" line of pastries. Specialty packaging, including "Via" and Keurig-compatible single-serve packages have done well also. Finally, Starbucks has joint ventures with PepsiCo and Dreyer's to develop bottled coffee drinks and coffee-flavored ice creams.

In the past year, however, Starbucks has invested a lot and expanded its leadership in the deployment of technology. Always a leader in providing connectivity to users in its stores, the company is now leading the way in mobile payment platforms, including its "Mobile Order and Pay" system where users can order and pay for their drinks using smartphones, then subsequently arrive at locations to pick up their drinks. Not only is this convenient for the customer, it effectively increases capacity and reduces wait time in the stores. The addition of technology and networking guru Kevin Johnson as president and Chief Operating Officer underscores this initiative.

The company's retail goal continues to be the unique Starbucks experience, which the company defines as a third place beyond home and work. The "experience" is built upon superior customer service and a clean, well-maintained retail store that reflects the personality of the community in which it operates—all aimed at building loyalty and frequent repeat visits.

The company also gets high marks for citizenship, continuing to offer health coverage, equity participation, and even college assistance for its 190,000 employees ("partners") and recent commitment to hire 10,000 veterans and military spouses over the next five years, among a list of other commitments to community service and social issues of the day.

Financial Highlights, Fiscal Year 2014

Okay, no puns about "percolating growth" or the usual other stuff in this narrative—Starbucks followers are probably weary of them by now. But any way you measure it, FY2014 was a strong brew (oops, sorry) that looks to stay hot (oops, sorry again) in FY2015, FY2016, and beyond.

Staying its excellent course, opening new stores (and even closing a few, once held as sacrilegious), and capitalizing on new food and technology initiatives all led to healthy same-store sales growth of 6 percent across the board, a growth driven equally by volume and "size of ticket"—the amount purchased per transaction. Operating margins improved a full 2.3 percent to 21.3 percent in FY2014, and, while expected to stay at that level for the next couple of years, are projected to rise further beyond the FY2016 timeframe.

All of this led to a 10.4 percent revenue growth and a 20 percent growth in net income, and with share buybacks a full 26 percent growth in per-share earnings. If that wasn't enough for a company thought to have maxed out its potential years ago, FY2015 revenue growth is projected at 15 percent, followed by another 11–12 percent in FY2016. Earnings and per-share earnings growth will track if not slightly exceed these figures. A 40–50 percent increase in the dividend is likely over the next two years as well, as the company has chosen this path to return cash to shareholders.

Reasons to Buy

Starbucks is still a great story. The company's stores continue to be more than coffee shops and are really that "third place" where professionals, students, moms, and other prosperous folks will meet and dole out a few bucks for quality drinks. The "third place" aura creates a lot of the brand strength and, in our view, represents the company's true strength—well beyond the quality of the coffee itself and related products. The company has a steadily (and profitably) growing presence on the world stage; it has trained its store-growth cannon on these markets rather than overbuilding in the U.S. New packaging and food products are broadening appeal to larger customer segments, as we thought would happen; the single-cup market has huge potential. And we believe the technology improvements hold a lot of promise, both for customers and operations.

The company is well managed, has an extremely strong brand, has solid financials, and, once again, a steady growth track record, and it is carving out an ever-stronger international footprint. Cash returns to investors are on the rise, and safety (as proxied by beta) has improved sharply. Starbucks offers both growth and, increasingly, cash and safety—a very nice beverage combination for investors indeed.

Reasons for Caution

The biggest risk—and maybe it's a good problem to have so long as you manage it well—is the temptation to overexpand (which they've done before), dilute the experience, and attract competition (which they've also done before and successfully dealt with). Coffee prices are volatile, but as experienced before, they don't really affect this story much since coffee is a small part of the company's total cost picture. Historically, coffee price surges have presented good share-buying opportunities. Perhaps our biggest fear is too much growth in the foodservice business—which could reduce margins, dilute the experience, and make the stores smell like a sandwich shop, far less appealing for most than the aroma of coffee. Too, it brings operational complexities. So we score the experience with food so far as mostly a success but are keeping our eyes (and noses) open for signs of stress.

SECTOR: **Restaurants** ❏ BETA COEFFICIENT: **0.77** ❏ 10-YEAR COMPOUND EARNINGS
PER-SHARE GROWTH: **20.0%** ❏ 10-YEAR COMPOUND DIVIDENDS PER-SHARE GROWTH: **NM**

	2007	2008	2009	2010	2011	2012	2013	2014
Revenues (mil)	9,412	10,383	9,774	10,707	11,701	13,299	14,892	16,448
Net income (mil)	673	525	598	982	1,174	1,385	1,721	2,068
Earnings per share	0.87	0.71	0.80	1.28	1.52	1.79	2.26	2.71
Dividends per share	—	—	—	0.23	0.52	0.68	0.84	1.04
Cash flow per share	1.54	1.46	1.53	2.00	2.28	2.58	3.11	3.71
Price: high	36.6	21.0	24.5	31.3	46.5	62.0	82.5	84.2
low	19.9	7.1	21.3	21.3	30.8	43.0	52.5	67.9

Website: *www.starbucks.com*

State Street Corporation

Ticker symbol: STT (NYSE) ❑ S&P rating: A+ ❑ Value Line financial strength rating: B++ ❑ Current yield: 1.5% ❑ Dividend raises, past 10 years: 8

Company Profile

Are you afraid of SPDRs? Not the eight-legged kind, but the original and one of three leading brands of exchange-traded funds (ETFs) out there rapidly gaining ground on the "traditional" fund industry? If you aren't afraid of SPDRs, and you aren't too afraid of financial stocks in general, State Street might make it onto your own personal buy list. In fact, we think State Street is, more than most, a safe and sane way to play the Financials sector, a sector which we continue to hold generally out of favor.

Like many financial powerhouses, State Street has a number of businesses under its umbrella. But unlike many, its core products are concentrated on offering services to other financial services firms and on offering the relatively new and growing ETF investment package to individual and institutional investors. It is often analyzed as a bank, but it acts more like a company providing services to other financial institutions and the public, receiving a steady and growing stream of fees for those services.

The company operates with two main lines of business: Investment Servicing and Investment Management:

■ *Investment Servicing* (66 percent of revenues) provides fee-based administrative, custody, analytic, and other value-add functions to investment companies—mainly mutual funds, hedge funds, and pension funds, including settlement and payment services, transaction management, foreign exchange trading and brokerage, and setting the NAV (net asset value, or price) of about 40 percent of U.S.-based mutual funds on a daily basis.

■ *Investment Management* (about 12 percent of revenues) provides investment vehicles and products through its State Street Global Advisors, or SSGA, subsidiary, including the well-known SPDR ETFs and some of the analytic tools and indexes supporting these products.

With these two fee-based business units accounting for 78 percent of total revenues, you might wonder where the rest of its $10.3 billion in revenues come from. The answer lies in interest and related income—some

22 percent of revenues are derived from the net interest generated on asset holdings.

State Street has operations in 29 countries, and about 64 percent of revenues come from assets managed in the U.S., 23 percent from the EMEA region, and 13 percent from Asia-Pacific.

Financial Highlights, Fiscal Year 2014

Despite a 6 percent rise in fund-servicing fees and a 9 percent rise in management (mostly ETF management) fees, total revenues advanced only 4 percent for FY2014. Currency effects in general, lower brokerage fees, and a 2 percent drop in net interest income were the main drags. Net earnings did not follow suit, as the company made major personnel and information technology investments to support the growing business base, and there were some one-time expenses related to its foreign exchange trading business. Net earnings dropped about 4.5 percent. Per-share earnings, however, on the back of a 4 percent share count reduction, were down only 1 percent.

The company projects that a more favorable interest rate environment and absorption of these new costs will move revenue forward about 3 percent in FY2015 and 3–5 percent in FY2016, with earnings ahead in the 5–10 percent range during this period. Continued aggressive share buybacks will help per-share earnings. By 2016, the company will have bought back about 25 percent of its float, most of which was issued to bolster finances during the Great Recession. Per-share earnings should rise in the low double digits for the foreseeable future, and dividends may follow suit in addition to the share repurchases.

Reasons to Buy

When there's a gold rush, the people who sell picks, shovels, and maps usually win. That's sort of the case with State Street. It makes a lot of steady money on selling services to other financial services firms. It's a steadier income stream absent some of the risks facing its other financial brethren. We think that State Street has a steady business with an innovative growth path in the ETF business, and we like the SPDR brand. We also like the fact that, unlike most financial firms, the company's income is more heavily based on fees and services than on interest margins and investment gains—more than 75 percent of revenues arise from fees and services. That said, the prospect for increased interest rates would bode well for interest income. The company continues to focus on financial strength, with a Tier One capital ratio exceeding 18.2 percent (anything over 10 percent is considered good; 8 percent is required under the new rules) and also continues to focus on investor returns, aggressively retiring shares and raising the dividend regularly.

Reasons for Caution

Despite the fact that State Street sells picks and shovels to other investment funds, many of its fees are based on asset valuations—which are in turn vulnerable to market downturns. The company estimates that a 10 percent drop in the markets would reduce total equity-based revenues about 2 percent and total fixed-income revenues about 1 percent, indicating vulnerability but at least some defense against market drops.

Like other financial firms, State Street is enormously complex and hard to understand—we almost gave up when we introduced this issue for 2014. If you insist on fully understanding how a business works, what it sells, how it delivers, and so forth, this one might not be for you. It's a bit murky, though it is easier to see how it makes money on the ETF business. Although the business is different than most financials, it could be swept up in another financial crisis. Likewise, a major market pullback and a decline in public interest could hurt. And the share price has finally caught up with its improved prospects. For all of these reasons, State Street is far from the least risky stock on our *100 Best Stocks* list, but it deserves a look if you have a taste for financials.

SECTOR: **Financials** ❑ BETA COEFFICIENT: **1.55** ❑ 10-YEAR COMPOUND EARNINGS PER-SHARE GROWTH: **6.5%** ❑ 10-YEAR COMPOUND DIVIDENDS PER-SHARE GROWTH: **6.5%**

		2007	2008	2009	2010	2011	2012	2013	2014
Assets (bil)		142.5	173.6	157.9	160.5	216.8	222.6	243.3	274.9
Revenues (mil)		8,336	10,693	8,640	8,953	9,594	9,649	9,881	10,235
Net income (mil)		1,231	1,811	1,803	1,559	1,920	2,061	2,136	2,037
Earnings per share		3.45	4.30	3.46	3.09	3.79	4.20	4.62	4.57
Dividends per share		0.88	0.95	0.04	0.04	0.72	0.96	1.04	1.16
Price:	high	82.5	86.6	55.9	48.8	50.3	47.3	73.6	80.9
	low	59.1	28.1	14.4	32.5	29.9	38.2	47.7	62.7

Website: *www.statestreet.com*

Steelcase, Incorporated

Ticker symbol: SCS (NYSE) ◻ S&P rating: BBB ◻ Value Line financial strength rating: B ◻ Current yield: 2.4% ◻ Dividend raises, past 10 years: 4

Company Profile

A newcomer to the *100 Best Stocks* list for 2015, Steelcase is the world's leading producer of office furniture, and more importantly, office systems. The company makes several lines of more traditional modular walls, chairs, desks, files, and other kinds of cabinets, etc. But in addition, in part through emerging subbrands such as Coalesse, Nurture, Workspring, and Turnstone, Steelcase is bringing to market new ideas and office concepts that we'd probably all like to see and work in. Call it office architecture if you will.

Imagine arriving at the office, heading to a small visible conference area with two glass walls, a floor-to-ceiling whiteboard, and display devices that connect immediately and wirelessly to your mobile device to display your work or your multimedia presentation. Imagine sitting (or standing) in small, comfortable work areas, again with a display, possibly built into the table in front of you, to work alone or with others. Impersonal, boring, paper-ridden, PC-based, space-consuming cubicle—be gone! And most in today's offices are empty anyway—so they might as well be gone. Steelcase continues to really be a bet on the demise of today's traditional office space. Why is that space going away? Several factors. One, today's new mobile worker, who doesn't spend so much time in the office. When she or he does, it's to get together, to collaborate, often on a ceramic or glass whiteboard, with other workers and to demonstrate their work. Most don't have traditional PCs. Less paper moves around, so workers don't need as much storage. What they need is a workbench, places to stash their backpacks, meet, ways to connect and display what they're working on and work together, places to rest and contemplate in ergonomic comfort, all the while connected to the business and to each other. "Work has been freed" is the slogan on the company's subbrand "Coalesse" website (*www.coalesse.com*).

Another factor in the death of the cube is the desire to reduce office space—and cost. Cubes, especially empty ones, take a lot of space. Just as the traditional four-walled, sometimes-windowed office went out in favor of the cubicle and cube farm when PCs took over and nobody needed a secretary pool any more, we think the office is ready for another transition. Steelcase has been studying and innovating in that space for quite some time, and it appears in our view to be ready to bring it to market, as a market leader. We think it could be big.

Steelcase doesn't just produce broad lines of office furnishings. It has conducted deep, customer-based studies of workplace activity, especially innovation, teamwork, and leadership, and it has studied and marketed to key vertical markets like health care, education, and hotels and hospitality—a case study for market-driven innovation. Former CEO Jim Hackett, in fact, is on the advisory board of the Mayo Clinic Center for Innovation, using that team as a test bed for highly creative workspaces as well as new medical workspaces. The company is also working with J.W. Marriott and others to develop innovative workspaces for business hotel guests. About 28 percent of sales come from overseas.

Financial Highlights, Fiscal Year 2014

Since the boom-and-bust cycle of the mid-2000s, the Great Recession, and emergence from it in 2011, the company continues to ready itself for the growth spurt that should result as the visions previously described become reality. For FY2014, revenues rose a modest 3.5 percent, helped along a bit by an improved product mix (a phrase we expect to repeat in future years as the traditional file cabinet slips into history) but also hurt a bit by currency shifts. Profits rose a slightly stronger 8 percent helped by some cost-reduction measures. The company, rather modestly, forecasts revenues to grow 4–5 percent in FY2015 and FY2016, with stronger growth in earnings in the high teens to low 20 percent range as product mix shifts continue to play in. Dividend raises are expected to become more steady and secure, in the 10–15 percent range annually.

Reasons to Buy

With Steelcase, we think we are in the early stages of an accelerating trend. A couple of trends, really. First, traditional organizations are looking for new ways to meet the needs and reduce the stress of today's mobile worker. They are also looking to optimize floor space, which the new designs tend to use less of. Second, new companies (and there are a lot of them) cater to the new "Millenenial" worker and aspire to create the perfect workspace for mobile collaboration and innovation. This trend is spreading around the world; currently, only 28 percent of sales are overseas, but the company's concepts are picking up particularly in the space-constrained Asia-Pacific region. In short, we think the update of today's traditional cube farm, born in the 1980s, is well under way. Steelcase gets this and has been investing in it for years. We like the designs and its approach to key vertical markets like health care, hospitality, and education, which have their own special needs. As these trends accelerate, we expect decent sales and earnings momentum going forward.

Reasons for Caution

Steelcase, and the office furniture/business in general, are extremely cyclical, subject to dramatic ups and downs tied to the level of business activity. Put simply, office furniture is one of the first expenditures to cut in bad times. As the following numbers show, the company took a huge hit in the Great Recession, one from which it hasn't fully recovered. That may be a blessing in disguise, as it appears to be the wake-up call to move forward beyond selling traditional office furniture. A fine example of creative destruction at work, we think.

Still, there is some risk—while the evolution of the modern office is underway, there may be some fits and starts, and competitive pressures and fickle investment attitudes of businesses do bear watching. Margins, at 8–10 percent for operating margin and 3–5 percent for net margins, are nothing to write home about. The company has invested a lot in development. However, we think Steelcase through their research efforts has at least something of a first-mover advantage, and as the world's largest single supplier, strength in scale and in distributor relationships as well. The scenario may require some patience, but investors are getting a decent dividend while they wait—which we expect to be more stable than it has been.

SECTOR: **Industrials** ❑ BETA COEFFICIENT: **1.33** ❑ 10-YEAR COMPOUND EARNINGS PER-SHARE GROWTH: **6.0%** ❑ 10-YEAR COMPOUND DIVIDENDS PER-SHARE GROWTH: **1.0%**

	2007	2008	2009	2010	2011	2012	2013	2014
Revenues (mil)	3,420	3,184	2,292	2,437	2,749	2,669	2,990	3,090
Net income (mil)	143	91	(12.2)	51	76	101	106	115
Earnings per share	1.00	0.68	(0.09)	0.38	0.58	0.79	0.84	0.90
Dividends per share	0.58	0.60	0.24	0.16	0.24	0.36	0.36	0.42
Cash flow per share	1.70	1.34	0.47	0.87	1.05	1.27	1.36	1.45
Price: high	20.7	16.7	7.7	10.9	12.1	13.3	17.0	18.8
low	14.0	5.0	3.0	6.2	5.4	7.3	12.2	13.6

Website: *www.steelcase.com*

AGGRESSIVE GROWTH

Stryker Corporation

Ticker symbol: SYK (NYSE) ❑ S&P rating: A+ ❑ Value Line financial strength rating: A++ ❑ Current yield: 1.5% ❑ Dividend increases, past 10 years: 9

Company Profile

Stryker Corporation was founded as the Orthopedic Frame Company in 1941 by Dr. Homer H. Stryker, a leading orthopedic surgeon and the inventor of several orthopedic products. The company now ranks as a dominant player in the global orthopedics industry with more than 59,000 products in its catalog and a strong innovation track record, with more than 5 percent of sales invested in R&D.

The Reconstructive segment, formerly known as Orthopedic Implants, comprising about 44 percent of sales, has a significant market share in such "spare parts" as artificial hips, prosthetic knees, implant products for other extremities, and trauma products. Within that group, knees are 15 percent, hips are 14 percent, and "Trauma & Extremities" are another 12 percent of sales, in case you were curious.

The MediSurg unit, about 37 percent of sales, develops, manufactures, and markets worldwide powered and computer-assisted (and now, thanks to a recent acquisition, robotic) surgical instruments, endoscopic surgical systems, hospital beds, and other patient care and handling equipment. Instruments (14 percent) and Endoscopy (13 percent) are the largest contributors.

The Neurotechnology & Spine segment, a large part of which was acquired from Boston Scientific in 2010, accounts for 19 percent of sales and sells spinal reconstructive and surgical equipment, neurovascular surgery equipment, and craniomaxillofacial products. This is the smallest but fastest-growing segment in the company.

Stryker's revenue is split roughly 66/34 percent domestic and international, with about 8 percent coming from emerging markets. The company scored a 19th position on the annual "Fortune 100 Best Companies to Work For" list for 2015, up a full 23 places from 2014 and one of the top players in the health-care industry.

Financial Highlights, Fiscal Year 2014

Despite currency effects that nagged many other health-care technology providers, Stryker flexed its joints quite well in FY2014, scoring a 7.2 percent sales gain. Some of their supported surgeries are naturally elective and thus rebounded as the Great Recession slips in to the past; equipment sales came back as well. Too, the company, with 66 percent domestic sales, is relatively less exposed to the strong dollar. Profits resumed "normal" growth after a sharp drop in net income reported in FY2013 due to product recalls and resulting restatements.

Going forward, Stryker projects a more moderate 3–4 percent revenue gain in FY2015 and 5 percent in FY2016. Improved operating leverage and resulting margin growth may lead to as much as a 30 percent net income growth in FY2015 and 10 percent in FY2016; per-share earnings should gain somewhat more with recently announced buybacks and could rise as high as $6.00 in FY2016. The company manages return on invested capital closely and strives for a capital allocation breakdown of $4.5 billion for driving growth, including mergers and acquisitions, $1 billion for dividends, and $1 billion for share buybacks. That all in place, the company authorized a $2 billion share repurchase in early 2015.

Reasons to Buy

Stryker's top line is driven largely by elective surgeries and hospital equipment purchases, and the Great Recession years turned out to be years for delaying whatever medical procedures could be delayed. Many consumers decided to wait and see how the medical care legislation would turn out, and some were simply deciding to hold on to their cash until economic conditions improved. That's all over now, and a resumed surgical calendar and international expansion bode well for the near-term future. We continue to see Stryker as an innovative health-care products company with relatively less entrenched competition than many others and a strong presence in the orthopedic market, which should capitalize on aging and the availability of health insurance to greater numbers under the Affordable Care Act. Emerging markets, particularly China, are strong, and recent acquisitions should strengthen the portfolio and brand worldwide. We also see ample buybacks and some dividend growth.

Reasons for Caution

Ongoing scrutiny of health-care costs and a continuation of small acquisitions bring some risks to the company, but we don't think they are excessive. The company makes fairly high-tech medical products and as such is exposed to legal, regulatory, and manufacturing risks, and the recent product recall did hurt. Ongoing efforts to contain medical costs could hurt the more elective orthopedic procedures, but that should be offset by the wider availability of covered care to more people. Finally, the stock price rose considerably in 2014, making it important to find good entry points for this long-term holding.

SECTOR: **Health Care** ❑ BETA COEFFICIENT: **1.00** ❑ 10-YEAR COMPOUND EARNINGS PER-SHARE GROWTH: **14.0%** ❑ 10-YEAR COMPOUND DIVIDENDS PER-SHARE GROWTH: **32.0%**

		2007	2008	2009	2010	2011	2012	2013	2014
Revenues (mil)		6,001	6,718	6,723	7,320	8,307	8,656	9,021	9,675
Net income (mil)		1,001	1,148	1,107	1,330	1,448	1,298	1,006	1,460
Earnings per share		2.44	2.78	2.77	3.30	3.72	3.39	2.63	3.85
Dividends per share		0.22	0.33	0.50	0.63	0.72	0.85	1.10	1.22
Cash flow per share		3.33	3.87	3.75	4.40	5.08	4.69	4.01	5.45
Price:	high	76.9	74.9	52.7	59.7	65.2	64.1	75.8	96.2
	low	54.9	35.4	30.8	42.7	43.7	49.4	55.2	74.0

Website: *www.stryker.com*

CONSERVATIVE GROWTH

Sysco Corporation

Ticker symbol: SYY (NYSE) ❑ S&P rating: A ❑ Value Line financial strength rating: A+ ❑ Current yield: 3.2% ❑ Dividend raises, past 10 years: 10

Company Profile

Sysco is the leading marketer and distributor of food, food products, and related equipment and supplies to the U.S. foodservice industry. The company distributes fresh and frozen meats, prepared entrées, vegetables, canned and dried foods, dairy products, beverages, and produce, as well as paper products, restaurant equipment and supplies, and cleaning supplies. The company might be familiar for its "institutional" number-ten-sized cans of food found in many high-volume kitchens, but the product line and customer base is much larger, including many specialty and chain restaurants, lodges, hotels, hospitals, schools, and other distribution centers across the country. Restaurants account for about 61 percent of the business; hospitals and nursing homes 9 percent; schools and colleges, and hotels and motels each 6 percent; and "other" categories make up the rest. You see their lift-gated "bobtail" delivery trucks continuously, but you may not notice them delivering and unloading a pallet or two of goods at a time for a broad assortment of foodservice venues in your area. If you eat out at all, you've most likely consumed Sysco-distributed products. Their slogan, "Good Things Come from Sysco," says it all.

Sysco was founded in 1969 with the goal of becoming a national foodservice network. By 1977, the company had become the largest foodservice supplier to the $255 billion restaurant market in North America, a position it has retained for more than 30 years. It has over 425,000 customers and distributes over 400,000 products, including 41,000 under its own label. Sysco operates 194 distribution facilities across the United States, Canada, the Bahamas, and Ireland and is kicking the tires in Costa Rica with a new joint venture there. From these centers, Sysco distributes 1.4 billion cases of food annually. The facilities include its 95 Broadline facilities, which supply independent and chain restaurants and other food-preparation facilities with a wide variety of food and nonfood products. It has 11 hotel supply locations, 25 specialty produce facilities, 17 SYGMA distribution centers (specialized, high-volume centers supplying to chain restaurants), 27 custom-cutting meat locations, and two distributors specializing in the niche Asian foodservice market.

The company also supplies the hotel industry with guest amenities, equipment, housekeeping supplies, room accessories, and textiles. By customer type, the company breaks down its revenues as 62 percent Restaurants, 18 percent Healthcare, Education, and Government, 8 percent to Travel, Leisure, and Retail, and 12 percent to "other." By product type, the top five are: 19 percent meat, 18 percent canned/dry, 13 percent frozen, 11 percent dairy, and 10 percent poultry, with produce, paper goods, seafood, beverages, and others making up the rest.

Sysco is by far the largest company in the foodservice distribution industry. Up until recently, it grew via small "bolt-on" acquisitions in specialty food companies (such as seafood) or new geographies, but for the most part avoided the "blockbuster" acquisition. Such acquisitions in 2013 added a billion dollars in net revenues. However, the "small" nature of these acquisitions changed dramatically in December 2013 with the announcement of a merger with its largest competitor, U.S. Foods, for some $8.2 billion. In mid-2015 the company, responding to pressure from U.S. antitrust authorities, terminated this acquisition.

Financial Highlights, Fiscal Year 2014

Sales and margins continued to be squeezed in the near term by softness in the restaurant sector (the recession taught a lot of people to "eat in") and despite lower fuel prices, there have been some inflationary pressures in processed foods and meats in particular; too, distribution costs have also risen. All taken together, and with a few small acquisitions, sales rose about 4.7 percent, but net income dropped a fairly substantial 7.1 percent. The company expects stronger top- and bottom-line performance as restaurant performance recovers and energy-related savings get into the mix into FY2015 and especially FY2016. Revenues should rise in the 6–7 percent range both years; net earnings are expected to serve up an 11 percent recovery in FY2015 and a gain in the high teens for FY2016. Dividend raises, which have been modest but consistent, may pick up a bit.

Reasons to Buy

Sysco continues to be a dominant player—and may become more dominant—in a niche that won't go away anytime soon. While the current food-service environment isn't great, the company has plenty to work on in the form of operational efficiencies. Meanwhile, we think the restaurant environment will get better as the economy improves and as "weak hands" are replaced by stronger ones.

Sysco's recent investments in technology continue to bear fruit, and we like to see innovation in an industry not known for it. New analytics, routing optimization, and recycling initiatives are being applied to realize savings in people, fuel, and other costs; the company still projects slight improvements in its net profit margin back into the 2.5 percent range and higher from a low of 2.0 percent in FY2014. New supply-chain tools —even a "MySyscoTRUCK" app—allow customers to view the location and status of the deliveries and more generally will expand efficiencies and extend the customer relationship. In sum, even with the merger, this is a steady and safe company with a pretty good track record for steady business, decent cash flow, and decent shareholder payouts.

Reasons for Caution

Although the trend is slowly reversing, the recession got many folks away from the habit of eating out, and many restaurants disappeared altogether during this period. Volatility in food and ingredient prices, and fuel costs too, can pressure margins; this is always a cause for concern. We also now worry that new dining trends and tastes of the Millennials and others will require more specialization in the restaurant market, something Sysco will need to adapt to at least to a degree.

As previously described, this is a low-margin business with not a lot of room for error. Share counts will rise slightly if the acquisition is completed, but we would expect resumption of buybacks after the acquisition period if the past pattern holds. Sysco, more than most, is a "sleep at night" kind of investment; investors seeking rapid growth might want to look somewhere outside of this steady and rather unsexy business.

SECTOR: **Consumer Staples** ◻ BETA COEFFICIENT: **0.77** ◻ 10-YEAR COMPOUND EARNINGS PER-SHARE GROWTH: **4.0%** ◻ 10-YEAR COMPOUND DIVIDENDS PER-SHARE GROWTH: **10.5%**

	2007	**2008**	**2009**	**2010**	**2011**	**2012**	**2013**	**2014**
Revenues (mil)	35,042	37,522	36,853	37,243	39,323	42,381	44,411	46,517
Net income (mil)	1,001	1,106	1,056	1,181	1,153	1,122	992	931
Earnings per share	1.60	1.81	1.77	1.99	1.96	1.90	1.67	1.58
Dividends per share	0.72	0.82	0.93	0.99	1.03	1.07	1.11	1.16
Cash flow per share	2.23	2.46	2.44	2.67	2.62	2.63	2.57	2.54
Price: high	36.7	35.0	29.5	32.6	32.6	32.4	43.4	41.2
low	29.9	20.7	19.4	27.0	25.1	27.0	30.5	34.1

Website: *www.sysco.com*

AGGRESSIVE GROWTH

Target Corporation

Ticker symbol: TGT (NYSE) ◻ S&P rating: A ◻ Value Line financial strength rating: A ◻ Current yield: 2.6% ◻ Dividend raises, past 10 years: 10

Company Profile

As you know by now, we take a long-term view when we include a company on our *100 Best* list. A good company with a good and long-standing business model will stay on our list despite a stumble; in fact, many a stumble can give a company strength, as we've seen over the years with the likes of Starbucks, Johnson & Johnson, and Procter & Gamble. If the business model, or marketplace changes for the worse, however, that's a different story; we cut our losses and say goodbye—Hewlett-Packard, or this year, McDonalds, and perhaps many of today's energy plays—come to mind. In Target we now have a classic example of a company stumbling badly and regaining its footing with good management and a sustaining brand. The stumbles included the well-publicized data breach in December 2013 and a less-publicized doomed venture into the Canadian market, which ultimately cost a billion dollars to earnings but the company cut its losses and exited that market in late 2014. Many a professional investor and "expert" jumped off this horse in 2014. Frankly, it never occurred to us—and we've been rewarded for our patience with a 39 percent gain on a total return basis. Let the lesson be learned here: The recognition of a company's core strengths—and patience—are true virtues of the successful investor. Anyway, let's get to the main story.

Target is the nation's second-largest general merchandise retailer and specializes in general merchandise at a discount in a large-store format. The company now operates 1,790 stores in 49 states (Vermont is the only state not represented), including 250 Super Targets, which also carry a broad line of groceries. The greatest concentration of Target stores is in California (15 percent), Texas (8 percent), and Florida (7 percent), with a combined total of about 30 percent of the stores. There is another concentration in the upper Midwest. With the sale of Marshall Field's and Mervyn's in 2004, the company has focused completely on discount retail in store locations and on the Internet.

Target positions itself against its main competitor, Walmart, as a more upscale and trend-conscious "cheap chic" alternative. The typical Target customer has a higher level of disposable income than that of Walmart, which the company courts by offering brand-name merchandise in addition to a series of largely successful house brands such as Michael Graves and Archer Farms. The company's revenues come from retail pretty much exclusively; it sold its credit card operations to TD Bank in late 2012.

The company is also investing domestically in its food lines, which now account for 21 percent of total 2014 sales. Food is sold in about 70 percent of stores. The total sales breakdown: 25 percent household essentials, 21 percent food and pet supplies, 19 percent apparel and accessories, 18 percent hardlines, and 17 percent home furnishings and décor. These percentages are largely unchanged from last year.

We'll treat the data breach and the Canada failure as "old news" and not dwell on the details; they've already been extensively covered in the trade press. Suffice it to say management handled both well, even with a transition to a new CEO and CIO midstream. The company showed above-average willingness to admit mistakes, maintain a positive customer experience, and cut losses (especially with the Canadian venture). The way both problems were handled strengthens our view of the management team, and ultimately, the Target brand.

What *is* news is a new "roadmap to transform business" shared by Target management in early 2015. Highlights include an emphasis on what other retailers call "omnichannel" development—combining web, mobile, and in-store experiences (and supply chains) to offer a better customer experience. The company estimates that "guests" who shop online generate three times the sales of guests who shop in stores only. We applaud this effort to differentiate customers by value and tailor experiences; far too few companies do this in our opinion. Target will also begin to tailor its merchandise assortments according to geography and demographic, and will prioritize Style, Baby, Kids, and Wellness categories in addition to Groceries as "targets" to improve merchandising and overall experience. The company has also admitted that its traditional store format is saturated. It's hard to find more locations (another "admission" we admire, since most retail managers have a hard time admitting this). The company will extend experiments with smaller TargetExpress and CityTarget formats. Finally, supply-chain and operational improvements will cut $2 billion in costs over the first two years of this plan.

Best of all, the traditional Target brand and merchandising will carry forward well beyond the mistakes of 2013.

Financial Highlights, Fiscal Year 2014

The numbers tell us that, post-2013, the business is pretty much back on track. Lingering effects of the data breach kept 2014 comparable store growth and overall sales growth pretty much flat; earnings recovered almost to pre-2013 levels after the writeoff of Canadian losses and data breach expenses. For FY2015 and FY2016, sales growth is expected to rebound into the 2–3 percent range, and a rebound in operating margins, driven in part by the operational improvements previously mentioned, will return earnings growth rates into the 7–10 percent range. Share counts continue to drop more than 1 percent each year, and dividends should grow in the high single- to mid-double–digit range. The overall picture is one of a return to stability with a stable growth component.

Reasons to Buy

We thought the long-term consequences of FY2013's problems would fade rather quickly, and so far, we've been right. The company handled both issues and particularly the data breach quite effectively, in fact used it as an opportunity to pioneer new technologies like smart chip cards, which we think in the long term will not only assuage its customers' concerns but attract new customers. The company is simply too strong in its brand and position to lose in the long term over an incident like this, particularly if handled well, which was the case.

Target remains a classic positioning success story. Customers understand and appreciate Target, and it has some of the highest customer satisfaction numbers in the industry. The company continues to take share away from specialty retailers in home lines, clothing, children's items, and other areas. People like the Target brand and associate it with well-managed stores and quality and good taste at a reasonable price with good locations. More recently they appear to be making more regular and frequent visits to the store because of the grocery department.

Better economic conditions and more spending on home and domestic goods should improve Target's market share. Share counts have dropped from 911 million in 2003 to about 640 million recently. We like the "roadmap" transition plan, and feel the overall story remains solid.

Reasons for Caution

Target is up against some very tough competitors: Walmart, Costco, and others. And it looks like international expansion is off the table, at least for now. We still see some risk in the grocery business, as groceries are very low margin, and the company hasn't really figured out how to make the grocery offering complete with meats and fresh produce. Gross and operating margins may continue to see some pressure from this business, depending on how valuable the generation of more frequent store visits turns out to be. And while we're thrilled at the recovery in the stock price, it does present some challenges to finding the right "target" price to make a new investment.

SECTOR: **Retail** ❑ BETA COEFFICIENT: **0.65** ❑ 10-YEAR COMPOUND EARNINGS PER-SHARE GROWTH: **8.0%** ❑ 10-YEAR COMPOUND DIVIDENDS PER-SHARE GROWTH: **18.5%**

	2007	2008	2009	2010	2011	2012	2013	2014
Revenues (mil)	63,367	64,948	63,435	67,390	69,865	73,301	72,596	72,618
Net income (mil)	2,849	2,214	2,488	2,830	2,829	2,925	2,060	2,734
Earnings per share	3.33	2.86	3.30	3.88	4.28	4.38	3.21	4.27
Dividends per share	0.56	0.60	0.66	0.84	1.10	1.32	1.58	1.90
Cash flow per share	5.51	5.37	5.90	6.98	7.46	7.82	6.77	7.60
Price: high	70.8	59.6	51.8	60.7	61.0	65.5	73.5	76.6
low	48.8	25.6	25.0	46.2	45.3	47.3	55.0	54.7

Website: *www.target.com*

Tiffany & Co.

Ticker symbol: TIF (NYSE) ❑ S&P rating: BBB+ ❑ Value Line financial strength rating: A+ ❑ Current yield: 1.7% ❑ Dividend raises, past 10 years: 10

Company Profile

All that glitters is not gold, as the saying goes, but some of the best of what glitters might be found at Tiffany. Tiffany is a jeweler and specialty retailer principally offering jewelry (accounting for 92 percent of FY2014 sales) but also timepieces, sterling silver goods (e.g., silver spoons), china, crystal, fragrances, stationery, leather goods, and other personal items. As of early 2015, the company operates some 295 retail locations worldwide, 122 of those in the Americas with a complementing online and catalog order operation.

The design of both product and packaging is distinctive, with a historic tradition and elegant simplicity that sets it apart. Ditto for the stores and catalog. Tiffany is probably the world's most recognized general jewelry brand (aside from Rolex and similar brands in the watch business).

The geographic tour of Tiffany's worldwide footprint is both interesting and insightful. First stop: Some 52 percent of FY2014 sales are from outside the Americas. There are 95 stores in the United States (up from 87 in 2012; the company has been expanding mainly in high-end malls), 11 in Canada, 11 in Mexico, and five in Brazil. Notably, the multistory flagship store on Fifth Avenue in New York City accounts for about 10 percent of Tiffany's business alone, albeit much of it from visiting foreign tourists craving the experience.

Now, moving on to the Asia-Pacific region, which accounts for 24 percent of sales, there are 35 stores in China (including Hong Kong), 14 in Korea, eight in Taiwan, seven in Australia, five in Singapore, two in Macau, and two in Malaysia. Oh, yes—what about Japan? Japan is so large it is accounted for as a separate region, with 13 percent of the business— slightly down from 14 percent in FY2013—and 56 stores. Do the Japanese appreciate quality and elegant simplicity? Always.

Finally, we come to Europe, which represents 12 percent of sales with ten stores in the U.K., seven in Germany, seven in Italy, five in France, two in Spain, two in Switzerland, and one each in five other countries. The company also does Internet sales in 9 European countries and in 13 overseas markets in all. Beyond Europe, the company also does business in the Middle East, Russia, and elsewhere through distributors. The Middle

East is a major growth market, and, interestingly, the sovereign wealth fund of Qatar apparently sees Tiffany as a crown jewel, owning almost 13 percent of the company.

In addition to retailing a broad line of luxury goods, Tiffany also designs and manufactures much of its branded jewelry. The Tiffany cachet raises margins on these items without significantly diluting brand strength, while at the same time driving store visits higher. Clearly, the company is a bastion for wealthy consumers, but it also works hard to attract so-called "aspirational" consumers seeking moderately priced $100–$300 items with that Tiffany cachet and experience. Internationally, and particularly in Asia, Tiffany appeals to the very wealthy, and the average selling price of items in Asia runs 8–10 times the average price of items sold in the Americas. That said, the growing middle class in that region is good news, too.

Financial Highlights, Fiscal Year 2014

Strong but somewhat diminished for 2014, 4 percent same-store comparisons and broad contributions from all regions with particular strength again in Asia-Pacific led to a 7 percent constant-currency revenue gain for FY2014, which was attenuated to 5 percent when currency was factored in. A better product mix, favorable input costs (the company buys a lot of gold and silver), and improved operating expenses led the way to a 13 percent gain in net profit and a similar gain in per-share earnings, as share counts remained largely unchanged.

The company expects continued strength in the fine and fashion jewelry categories, with another favorable new product launch in a boldly contemporary-styled line called "Tiffany T" as well as an expansion of its traditional and highly aesthetic Atlas line. At the end of FY2014 and into 2015, the company hit a bit of a soft spot, as the strong dollar cut into foreign visits to the U.S. (a big driver for the Fifth Avenue store), Japan and China softened, and better economic times failed to translate directly one-for-one into U.S. consumer purchases. As a result, FY2015 predictions for sales and profits are in the flat-to-2 percent range. The company expects better results in key overseas countries as well as scale in its newer product lines to bring growth back for FY2016; sales are projected back up in the 6–8 percent range while earnings up a stronger 15 percent with operational improvements and continued moderated input costs. Dividends should rise moderately; however, the company isn't planning major net share count reductions at present.

Reasons to Buy

"We deliver the promise of the blue box." Tiffany is a classic branding story, where brand image supports the product and the product (and packaging) supports the brand image. People buy Tiffany because it is Tiffany and because they are attracted to the brand's distinctive cachet and elegant simplicity. While the company is working to offer more moderately priced items for the "aspirational" market, we don't expect it to lower quality and damage the brand prestige. We also see the edgier Tiffany T line and other product line enhancements as effectively targeted toward Millennial tastes—and pocketbooks—both good ideas in today's marketplace. Pricing power appears strong, and the sales mix has improved recently.

Although it's been in a bit of a holding pattern currently, we are still very strong on the company's international footprint and the ability to grow sales and leverage the brand, particularly in Asia. That softness has created a buying opportunity; we'll see if it lasts into the latter parts of 2015.

Finally—and one might not expect this in the typically sales-y jewelry industry—the company makes a notably complete and digestible presentation of its own business in its annual reports and other releases—elegant and simple. We like that and think it reflects good management overall.

Reasons for Caution

Naturally, Tiffany is somewhat exposed to economic cycles, particularly economic circumstances that affect the rich, as the Great Recession clearly did. It is also exposed to the volatility of gold and silver—although this volatility actually creates some demand as buyers, particularly in Asia, look at fine jewelry and its precious metals as a store of value. Recently, lower precious metals prices have given a boost to results, and the future for these prices looks favorable, but this could change at any time. Also we would be cautious of any major departure from the company's core "elegant simplicity" style, particularly toward becoming a jeweler and retailer to the masses. Current conservative store expansions and expansion plans allay this fear. Also, we would expect not to see any acquisition activity, which would dilute the distinctive brand and style.

SECTOR: **Retail** ❑ BETA COEFFICIENT: **1.81** ❑ 10-YEAR COMPOUND EARNINGS PER-SHARE GROWTH: **10.5%** ❑ 10-YEAR COMPOUND DIVIDENDS PER-SHARE GROWTH: **21.5%**

	2007	2008	2009	2010	2011	2012	2013	2014
Revenues (mil)	2,938	2,860	2,709	3,085	3,643	3,794	4,031	4,250
Net income (mil)	322	294	266	378	465	416	481	545
Earnings per share	2.33	2.33	2.12	2.93	3.61	3.25	3.73	4.20
Dividends per share	0.52	0.66	0.68	0.95	1.12	1.25	1.34	1.48
Cash flow per share	3.50	3.44	3.21	4.13	4.82	4.57	5.15	5.72
Price: high	57.3	50.0	44.5	65.8	84.5	74.2	93.0	110.6
low	38.2	18.8	16.7	35.6	54.6	49.7	57.1	82.6

Website: *www.tiffany.com*

CONSERVATIVE GROWTH

Time Warner Inc.

Ticker symbol: TWX (NYSE) ❑ S&P rating: BBB ❑ Value Line financial strength rating: A ❑ Current yield: 1.7% ❑ Dividend raises, past 10 years: 9

Company Profile

Time Warner is a $28 billion media and entertainment company aimed squarely at producing and distributing media in both traditional and innovative ways. Six years ago, the company undertook a well-publicized—and necessary—downsize, untying itself from America Online (AOL) and separated from its Time Warner Cable business too, and went back to working in the areas it knows best—content—and working on new ways to make more money producing and delivering that content. Last year, it spun off its print media—translation, "magazine"—unit into a separate company, Time Inc., to focus on its core film, television, and digital businesses. We continue to like this movie.

With the disposal of much of the publishing operation, and an expansion in digital and content services, the company reorganized itself into three reporting business segments during 2013, to take effect with the Time separation, which was completed in mid-2014:

■ *Turner* (38 percent of 2014 revenues), which brands itself "The Best in Entertainment, Sports, Kids, and News," includes industry-leading properties formerly part of the Turner Broadcasting System, including CNN, TBS, TNT, Turner Classic, as well as other standards such as Cartoon Network, Adult Swim, Boomerang, and a series of digital sports networks including NBA.com, PGA.com, TMZ, and others. The unit is investing heavily in on-demand viewing and live streaming of content, which they now estimate to be available to 82 million U.S. households. The unit, in all, has 165 channels broadcast in 36 languages in 200 countries worldwide. TBS, TNT, and Adult Swim had three of the top ten primetime ad-supported viewing slots for adults 18–49 in 2014.

- *HBO* (19 percent of revenues), which brands itself as "the World's Most Successful Premium Television Company," delivers premium pay-TV services in the U.S. with an estimated 43 million subscribers, and premium and basic pay services internationally (direct in 60 countries, licensed in 150) with about 127 million subscribers. The unit has had increasing success in producing its own shows—its *Game of Thrones, The Sopranos*, and *True Detective* are long-standing favorites with several new series coming on line, including *Citizenfour, The Leftovers*, and *Silicon Valley*.

- *Warner Bros.* (43 percent) brands itself "The Global Leader in Entertainment," and includes Warner Bros. Pictures and New Line Cinema. Warner Bros. produces more than 60 TV shows (including *The Big Bang Theory* and *Gotham*) and about 20–30 feature films a year and distributes hundreds of others. *American Sniper* was one of 2014's biggest titles. The unit also produces and licenses content for video games (*The LEGO Movie Videogame* is an example) and other delivery modes, and distributes its content in more than 125 countries, many in local languages.

The details of these businesses and sub-businesses expand far beyond what is described here; suffice it to say TWX has a huge presence in the creation and distribution of many forms of media. The company has two major strategic directions. The first, to expand global reach, and the company now tallies 32 percent of its revenues from outside the U.S. The second, and perhaps most important, to get more content to more people in more places at more times than ever before—mostly digitally ("Content Everywhere," as they refer to it). The company is leading the way in live streaming of all of its TV content to valid subscribers through a "TV Everywhere" initiative to a variety of devices, including mobile. "HBO NOW" is one branding of this service. A new "UltraViolet" cloud content service now makes 110 movies and TV shows available to 21 million users worldwide; the service grew 40 percent in 2014, and there are many more innovations in the digital space.

Financial Highlights, Fiscal Year 2014

Time Warner successfully executed its Time spinoff (we do wonder whether they will change the corporate name to "Turner Warner" or some such to reflect the disposition of Time and Time Warner Cable years earlier). The spinoff had its expected effects on financial results—revenues down, net income up, as the more profitable content businesses emerged even stronger. Reported revenues dropped about 8.2 percent, not unexpected with Time's contribution of about 10 percent to the business. Net income rose 9.6 percent, and a substantial 7 percent share repurchase generated a per-share increase of 17 percent. The company repurchased another $1.1 billion in the first quarter of FY2015 and has $3.4 billion left in the authorization, so it appears that share counts are headed at least another 3–5 percent lower. That, on top of 3–5 percent revenue increases and 2–6 percent earnings increases in FY2015 and FY2016 should reward shareholders well in 2016. Earnings increases would probably be higher without digital investments; estimates call for even stronger earnings and cash-flow growth in 2017 and beyond.

Reasons to Buy

By splitting from AOL, then selling the cable business and now the magazine business, we think Time Warner has gotten to where it wants to be, particularly as it makes headway in the digital space. Especially considering the "everywhere" digital expansion, we think the demand for content will only go up, and TWX has some of the great properties and brands, such as CNN, HBO, and TBS, to leverage as platforms to develop and deliver this content in traditional and new, multichannel formats. The content appears to play well with the younger Millennial generation and their slightly older brethren, and the digital "when you want it, where you want it, how you want it" delivery should only make this better. Finally this is a cash-generating business, and the cash returns to investors, especially the buybacks, which have dropped share counts 40 percent since 2005, should receive an Academy Award.

Reasons for Caution

The entertainment business is complex, fickle, and ever changing, which in part explains why we had no such companies on our *100 Best* list until 2013—and why we have only one today. It's a struggle to keep up with what's new and what's changing, and in particular, what's working, but we've admired this company's ability to build good brands, put good products on the market, and achieve lasting revenue streams from all of it. Others have also recognized the more focused operating model that has emerged since the AOL and print-publishing days. As a consequence of this and strong operating performance, the stock price has risen considerably. We've said it before: Investors should look for matinee pricing.

SECTOR: Entertainment ❑ BETA COEFFICIENT: **1.16** ❑ 10-YEAR COMPOUND EARNINGS PER-SHARE GROWTH: **9.0%** ❑ 10-YEAR COMPOUND DIVIDENDS PER-SHARE GROWTH: **17.0%**

	2007	2008	2009	2010	2011	2012	2013	2014
Revenues (mil)	46,482	46,894	25,785	26,888	28,944	29,729	29,795	27,359
Net income (mil)	4,051	3,574	2,079	2,578	2,886	3,019	3,554	3,894
Earnings per share	2.97	2.88	1.74	2.25	2.71	3.09	3.77	4.41
Dividends per share	0.71	0.75	0.75	0.85	0.94	1.04	1.15	1.27
Cash flow per share	7.07	6.83	2.66	3.20	3.91	4.20	4.96	5.56
Price: high	69.5	50.7	33.5	34.1	38.6	48.5	70.8	88.1
low	45.5	21.0	17.8	26.4	27.6	33.5	48.6	60.7

Website: *www.timewarner.com*

AGGRESSIVE GROWTH

NEW FOR 2016

The Timken Company

Ticker symbol: TKR (NYSE) ❑ S&P rating: BBB- ❑ Value Line financial strength rating: B++ ❑ Current yield: 2.6% ❑ Dividend raises, past 10 years: 8

Company Profile

When you operate a 140-ton loaded railroad car, a giant windmill, or a rolling mill in a steel-fabricating plant, you have tremendous frictional forces to overcome, often in harsh environments, for long periods of operating time and with 100 percent reliability required. Without a dependable and efficient friction solution to these moving parts, they can overheat, fail, get out of alignment, and otherwise wreak havoc on your mobile system or stationary machine—not to mention make it cost more to operate. That's where premium-engineered, replaceable bearing assemblies come into play.

On rail cars, for instance, roller bearings—small, tapered, hardened steel bearings "rolling" between the rotating axle and the wheel housing—solved years of headaches (and fires and accidents) caused by oiled brass bearings. Years ago roller bearings became mandatory for U.S. railroad operation. Similar gains in performance, reliability, reduced friction, and cost came to other businesses. These specialized, high-value-add bearings—and now application-specific bearing assemblies and housings that hold them—are a critical manufactured and serviced component of most of today's mobile and many of today's stationary systems.

Founded in 1899, the Timken Company is the oldest, most established and focused, and largest producer of bearings and bearing products. Over time, they have evolved the product line from relatively simple tapered and ball bearings to a greater number of protected bearing assemblies, or "housed units" which enable solutions in harsher operating environments and create maintenance cost savings for the customer.

The company, after spinning off its steelmaking business in 2014, is made up of two business segments:

- *Mobile Industries* (55 percent of 2014 sales) offers bearings, bearing systems, seals, lubrication devices, and power transmission systems mainly to OEMs and operators of trucks, automobiles, rail cars and locomotives, rotor and fixed-wing aircraft, construction and mining machinery, and certain military items. There had been a separate Aerospace segment; it is now part of Mobile.
- *Process Industries* (45 percent of sales) supplies industrial bearings, bearing systems and assemblies, and power transmission components to OEMs and operators in metals, mining, cement, aggregates production, food processing, wind energy, turbine and oil drilling equipment, material handling equipment, and certain marine applications among many applications. These are stationary machines without wheels, whereas Mobile mainly supports things *with* wheels (or rotors or wings).

The company has added, and still intends to add, a few bolt-on acquisitions for adjacent machinery and mechanical power transmission parts, including chains, belts, gear drives, couplings, brakes, sprockets, clutches, including sales but also service and reconditioning businesses. Like bearings, these are relatively mission-critical, high-value–add components with serviceable lives requiring replacement, and Timken would like to expand its position as a single-source, branded, full-service vendor for such components. The company has also been exiting a few low-end businesses, mainly in the automotive sector.

More significantly, in 2014 the company spun off its steel-producing business into a separate company—TimkenSteel—at once becoming a more focused and higher-value-add business but also smoothing out financial results considerably; the steel business had been a revenue and earnings wild card especially in recent years.

The top five end-user markets are Industrial Machinery (19 percent), Automotive (15 percent), Rail (11 percent), Heavy Truck (8 percent), and Energy (7 percent). About 57 percent of Timken's business originates in North America; EMEA (18 percent), Asia (17 percent), and Latin America (8 percent) make up the rest. The company projects that 26 percent of revenue comes from developing markets.

Financial Highlights, Fiscal Year 2014

In the numbers in the following table, the TimkenSteel spinoff accounted for roughly $1.6 billion in sales and $100 million in net profit starting in 2014—although these numbers and especially the net profit number had been highly erratic. Apart from that and adjusting for the spinoff, revenues rose 1 percent in FY2014, but this number would have been closer to 6 percent absent currency effects and a few other small business exits. The strongest units were rail, wind energy, and the industrial aftermarket. Operating and net profit margins advanced about 1.4 percent, a healthy post-acquisition sign, and adjusted per-share earnings advanced to $2.55 from $2.07 (reported $2.55 including TimkenSteel), a gain of 23 percent, mainly due to margin expansion and a more favorable business mix. For FY2015 and FY2016, the company projects a much steadier 8–10 percent revenue growth, continued margin strength, and earnings gains in the 7–15 percent range annually.

A 2014 authorization calls for a repurchase of 10 million common shares—more than 10 percent of its float. About 8.9 million shares of this authorization remain. The company has been paying dividends since its IPO in 1922, and has been raising dividends roughly 10 percent a year recently and projects raises in the high single digits ongoing. The company has also suggested a plan to reduce long-term debt to zero.

Reasons to Buy

We like companies with strong brands and legacies that also happen to supply very key high-value-add components to a value chain. Timken offers such key components in several important value chains, and these components wear out and must be replaced periodically—they aren't just depending on new capital investment for business. Timken's presentations drive this home—one highlights the rail car example, where a given rail car has a 35-year life and requires bearing replacement every five years—bringing $800,000 in lifetime revenue to Timken for a 100-car train (or $8,000 per rail car for life for the million-and-a-half plus of them out there if you'd prefer to look at it that way). Lifetime value calculations like this, spread across many industries, really bring Timken's value proposition home for us. We think the TimkenSteel divestiture will remove a distraction and make the best parts of this company better; we see a lot of opportunity for international growth downstream. The net profit margin of roughly 8 percent indicates a differentiated industry (not a commodity) and a strong market position. Cash flows are strong and cash returns to investors should improve steadily.

Reasons for Caution

Economic cycles, of course, will affect Timken's fortunes, although the TimkenSteel divestiture makes results far less sensitive to these cycles. Despite the recognized brand and market leadership position, the company still has only 5 percent of the overall bearing and 30 percent of the tapered bearing market; competitors are out there. Some of the company's products go into the now-depressed energy extraction and mining industries—maintenance and replacement volume from these industries will probably soften in 2015 at least. On the other side, the mining slowdown could reduce the cost of key steel and other resource inputs.

SECTOR: **Industrials** ❑ BETA COEFFICIENT: **1.88** ❑ 10-YEAR COMPOUND EARNINGS PER-SHARE GROWTH: **23.5%** ❑ 10-YEAR COMPOUND DIVIDENDS PER-SHARE GROWTH: **4.5%**

		2007	2008	2009	2010	2011	2012	2013	2014
Revenues (mil)		5,236	5,664	3,142	4,056	5,170	4,987	4,341	3,076
Net income (mil)		230	313	51	289	457	456	263	234
Earnings per share		2.40	3.26	0.53	2.95	4.59	4.66	2.74	2.55
Dividends per share		0.68	0.70	0.45	0.53	0.78	0.92	0.92	1.00
Cash flow per share		4.68	5.64	2.61	4.89	6.65	6.81	4.93	4.19
Price:	high	38.8	38.7	26.1	49.3	57.8	57.9	64.4	69.5
	low	27.4	11.0	9.9	22.0	30.2	32.6	47.7	37.6

Website: *www.timken.com*

GROWTH AND INCOME

Total S.A. (ADR)

Ticker symbol: TOT (NYSE) ❑ S&P rating: AA- ❑ Value Line financial strength rating: A++ ❑ Current yield: 6.3% ❑ Dividend raises, past 10 years: 8

Company Profile

Total S.A. (S.A. is short for Société Anonyme, which is the French equivalent of "incorporated") is the fifth-largest publicly traded oil and gas company in the world. Headquartered in France and primarily traded on the French CAC stock exchange, the company has operations in more than 130 countries. Total is vertically integrated with upstream operations engaged in oil and gas exploration and downstream operations engaged in refining and distribution of petroleum products; the company also has a chemicals subsidiary.

Upstream activities are geographically well diversified, with exploration occurring in 50 countries and production happening in 30 of them. Many of the E&P projects are done through partnerships to spread risk. The largest production regions are (in production-volume sequence) in the North Sea, North Africa, West Africa, and the Middle East, with smaller operations in Southeast Asia and North and South America. Liquids (oil) account for about 61 percent of production, while natural gas is 39 percent. The company is a leader in the emerging liquefied natural gas (LNG) market for export, and recently strengthened an agreement to supply LNG to the China National Offshore Oil Corporation (CNOOC).

Downstream operations are also worldwide and centered in Europe. Operations include interests in 21 refineries worldwide, with 11 refineries and 85 percent of total refining capacity in Europe. There are also 20 petrochemical plants. Total also operates 14,820 service stations in 60 countries, mainly under the Total, Elf, and Elan names, again weighted toward Europe and North Africa. The downstream presence is also growing in Asia-Pacific (including China), Latin America, and the Caribbean. The company now has a leading market presence in those regions.

Total also has ventures in alternative energy, notably solar. It owns a 65 percent interest in global solar leader Sunpower. With two major partners it brought online in 2013, it also has an interest in what is thought to be the world's largest concentrated solar power plant at 100 megawatts in Abu Dhabi. The company started an initiative known as Awango, to sell solar-powered lamps in remote regions of Indonesia and Africa along with traditional energy products.

Financial Highlights, Fiscal Year 2014

To say the least, FY2014 was a challenging year for Total due to turmoil in the oil markets with a backdrop of general business malaise in Europe. Add to that, the sudden death and loss of highly regarded CEO Cristophe de Margerie in an airplane accident during a visit to Russia—and weakness in the euro, which makes Total's dividends less attractive to U.S. investors—and truly, you have a year to forget.

Low oil prices took their toll on revenues, not surprisingly, with a 7 percent drop in the top line and a 10 percent skid in net profits, a feat that will be more than matched in gloom by FY2015's estimated 15 percent drop in revenues and 33 percent drop in net income. What's there to like here, anyhow? The company has cut capital spending, exploration, and seeks other efficiency opportunities—and maybe, just maybe, the European Central Bank's "quantitative easing" program will stimulate European spending. Sales are currently projected to rebound to FY2014 levels, although this depends a lot on oil prices, and better unit volumes will once again help profitability with a rebound halfway to 2014 levels.

Reasons to Buy

Even with the unfortunate CEO transition, we still think this is a well-managed company, well positioned and quite capable of making adjustments to market conditions and making wise investments in fossil fuel and alternative energy sources. If oil prices rebound (and we think they will gradually), efficiencies gained through this "crisis" will bear more fruit in the future. We like their branding and dominance in the key worldwide markets they serve. Total has done better than most "big oils" in reserve replacement. The down cycle in the oil business offers a good buying opportunity for those who can stomach the ups and downs; we think long-term prospects are bright for a solid recovery, persistent and growing cash returns, and growth beyond that. We hope we're right, and we hope our patience as investors is rewarded with a solid thumbs-up for next year's *100 Best Stocks* list.

Reasons for Caution

Clearly, the current situation is a test of our patience and appetites for risk, and it appears likely to continue into FY2016, although we do view the year as a recovery year. Generally, the level of risk is higher with (1) oil prices, (2) dollar versus euro fluctuations, and (3) Vladimir Putin and his dogs barking practically just down the street. More aggression on Russia's part, both militarily and economically, would add risk to a situation already destabilized by the usual Middle East tensions, European economic woes, and European Central Bank adventures. Finally, the company appears to be taking on more long-term debt to get it through the bump.

More generally, we remain cautious on investing in foreign companies because of differences in management style and accounting rules; they aren't necessarily bad but are difficult to understand and follow. Antiquated European pension rules and other labor practices could also be a disadvantage. All of these risks and downsides appear to be priced into the stock as of early 2015, but Total would not qualify as one of our "sleep at night" stocks—not now, anyway.

SECTOR: **Energy** ❑ BETA COEFFICIENT: **1.35** ❑ 10-YEAR COMPOUND EARNINGS PER-SHARE GROWTH: **10.5%** ❑ 10-YEAR COMPOUND DIVIDENDS PER-SHARE GROWTH: **13.5%**

	2007	2008	2009	2010	2011	2012	2013	2014
Revenues (bil)	167	236	157	186	216	234	228	212
Net income (bil)	16.7	18.2	11.6	14.0	15.9	15.9	14.2	12.8
Earnings per share	7.35	8.55	5.31	6.24	7.05	7.01	6.28	5.63
Dividends per share	2.81	3.10	3.28	2.93	3.12	2.98	3.10	3.21
Cash flow per share	10.73	12.42	9.49	11.25	11.37	12.46	11.57	10.90
Price: high	87.3	91.3	66.0	67.5	64.4	57.1	62.4	74.2
low	63.9	42.6	42.9	43.1	40.0	41.8	45.9	48.4

Website: *www.total.com*

CONSERVATIVE GROWTH

Union Pacific Corporation

Ticker symbol: UNP (NYSE) ❑ S&P rating: A ❑ Value Line financial strength rating: A++ ❑ Current yield: 1.9% ❑ Dividend raises, past 10 years: 10

Company Profile

Union Pacific has been a familiar name and logo in the railroad business since its inception during the Civil War. With about 32,000 miles of track covering 23 states in the western two-thirds of the United States, today's Union Pacific Railroad, the primary subsidiary of the Union Pacific Corporation, describes itself as "America's Premier Railroad Franchise." The route system is anchored by Gulf Coast and West Coast ports and areas in between and has coordinated schedules and gateways with other lines in the eastern U.S., Canada, and Mexico.

With 10,000 customers, a large number in today's era of trainload-sized shipments, UNP has a more diversified customer and revenue mix than the other rail companies, including the other three of the "big four" railroads: Burlington Northern Santa Fe, Norfolk Southern, and CSX. Energy (mainly Powder River Basin and Colorado) accounts for 18 percent of revenues; Intermodal (trucks or containers on flatcars), 20 percent; Agricultural, 17 percent; Industrial, 20 percent; Chemicals, 16 percent; and Automotive, 9 percent of FY2014 revenues. These figures represent a slight shift away from coal and autos and toward agriculture and industrial, following industry trends and reflecting an even more diversified traffic base and a probable gain in market share versus trucking.

The company has long been an innovator in railroad technology, including motive power, communications and technology automation, physical plant, community relations, and marketing. The company functions with the lowest operating ratio in the industry, 63.5 percent, meaning that operating costs account for 63.5 percent of total costs (65.0 percent in FY2013, 67.8 percent in FY2012, 70.6 percent in FY2011—you can see the trend). This allows a solid contribution to the substantial fixed costs of owning and running a railroad. This success has translated to continued strong operating margins, which of course have helped earnings and cash flows and in turn have funded physical plant improvements and shareholder returns.

The company also invests a lot in marketing and community relations. One example is the Heritage Fleet Operations program, through which the company operates steam-powered and other excursions on selected lines. The company just began a five-year program to restore a "Big Boy" steam locomotive, the largest ever used in regular service (of course, for the UP originally) for a Golden Spike sesquicentennial rollout in 2019. Such public relations efforts show an extraordinary measure of pride and appreciation for heritage and community. We loudly applaud this effort.

Railroads have quietly been learning to use technology to improve operations and deliver better customer service. New tools can track shipments door-to-door using GPS-based technology, and the railroad will accept shipments and manage them door-to-door, even over other railroads or with other kinds of carriers. Customers can check rates and routes and track shipments online. These services, combined with high fuel prices, have led to a continuing migration from trucks back to rail and intermodal rail services.

Financial Highlights, Fiscal Year 2014

The company continues to deal with a shift in mix away from the profitable coal segment, as more power plants convert to gas, but has made up for that in most of its other categories. New export coal shipments, especially to Japan, which has downsized its nuclear exposure in favor of coal, may make up for some of the U.S. coal decline. For FY2014 and in the near term, the company will experience some tailwind in the form of lower fuel prices but also some headwind in the form of reduced oil and oil supply shipments (although competitor BNSF will be hit harder as a matter of geography). There may also possibly be a rebound in the competitiveness in trucking, again due to lower fuel prices. It's too soon to decipher the net effect of all of this.

Regardless of whether headwinds or tailwinds prevail, the good news really lies in the payoff from previous investments in physical plant and equipment, which continue to deliver operating efficiencies. The drop in operating ratio in four years from 70.6 percent to 63.5 percent is remarkable and probably an industry first—and most of this efficiency drops straight to the bottom line. FY2014 revenues were up 9.2 percent, a faster rate of increase than in previous years. On top of that, operating margins advanced a full 2.4 percent to an all-time high (from 21.9 percent in 2005 to 44.4 percent in 2014 if you're keeping track), A 3 percent share buyback highballed FY2014 per-share earnings forward at an even faster clip—22.1 percent higher than FY2013. Cash flow per share has almost quadrupled since 2005, and the company chipped in a 29 percent dividend increase for the year as well.

Although we do see some yellow signals in the form of lower oil and coal shipments (and lingering effects from the West Coast port strike too, also an unknown), we see continued strength into FY2015 and FY2016— 5–6 percent revenue gains in both years, 12–15 percent gains in per-share earnings, near double-digit dividend growth and steady share buybacks.

Reasons to Buy

Put simply—whether or not you enjoy watching trains, this company has been as exciting as any tech stock, and it is also returning plenty of cash to share-holders. UNP is an extraordinarily well-managed company and has become more efficient and at the same time more user-friendly to its customers and to the general public. The company continues to make gains at the expense of the trucking industry, and new short- and long-distance intermodal services move higher-valued goods more quickly and cost-effectively; we see a steady shift toward this business. The company has a solid and diverse traffic base and continues to have a good brand and reputation in the industry. The company got an early start expanding and modernizing its physical plant and technology base; that has paid off well and will continue to do so.

Reasons for Caution

Railroads are and will always be economically sensitive because of commodity revenue and their high fixed-cost structure. They also have significant headline risk—a single event like a derailment or spill can put them in a bad public eye, or worse, tangle them up in regulation, lawsuits, and unplanned costs. Regulation and mandates for Positive Train Control and other safety features can be expensive. Another longer-term factor may be the widening of the Panama Canal, which may shift some Asian import/export traffic to southern and eastern ports and away from the West Coast. The recent West Coast port strike may have accelerated this effect somewhat. For most railroads, recent success has created traffic volumes that put physical capacity to the test, and UP has had some service problems and delays, but fewer than most, again due to early and well-executed plant expansions. Finally, the increase in profitability has been reflected "full throttle" in the share price, and further gains may be attenuated a bit, particularly if coal and oil remain soft, if truckers recapture some business, or some other traffic segment runs into problems.

SECTOR: **Transportation** ❑ BETA COEFFICIENT: **0.90** ❑ 10-YEAR COMPOUND EARNINGS PER-SHARE GROWTH: **18.0%** ❑ 10-YEAR COMPOUND DIVIDENDS PER-SHARE GROWTH: **20.5%**

	2007	2008	2009	2010	2011	2012	2013	2014
Revenues (mil)	16,283	17,970	14,143	16,965	19,557	20,926	21,953	23,988
Net income (mil)	1,856	2,338	1,826	2,780	3,292	3,943	4,388	5,180
Earnings per share	1.73	2.27	1.81	2.77	3.36	4.14	4.71	5.75
Dividends per share	0.34	0.47	0.54	0.66	0.97	1.25	1.48	1.91
Cash flow per share	3.04	3.70	3.24	4.34	5.11	6.07	6.76	8.02
Price: high	34.4	42.9	33.4	47.9	53.9	64.6	84.1	123.6
low	22.4	20.9	16.6	30.2	38.9	52.0	63.7	82.5

Website: *www.up.com*

`AGGRESSIVE GROWTH`

UnitedHealth Group Inc.

Ticker symbol: UNH (NYSE) ❑ S&P rating: A- ❑ Value Line financial strength rating: A++ ❑ Current yield: 1.3% ❑ Dividend raises, past 10 years: 5

Company Profile

UnitedHealth Group is the parent company of a number of health insurers and service organizations. It is the largest publicly traded health insurance company in the United States, with more than $130 billion in revenue reported in 2014 and a Number 14 ranking on the *Fortune* 500 list.

The company has reorganized and rebranded part of its business and now operates in two major business segments: UnitedHealthcare (health insurance and benefits) and Optum (health services), which, combined, touch about 85 million people worldwide in 50 U.S. states and 125 countries globally.

UnitedHealthcare provides traditional and Medicare-based health benefit and insurance plans for individuals and employers, covering approximately 27 million individuals, with about 400 national employer accounts and many other smaller employer accounts. The company estimates that it serves more than half of the *Fortune* 100 companies list. The company, mainly through this unit, has been an active acquirer of other familiar health-care and insurance brands, including Oxford Health in 2004, PacifiCare in 2005, Sierra Health Plans and Unison Health Plans in 2008, AIM Healthcare Services in 2009, and more recently an assortment of small, mostly Medicare-related providers. The UnitedHealthcare insurance business in total accounts for 72 percent of FY2014 revenues and 69 percent of profits.

The UnitedHealthcare business unit actively markets traditional individual and employee health plans, and is also very active in the senior and military market, with a growing assortment of Medicare Advantage, Medicare Part D, and Medicare supplement plans. Revenues in this subsegment accounted for 29 percent of UNH's total business. The recently added TRICARE insurance program for active and retired military is another large subsegment. It is a $3 billion business at present and will grow as a five-year transition plan moves forward.

The "other side" of the business is its health services businesses, which it markets under the Optum brand umbrella. This segment, which touches some 64 million customers, is far and away big enough to be a separate company, and is an increasingly important part of the overall UNH business offering. Optum delivers service through three separate businesses. OptumHealth is an "information and technology"–based health population management solution, deploying mostly remote telesupport for well care, mental health, ongoing disease management, and substance abuse programs. The OptumRx business is a pharmacy benefits provider serving 30 million customers with about 600 million prescriptions annually, while OptumInsight is a management information, analytics, and process-improvement arm providing an assortment of services for health plans, physicians, hospitals, and life science research, formerly marketed under the Ingenix brand. Of the total Optum-branded business of $47 billion (25 percent ahead of FY2012), Rx accounts for the lion's share at $31 billion, while OptumHealth, which grew 13 percent in FY2014, weighs in at $11 billion and OptumInsight at $5.2 billion with 11 percent annual growth. Although these numbers may seem small in the context of UNH's total $130 billion annual revenue footprint, they are sizeable businesses when looked at individually. The Optum umbrella brand is gaining in prominence, and even has its own unique web presence at *www.optum.com*.

UnitedHealthcare has been a leader in process, delivery, and cost improvement and a recognized innovator in the industry. Currently, while not participating in all Affordable Care Act exchanges, the company is learning to adapt to the new environment and has moved aggressively to offer tools to manage and contain costs in the health-care system, mostly through the Optum business. The company sits on top of a mountain of health-care data and is putting it to good use, and has emerged as a leader in developing remote and preventative care models.

Financial Highlights, Fiscal Year 2014

A combination of healthy existing and new businesses drove another solid year in FY2014, with a 6.5 percent revenue gain, substantial on this size of base. However, continued cutbacks in Medicare reimbursements, other reforms, and investments in the new Optum businesses attenuated growth in per-share earnings to a roughly flat earnings performance (though still, with a substantial 3 percent share buyback, to a 4 percent gain in per-share earnings). For FY2015 and beyond, the company has adapted to ACA and Medicare changes, and has added size and scale particularly to its Medicare-related and Optum businesses; forecasts call for revenue gains in the 7–9 percent range through FY2016 and per-share earnings gains in the 8–12 percent range. Dividend growth prospects are equally healthy, and share repurchase, while attenuated somewhat from 2014, should chip in as well.

Reasons to Buy

This bellwether company is one of the most solid, diverse, and innovative enterprises in the health insurance industry. Health insurers such as Aetna, included on our *100 Best* list, seem to be getting past many of the fears of reform and other contrary public opinion; these companies by design simply pass costs through but are doing more to control and reduce costs through utilization management and other initiatives, and these efforts are paying off. Meanwhile, like Aetna, UNH brings a fair amount of innovation to the marketplace, primarily through its Optum offerings. We like its initiatives to make use of its own "big data" with analytics; the size of its database and the tools it possesses can deliver efficiency improvements, and even slight efficiency improvements can help the bottom line substantially. If price competition eventually dictates lower premiums, UNH will be in good position with cost-side improvements.

The scale of UNH's operation gives it tremendous leverage when negotiating for the services of health-care providers. Hospitals and physicians are strongly motivated to join UNH's network, as doing so will provide assurance of steady referrals. The Optum360 venture—a combination of payer (UNH) and provider (Dignity Health, a western U.S. hospital chain) to optimize service and cost—shows a new level of partnering between payer and provider; we await the outcome.

UnitedHealth continues to easily score the "quintuple play," with ten-year compounded growth in revenues, earnings, cash flow, dividends, and book value well into double digits; in fact, each has grown over 15 percent over the ten-year period. And cash returns haven't been too bad either—through increased dividends and share buybacks, the company is growing its cash returns to shareholders.

Reasons for Caution

The outcomes of the Affordable Care Act are still not certain on both the cost and the revenue side; like others, the company is stepping through these changes at a deliberate pace while the final imprint on the business is far from clear. The company is vulnerable to shifts in public opinion and to new regulation, as well as economic downturns, which can hurt employer participation. The company also has demonstrated a fairly aggressive acquisition strategy in the past; this seems to be on the back burner as focus has shifted to the Optum offerings. That's probably a good thing.

SECTOR: **Health Care** ❑ BETA COEFFICIENT: **0.58** ❑ 10-YEAR COMPOUND EARNINGS PER-SHARE GROWTH: **17.0%** ❑ 10-YEAR COMPOUND DIVIDENDS PER-SHARE GROWTH: **58.5%**

	2007	2008	2009	2010	2011	2012	2013	2014
Revenues (bil)	75.4	87.1	87.1	94.1	101.9	110.6	122.5	130.5
Net income (mil)	4,654	3,660	3,822	4,633	5,142	5,526	5,625	5,619
Earnings per share	3.42	2.95	3.24	4.10	4.73	5.28	5.50	5.70
Dividends per share	0.03	0.03	0.03	0.41	0.61	0.80	1.05	1.41
Cash flow per share	4.35	3.86	4.20	5.25	5.86	6.67	7.09	7.44
Price: high	59.5	57.9	33.3	38.1	53.5	60.8	75.9	104.0
low	45.8	14.5	16.2	27.1	36.4	49.8	51.4	69.6

Website: *www.unitedhealthgroup.com*

CONSERVATIVE GROWTH

United Parcel Service, Inc.

Ticker symbol: UPS (NYSE) ❑ S&P rating: A+ ❑ Value Line financial strength rating: A ❑ Current yield: 3.0% ❑ Dividend raises, past 10 years: 10

Company Profile

UPS is the world's largest integrated ground and air package delivery carrier. UPS and rival FedEx have converged on the same business from different directions—FedEx being an air company getting ever more into the ground business; UPS being a ground business taking to the air. That convergence is now nearly complete. Both companies continue to build international capabilities, invest in technology to track shipments, and provide logistics services beyond basic assortments of transportation services. UPS derives just over 61 percent of revenues from U.S. package operations, 22.5 percent from international, and 16 percent from Supply Chain & Freight, an assortment of bundled logistics and supply-chain services and solutions. The company operates 625 aircraft and almost 103,000 ground vehicles ("package cars"), most of the familiar brown variety. They serve more than 220 countries with an assortment of priority to deferred services, with 154,000 domestic and international entry points including 39,000 drop boxes, 1,600 customer service centers, and 4,800 independently owned "UPS Store" (formerly "Mailboxes Etc.") storefronts.

Once thought to be old-fashioned and averse to innovation, the company has invested in sophisticated package-tracking systems and links for customers to tie into them. An example is the recently introduced My Choice service, which allows a customer to control the timing of deliveries mid-service—by smartphone if they choose—so no more waiting half a day at home for a delivery that might come anytime (hallelujah!), a nice perk for a consumer waiting for an e-commerce shipment as well as a savings for the company, avoiding multiple delivery attempts. The company is also creating specialized logistics services for vertical markets, such as the auto industry "Autogistics" and the health-care industry, retail, high tech, and more.

Now, despite higher volumes and a favorable turn in fuel costs, "Big Brown" has delivered two subpar years in the profitability front. Why? Because they've been unable to properly adjust their capacity to handle the traditional spike in holiday demand—an industry "feature" increasingly important as the volume of "one-off" individual shipments spikes higher during this critical period. Effectively, UPS missed on the downside, by not having enough capacity in place at the end of 2013, causing major service delays, disruptions, and extra last-minute costs to remedy. Then, in 2014, the company overreacted, putting too much capacity in place. It's a Goldilocks scenario—first, not hot enough, then too hot. Both were expensive and were a direct hit on earnings; UPS will have to get it "just right" going forward. Interestingly, rival FedEx (another *100 Best* company) did not have these problems, causing some to call into question UPS's flexibility and ability to use and deploy its analytical tools. We keep this stock on the *100 Best* list, anticipating that eventually it'll find the sweet spot and for other reasons we'll present. Solving the end-of-year problem is far from the only efficiency improvement initiative on UPS's plate. The company has embarked on numerous revenue- and cost-optimization campaigns, among them a detailed analysis of the cost drivers for their businesses. As an example, they report that one mile saved in their Small Package Pickup & Delivery business across all delivery routes would save $50 million per year; one minute saved would save $14.6 million per year, and one minute of idle time reduced would save $515K. From this point, the company is working to improve these metrics one step at a time through technologies and analytics designed to predict and optimize route selection and other aspects of the delivery network. One such project, called "Orion," is dubbed as the "world's largest operations research project."

Financial Highlights, Fiscal Year 2014

Economic recovery, improved international volumes, and better pricing led to a 5 percent increase in FY2014 revenues. Net profits, however, remained almost flat as the "miss" excess holiday capacity cost some $200 million—without that, profits would have advanced in line with revenues. Buybacks drove per-share earnings up 3 percent, but profit figures in general disappointed those who follow the company. The company continues to project a steady climb in what it refers to as the "B2C" mix—that is, commercial businesses to individual consumers—to more than 50 percent of the business mix by 2019. This means a big rise in the number of individually packaged e-commerce shipments. The upside, of course, is more volume and a potentially more lucrative mix of small packages. The downside: lots of small shipments create additional demand on existing capacity because the company has to deliver more and smaller shipments to more individual addresses. This factor gets better over time as the volume on those more dispersed routes increases. We think the company may be in that trough—first, greater costs and more capacity utilization "challenges" short term, and then better utilization and productivity long term as the company rationalizes capacity and puts more volume through its machine.

Indeed, while the company is holding to roughly 5 percent growth projections for FY2015 and FY2016, they project an upswing to something closer to 7 percent out to the end of the decade—substantial for a company this size. Efficiencies (and now lower fuel costs) lead to margin improvements, and UPS expects earnings up something in the 7 percent range through FY2016, and per-share earnings, driven by substantial buybacks ($15 billion by the end of the decade), to grow somewhere in the 9–13 percent range.

The effects of this are too early to tell.

Reasons to Buy

The "fastest ship in the shipping business" continues to also be one of the most stable; UPS continues to position itself as the standard logistics provider of the world. As we mentioned, we think the company may be in a downside "knee" on its profitability curve in terms of optimizing capacity; better utilization added to its relatively stable core traditional commerce service makes UPS a relatively safe growth investment with improving prospects driven by one of today's big megatrends—the shift toward e-commerce (rival FedEx projects a doubling of e-commerce revenues in the five-year period 2012–2017). In general, we applaud the use of technology to get "details" right on the cost front.

We think the company will eventually get the year-end capacity puzzle right. We are also fans of its logistics and supply-chain management businesses and the many innovations in that space, as the push for many customers to optimize this part of their business will lead them to UPS's front door.

Reasons for Caution

The inability to properly balance year-end capacity gives us as well as other industry observers some pause for concern: Why can't management—with all of its analytical tools—get this right? Is the company to big and bureaucratic? Are they unable to come up with the right answer, or is there a problem getting the right answer through the bureaucracy, unions, and established ways? Are they flexible enough? Do they believe their own analysis and have the flexibility to act on it? Such questions circle companies like UPS and IBM—who appear to "see" the right answers but never really get there, not as fast as others in their industry. We'll wait and see . . . and hope for a little more holiday cheer in the years to come, starting with FY2015.

Competition in this industry is fierce. Too, the Postal Service is getting more aggressive in marketing its small package and logistics services as it sees the writing on the wall for traditional mail services. Of about 400,000 employees, 62 percent are union, so labor relations and pension funding both bear watching. Of course, fuel prices are a wild card, and can reverse back upward at any time.

SECTOR: **Transportation** ❑ BETA COEFFICIENT: **0.97** ❑ 10-YEAR COMPOUND EARNINGS PER-SHARE GROWTH: **7.0%** ❑ 10-YEAR COMPOUND DIVIDENDS PER-SHARE GROWTH: **11.0%**

	2007	2008	2009	2010	2011	2012	2013	2014
Revenues (mil)	49,692	51,466	45,297	49,545	53,105	54,127	55,438	58,232
Net income (mil)	4,369	3,581	2,318	3,570	4,213	4,389	4,372	4,389
Earnings per share	4.11	3.50	2.31	3.56	4.25	4.53	4.61	4.75
Dividends per share	1.64	1.77	1.80	1.88	2.08	2.28	2.48	2.68
Cash flow per share	5.91	5.42	4.09	5.43	6.60	6.90	6.75	7.00
Price: high	79.0	75.1	59.5	73.9	77.0	84.9	105.4	113.1
low	68.7	43.3	38.0	55.6	60.7	75.0	75.0	93.2

Website: *www.ups.com*

CONSERVATIVE GROWTH

United Technologies Corporation

Ticker symbol: UTX (NYSE) ❑ S&P rating: A ❑ Value Line financial strength rating: A++ ❑ Current yield: 2.2% ❑ Dividend raises, past 10 years: 10

Company Profile

United Technologies is a large and diversified provider of mostly high-technology products to the aerospace and building systems industries throughout the world, selling to an assortment of mostly commercial and public-sector customers. To many, it is an aerospace company; to many others it is a producer of key pieces, parts, and systems for the building industry; to investors, it is a broadly diversified industrial conglomerate.

In 2012, the company made a significant $18.4 billion acquisition of aerospace material and system provider Goodrich Corp. The mix of businesses is likely to change again as the company seeks more acquisitions along the lines of their two major business units. The third, Sikorsky, appears to be on the auction block based on company comments and the fact that it wasn't combined into the Aerospace unit. Here are the three major units as they line up today:

- *UTC Propulsion & Aerospace* (44 percent of FY2014 revenues) combines the former Aerospace division with the Pratt & Whitney jet engine division and most of the Goodrich assets. Aerospace, formerly known as Hamilton Sundstrand, produces aircraft electrical power generation and distribution systems; engine and flight controls; propulsion systems; environmental controls for aircraft, spacecraft, and submarines; auxiliary power units; space life-support systems; and industrial products including mechanical power transmissions, compressors, metering devices, and fluid handling equipment. It also provides product support and maintenance and offers repair services. Pratt & Whitney produces large and small commercial and military jet engines, spare parts, rocket engines and space propulsion systems, and industrial gas turbines, and it performs product support, specialized engine maintenance and overhaul, and repair services for airlines, air forces, and corporate fleets.
- *UTC Building & Industrial Systems* (47 percent of FY2014 revenues) also combines two former divisions, Climate Controls and Security, and Otis. Climate Controls and Security, formerly known as Carrier, produces heating, ventilating, and air conditioning (HVAC) equipment for

commercial, industrial, and residential buildings; HVAC replacement parts and services; building controls; and commercial, industrial, and transport refrigeration equipment. The Climate Controls and Security group also includes the old UTC Fire and Security business, which provides security and fire protection systems; integration, installation, and servicing of intruder alarms, access control, and video surveillance and monitoring; response and security personnel services; and installation and servicing of fire detection and suppression systems. Otis is probably one of the most recognizable brands. It designs and manufactures elevators, escalators, moving walkways, and shuttle systems, and performs related installation, maintenance, and repair services; it also provides modernization products and service for elevators and escalators.

- *Sikorsky* (10 percent of FY2014 revenues) remains a standalone division (for how long we don't know) and designs and manufactures military and commercial helicopters and fixed-wing reconnaissance aircraft, and it provides spare parts and maintenance services for helicopters and fixed-wing aircraft.

The company provides another useful breakdown to help understand its businesses:

- Commercial & Industrial: 45 percent
- Commercial Aerospace: 35 percent
- Military Aerospace & Space: 25 percent

These figures reveal that UTX is not as tied to military and government contracts as many think. The disposal of the Sikorsky unit, which is primarily military, would shift their mix even farther toward the commercial side. About 62 percent of sales are overseas.

Financial Highlights, Fiscal Year 2014

Currency headwinds were strong, but FY2014 gained some altitude anyhow, reflecting a well-executed acquisition of Goodrich. Led by strong aviation and construction markets, organic revenues rose 4 percent, although currency headwinds hampered the Pratt & Whitney and Climate businesses in particular. Led by strength in its higher-margin Otis, Commercial Aerospace, and Climate businesses, and helped along by cost reductions, earnings rose a more substantial 9.5 percent for the year. Going forward, and assuming continued currency headwinds, the company is projecting a relatively flat to plus 2 percent revenue and earnings performance, helicoptering back up to gains in the 4–5 percent range for revenue and 9–10 percent for earnings. Dividend growth should pick up a bit into the 8–10 percent range, while share buybacks will continue only at a moderate pace for the time being as acquisitions are made.

Reasons to Buy

With Honeywell and GE already on our *100 Best* list, and with a fairly soft projection for FY2015 and the apparent thirst for acquisitions and business realignment, we felt the need to take a pretty close look at UTX for the 2016 list. Based on how the business mix is evolving and on the strength of its projections beyond 2015, we felt that having UTX as a third pick in this genre was still a good idea.

UTX is a classic industrial conglomerate play. The separate and loosely related or unrelated businesses buffer each other in line with what's happening in the economy, both in the private and public sectors, and the economic recovery should continue to help most, if not all, of the businesses. As it is not a pure defense play like many of its competitors, United Technologies can maintain a global presence, benefitting from global and emerging-market infrastructure and other construction and even from defense spending by other countries.

The recent surge in the airline industry will help the business going forward. The company's brands, particularly Otis, are well known and very well-supported worldwide, and a return of strength in global construction should help its two largest businesses. The stock price is on a very stable upward growth track. The company is focused on shareholder returns, and while it is "acquisitive," it seems to have managed the Goodrich acquisition well and, indeed, without adding share count. In all, UTX is a well-managed company that presents itself well in the market and to investors.

Reasons for Caution

The stability of the public-sector portion of the business is always a question as Congress wrestles with the budget deficit. The rest of the business is still sensitive to construction, and construction may not be out of the woods yet and there is plenty of competition in most of its construction businesses. If the recent airline boom falters, that too could bring UTX back to earth. While Goodrich was a good fit, we would hope the company doesn't get too intoxicated with acquisitions, for, like all conglomerates, UTX is a very complex business to manage. It can also be vulnerable to headline risk, such as aviation accidents resulting from failure of its jet engines.

SECTOR: Industrials ◻ **BETA COEFFICIENT: 1.12** ◻ **10-YEAR COMPOUND EARNINGS PER-SHARE GROWTH: 9.5%** ◻ **10-YEAR COMPOUND DIVIDENDS PER-SHARE GROWTH: 14.0%**

	2007	2008	2009	2010	2011	2012	2013	2014
Revenues (mil)	54,759	58,681	52,920	54,326	58,190	57,708	62,626	65,100
Net income (mil)	4,224	4,689	3,829	4,373	4,979	4,840	5,685	6,220
Earnings per share	4.27	4.90	4.12	4.74	5.49	5.34	6.21	6.82
Dividends per share	1.28	1.55	1.54	1.70	1.87	2.03	2.20	2.36
Cash flow per share	5.50	6.38	5.43	6.22	6.97	6.93	8.19	8.94
Price: high	82.5	77.1	70.9	79.7	91.8	87.5	113.9	120.7
low	61.8	41.8	37.4	62.9	66.9	70.7	92.1	97.2

Website: www.utc.com

AGGRESSIVE GROWTH

Valero Energy Corporation

Ticker symbol: VLO (NYSE) ◻ S&P rating: BBB ◻ Value Line financial strength rating: A ◻ Current yield: 2.6% ◻ Dividend raises, past 10 years: 9

Company Profile

Valero Energy is the largest independent oil refiner in the United States. The company owns 15 refineries and distributes primarily through a network of 7,400 retail combined gasoline stations and convenience stores throughout the United States, the U.K. and Ireland, and Canada, most of it under the Valero, Ultramar, Shamrock, Diamond Shamrock, and Texaco brands. In 2013 the company spun off 80 percent of the retail operations, mostly U.S. based, to shareholders in the form of an independent public company called CST Brands but still maintains distribution to most of these outlets. Aside from unlocking capital and increasing focus on refining, the separation of these businesses allows more refining sales to other channels, and allows the retailers to source from their lowest cost supplier—improving the performance of both.

Most of the 15 Valero refineries are located in the United States, centered in the South and on the Texas Gulf Coast with others in Memphis, Oklahoma, and on the West Coast. Others are located in Quebec and Wales in the U.K. The refinery network was mostly assembled through a series of acquisitions from Diamond Shamrock in 2001; El Paso Corporation in the early 2000s; and, more recently, the Pembroke (Wales) refinery from Chevron in 2011. The refining operations produce the full gamut of hydrocarbon products: gasoline, jet fuel, diesel, asphalt, propane, base oils, solvents, aromatics, natural gas liquids, sulfur, hydrogen, middle distillates, and special fuel blends to meet California Air Resources Board requirements. The company markets these products where the refineries are located, plus in the Caribbean and in Ireland.

Valero is strictly focused on downstream operations—now just the refining portion, not retail—and owns no oil wells or production facilities. Instead, they purchase a variety of feedstocks on the open market and can adjust those purchases to market conditions while using contracts and hedging tools to manage input prices to a degree—and rail transport to get it to the refinery. About 46 percent of feedstocks are purchased under contracts, with the remainder on the spot market (this figure was 51 percent in FY2013, reflecting a greater reliance on the now–less expensive spot market). Most of these refineries are legacy operations and have been in place for many years, as far back as 1908. The company has invested heavily in upgrading these refineries to improve capacity, efficiency, and environmental compliance and in recent years has grown its utilization rates to an industry-leading 96 percent. The company has also added capacity in two plants to produce high-quality distillates from low-quality feedstocks and natural gas.

The company is increasing its activities in transportation and logistics, where it already owns key pipelines—by adding approximately 4,100 rail cars to its fleet as part of a 5,300-car expansion, all using the new accident-resistant designs. With today's rapidly transformed domestic crude production activities, this logistics flexibility represents a key strategy toward optimizing input costs. The company now imports about half the amount of crude that it did back in 2006.

Bulk sales to other retail, commercial distributors, and large-end customers like airlines and railroads are also important. The company also owns and operates 11 ethanol plants in the U.S. Midwest, producing and shipping 1.3 billion gallons per year, and a 50 percent interest in a 10,500-barrels-per-day renewable diesel plant.

Financial Highlights, Fiscal Year 2014

With the effects of the retail spinoff not quite behind it, Valero posted a modest 6 percent revenue decline. But in this business, revenue will fluctuate based on energy prices. What's really important is profits—the difference between revenue and costs. Lower oil prices led to a dramatic increase in net margins (from 1.7 percent to 2.8 percent—small numbers but huge impact). As such, net income rose a whopping 52 percent, and with the buybacks, per-share earnings rose 57 percent.

The company continues to benefit from lower oil prices and strategic domestic sourcing ("strategic" because rail car shipments bind the company less to fixed sources); this looks to continue particularly as worldwide and domestic oil inventories rise. That said, the spinoff will cut into total revenues and earnings—the company now predicts that revenues will settle at $100 billion (again, without the retail operations) with a more moderate $2.8 billion level of profit. That's still good for $5.50 per share in FY2015 earnings and $6.00 in FY2016—and we think these numbers could be much higher if low oil prices linger. The company repurchased over 10 million of its shares (2 percent) during the fourth quarter FY2014 alone, a period where its stock price was depressed; we applaud this "smart" repurchase activity. It also raised the dividend some 45 percent in early FY2015, a strong nod to projected continued success.

Reasons to Buy

The profitability of this business, like other refining businesses, depends on the supply and cost of feedstocks and the wholesale and retail prices of finished products. In addition, the availability of refining capacity is also a factor; when markets get tight, it is extremely difficult to put another refinery on the ground to handle demand. These two factors together work very favorably for Valero—lower input costs, no new competition—it's an oligopolistic dream and should bode well for profits for years to come, especially in today's new world of crude oil (over)abundance.

Flexibility is the key, and is a key part of Valero's strategy. Rail transport provides excellent flexibility, and some say flexible methods, not fixed pipelines, are the optimal way to distribute crude from multiple sources in the future. Valero's investments in rail cars will help to capitalize on this trend.

We like Valero's leading position in the refining business, and having 15 well-distributed, efficient, and largely successful operating refineries on the ground already is a good thing. We also like the branding, abundance, look, and feel of the retail presence—even though the company no longer owns the stations outright.

Reasons for Caution

The refining business in particular is inherently volatile and complex, and what may appear today as an advantageous input and output pricing profile might disappear in a minute. Gross, operating, and net margins are very thin, typically in the 1–2 percent range—although Valero appears to be breaking above that range at about 2.8 percent currently. Refiners also endure the headline risk of refinery mishaps, a few of which have already come Valero's way in recent years. And now we incur more risks in rail transport of crude and saw what can happen in recent mishaps (neither of which affected Valero directly). We doubt if rail shipment of crude will be shut down, but it could become more expensive as mandates for safer cars, slower speeds, track improvements, etc., come into play.

The retail spinoff seems to be working even though we were a bit skeptical originally—we like some brand equity in this commodity business, and there is value in having a captive retail market for your product. Valero seems to have retained most of the advantage while allowing itself more focus on the refining business.

SECTOR: **Energy** ❑ BETA COEFFICIENT: **1.89** ❑ 10-YEAR COMPOUND EARNINGS PER-SHARE
GROWTH: **12.5%** ❑ 10-YEAR COMPOUND DIVIDENDS PER-SHARE GROWTH: **20.0%**

	2007	2008	2009	2010	2011	2012	2013	2014
Revenues (bil)	94.5	118.3	87.3	81.3	125.1	138.3	138.1	130.8
Net income (mil)	4,565	(1,131)	(352)	923	2,097	2,083	2,395	3,630
Earnings per share	7.72	(2.16)	(0.65)	1.62	3.69	3.75	4.37	6.85
Dividends per share	0.48	0.57	0.60	0.20	0.30	0.65	0.85	1.05
Cash flow per share	11.04	0.67	1.91	4.10	6.52	6.60	7.65	10.30
Price: high	75.7	71.1	26.2	23.7	31.1	34.5	50.5	59.7
low	47.7	13.9	16.3	15.5	16.4	16.1	33.0	42.5

Website: *www.valero.com*

Valmont Industries, Inc.

Ticker symbol: VMI (NYSE) ❑ S&P rating: BBB ❑ Value Line financial strength rating: A+ ❑ Current yield: 1.3% ❑ Dividend raises, past 10 years: 10

Company Profile

Every portfolio has a few near-term clunkers that for one reason or another, or for a perfect storm of reasons, had a bad stretch. When we review such companies, we take the long-term view: Has the business changed? Has the business model been disrupted? Has the company lost a key position in its marketplace? Have its products been commoditized? Has it restructured itself or acquired its way into mediocrity or excess complexity?

Naturally, we asked these questions of Valmont, one of our year's poorest performers, down 16.4 percent on a total return basis for our measurement year. The company has indeed hit a soft spot, hit by a perfect storm of lower volumes driven by reduced public spending, uncertainty in the agriculture markets, and low steel prices (which both hurt and help the company). But the company is a quiet and prosperous leader in three businesses we like a lot: food, water, and infrastructure. So we're keeping it on the 2016 *100 Best* list as both a long-term play and as an attractive short-term buying opportunity—frankly, one of the few on our list this year.

Valmont Industries was founded in 1946 as a supplier of irrigation products and became one of the classic postwar industrial success stories, growing along with the need for increased farm output. It was an early pioneer of the center-pivot irrigation system, which enabled much of that growth and now dominates the high-yield agricultural business. These machines remain a mainstay of its product line. But the company has expanded on that core expertise in galvanized metal to make such familiar infrastructure items as light poles, cell phone towers, and those familiar high-tension electric towers that crisscross the landscape, and to provide such galvanizing services to other product manufacturers.

Valmont products and product lines now include:

- *Engineered Infrastructure Products* (34 percent of FY2014 revenues, 29 percent of operating incomes)—Lighting poles, including decorative lighting poles, guard rails, towers, and other metal structures used in lighting, communications, traffic management, wireless phone carriers, and other utilities. Products are available as standard designs and engineered for custom applications as needed for industrial, commercial, and residential applications. If you've ever sat at a stoplight and wondered how a single cantilevered arm could support four 400-pound traffic signals, these are the folks to ask.

- *Utility Support Structures* (20 percent, 26 percent)—This segment produces the very large concrete and steel substations and electric transmission support towers used by electric utilities. We like this unit's prospects as utility infrastructure is replaced and modernized in the interest of grid efficiency.

- *Irrigation* (24 percent, 36 percent)—Under the Valley brand name, Valmont produces a wide range of equipment, including gravity and drip products, as well as its center-pivot designs, which can service up to 500 acres from a single machine. Valmont also sells its irrigation controllers to other manufacturers.

- *Coatings* (9 percent, 17 percent; note: division numbers don't quite add up because of corporate eliminations and operations selling to other operations internally)—Developed as an adjunct to its other metal products businesses, the Coatings business now provides services such as galvanizing, electroplating, powder coating, and anodizing to industrial customers throughout the company's operating areas.

There is also an "other" segment comprising about 7 percent of the business. Among the small acquisitions in 2014, Valmont acquired a 51 percent interest in AgSense, a maker of electronic remote monitoring devices for irrigation systems, and a manufacturer of fiberglass composite support structures.

Financial Highlights, Fiscal Year 2014

With the aforementioned headwinds (and currency was another), Valmont revenues dropped, and as a relatively small enterprise with relatively fixed manufacturing costs, scale wasn't sufficient to maintain previous profits levels, or even measure up to the company's own forecasts. FY2014 revenues slipped a little over 5 percent and a 2.5 percent dip in the operating margin percentage (from 16.7 percent to 14.3 percent) led to an overall earnings decline of 34 percent after a couple of particularly strong years. More of the same is forecast for the next couple of years on the top line, barely maintaining to slightly increasing revenues (leaving opportunity, of course, for a positive surprise), but efficiency measures and a more favorable product mix should start to creep earnings back upward in the 10 percent range annually by FY2016.

The company "irrigated" investor portfolios with a stepped-up 40 percent dividend increase in FY2014, and looks to be set to follow with further decent increases. Also, in early FY2015, Valmont announced a new $250 million share repurchase authorization—which may not seem that large compared to other large-cap companies. But with VMI's $3 billion market cap (making it a "mid-cap" player), it's significant, accounting for 8 percent of its share float; moreover, with this year's soft patch for the company, unlike many others, the timing of these repurchases looks to be favorable for investors. Many companies tend to repurchase when they're doing well and generating lots of cash, which is also when their stock prices are highest. Kudos to Valmont.

Reasons to Buy

As long-term investors, we must look the other way for FY2014 and FY2015—remember, this book is *The 100 Best Stocks to Buy in 2016*! As you will likely read this before the year 2016 becomes reality—or at least in the early part of the year—we think your timing is right, and that our "chestnuts will be taken out of the fire" by the time we tally 2016 results. That, and the fundamental strength of Valmont and the attractiveness of its core business, keep us going.

We continue to view Valmont as a key infrastructure play. America's infrastructure needs to be replaced, as does infrastructure in much of the developed world. As for the less-developed world, that infrastructure needs to be built in the first place. We think, long term, that Valmont is in the right place to capture a decent share of this replacement business, including electric utility infrastructure. The original irrigation business should also do well in the long term as global food consumption increases and as agriculture, farmland, and farm commodity prices eventually strengthen— and as droughts in key "ag" markets like California persist. Valmont has retained market share and remains the leader among the four dominant U.S.-based players in the large-scale irrigation market. The company's continued emphasis on growth into new geographies should pay dividends as India and China begin to build infrastructure and adopt more modern agricultural methods. We also like the relatively simple, straightforward nature of this business and the way the company presents itself online and in shareholder documents. Frankly, as the company is headquartered in Omaha, we wonder out loud why it hasn't garnered the interest of its prosperous and acquisitive neighbor, Berkshire Hathaway. Perhaps it has.

Reasons for Caution

Many Valmont products are purchased by public sector and government agencies, and these agencies will be scrutinizing purchases to a greater degree than in the past. Sectors that have recently showed strength sell to agriculture and utility interests, not government agencies—and now even these sectors are running into challenges as farmers scale back investments. Of course, we could be wrong about the long-term fundamentals of Valmont's businesses. That, playing together with low share counts—sometimes an advantage with smaller and highly successful businesses that everyone wants shares of—can work the other way if things don't work out. We think that's part of the story already baked in as we move through 2015.

SECTOR: **Industrials** ▫ BETA COEFFICIENT: **1.01** ▫ 10-YEAR COMPOUND EARNINGS PER-SHARE GROWTH: **22.0%** ▫ 10-YEAR COMPOUND DIVIDENDS PER-SHARE GROWTH: **13.5%**

		2007	2008	2009	2010	2011	2012	2013	2014
Revenues (mil)		1,500	1,907	1,787	1,975	2,661	3,029	3,304	3,123
Net income (mil)		94.7	132.4	155.0	109.7	158.0	234.1	278.5	184.0
Earnings per share		3.63	5.04	5.70	4.15	5.97	8.75	10.35	7.09
Dividends per share		0.41	0.50	0.58	0.65	0.72	0.88	0.98	1.38
Price:	high	99.0	120.5	89.3	90.3	116.0	141.2	164.9	163.2
	low	50.9	37.5	37.5	65.3	73.0	90.2	129.0	116.7

Website: *www.valmont.com*

Verizon Communications Inc.

Ticker symbol: VZ (NYSE) □ S&P rating: BBB+ □ Value Line financial strength rating: A++ □ Current yield: 4.5% □ Dividend raises, past 10 years: 9

Company Profile

Verizon operates two telecommunications businesses: Domestic Wireless, which provides wireless voice and data services, and Wireline, which provides voice, broadband data and video, Internet access, long-distance, and other services, and which owns and operates a large global Internet protocol network. The wireless business represents about 67 percent of the total; Wireline is about 33 percent of the total by revenues. As we'll get to shortly, the company's data and cloud computing business is one of its more exciting prospects.

In the consumer space, the Wireline segment also supplies Verizon's fiber-to-the-home (FiOS) broadband data infrastructure. One of Verizon's largest investments, FiOS provides a very high bandwidth link to the Internet, easily surpassing DSL and even cable. Over this network, Verizon can provide hundreds of HD video streams, high-speed data, and voice all simultaneously. This service competes head-to-head with AT&T's (a *100 Best* stock) U-verse and Comcast's (another *100 Best* stock) Xfinity services among others.

The Domestic Wireless segment is served by the now wholly owned Verizon Wireless, the remaining unowned 45 percent acquired from Vodafone in a $130 billion deal that closed in early 2014. Verizon Wireless is now the largest wireless carrier in the United States, and it operates in 19 countries outside the United States as well. The wireless side of the business has been rolling out its new LTE mobile broadband network, a leading-edge 4G network designed to be ten times faster than the standard 3G network, and now available in some 500 U.S. markets to more than 97 percent of the U.S. population.

Adding hardware products and wireless capacity hasn't been the only growth strategy employed at Verizon—the company has a healthy appetite for acquisitions, growing its footprint in advanced networking, private networks, and cloud computing, with the 2011 acquisition of IT and cloud services provider Terremark Worldwide, and a small but interesting partnership with a company called eMeter, which markets devices that automatically read and transmit energy usage for utilities using Verizon's wireless network. The company is leveraging its investment in the 4G LTE network for corporate customers to offer secure wireless private IP networks. In mid-2012, the company acquired Hughes Telematics, expanding its offerings in vehicle telematics (more popularly known as OnStar in GM cars) and other machine-to-machine communications. In 2013, Verizon acquired upLynk, a television cloud company, and in early 2014 it acquired the Intel Media arm of Intel, which develops cloud TV products and services, and EdgeCast Networks, a fast-content delivery network originally funded by Disney. In all, you can see where these additions are going—they provide more pipe, new kinds of pipe, and some of the content that flows through the pipe.

But acquisitions aren't the whole story—there are divestitures and asset sales too. In early 2015 the company moved to sell local wireline services in California, Florida, and Texas and to sell a big chunk of cell phone tower rights and some complete towers to American Tower. These transactions alone amount to some $15 billion and will be used for other acquisitions and to accelerate share buybacks (that is, to buy back 500 million of the 1.3 billion shares issued to acquire the strategic other half of the Verizon Wireless business).

Financial Highlights, Fiscal Year 2014

Top- and bottom-line figures have been a difficult read over the past two years as VZ digests the rounding out of Verizon Wireless and the divestiture of less profitable wireline businesses. Suffice it to say that revenues and per-share earnings are moving in the right direction and look to continue to do so—at a faster pace—through FY2016.

Strength in new subscriber additions, per-subscriber profitability, the 4G smartphone business and related data plans, and the FiOS business should drive revenues ahead 2–4 percent for the next two years, but with increased profitability. Even better news: Net margins are expected to ring in at 10 percent for the first time in FY2015, up from the 5–7 percent range in recent years. That with reduced share counts (a bit artificially so in the short term) will grow per-share earnings to $3.75–$4.00 by FY2016—a nice jump from today's levels especially for a large and steady player like Verizon. Dividend raises look to continue in the 4 percent range annually.

Reasons to Buy

Verizon continues to offer a good combination of stability, financial strength, and income with a play in the growth of the "new economy" and supporting technology. After a few years of lean profit growth as the company invested in infrastructure and iPhones, earnings growth is now well ahead of top-line growth. We especially like the new cloud and wireless data services for the commercial market, which offer good promise and significant leverage of existing investments, and the promise of emerging services in the consumer space such as video-on-demand.

We're glad the Vodafone acquisition is finally behind the company. This cast some uncertainty for quite a while: whether or not it would happen and what the price would be. Check that box. The recent divestitures to help pay for that and other acquisitions make a lot of sense to us, as we mortals often have to sell things to raise cash to buy the things we want, too! Seriously, better to raise it this way than to take it out of shareholder returns.

The company has typically paid out a high portion of earnings as dividends and has increased its dividend regularly. The high payout and low beta of 0.36 make the stock a safe core holding.

Reasons for Caution

The telecommunications business is always capital intensive, and Verizon, like others, must spend heavily just to keep up with technology and competition. The business environment is extremely competitive, and Verizon's sheer size may hamper its flexibility to compete. Finally, on the acquisition front, Verizon has gobbled up a lot, and while we think the add-ons make sense, they add to risk and perhaps make the company a bit unwieldy to manage.

SECTOR: **Telecommunications Services** ❑ BETA COEFFICIENT: **0.36** ❑ 10-YEAR COMPOUND EARNINGS PER-SHARE GROWTH: **3.0%** ❑ 10-YEAR COMPOUND DIVIDENDS PER-SHARE GROWTH: **3.0%**

		2007	2008	2009	2010	2011	2012	2013	2014
Revenues (mil)		93.4	97.4	107.9	106.6	110.9	115.8	120.6	127.1
Net income (mil)		6,854	7,235	6,805	6,256	6,087	5,970	11,497	9,625
Earnings per share		2.36	2.54	2.40	2.21	2.15	2.32	2.84	3.35
Dividends per share		1.65	1.78	1.87	1.93	1.96	2.02	2.09	2.16
Cash flow per share		7.40	7.65	7.70	7.60	7.96	7.35	6.79	5.45
Price:	high	46.2	44.3	34.8	36.0	40.3	48.8	54.3	53.7
	low	35.6	23.1	26.1	26.0	32.3	36.8	41.5	45.1

Website: *www.verizon.com*

Visa Inc.

Ticker symbol: V (NYSE) □ S&P rating: A+ □ Value Line financial strength rating: A++ □ Current yield: 0.7% □ Dividend raises, past 10 years: 6

Company Profile

If we wrote about a company with a 42 percent net profit margin—and growing rapidly—and a global brand that was in the business of collecting small fees on every one of the billions of transactions worldwide; a company that required almost no capital expenditures, plant, equipment, or inventory; a company that brought in almost 1.3 million dollars per employee in revenue and $570,000 per employee in net profit (the company refers to this as "people light and technology heavy"); a company growing earnings 10–30 percent a year; a company with a time-tested business model and absolutely zero long-term debt—would you believe that it existed? Not to mention a company with a share price that rose from $74 to $118 in our 2011 measurement period, to $168 in 2012, to $220 in 2013, and to $270 in 2014—before it split four-for-one in early 2015?

It's all true. And the company, formed in a 2007 reorganization and taken public in 2008, is Visa. Yes, the same Visa whose emblem has traditionally appeared on a majority of the world's credit cards—and now debit cards. In fact, there are about 2.3 *billion* such cards dispersed through 200 countries worldwide. The company operates the world's largest retail electronic payment network, providing processing services; payment platforms; and fraud-detection services for credit, debit, and commercial payments. The company also operates one of the largest global ATM networks with its PLUS and Interlink brands. In total, the company processes 98.4 billion transactions per year (which works out to about 3,100 transactions *per second*) and estimates that it can process about 15 times that amount in a peak scenario—while being operational 99.999999 percent of the time!

For years, Visa has been synonymous with credit and credit cards, but in recent years it has become more of a digital currency company, stitching together consumers, retailers, banks, and other businesses in a giant global network. Really, Visa is a global payments technology business that not only develops and supplies the technology but also collects fees upon its use.

The shift from traditional cash and check forms of payment to debit cards and other digital forms is growing at about a 12 percent annual rate, driven by the security and convenience of these transactions as well as a shift away from consumer debt to more "paid for today" debit transactions. Debit transactions now account for more than half the company's overall business volume, albeit at a small penalty, as average transaction sizes are smaller.

The company is an active innovator, with several initiatives in what it calls an "evolving payments ecosystem" and in network security. Mobile payment and mobile wallet innovations include "V.me" and "payWave" licensed products, and, not surprisingly in light of recent news events, the company is also working on new payment and card security initiatives. A new platform called Visa Checkout makes it easier for merchants to integrate Visa payment into websites and mobile platforms, and the company has partnered with Apple to create new connections with Apple Pay, which should prove to be quite important going forward. A new fraud protection tool is estimated to reduce fraud by as much as 23 percent.

More than its rivals, Visa derives a significant percentage of transaction revenues, about 46 percent, overseas. International revenues are growing faster than in the United States, about 9 percent compared to 7 percent, as cash electronic payments gradually replace cash as a payment method especially in emerging markets.

Financial Highlights, Fiscal Year 2014

Helped by international expansion, increased economic activity, and e-commerce, Visa continued to deliver in FY2014 and will for the immediate future in our opinion. Despite a 2 percent currency headwind, total revenues advanced just under 8 percent; earnings advanced 9 percent and per-share earnings advanced almost 20 percent on the back of share repurchases. Current projections call for revenue growth in the 8–10 percent range through FY2016, with a slight pause in earnings growth in FY2015 to 4 percent due mostly to litigation expenses (settling a large payment fees dispute in 2014), and should recover to a 17 percent growth rate FY2016 over FY2015. The company authorized another $5 billion to repurchase shares—enough to retire 3–4 percent of the float—and has already retired 18 percent of its float since going public in 2008.

Reasons to Buy

Simply, it continues to be difficult to come up with a better business model—a company that develops and sells the network and collects fees every time it's used. It would be like Microsoft collecting fees every time a file is created and saved, or an e-mail platform that charges fees for every message. Visa is in a great position to not only capitalize on overall world economic growth, as most companies should be, but also to capitalize on a shift in this growth toward electronic and mobile payments. Even as debt-conscious consumers pull back on using credit cards, debit card usage continues to advance. This reinforces one of Visa's big strengths—unlike most other financial services businesses, Visa is relatively immune to downturns, as it makes its money by processing payments, not by extending credit. On the growth side, the company is expanding its footprint in emerging markets, and there is plenty of innovation opportunity in this business. Overall, while Visa has competitors (MasterCard, American Express, and Discover), it has the strongest franchise, technology leadership, and pricing power at its back.

Reasons for Caution

The company has pricing power, but as with many companies that do, that power has come under government, merchant, and public scrutiny; the company must tread lightly or face possible consequences. Recent litigation and regulatory actions have presented some headline and profit risk and may be construed as a threat to the franchise—perhaps if it sounds too good to be true, it may be. But even after some legal and regulatory bumps, Visa has emerged rock solid. In fact, it's good to confront these issues and get past them even if they do cause some short-term stomach pain for investors—as they have recently with the fee settlement. The stock has recognized a lot of this excellence and has risen sharply, splitting 4:1 recently; proper entry points are still required and have become available from time to time as legal and security challenges have come and gone.

SECTOR: **Financials** ❑ BETA COEFFICIENT: **0.80** ❑ 10-YEAR COMPOUND EARNINGS PER-SHARE GROWTH: **NM** ❑ 10-YEAR COMPOUND DIVIDENDS PER-SHARE GROWTH: **NM**

	2007	2008	2009	2010	2011	2012	2013	2014
Revenues (mil)	—	6,263	6,911	8,065	9,188	10,421	11,776	12,702
Net income (mil)	—	1,700	2,213	2,966	3,650	4,203	4,980	5,438
Earnings per share	—	0.56	0.73	0.98	1.25	1.55	1.90	2.27
Dividends per share	—	0.03	0.11	0.13	0.15	0.22	0.33	0.42
Cash flow per share	—	0.63	0.80	1.09	1.39	1.67	2.05	2.44
Price: high	—	22.5	22.4	24.3	25.9	38.1	55.7	67.3
low	—	10.9	10.4	16.2	16.9	24.6	38.5	48.7

Website: *www.corporate.visa.com*

Wal-Mart Stores, Inc.

Ticker symbol: WMT (NYSE) ▫ S&P rating: AAA ▫ Value Line financial strength rating: A++ ▫ Current yield: 2.5% ▫ Dividend raises, past 10 years: 10

Company Profile

"Helping people save so they can live better" is the guiding philosophy of Wal-Mart, the world's largest retailer. At 2.2 million employees, it is also the world's largest private employer, ranked overall behind only the U.S. Department of Defense and the People's Liberation Army of China. This "army" of employees serves more than 260 million customers each week in 27 countries from over 11,400 stores and one of the world's largest e-commerce operations. To clear up some confusion before it occurs, the Wal-Mart company operates stores under the "Walmart" brand, so if you feel like you're seeing two spellings of the same thing in error, that's the explanation (we still expect they will clear this up some day by changing the corporate name). In the U.S., Wal-Mart operates 3,407 Walmart Supercenters (up from 3,288 last year), 647 Sam's Club stores (up from 632), 470 Walmart Discount Stores (down from 508, reflecting some conversion to Supercenters), and 639 Walmart Neighborhood Markets and other small formats (up dramatically from 407 last year and 286 two years ago). Rest-of-world retail locations total 6,290 medium and smaller footprint stores (up from 6,107), mostly in Latin America, Canada, Japan, China, India, and the U.K. Nearly all of the stores are owned by the company, with the exception of those in India and China, which are joint ventures.

Wal-Mart operates in three business segments: the Walmart U.S. segment, the Walmart International segment, and the Sam's Club segment. In 2014, the Walmart U.S. segment (which includes the online retail presence at Walmart.com) accounted for approximately 60 percent of revenue. The Walmart International segment accounted for 28 percent of sales, while the Sam's Club segment and its own online presence accounted for approximately 12 percent of net sales. Walmart's mainline stores operate on an "everyday low price" (acronym: "EDLP") philosophy. The idea is that customers need not wait for sale prices, as Walmart's normal price is at or near the bottom of the competitive market at all times.

The Sam's Club stores are membership clubs, focused on selling brand-name and private- label goods in larger quantities to individuals and businesses. They compete with Costco and other warehouse merchandisers.

The Walmart U.S. segment does business in six merchandise units, including Grocery, Entertainment, Hardlines, Health and Wellness, Apparel, and Home. Grocery, which accounted for some 55 percent of U.S. sales, is typically available at its Superstore and Neighborhood Market formats; the grocery section is quite large although oriented toward packaged and frozen goods. Other lines found in Superstores include Entertainment, which contains electronics, toys, cameras and supplies, cell phones, service plan contracts, and books; Hardlines includes stationery, automotive accessories, hardware and paint, sporting goods, fabrics and crafts, and seasonal merchandise; Health and Wellness, which includes pharmacy and optical services; Apparel includes apparel for women, girls, men, boys, and infants, shoes, jewelry, and accessories; Home includes home furnishings, housewares and small appliances, bedding, home decor, outdoor living, and plants. The Walmart U.S. segment also offers financial services and related products, including money orders, wire transfers, check cashing, and bill payment. It has a private-label store credit card issued by a third-party provider and accepts online payments through PayPal. In addition, its pharmacy and optical departments accept payments for products and services through its customers' health-benefit plans.

Overall, Walmart delivers a four-element "customer proposition" including Price, Access, Assortment, and Experience. The company is embracing a segment of the market less inclined to do a full, supersized "big-basket" trip and more inclined to more frequent, convenience-oriented "stock-up" trips. To that end they plan to open more Neighborhood Markets, which concentrate on groceries, and a number of "Walmart Express" locations. By sheer scale, the e-commerce site is one of the world's largest, and grew 22 percent last year. The company runs e-commerce sites in 11 countries, and, like many others, is beginning to work on an "omnichannel" approach (shop online or from a mobile device, pick up in store, fulfill from store inventories where it makes sense) to integrate e-commerce into its total offering. In mid-2014 the company announced a major strategic move to raise pay for approximately 500,000 employees from minimum wage (typically $7.25) to $9.00 per hour, and to raise pay for some store managers $2.00/hr. to $15.00. Although projected to cost about $1 billion, the company expects improved morale, lower turnover, and a better public image going forward.

Financial Highlights, Fiscal Year 2014

The company calls it Fiscal Year 2015 because it ends on January 31, 2015. To make it more comparable to other businesses, we will refer to it as "2014" and drop the "FY."

Same-store sales growth of 0.5 percent (0.6 percent without fuel) and moderate store expansion drove total revenue 2 percent higher in 2014—a figure that would have been larger without currency headwinds. As we've noted in the past, that number sounds small, but represents a gain of almost $10 billion on the top line. The figure reflected growth in e-commerce and a long-awaited return of Wal-Mart's post-recession core customer base to its stores—comps for 2014 over 2013 had *declined* 0.5 percent. A resumption of higher payroll taxes, health-care costs, bad weather, and a reduction in government food assistance programs led to a slight 0.1 percent margin contraction—which in turn led to a 6.7 percent drop in net profits—in a high-volume, low-margin business such sensitivity is no surprise.

For 2015 and 2016, we've already mentioned the $1 billion earnings hit for the higher wages. Revenues are projected to grow in the 1–2 percent range, with earnings taking the hit to the tune of 4–5 percent in 2015, recovering most of that in 2016. Modest dividend growth should continue, but buybacks will attenuate to less than 1 percent as the effects of lower profits and some capital investments, particularly in e-commerce, are absorbed. The company has already retired about a quarter of its outstanding float in the past ten years.

Reasons to Buy

Although it will hit short-term earnings, we applaud the company's "invest-ment" in paying its people more both from a public relations standpoint, and perhaps even more, a stimulus to morale, productivity, and ultimately, support of the brand. Progressive retailers like Starbucks and many smaller mom-and-pop businesses have paid a bit more to employees, even share profits, with favorable results for the business. We see no reason why this can't have a positive effect on a business as large as Wal-Mart. We see a company that has shifted focus from internal operational improvements and growing stores to employee excellence and customer experience—we like both of these particularly if they can keep "EDLP" to boot.

Wal-Mart is a well-run company that seems to be taking the right steps to improve both its business and its brand image. We like the safety and low-volatility profile of both the business and the stock, as the long-term share-price chart and the beta of 0.45 would indicate.

Reasons for Caution

Wal-Mart is very large, with few major growth vectors. Although international growth does provide one, it's encountered some tough sledding in China. Its size may also make it difficult to manage, though today's management operates with near-military precision and does it well. Increasing reliance on the low-margin and sometimes-fickle grocery business is a minor concern. Overall, while they seem more dedicated to improving their image than in past years, the brand doesn't always fare so well in the court of public opinion.

SECTOR: **Retail** ❑ BETA COEFFICIENT: **0.45** ❑ 5-YEAR COMPOUND EARNINGS PER-SHARE
GROWTH: **10.5%** ❑ 10-YEAR COMPOUND DIVIDENDS PER-SHARE GROWTH: **18.0%**

		2007	2008	2009	2010	2011	2012	2013	2014
Revenues (bil)		378.8	405.6	408.2	421.8	447.0	469.2	476.3	485.7
Net income (bil)		12.9	13.6	14.2	14.9	15.5	17.0	16.7	16.4
Earnings per share		3.16	3.42	3.66	4.07	4.45	5.02	5.11	5.04
Dividends per share		0.88	0.95	1.09	1.21	1.46	1.59	1.88	1.92
Cash flow per share		4.83	5.16	5.64	6.42	6.92	7.69	7.92	7.93
Price:	high	51.4	63.8	57.5	56.3	60.0	77.6	81.4	88.1
	low	42.1	43.1	46.3	47.8	48.3	57.2	67.7	72.3

Website: *www.walmart.com*

Waste Management, Inc.

Ticker symbol: WM (NYSE) ❑ S&P rating: A- ❑ Value Line financial strength rating: A ❑ Current yield: 2.8% ❑ Dividend raises, past 10 years: 10

Company Profile

You may refer to it as a "garbage company" if you want—we won't take offense. Waste Management is the largest and steadiest hand in the North American solid waste disposal industry. Like most large waste firms, WM has grown over time by assembling smaller, more local companies into a nationally branded and highly scaled operation with a notable amount of innovation on several fronts in the core business and especially in material recovery—translation, recycling.

The business is divided into three segments:

- *Collection,* which accounts for 54 percent of the business, includes the standard dumpster and garbage truck operations. The company has about 400 collection operations, many of which have long-term contracts with municipalities and businesses. About 40 percent of the collection business is commercial, 30 percent residential, and 26 percent industrial. For the industry, WM is considered an innovator even in its traditional collection operations; examples include the Bagster small-scale disposal units now sold through retail home-improvement outlets and 3,700 collection trucks converted to natural gas (some of which the company produces from waste). The company perceives itself as a world-class logistics company (and why not?) and has equipped its trucks with the latest in onboard computers, centralized dispatching, and routing processes, reducing collection costs an additional 1 percent during FY2015.

- *Landfill* (18 percent of revenues). The company operates 247 landfills across North America, servicing its own collection operations and other collection service providers. Among these sites, there are 134 landfill-gas-to-energy conversion projects producing fuel for electricity generation—currently enough to power 500 million homes each year. There are also five active hazardous waste landfills and one underground hazardous waste facility.

- *Transfer, Recycling, and Other* (28 percent). These operations perform specialized material recovery and processing into useful commodities. There are 298 transfer stations set up for the collection of various forms of waste, including medical, recyclables, and e-waste. The company has also pioneered single-stream recycling, where physical and optical sorting technologies sort out unseparated recyclable materials. Single-streaming has greatly increased recycling rates in municipalities where it is used and provides a steady revenue stream in recovered paper, glass, metals, etc., for the company. WM also further refines these materials into industrial inputs, e.g., glass or plastic feedstocks in certain colors. In total there are 76 traditional and 50 "single-stream" operations, recycling some 13 million tons of commodities annually today, a figure expected to grow to 20 million by 2020. "Capture Value from Waste" is a popular company slogan.

In 2014, the company sold its Wheelabrator Technologies subsidiary, which operated a network of waste-to-energy gasification plants at landfills. While we were initially disappointed with the sale, the business was more of a good idea than a solid contributor to profits, especially with the recent abundance of natural gas. The sale had only a minor effect on their numbers, but did cut the number of homes supplied with power in half. Recycling operations in general produce 9 percent of revenues and are not big profit producers with today's soft commodity prices and diminished China demand, but the company remains strategically committed to these operations for the long term.

Financial Highlights, Fiscal Year 2014

While the Wheelabrator sale and softness in the recycling business provided a headwind for FY2014, operational improvements, a reduction in capital expenditures, and core business strength led to a not-so-trashy year. Revenues were roughly flat, but earnings and per-share earnings advanced around 15 percent, and the Wheelabrator sale for almost $2 billion injected cash to use for buybacks and more small acquisitions—it appears to be a good move all in all. FY2015 reported revenues will back off a bit over 2 percent with the divestiture but reclaim that (oops, sorry) in FY2016 to regain the $14 billion level. The better story is margins, which with operational improvements and a downsizing in less profitable waste-to-energy operations are expected to rise about 1 percent (a big deal on a 7.2 percent base). This delivered some of the FY2014 gains and will continue into FY2015 and FY2016; per-share earnings should rise to $2.70 per share, and the "miss" would likely be on the upside if recycled commodity prices improve. Dividends look to rise steadily, and share buybacks will continue to come down the conveyor belt.

Reasons to Buy

WM is the strongest and most entrenched player in a business that isn't going away anytime soon. "Strategic" waste collection, particularly with the high-value-add material recovery operations that have become core to WM's business, is not only here to stay but also will only become more important to residential, industrial, and municipal customers as time goes on. Despite today's low energy and material prices, we feel the "sweet spot" in this trend is yet to come.

WM exhibits a lot of innovation in an industry not particularly known for it. We feel that WM's performance is solid, and could break out of the doldrums as operational improvements take effect, lower fuel costs weigh in, and as material recovery becomes an even more strategic and profitable enterprise. WM is a slow, steady, safe, well-managed investment with decent cash returns to shareholders.

Reasons for Caution

With earnings doubling in ten years and an improved track record for shareholder returns, we were surprised through 2013 that WM's share price had remained in the doldrums for so long. It finally broke out of that pattern in 2014, making it more important to shop for a good entry point. The company does rely on acquisitions for a lot of its growth. In this business, that might not be so bad, for existing companies have captive markets and disposal facilities and can likely benefit from proven management processes and reduced overhead costs. The recycling operations, while cool and sexy, aren't always profitable as we've seen, especially when competing material prices, like natural gas these days, are soft. The right combination of factors to drive improved recycling profitability may be close at hand or a ways off—you can have a clear environmental conscience (and collect your dividends) while you wait for better times. Additionally, any waste company runs the risk of going afoul of environmental regulations; WM has largely steered clear of trouble thus far (and has indeed been in most ethical companies for the past eight years), but there are no guarantees. More stringent regulations could also pose problems.

SECTOR: **Business Services** ❑ BETA COEFFICIENT: **0.67** ❑ 10-YEAR COMPOUND EARNINGS PER-SHARE GROWTH: **5.5%** ❑ 10-YEAR COMPOUND DIVIDENDS PER-SHARE GROWTH: **5.5%**

	2007	2008	2009	2010	2011	2012	2013	2014
Revenues (mil)	13,310	13,388	11,791	12,515	13,375	13,649	13,983	13,996
Net income (mil)	1,080	1,087	988	1,011	1,007	968	1,008	1,155
Earnings per share	2.07	2.19	2.00	2.10	2.14	2.08	2.15	2.48
Dividends per share	0.98	1.08	1.16	1.28	1.36	1.42	1.46	1.50
Cash flow per share	4.68	4.74	4.43	4.64	4.85	4.88	5.04	5.34
Price: high	41.2	39.3	34.2	37.3	36.7	36.3	46.4	51.9
low	32.4	24.5	22.1	31.1	27.8	30.8	33.7	40.3

Website: *www.wm.com*

AGGRESSIVE GROWTH

WD-40 Company

Ticker symbol: WDFC (NASDAQ) ◻ S&P rating: NR ◻ Value Line financial strength rating: A ◻ Current yield: 1.2% ◻ Dividend raises, past 10 years: 7

Company Profile

Want to keep squirrels from climbing the poles to your bird feeders? We did, and we always have. And we found the solution through WD-40's website—spray the pole with WD-40.

Turns out, people have been spraying WD-40 on plenty of other things over the years to get them to work right, stop squeaking, dry out properly, or to be just plain in good repair. In fact, they've been spraying WD-40 for 61 years—just a few years after the Rocket Chemical Company first invented the stuff for the aerospace industry in 1953 to protect the outer skin of the SM-65 Atlas missile. And what is "WD-40"? It was the fortieth attempt to develop a good Water Displacement formula. It was so good, and had so many uses in unsticking stuck things, that employees started sneaking it out of the factory in lunch buckets. Shortly thereafter, in 1958, the product made its first appearance on store shelves as a spray.

Fast-forward to now: the professional and now-consumerized WD-40 remains a product of a thousand uses—2,000 in fact, according to their website—and a lesson in building a very effective brand around a fairly plain consumer product for distribution into what the company estimates to be four out of five U.S. households and into 188 countries worldwide.

The base WD-40 product, in its familiar blue and yellow spray can of various sizes, is still the brand cornerstone, even though the company doesn't make a drop of it. They do the research and lab work but outsource production to other specialty chemical companies. In fact, the company in total has only 369 employees, probably the fewest on our *100 Best Stocks* list. In the late 1990s, they sought to extend their presence in the maintenance and repair market by acquiring canned light oil maker 3-IN-ONE, then went further into this market to acquire the maker and distributor of Lava soap and Solvol heavy-duty hand cleaner. After initial successes with these acquisitions, and as their products were adopted in greater quantities as consumer products for use in the home, not just the repair shop, they started adding cleaning products, including X-14 stain removers and 2000 Flushes bath cleaners, Carpet Fresh and Spot Shot carpet cleaners, and a handful of other products, some with only international distribution.

In 2003 they added a 3-IN-ONE Professional line, and in 2011 they sought to extend the WD-40 name itself beyond the namesake light oil spray with the addition of a WD-40 Specialist line for especially challenging jobs in maintenance and repair operations for the trade professional and the "doer enthusiast" like rust removal, engine degreasing, corrosion prevention, and electrical contact cleaning. They also introduced specialty lines for motorcycle maintenance, home maintenance, and a WD-40 Bike line specifically produced and packaged for bicycle maintenance. New packages, spray tubes, and injectors help users get the product into difficult spaces. The Multipurpose Maintenance Products line, which includes the broad family of lubricants, now accounts for 85 percent of the revenue.

In short, WD-40 is a classic case study in *brand extension*, with new ways to package and position its core WD-40 and 3-IN-ONE lubricants for new and existing markets, and *business model extension*, where they leverage their operating and marketing model into other useful product lines as exemplified by their cleaning products. That said, the company is considering a sale of some of the homecare brands to focus more on the niche it dominates—multipurpose maintenance products.

Financial Highlights, Fiscal Year 2014

The numbers in the following table reflect a steady and gradually accelerating business success. FY2014 revenues rose about 3.9 percent in total, although notably revenues in the core Multipurpose Maintenance products segment grew 5 percent, while the Homecare and Cleaning Products segment dropped 5 percent—hence the previous note about the company exploring strategic opportunities. Of the $383 million in sales, about 52 percent came from outside the Americas; of that, about three-quarters are from EMEA and about a quarter are from Asia. Gross margins increased about 0.6 percent to 51.9 percent; operating margins increased from 17.7 percent to 18.9 percent, and net profit margins rose from 10.8 percent to 11.4 percent—all healthy figures to begin with—delivering an almost 10 percent gain in net earnings. As a result of buybacks, per-share earnings rose 13 percent. Buybacks are small, fewer than 1 million shares per year, but so is the base—the company currently has only 14.75 million shares outstanding.

Increased brand leverage and penetration (sorry) into new markets like China are expected to bring FY2015 sales about 5–6 percent higher; margins may rise just a bit with the attenuation of oil prices (petroleum products make up about a third of cost for the WD-40 product) leading to steady 6–9 percent increases in per-share earnings. Buybacks will continue at a moderate pace.

Reasons to Buy

We wish we had come on to this story a little sooner; WD-40's share price has risen substantially in the past two years. We see why but think this story has room to run. We like the branding leverage and niche dominance of any business we see like this. Moreover, we like the way this company is run. A visit to their website and their "About Us" page will uncover their view of the world and clearly stated values: This is a leaner and better culture—or "tribe" as they refer to it—than we've seen in most consumer brand companies. Too, a trip through their investor presentations will shed an unusual amount of positive light on their concise management style. Management respects its employees . . . and respects its shareholders too. Finally—we can't ignore this—it has all the hallmarks of a Buffett acquisition: a simple business model, strong brand, and good management in place.

Reasons for Caution

A possible sale of some of the homecare brands brings some uncertainty, and clearly a major economic breakdown or rise in input prices will hurt. But given their niche dominance and the unlikelihood that squeaks and rusty bolts will go away anytime soon, we think this company is protected better than some from bad business cycles. With only 369 employees on staff, and an "asset-light" strategy, there's little excess fat to worry about. At this point we'd mainly be concerned about the high stock price against the relatively modest, albeit steady, growth prospects.

SECTOR: **Industrials** ❑ BETA COEFFICIENT: **0.79** ❑ 10-YEAR COMPOUND EARNINGS PER-SHARE GROWTH: **4.5%** ❑ 10-YEAR COMPOUND DIVIDENDS PER-SHARE GROWTH: **NM**

		2007	2008	2009	2010	2011	2012	2013	2014
Revenues (mil)		308	317	292	322	336	343	369	383
Net income (mil)		31.5	28.5	26.3	36.1	36.4	35.5	39.8	43.7
Earnings per share		1.83	1.69	1.56	2.15	2.14	2.20	2.54	2.87
Dividends per share		1.00	1.00	1.00	1.00	1.06	1.14	1.22	1.33
Cash flow per share		2.09	1.96	1.82	2.42	2.49	2.57	2.96	3.36
Price:	high	42.7	40.0	34.6	41.8	48.0	54.4	79.3	87.1
	low	30.8	23.1	21.6	29.3	35.4	39.4	47.0	65.2

Website: *www.wd40.com*

GROWTH AND INCOME

Wells Fargo & Company

Ticker symbol: WFC (NYSE) ❑ S&P rating: A+ ❑ Value Line financial strength rating: A ❑ Current yield: 2.7% ❑ Dividend raises, past 10 years: 8

Company Profile

Wells Fargo & Company is a diversified financial services company, providing banking, insurance, investments, mortgages, and consumer finance from more than 8,700 offices (more than any other bank but down from 9,000 last year due to some efficiency measures) and other distribution channels, including mortgage, investment management, commercial banking, and consumer finance branches across all 50 states and 36 countries including locations in Canada, the Caribbean, and Central America.

The business is divided into three segments. First and largest is Community Banking, which provides traditional banking and mortgage services in all 50 states through a combination of branches, ATMs, and online services. Wholesale Banking provides commercial banking, capital markets, leasing, and other financing services to larger corporations. Wealth, Brokerage, and Retirement provides financial advisory and investment management services to individuals.

As of the end of 2014, Wells Fargo had $1.75 trillion in assets, loans outstanding of $850 billion, and shareholder equity of $184 billion (this latter figure is up 46 percent from the end of 2010, a sign of health). Based on assets, it is the third-largest bank holding company in the United States. The company expanded its footprint and market share—which is close to 10 percent of all U.S. banking services—considerably with the 2009 acquisition of Wachovia. At present, it is the U.S. market-share leader in commercial real estate, middle-market commercial lending, mortgage origination and servicing, small-business landing, auto loans, and retail deposits. It holds the number two position in debit card issuance, number three in total deposits and full-service retail brokerage, and number four in wealth management.

Wells Fargo is currently making a big push into eastern U.S. markets, particularly the New York area. It also recently announced the opening of an Asset Management office in Paris, to add to an already sizeable international footprint with offices in some 36 countries. The company is also an innovation leader, for instance, with experiments with a new 1,000-square-foot "minibank" with personalized service, interactive technologies, and large-screen ATMs and in mobile banking, which, it estimates, 15 million customers are using at present.

The bank's success is more based on fees and services than most. About 52 percent of income originates from interest margin (the difference between interest charged and interest cost); 48 percent originates from an assortment of fees. Of that 48 percent, the brokerage and financial advisory operations generate 31 percent, deposit service charges 12 percent, mortgage origination fees 10 percent, card fees 9 percent, and 12 other small categories account for as much as 5 percent apiece.

Financial Highlights, Fiscal Year 2014

Wells Fargo continues to rebound from the Great Recession more successfully than most of its brethren. Loan losses and nonperforming assets continue to drop, and the so-called "Tier 1" ratio, a measure of equity to total assets, has improved from 8.3 percent in 2010 to 10.53 percent at the end of 2014, healthy by banking standards. The company also reported charge-offs for nonperforming assets of 0.33 percent compared to 0.47 percent last year and 1.36 percent in 2011; allowance for loan losses of 1.51 percent down from 1.81 percent last year and 2.56 percent in 2011; and nonperforming assets down to 1.72 percent from 2.37 percent in 2014 and 3.37 percent in 2011. In line with these numbers, the loan loss reserve has dropped from $15.7 billion at the end of 2010 to $2.1 billion at the end of 2014. These figures all deliver a picture of vastly improved financial health and asset quality, and we like the fact that the company presents these figures clearly on their "Investment Profile" page (*www.wellsfargo.com/about/investor_relations/investment_profile*).

These figures, while indicating health, also brought improved performance. Strong loan growth in commercial and industrial segments and in credit cards was offset by a decline in interest margin; together these led to a 3.2 percent revenue gain for FY2014. Per-share earnings for the year were up a respectable 5.4 percent after a 16 percent gain in FY2013 and a 19 percent gain in FY2012. The company projects a further leveling off in FY2015 with largely flat earnings results partly due to salary, benefits, and commissions increases, then an 8–10 percent earnings growth on a 5–6 percent revenue gain for FY2016. Another substantial 17 percent bump in the dividend accompanied a 1.5 percent share count reduction in FY2014. Fully blessed so far by the Federal Reserve, the dividend should rise above $2.00 by the end of the decade if not before.

Reasons to Buy

Wells Fargo has cleaned house with its Wachovia purchase, its mortgage lending, and other overhang from the financial crisis and has become more of a global brand and steady player in the consumer and commercial banking industry. We like its solid financial base and its growth in noninterest income (fees, etc.) that insulate it against possible interest rate hikes, and its reputation in the marketplace.

Especially as the macroeconomic environment improves, we think WFC is well positioned to take advantage. Shareholders will be rewarded with ample return in the form of share price appreciation, dividends, and buybacks as time goes on, although buybacks may attenuate in an effort to retain strong capital ratios—in this industry, that's not a bad thing. And we also don't think it's a bad thing that Warren Buffett, through his Berkshire Hathaway business, recently upped his stake 1.5 percent to 470 million shares, or 24 percent of his stock portfolio—his largest position.

Reasons for Caution

Headline risk continues to abound in the banking industry. Wells Fargo is still deeply involved in mortgages, and any sign of trouble on the mortgage front will obviously hurt, although recent settlements of litigation related to mortgage-lending operations reduce this risk somewhat. Banking is a complex business—more complex than we like—and hence our minimal inclusion of financial firms on the *100 Best Stocks* list; only the best, as they say. The changing interest rate landscape in the wake of Fed "tapering" is a bit hard to predict and may cause some short-term profitability hiccups as "wholesale" interest rates rise faster than "retail," but in the long term, the company is well positioned to handle any rise in interest rates and may even benefit from it.

SECTOR: **Financials** ◻ BETA COEFFICIENT: **1.12** ◻ 10-YEAR COMPOUND EARNINGS PER-SHARE GROWTH: **5.5%** ◻ 10-YEAR COMPOUND DIVIDENDS PER-SHARE GROWTH: **12.0%**

		2007	2008	2009	2010	2011	2012	2013	2014
Loans (bil)		344.8	843.8	758	734	750	783	811	850
Net income (mil)		8,060	2,655	12,275	11,632	15,025	17,999	20,889	21,821
Earnings per share		2.38	0.70	1.75	2.21	2.82	3.36	3.89	4.10
Dividends per share		1.18	1.30	0.49	0.20	0.48	0.88	1.15	1.35
[Price:	high	38.0	44.7	31.5	34.3	34.3	36.6	45.6	55.9
	low	29.3	19.9	7.8	23.0	22.6	27.9	34.4	44.2

Website: *www.wellsfargo.com*

CONSERVATIVE GROWTH

Whirlpool Corporation

Ticker symbol: WHR (NYSE) ❑ S&P rating: BBB ❑ Value Line financial strength rating: A+ ❑ Current yield: 1.9% ❑ Dividend raises, past 10 years: 5

Company Profile

Whirlpool is the world's leading home appliance manufacturer in a $120 billion global industry. The company manufactures appliances under familiar and recognized brand names in all major home appliance categories including fabric care (laundry), cooking, refrigeration, dishwashers, water filtration, and garage organization. Familiar brand names include Whirlpool, Maytag, KitchenAid, Amana, Jenn-Air, Gladiator, and international names Bauknecht, Brastemp, and Consul. The Whirlpool brand itself is the number one global appliance brand and is number one across all four major world geographic regions. Seven brands within the branded house generate over $1 billion in annual sales. Based on FY2014 sales, the product breakdown is about 28 percent refrigerators and freezers, 27 percent fabric care, 18 percent home cooking appliances, and 27 percent "other." About 54 percent of Whirlpool's sales come from overseas, a growth of 13 percent since 2008. Latin America has been the most dynamic player at 26 percent of sales, up from 19 percent in 2008. The total overseas percentage will be on the rise with the acquisition of two moderately sized international firms: Europe's Indesit (another billion-dollar brand) and China's Hefei Sanyo.

In an industry not known for innovation, Whirlpool has striven to be an innovation leader in its industry. This has manifested itself both in new products, product platforms, and contemporary styling within those platforms; and in manufacturing and supply-chain efficiencies, such as a global platform design for local manufacture of washing machine products, recalling similar achievements in the auto industry. Such gains are key in this competitive, price-sensitive industry. The company also has initiatives to build lifetime brand loyalty and product quality, improve energy efficiency, and to expand in key developing markets such as Brazil (where the Brastemp brand is sold) and India. Once a major maker of OEM products for such names as Sears (Kenmore), the company has shifted focus to its own brands: 95 percent of sales are from its brands compared to 80 percent in 2000. Overall, the strategy is to expand the business through brand strength and geographic coverage; then to expand margins through supply-chain and cost-structure efficiency.

Financial Highlights, Fiscal Year 2014

The company rode the tailwinds of an improving economy, an improved replacement cycle for old units, improved demand for today's more efficient appliances, and operational improvements to another very successful year in FY2014 with a respectable 6 percent top-line growth (especially with currency headwinds) and a stronger 7.5 percent earnings growth led by cost efficiencies. Operational improvements, higher-product value add, and a gradual increase in premium brands have driven operating margins from the 6–8 percent range five years ago into the 10–12 percent range; these improvements look to be permanent.

The company expects these conditions to continue through FY2015: revenues on medium heat, earnings on full boil. Sales, helped along by acquisitions, are expected to rise about 17 percent; earnings, helped along by increased overseas manufacturing and lower raw materials prices, appear headed to a 20–22 percent gain, with another 14 percent earnings gain on a 5 percent revenue rise forecast for FY2016.

Reasons to Buy

Three years ago we added Whirlpool because we had a good feeling about the company, its management, its markets, and the health of the economy in general. We haven't been disappointed; the stock has almost quadrupled in three years—not bad.

Now we can add to the mix the fact that so many have put off basic appliance purchases for so long. What's more, if you shop for an appliance today—take washers and dryers, for example—they work better, they're more energy efficient, they use less water, and are more technology enabled. In short, they're better products, and guess what: They're more expensive and more profitable for the manufacturers, too. Operating margins have expanded from the 5–7 percent range to the 9–11 percent range in the past five years. We think some of the company's success is permanent, beyond the effects of a strong business cycle.

We like market leaders, particularly companies not content to sit on their laurels while others close in around them. Whirlpool used the recession and ensuing recovery as a wake-up call and an opportunity to streamline its businesses and to put some real strategic thought into how to drive its brand assortment and international portfolio to achieve better results.

The company continues to innovate toward better products and internal processes. We like their "Purposeful Innovation" motto. Long term, we see more opportunities to develop "smart" appliances, which can work together with smartphones and other residential management applications to deliver better, more energy-efficient results. Too, the company is building critical mass in overseas markets. Cash flows and investor returns are solid. More than most, the management team is a plus with a recognizable pragmatic and strategic approach to managing this business.

Reasons for Caution

By nature, the appliance business is highly competitive and cyclical. In addition, consumers with more disposable income have of late been opting for fancier, more expensive foreign brands, like Bosch and LG, a trend that could hurt if it continues. We believe that Whirlpool is countering this trend by adding elegance, advertising, and channel support for its top-tier brands and products—as well as a few "foreign" brands of its own. That plus a reversal of customer preferences toward American brands as seen to a degree in the auto industry should help. Commodity costs, labor issues, quality issues, and shifts in consumer preferences, while favorable now, are perpetual risks. Finally, the share price has been on a roll—while there is little dirty laundry to be found in this story, the rapid rise makes this one of the more aggressive names in our *100 Best* portfolio.

SECTOR: **Consumer Durables** ▫ BETA COEFFICIENT: **1.50** ▫ 10-YEAR COMPOUND EARNINGS PER-SHARE GROWTH: **4.0%** ▫ 10-YEAR COMPOUND DIVIDENDS PER-SHARE GROWTH: **4.5%**

		2007	**2008**	**2009**	**2010**	**2011**	**2012**	**2013**	**2014**
Revenues (mil)		19,408	18,907	17,099	18,366	18,666	18,143	18,768	19,872
Net income (mil)		647	418	328	707	699	559	810	907
Earnings per share		8.10	5.50	4.34	9.10	8.95	7.05	10.03	11.39
Dividends per share		1.72	1.72	1.72	1.72	1.93	2.00	2.38	2.88
Cash flow per share		16.32	13.90	11.37	16.91	16.54	14.05	17.53	18.80
Price:	high	118.0	98.0	85.0	118.4	92.3	104.2	159.2	196.7
	low	72.1	30.2	19.2	71.0	45.2	47.7	101.7	124.4

Website: *www.whirlpoolcorp.com*

Currently available from Value Line for individual investors

THE VALUE LINE INVESTMENT SURVEY®

The signature publication from Value Line is one of the most highly regarded comprehensive investment research resources. Published weekly, it tracks approximately 1,700 stocks in more than 90 industries and ranks stocks for Timeliness™ and Safety™.

THE VALUE LINE INVESTMENT SURVEY® — SMALL & MID-CAP

The Small & Mid-Cap Survey applies Value Line's data and analysis protocols to a universe of approximately 1,800 companies with market values from less than $1 billion up to $5 billion.

THE VALUE LINE INVESTMENT SURVEY® — SMART INVESTOR

This internet version of the Value Line Investment Survey tracks approximately 1,700 stocks and offers sorting functions and custom alerts.

THE VALUE LINE INVESTMENT SURVEY® — SAVVY INVESTOR

The internet counterpart of the preceding three Surveys, Savvy Investor includes every one of our 3,500 stock reports plus updates during Stock Exchange hours.

THE VALUE LINE® 600

Provides stock reports from The Value Line Investment Survey on 600 large, actively traded and widely held U.S. exchange-listed corporations, including many foreign firms, spanning over 90 industries.

VALUE LINE SELECT®

Once a month, subscribers receive a detailed report by Value Line senior analysts, recommending the one stock that has the best upside and risk/reward ratio.

VALUE LINE SELECT®: DIVIDEND INCOME & GROWTH

A monthly, in-depth report recommending one dividend paying stock, providing extensive information about the company's finances, prospects, and projected earnings, along with follow-up on numerous alternate selections.

THE VALUE LINE SPECIAL SITUATIONS SERVICE®

The Value Line Special Situations Service is designed for those seeking investment ideas in the small-cap arena. It includes both aggressive and conservative selections every month.

A special 14-day trial of The Value Line Investment Survey — Smart Investor is available to individual investors with the code "100STOCKS" at *www.valueline.com/100STOCKS*.

485 Lexington Avenue, 9th FL, New York, NY 10017
www.valueline.com
1-800-VALUELINE